T0389600

From Tribalism to Nationalism

NIAS – Nordic Institute of Asian Studies
NIAS Studies in Asian Topics

66 *Departing from Java: Javanese Labour, Migration and Diaspora* • Rosemarijn Hoefte & Peter Meel (eds)

67 *Engaging Asia: Essays on Laos and Beyond in Honour of Martin Stuart-Fox* • Desley Goldston (ed.)

68 *Performing the Arts of Indonesia: Malay Identity and Politics in the Music, Dance and Theatre of the Riau Islands* • Margaret Kartomi (ed.)

69 *Hearing Southeast Asia: Sounds of Hierarchy and Power in Context* • Nathan Porath (ed.)

70 *Asia Through Nordic Eyes: Fifty Years of Nordic Scholarship on Asia* • *Geir Helgesen & Gerald Jackson* (eds)

71 *Everyday Justice in Myanmar: Informal Resolutions and State Evasion in a Time of Contested Transition* • Helene Maria Kyed (ed.)

73 *East–West Reflections on Demonization: North Korea Now, China Next?* • Geir Helgesen and Rachel Harrison (eds)

74 *Spirit Possession in Buddhist Southeast Asia: Worlds Ever More Enchanted* • Bénédicte Brac de la Perrière and Peter A. Jackson (eds)

75 *Fragrant Frontier: Global Spice Entanglements from the Sino-Vietnamese Uplands* • Sarah Turner, Annuska Derks & Jean-François Rousseau (eds)

76 *From Tribalism to Nationalism: The Anthropological Turn in Laos – A Tribute to Grant Evans* • Yves Goudineau and Vanina Bouté (eds)

77 *Community Still Matters: Uyghur Culture and Society in Central Asian Context* • Aysima Mirsultan, Eric Schluessel and Eset Sulaiman (eds)

78 *Jin Ping Mei – A Wild Horse in Chinese Literature: Essays on Texts, Illustrations and Translations of a Late Sixteenth-Century Masterpiece* • Vibeke Børdahl and Lintao Qi (eds)

79 *Electoral Reform and Democracy in Malaysia* • Helen Ting M. H. and Donald L. Horowitz (eds)

NIAS Press is the autonomous publishing arm of NIAS – Nordic Institute of Asian Studies, a research institute located at the University of Copenhagen. NIAS is partially funded by the governments of Denmark, Finland, Iceland, Norway and Sweden via the Nordic Council of Ministers, and works to encourage and support Asian studies in the Nordic countries. In so doing, NIAS has been publishing books since 1969, with more than two hundred titles produced in the past few years.

From Tribalism to Nationalism

The Anthropological Turn in Laos – A Tribute to Grant Evans

Edited by
Yves Goudineau and Vanina Bouté

NIAS PRESS

From Tribalism to Nationalism
The Anthropological Turn in Laos – A Tribute to Grant Evans
Edited by Yves Goudineau and Vanina Bouté

Nordic Institute of Asian Studies
Studies in Asian Topics, no. 76

First published in 2022 by NIAS Press
NIAS – Nordic Institute of Asian Studies
Øster Farimagsgade 5, 1353 Copenhagen K, Denmark
Tel: +45 3532 9503 • Fax: +45 3532 9549
E-mail: books@nias.ku.dk • Online: www.niaspress.dk

Publication of this volume was assisted by generous financial support received from l'École française d'Extrême-Orient (EFEO), Paris, for which the editors express their warm thanks.

A CIP catalogue record for this book is available from the British Library

ISBN: 978-87-7694-296-0 (hbk)
ISBN: 978-87-7694-303-5 (pbk)

Typesetting and cover design by NIAS Press

Printed and bound in the United States by Maple Press, York, PA

Cover image: Vanina Bouté, 2008: 'Painting of ethnic minorities at Phongsaly market'.

IN MEMORY OF GRANT EVANS AND BOIKE REHBEIN

While the editing of this book was in its final stages, we were dismayed and saddened to learn of the sudden death of Boike Rehbein, who was pleased to participate in this tribute to his close friend Grant Evans. We wish to associate their memories with this collection of Laos Studies of which they were such distinguished representatives.

Contents

List of Maps, Figures and Tables

(**bold** = colour version of image)

Maps

Figures

Tables

Foreword

YVES GOUDINEAU AND VANINA BOUTÉ

For many years, fieldwork in Laos was made impossible by wars, the overthrow of royal power and the establishment of a revolutionary regime. Yet the country has long been regarded by anthropologists as a unique place to study, not least because very diverse ethnic minorities make up about half the population. There were a limited number of good ethnographical surveys conducted during the colonial period and after independence, up to the 1960s, both among Lao villagers and among some ethnic minorities. But most of these took a rather narrow approach, producing monographs on specific ethnic groups or village studies. After the establishment of the new regime in 1975, a few international researchers were able to return to the field in Laos, often under difficult and precarious conditions, and to carry out further studies. Most of these date from the 1990s onwards.

The book brings together a number of anthropological studies that are representative of this new generation of researchers engaged in fieldwork, often in joint projects with Lao partners. The aim of gathering these contributions was to meet the demand for a wider audience for texts that had had limited circulation, some because the book or journal in which they appeared was now difficult to obtain, others because they had not been translated into English. This is particularly the case of chapters that were first published in the volume *Recherches nouvelles sur le Laos / New Research on Laos* (EFEO 2008), but also of others that appeared in Asian Studies journals (see below, 'Credits and acknowledgements').

The drive to increase the availability of these texts was first led by the late Grant Evans, certainly still the most renowned anthropologist who has worked on Laos, who wished for a better dissemination of what he considered to be a body of valuable and innovative research in the field of Lao studies. He had himself undertaken the project of having several of the chapters of the anthropological section of *New Research on Laos* translated into Lao, in the hope that this might inspire Lao colleagues with new approaches and questions. However, his sudden demise in 2014 meant not only that we lost a leading Southeast Asian scholar and a close friend, but also that his last project could not be pursued. Thus, this collection of texts that he wanted to make more available, written by colleagues who knew him well or even collaborated with him in Laos, is also a tribute to his work and the recognition of a debt of friendship.

Grant Evans paved the way for new field research in Laos, with his initial work *Laos Peasants under Socialism* (Evans 1990). From the outset, he sought to place all social dynamics in a broader context, taking into account the determining role of political factors. At the same time, he did not approach the issue of ethnicity in Vietnam and Laos from a narrow perspective based on studies by ethnic group or 'tribe', as official ethnography did, but analysed the way in which ethnicity was managed from an ideological point of view in the context of nationalism. Hence the title of this book, *From Tribalism to Nationalism*, which is partly borrowed from him. He had a great interest in the making of nationalism, which led him to study, in the case of the Lao communist regime, the reclamation of ancient symbolic forms of legitimisation (Evans 1998) and to deconstruct the official discourse on national history (Evans 2002a, 2009).

For all these reasons, the perspective pioneered by Grant Evans is emblematic of an 'anthropological turn' in Lao studies, of which the chapters in this book are part. Among other themes, and in contrast to past studies, a number of these chapters include investigation of the political role of the state in the management of ethnicity and of religion, revealing its openly nationalistic intention. They also consider the study of Lao society and of specific ethnic minorities in the broader context of inter-ethnic relations at the national or regional level, particularly in some of the contributions, which are marked by an overtly ethnohistorical approach. This does not mean, of course, that the national framework is the only relevant one – ethnic and religious identities cross borders as easily as goods – but not taking into account national determinants would make any serious comparative studies impossible. The chapters included here do not claim to represent the entirety of anthropological work in Laos (see the Introduction below), but they do provide an understanding of the different directions that field research has taken there to date. More generally, this 'anthropological turning point' illustrates the need to bring – especially in local research – a critical spirit to the analysis of social facts.

Credits and acknowledgements

Versions of a number of the chapters in this book originally appeared in Yves Goudineau and Michel Lorrillard (eds), *Recherches nouvelles sur le Laos / New Research on Laos*, Editions EFEO, coll. Etudes thématiques n°18, 2008. They are reproduced here with the kind permission of the publisher, École française d'Extrême-Orient (EFEO) and the friendly approval of Michel Lorrillard. The original titles of these are: Grant Evans: 'Lao peasant studies today'; Boike Rehbein: 'The modernization of Lao'; Vanina Bouté: 'Cultes aux esprits et bouddhisme chez les Phounoy du Nord-Laos'; Ian Baird: 'The case of the Brao: Revisiting physical borders, ethnic identities and spatial and social organisation in the hinterlands of Southern Laos and Northeastern Cambodia'; Yves Goudineau: 'L'anthropologie du Sud-Laos et l'origine de la question kantou.'

In addition, permission has been given by the journals in which versions of the following were originally published: N. J. Enfield: 'Language and culture in Laos: An agenda for research', *Journal of Lao Studies*, Vol. 1, No.1, 2010, pp. 48–54; Yves Goudineau: 'The ongoing invention of a multi-ethnic heritage in Laos', *Journal of Lao Studies*, Special issue, 2, 2015, pp. 33–53; Patrice Ladwig: 'The genesis and demarcation of the religious field: Monasteries, state schools and the secular sphere in Lao Buddhism', *Sojourn: Journal of Social Issues in Southeast Asia*, Vol. 26, No. 2, 2011, pp. 196–223; Vatthana Pholsena: 'The early years of the Lao revolution (1945–1949): Between history, myth and experience', *South East Asia Research*, Vol. 14, No. 3, 2006, pp. 403–430; Guido Sprenger: 'The end of rituals. A dialogue between theory and ethnography in Laos', *Paideuma*, Vol. 52, 2006, pp. 51–72.

The editors would like to thank Keomany Somvandy-Evans for her support and encouragement, Alexandra Céalis, Maureen Phillips and Mark McGovern for their translations, Monica Janowski for her meticulous reading and finally Gerald Jackson for his patience.

INTRODUCTION

In the Field in Laos

YVES GOUDINEAU

The main common feature of all the contributors to this volume, whether they be linguists, anthropologists or historians, is their experience of field research in Laos. This is all the more noteworthy as it has not always been possible to do field work in the country, as both during the war and in the post-war period it was largely inaccessible to international researchers, who were obliged to fall back on material from French or American archives or to work amongst refugee populations. Even today, there are still difficulties in carrying out research *in situ*, partly because of the rugged terrain and the lack of infrastructure in much of the country and partly because there is limited interest within Laos in research, particularly anthropological research – which may, at times, even be viewed with suspicion.

Linguistic and ethnographic work done by foreign researchers in Laos, which for the most part resumed properly in the 1990s, has been characterised by new approaches in social and cultural anthropology. Analysis of the evolution of the Lao language has shown how, over a relatively short period of time, it has undergone accelerated change linked to educational reform and, even more importantly, due to external influences – particularly from the Thai language, which is favoured by the media and within social networks. Ethnographic surveys, which had not been possible in the country for many years, have resumed, and these have enabled researchers to study or revisit certain societies both in the north and in the south of the country (Lamet, Khmu, Phunoy, Brao, Kantu...) that have become 'ethnic minorities'.

Today, the perspective of anthropological research is no longer the same as in the past. The aim is not so much to produce monographs on villages or ethnic groups as to focus on contemporary social dynamics (local, regional and transnational) that link people – both those who belong to closely related groups or those who are very different from each other culturally. Today, ethnographers study not only the changing situation of Lao peasants or of the so-called ethnic minorities, who have been affected by the restructuring of the rural world and by development projects, but also topics such as the evolution of Buddhist communities, or the discourses and practices of local officials. Moreover, it is important to note that anthropologists working in the field of 'Lao studies' do not limit themselves to looking at what is happening within the Lao national context – although this is certainly key to understanding social dynamics more widely – but extend their horizon beyond the frontiers of the modern state, as attested to here by several contributions that focus on cross-border situations.

The Long Road to Field Research in Laos

The earliest academic field research in anthropology was conducted by the Swedish ethnologist Karl G. Izikowitz, who spent eight months in a Lamet village (Upper Mekong province, now Luang Nam Tha) during a stay in Northern Laos between 1936 and 1938. His work, which broke with colonial ethnography, remains pioneering in its consideration of 'hill peasants' rather than 'tribes' and in its analysis of interethnic relations, particularly those between groups speaking Austroasiatic languages and the Northern Tai groups.[1]

However, it was Charles Archaimbault who first undertook, between 1951 and 1956, an in-depth study of Lao society. Trained both in anthropology and philology, and refusing to comply with disciplinary divisions, he collected during almost 6 years oral and written traditions throughout the country. From this considerable ethnographic material, he proposed an analysis of Lao society, until then mainly considered through its literary traditions, with a theoretical perspective combining Freudian psychoanalysis and a structuralism inspired by the work of Georges Dumézil.[2] Laos had yet to benefit from research in human geography comparable to Pierre Gourou's work on village life and vil-

1. For a good overview of his work, see the collection of articles published in Izikowitz 1985.

2. See bibliography of Charles Archaimbault in Goudineau 2002.

lage economies in the Red River plain in Vietnam. However, this need was addressed in 1959 by the collaboration between agronomist Claude Gaudillot and anthropologist Georges Condominas and the launch of a vast study of the Vientiane plain, a study that, for the first time, included an important rural sociology component.[3]

Thereafter, social anthropological research was mainly carried out by American researchers, who saw Laos as a field in which to extend the studies undertaken on Thai village life. This was the point of departure for the 'Laos Project' (UCLA and Yale) coordinated by Joel Halpern, which, in the space of a few years, produced a series of papers (published between 1960 and 1965), many of them written by Halpern himself, on various issues relating to Lao society at this time: education, health, agriculture, local elites, etc.[4] Several village monographs were also produced, some of which resulted from collective surveys with Japanese researchers from the 'Japanese Mekong Expedition' (G. L. Barney, Howard K. Kaufman, Tsuneo Ayabe, Keiji Iwata, etc.).[5]

Although limited by the progressive closure of the provinces due to the war, fieldwork continued in the 1960s and 1970s, and in particular studies were carried out by French researchers through Cedrasemi.[6] Notable ethnological research from this period includes field work by Barbara Wall in the south on the Nya Heun; by Jacques Lemoine in the north on the Hmong; by Richard Pottier on health systems and traditional Lao therapeutic practices; by Amphay Doré on ancient Lao elites; and by Sophie Clément-Charpentier and Pierre Clément on the habitat and dwellings in the Luang Prabang area. Research in the field of language studies includes that carried out by Michel Ferlus on Austroasiatic languages; by James Chamberlain on Tai-Kadai; and by Pierre-Bernard Lafont on Tai scripts. In the field of social geography, Christian Taillard studied village economies in the Nam Ngum valley, while American psychiatrist Joseph Westermeyer conducted innovative investigations on the impact of drugs and mental disorders.

3. See Condominas 1962, 1998; Condominas et Gaudillot 2000.
4. See, for example, Halpern 1964.
5. See Gunn 1998: 3–24.
6. Documentation and Research Centre on Southeast Asia and the Austronesian World (CNRS). See Lemoine 1972, Doré 1972, Wall 1975, Clément-Charpentier and Clément 1990, Pottier 2007; also Lafont 1962, Ferlus 1974, Chamberlain 1975, Taillard 1977, Westermeyer 1983.

After 1975, the Lao government, which was keen to demonstrate its Marxist interest in economic and social issues, established a national Committee for Social Sciences (CSS). It also set up a Nationalities Committee within the Lao Front for National Construction (*Neo Lao Sang Sat*), to deal with policies relating to ethnic minorities. At the same time, a few Western researchers were able to work briefly *in situ* or managed, indirectly, to obtain reliable data on the social situation in the country. These included Geoffrey Gunn, whose historical anthropology was Marxist-inspired and combined findings from short field trips with extensive archival work; the Iresons, who carried out a study of ethnicity in a socialist context; and, above all, Martin Stuart-Fox, who produced a pioneering socio-political synthesis, based on interviews that he carried out himself in Vientiane in 1985 and also on material from good informants within Laos.[7] However, Grant Evans was, in the 1980s, the first researcher to be able to carry out real field studies, as part of his research on Lao peasant society after collectivisation. Thereafter, Yves Goudineau began his study of Austroasiatic-speaking peoples in Saravane and Sekong in 1991, while Andrew Walker undertook research on cross-border merchant communities in Bokeo from 1993 (Walker 1999, 2000). In a separate development, Mayoury Ngaosyvathn conducted the first survey on the place of women in Lao society around this time (1995), while some foreign researchers were able to conduct short studies commissioned by ministries or international development projects.[8]

In the wake of the 1996 UNESCO recommendation to make the study and preservation of the intangible heritage of ethnic minorities a priority for Laos,[9] the Institute of Cultural Research (ICR) initiated several collaborative projects with Japan, Australia, France, Canada and Germany, which paved the way for authorisation for doctoral students and foreign researchers, including several of the contributors to this

7. See in particular Ireson and Ireson 1991 and Stuart-Fox 1986, 1996.

8. For instance, Trankell 1993; Ovesen 1995; Hours and Selim 1997; Proschan 1997; Lyttleton 1999; Cohen P.T. 2000; Cohen P.T. and Lyttleton 2002, 2008. Mention should also be made of surveys conducted from neighbouring Thailand, especially the multi-year research programme on the Kammu (Khmu) by Kristina Lindell and Damrong Tayanin (see Damrong 1994, Lindell and al. 1995), or some short comparative fieldworks (see Cohen P.T. 1998, 2000; Hinton 2000; Keyes 2019: 273–274).

9. See Goudineau (ed.) 2003.

book, to conduct fieldwork in the country. Over the last 15 years, cooperation with the National University of Laos, the Institute of Statistics and various government ministries has made it possible to broaden certain fields of investigation, for example in geography (urban geography, health, etc.), and to open up new ones (psychology, sociology, etc.). As part of development projects, numerous studies using social science methods have often been initiated by international organisations (UNDP, FAO, WHO, UNICEF, etc.) or NGOs. There is therefore a vast literature of reports on Laos that has a role to play in the analysis of current social dynamics. But it is up to researchers to evaluate the rigour and objectivity of these documents and to see what use can be made of them in a broader context (Evans this volume, Chapter 3).

Tribalism and Nationalism

The first attempt to conduct a systematic ethnographic survey of Laos and the rest of French Indochina dates back to 1903, when the colonial power decided to draw up a list of all the peoples under its rule. On the orders of the Governor General, the heads of local administrations and the commanders of 'military territories' were charged with creating an initial inventory of all the different ethnic groups residing in their districts and of the different languages spoken there. A rather rudimentary questionnaire was distributed, the results of which were uneven and often very superficial.[10] In Laos, only the provincial commissioners of Attapeu and Khammuane submitted a report with fairly detailed data. Although these reports provide the first notes on certain forms of social organisation (domestic structure, etc.) and the first known lexicons for certain languages, the overall results were not sufficient to 'provide the basis for ethnic statistics', and the linguistic data collected were too patchy for any 'attempt at an ethnographic map of Indochina'.[11] Moreover, during the colonial era, there were only a few

10. A manual for in-depth ethnographic investigation, entitled 'Instruction pour les collaborateurs de l'École française d'Extrême-Orient', was written by the EFEO in collaboration with Marcel Mauss, but it was ignored by the colonial administration (Michaud 2013: 12f.).

11. The only two publications resulting from the 1903 surveys are those of Étienne-Edmond Lunet de Lajonquière. One as editor: *Ethnographie des territoires militaires* (1904) – of which Claude E. Maître, then director of the EFEO, in a long review published in the *BEFEO*, 1905, praised the effort to learn about the 'uncivilised

general population censuses that collected ethnic data – in 1921, 1931 and 1936 – and these were conducted with limited means and provided only partial results, which omitted large mountainous areas (Pholsena 2009). In fact, the first relatively detailed ethno-linguistic map of Indochina was not published until 1949 by the EFEO.

Notwithstanding the limitation and inadequacy of the data collected, the colonial state nevertheless wanted to classify populations not only in terms of race, but also as tribes, each of which was supposed to form a distinct unit that could be categorised according to scientific criteria, both classificatory and evolutionary. A fundamental distinction, common to all colonisers, was drawn between 'centres' and 'peripheries'. On the one hand, there were the 'civilised' peoples, who had writing and notable monuments, such as the Viet, the Khmer, and the Lao, and on the other there were the 'savage' tribes ('*Kha*'), whose linguistic affiliations needed to be understood, as well as the differences between them in terms of customs. At the same time, an effort was made to distinguish, within 'tribes', between groups that were primitive and rebellious, and others that were considered to be more evolved because they had been in contact with literate cultures, particularly, in the north, the Meo (Hmong) and the Man (Yao), who had come from China. In Laos, a tripartite division arranged in order of decreasing cultural level – descending from 'Lao-Tai' to 'Meo' and then 'Kha' – was quickly established during the colonial period, and persisted in various forms, both explicit and implicit, from independence up until 1975. It is still firmly rooted in the popular imagination in most of the provinces across the country (Goudineau 2000, and Chapter 12 in this volume).

The colonial archives also show that this 'tribalisation' was intended to serve utilitarian or political aims. This started with the identification of local chiefs, who were unilaterally promoted to be intermediaries between their people and the colonial power. In periodic reports sent by provincial administrators to the 'Résident-supérieur' in Vientiane, there are supposedly ethnographic observations which have overt practical and strategic purposes. Some reports focus on the need to 'pacify' insubordinate Kha tribes or bellicose Meo villages, while others describe projects to move

tribes' but underlined all the shortcomings and inadequacies of the surveys. And the other, as author: *Ethnographie du Tonkin septentrional* (1906) – with a review by Marcel Mauss in *L'Année Sociologique*, 1906 (see Michaud, 2013: 28, 36).

populations considered to be 'more evolved' into savage territories, or to facilitate the economic development of small regions (through plantations, etc.) by displacing tribal villages in order to generate a workforce. The Hmong developed a special status, and it is clear that the reasons for this were strategic. Although they were initially responsible for an anti-colonial rebellion linked to the control of opium, they were nonetheless allowed to benefit from a degree of territorial independence from the 1920s onwards in Xieng Khouang, and subsequently many of them became allies of the French forces during the Indochina War.

Unlike other colonised countries, Laos did not really experience the period of radical change that is usually characteristic of 'decolonisation'. The formation in 1946 of a constitutional monarchy centred on the sovereign of Luang Prabang, reigning over a theoretically unified country, was set up and then supported by the French (who returned to Laos militarily after 1945), who nevertheless retained prerogatives in matters of defence and foreign policy. In 1949, a constitution confirmed the Royal Lao Government (RLG), which gained full autonomy in 1953, when a centralised and independent state was formed – although French economic, educational and cultural aid was still important.[12] However, when it came to 'ethnic policy' the new government struggled to define principles and objectives that truly distinguished it from previous governments. Although the territorial unity of the country, with internationally recognised borders, was accepted in principle, between 1945 and 1975 the Lao state's room for manoeuvre was considerably reduced, in the context of a region saturated by wars and internal conflicts.

For 30 years, Laos was crossed by a kind of longitudinal divide – although this divide changed according to the region and the period considered. On the one side, were the easily accessible areas, mainly located in the Mekong Valley. On the other side, the potentially dangerous mountainous areas where the military situation remained uncertain. Issues of ethnicity and inter-ethnic relations were seized upon and exploited by all the different factions during the war. The way in which

12. The publication *Présence du Royaume Lao,* edited by René de Berval (Berval [ed.] 1956), brought together more than 40 Lao and French authors. It has several chapters written by Charles Archaimbault. The book is significant in terms of demonstrating the ways in which Lao national culture was promoted and in terms of showing how explicit support was given by the French to the RLG (see Berval 1956).

this played out depended largely on the 'position' of the ethnic groups concerned – their geographical position often determining which side they found themselves on in conflicts. For researchers, most fieldwork among 'ethnic' populations became impossible, both in the north and in the Annamese Cordillera in the south. Surveys that were carried out were thus conducted mostly among peoples displaced from their traditional habitat by the war and therefore easier to access, whether in the plains or on the other side of the border, in Thailand.

What really distinguished the RLG period from the colonial period was its official affirmation of Lao nationalism. The colonial power, when considering the different 'races' and 'tribes', reasoned first of all on a scale that included the whole of Indochina, as colonial administrators were well aware that many peoples lived in areas that crossed borders between countries within the region.[13] However, this was set to change after 1945, when the advent of independence in Laos raised two nationalistic concerns that persist to this day. On the one hand, there was external pressure to create a Lao national culture that was distinct from Thai culture, but which could nonetheless include Tai highlanders (Black Tai, White Tai, etc.).[14] On the other, there was the internal need to recognise the multiplicity of ethnicities within the national territory, while at the same time establishing and reinforcing Lao culture as the national culture. This led certain nationalists to propose a new tripartite division of the population of the country, into three ecological strata – Lao Loum, Lao Theung, Lao Soung – so as to show that, regardless of any internal ethnic distinctions, all of the groups in the country were 'Lao', and that ancient relationships existed between these three components of national unity.[15]

13. The administrative division of peoples by country was mainly used, after a census, to identify those who were liable to pay taxes in each province (Pholsena 2009).

14. In support of the new Lao nation, the historical and ethnographic work of Charles Archaimbault aimed to show that there was a specific Lao culture, although with regional variations, and that there was an essential ritual complementarity between the Lao principalities and the tribal populations (see Goudineau this volume, Chapter 12).

15. *Lao Loum*: Lao 'of the plains', corresponding to the Lao-Tai; *Lao Theung*: Lao 'of the foothills', supposedly including all of those speaking Austroasiatic languages; *Lao Soung*: Lao 'of the summits', applied broadly to the Hmong-Yao and to the Tibeto-Burman speaking groups.

In fact, tribalism and nationalism are not inherently opposed, but are in a dialectical relationship, where state control of ethnicity also aims to impose limits on multiculturalism (Evans 1999: 175). Compared to the colonial administration and the Royal Lao Government, the communist government, which took power in 1975, has shown unprecedented zeal in its drive to classify and categorise 'ethnic minorities', which has been facilitated by its rule over a pacified country with fixed borders and a population that is more or less stable. It is also clear that the Lao communist regime has directly inherited this obsession with classification from its Vietnamese mentors. During the period of the war, and subsequently in the 1980s, Vietnamese ethnographers conducted a number of surveys inside Laos territory, particularly in the north. This was a sort of extension of those they had conducted in Vietnam itself with the express aim of drawing up an inventory of national 'ethnic groups'. Among these researchers were Pham Duc Duong, Le Cu Nam, Cam Trong, Dang Nghiem Van and Nguyen Duy Thieu, who introduced their Lao colleagues to ethnographic data collection. As a result, a Lao Institute of Ethnography was established in 1988 and given the similar task of compiling a national inventory of 'national ethnic groups' in Laos. A first generation of Laotian 'apprentice ethnographers', Khampheng Thipmuntaly (Northern Tai), Khamsao (Hmong) and Souksavang Simana (Khmu), received training here – training that was later completed in Hanoi, and even in Moscow in some cases (Evans 1999a: 161f.).[16]

Since then, the counting of ethnic groups in Laos, which is a concern of the Communist Party, has been a major mission for the few local specialists. Initially, the government focused its nationalist propaganda on images showing the unity of the three Lao ethnic families (large illustrated posters, etc.); then, no doubt aware of the limits of this very broad categorisation, it decided to create a Nationalities Committee within the framework of the Lao Front for National Construction (LFNC), a mass organisation led by the Party.[17] The official task of the committee

16. Among the works of Lao ethnographers, see the publications by Khamluan Sulavan, Thongpheth Kingsada and Costello 1995, Houmphanh Rattanavong 1997, Suksavang Simana and Elizabeth Preisig 1999, Khampheng Thipmuntali 1999 and several other Lao contributors in Goudineau 2003.

17. Khambay Nyundalath, a former director of the Lao Institute of Ethnography, was appointed to head the Nationalities Committee in 1999.

was to establish a precise inventory of minorities on a 'scientific basis', which it did by firstly abandoning the old tripartite division and then by replacing this with recognition of the four major ethno-linguistic families represented in Lao territory: Lao-Tai, Mon-Khmer (Austroasiatic), Hmong-Mien and Tibeto-Burman.

As for the classification of ethnicities, this has been reworked several times, with varying results depending on the criteria used, to arrive at the 49 'ethnicities' officially listed by the LFND in 2000, confirmed in 2005 and then in 2015, and still in use today (although a 50th category labelled 'other' has now been added). Worth noting here is both the obviously arbitrary nature of these inventories and the fact that this zeal for categorisation taken to extremes has been accompanied by an equally zealous 'scientific' quest to attribute 'exact' ethnic names (Chinese heritage via Vietnamese ethnography?), which has led to the listing of some 160 names for sub-groups. Within this system, the 'right' name is supposed to express the essence of a group, and the main task of ethnographic work, once the name is fixed, is to determine characteristics and attributes related to this 'essence' (Goudineau 2000: 22–23).

As a consequence, most of the ethnographic work published in Lao has been little more than catalogues of ethnic groups. Although classification by stages of civilisation according to Engels has now been abandoned in Laos, as it has in Vietnam, the criterion of 'backwardness' continues to play a key role in educational programmes designed by the Lao Front for National Construction that aim to combat 'bad' customs and superstitions among ethnic minorities, which provincial cultural services put into practice in 'cultural villages' (Goudineau this volume, Chapter 12). In these villages, ethnic diversity is presented through folkloric markers that supposedly represent the 'good' customs (architecture, costumes, songs, dances, etc.) of each group, which are frequently reworked in accordance with a so-called 'national' aesthetic judged to be compatible with progress and socialist modernity. This zeal for categorisation, driven by a culturalist reconstruction of what purports to be ethnic identity, goes hand in hand with a normative and instrumental practice of ethnography that implies a cultural reductionism far removed from the ethnographic fieldwork and faithful observation that should be at the basis of all anthropological questioning.

Grant Evans and the Anthropological Turn in Laos

The 1970s and 1980s in Europe and the United States saw a reflexive return to ethnography, which had been accused of being confined to local, ethnic and communal spheres (villages, tribes, collectives, etc.), and of failing to pay attention to socio-historical dimensions and theoretical questions. The 'anthropological turn' that emerged in the wake of the 'linguistic turn' of the 1960s and before the 'ontological turn' of the 2000s called into question the method and content of ethnography – not only the practice of fieldwork by certain researchers, but also the analysis of identities and representations of otherness. There were a number of reasons for this crisis in anthropology. It was a consequence of decolonisation, but also of an increased political awareness of the relationship to the Other and of a broadening of research fields. However, in Laos the impact of the anthropological turn was not really felt until the 1990s. Before then, particularly following the change of political regime in 1975, the only research done by anthropologists was a handful of short surveys, carried out both by Lao and foreign ethnographers. As noted above, they had to restrict themselves to very localised questions; and the small number of sociologists and historians who wanted to take a more comprehensive view of Lao society and the issues that it faced had limited empirical data, which was often second-hand.

In this respect, Grant Evans was an exception since he was able to do long-term fieldwork in Laos from the 1980s onwards. He also emerged as the main representative of this anthropological turn, as attested to in the opening chapter of his edited book *Laos: Culture and Society* (Evans [ed.] 1999: 1–34), which highlighted the urgent need for the exploration of more theoretical questions in the field of Lao Studies.[18] In many ways, Grant Evans' multi-faceted research outlines a general anthropology of Laos: economic anthropology (on the Lao village economy and the failure of collectivisation), social anthropology (on the impact of Lao-isation and on interethnic relations), cultural anthropology (on the self-legitimisation of the communist state by means of cultural symbols from the past) and more generally a historical anthropology that seeks

18. On Grant Evans, see two special issues: 1/ Peter Cox and Boike Rehbein (eds), *Journal of Laos Studies* (*JLS*), Special issue 2016, Vol 3, 1, with an extensive bibliography of Grant Evans' publications (Cox and Rehbein 2016); 2/ Paul T. Cohen and Olivier Évrard (eds), *The Australian Journal of Anthropology* (TAJA), Special issue 2019, Vol. 30, 2 (Cohen and Évrard 2019).

to historicise social fact but rejects any official rewriting of history. All of these angles of attack converge towards a political anthropology that questions the various components of the national identity constructed by the Lao PDR.

Grant Evans was initially interested in Laos as a kind of observatory within which the transformations of society in a country that had just entered communism could be viewed. A sociology tutor at La Trobe University and a committed journalist and activist for the Australian 'New Left', his personal political itinerary had gradually led him from strong opposition to the American war in Vietnam to a critique of certain dogmatic applications of Marxism. His interest in the communist future of the societies of former Indochina, including the tragic fate of Cambodia, led him to conduct his first surveys in peninsular Southeast Asia (Rowley 2016). Following the publication of his book *The Yellow Rainmakers* (Evans 1983), which was particularly well received in the Lao PDR,[19] he was authorised to go and do research in some rural areas, conducting the first field study by a Western researcher in the country since 1975. In the course of a series of surveys between 1982 and 1987, lasting several weeks each and sometimes as long as two or three months, he followed the creation and development of agricultural cooperatives in the Vientiane region.

As a result of this work, he became a first-hand observer of the failure of attempts at collectivisation in rural areas.[20] In his book *Lao Peasants under Socialism* (1990), Grant Evans showed how the dogmatic application of an orthodox communist macro-economic model to Lao peasants had led to absurdities in terms of crop productivity and cooperation between villagers.[21] Not only did yields fall dramatically, but the bureaucratic organisation of cooperatives, which privileged Party members, greatly disrupted village social structure. Opposing the economic

19. In this first book, Grant Evans, after interviewing many Hmong people in refugee camps in Thailand, showed that there was no real evidence for the allegations that Pathet Lao air force planes fired rockets containing Soviet chemical weapons to kill the Hmong of the 'CIA army' (see Cox and Rehbein 2016: 1–5).

20. See the insightful analysis by Christopher Hutton and Dominique Blaettler, 'From Peasants to Lords. The Intellectual Evolution of Grant Evans' (Hutton and Blaettler 2016: 24–36), see also Cole and Rigg (2019).

21. The book is also a theoretical discussion of the theses of James C. Scott (Scott 1976), Samuel Popkin (Popkin 1979) and A.V. Chayanov (Chayanov 1986) on the nature of the peasant economy.

irrationality of the agricultural structures imposed by the state, Grant Evans, himself the son of an Australian farmer, defended the rational character of the 'natural economy' of the Lao peasants, whose production is adapted to their needs, and which benefits, when necessary, from traditional mutual aid among villagers. The end of the agricultural cooperatives in the mid-1980s, and the promotion of a 'New Economic Mechanism', amounted to an admission of the powerlessness of the socialist economy to replace the peasant economy in Laos, a country that was essentially rural at the time. More generally, through his analysis of the failure of collectivisation he questioned the very socialist identity of Laos, as expressed in its economic organisation. The opening of the country to the market economy in the 1990s, which led to corruption and nepotism, appeared to confirm that the regime had renounced its main socialist ideals, and that it was more appropriate to speak of a 'post-socialist' identity (Evans 1995).[22]

The ethno-cultural identity postulated by the Lao nation-state, including the fate of 'minorities', was another research theme for Grant Evans, who explored it in various articles and book chapters. Despite a heavy teaching load in anthropology and sociology at the University of Hong Kong – where he had been appointed in 1989 – he carried out further fieldwork, making several visits between 1988 and 1993 to the district of Muang Xieng Kho in Huaphanh province on the border with Vietnam. These visits enabled him to observe the evolution of interethnic relations at the local level. Rejecting any fixed or 'fixist' vision, he went on to insist on the plasticity of ethnicities, citing the example of the Black Tai, whom he considered typical of a group living in an intermediate geographical and cultural space.[23] Although they are an upland and non-Buddhist ethnic group, the Black Tai belong to the Tai-Lao (Indianised) world through their language as well as through their hierarchical social and political organisation in *müang* – which have long been characterised as 'fiefdoms' that are dominated by aristocratic lineages. On the other hand, numerous cultural borrowings, mainly through their elites, had

22. In the second edition of his book published in 1995: '*and Post-Socialism*' was added to the original title (*Lao Peasants Under Socialism*). On the discussion of a 'post-socialist era', especially in China and Laos, see Peter Hinton 2000.

23. His analysis starts from the theoretical discussion of earlier works on Tai political systems by Leach (1954) and Condominas (1990), from whom he borrows the notion of social space.

also brought them closer to the (Sinicised) Vietnamese world. Thus, the Black Tai had constructed and negotiated a dual identity throughout their history. Furthermore, Grant Evans showed how the Sing Moon, a small group that had been subdued and paid tribute to the Black Tai, had been partly Tai-ised. His long-term study of such local interethnic situations, including complex and ancient forms of interdependence, revealed identities that were not bounded but flexible and evolving, in the context of which borrowings and the affirmation of different traditions co-existed to varying degrees; as he pointed out this was, for example, true in relation to matrimonial rules and funeral rituals (Evans 1999b: 125f.).

In this context, Grant Evans notes that with its decision to make the Lao majority culture the sole basis of national culture and with the dissemination of Lao culture throughout the country as a priority, the communist government has denied recognition of cultural (and spatial) autonomy to 'minorities'. Instead, it has imposed an arbitrary categorisation into different 'ethnicities', all considered to be equal and to be, in some way, juxtaposed within the nation-state. This denies the natural fluidity of interethnic relations and amounts to a purely ideological vision, one that obscures real social and cultural differences between ethnicities and, moreover, ignores the reality of economic inequalities.

Not only have unequal relations persisted, including contempt for groups deemed to be 'backward' with regard to socialist modernism, but many ethnic minorities who played a vital role in supporting the Pathet Lao during the war have never benefited from the economic development that they were promised, as Grant Evans pointed out. They even had to leave their ancestral lands in order to survive, and these large-scale resettlements throughout the country, whether forced or voluntary, have significantly redistributed intercultural relations (Goudineau 1997a, 2000b). This means that anthropologists, when they are investigating ethnocultural identity in contemporary Laos, must analyse state intervention in matters of ethnicity and must also take into account the existence of a complex hierarchy of cultural identifications on the part of peoples who, through their mobility, have access to increasingly wider social spaces (Evans 2000).

Grant Evans argued that the creation of a strong national identity was intended to compensate for the fact that a socialist identity had been undermined by the abandonment of any socialist economic programme. This was also intended to strengthen ethnocultural identity, which remained fragile due to the difficulty of reconciling the presence of numerous 'minorities' to the creation of a truly multi-ethnic nation and of cultural unity. Hence the recourse on the part of the state to powerful symbols, mainly borrowed from Buddhism and history, which Grant Evans has documented in *The Politics of Ritual and Remembrance* (1998). After an initial period during which the monastic community (*sangha*) was strictly controlled and was obliged to support the actions of the communist regime, Buddhist ceremonies were tolerated from the mid-1980s onwards and quickly regained a prominent place in the public sphere, to the extent that Party leaders were eager to endorse and even patronise them ostentatiously by their presence. As a result, Buddhism was (re)established as a central pillar of national culture, while some Lao popular rituals were tolerated as secondary beliefs, particularly *baci* or *sukhuan* ('souls recall') and certain mediumistic practices.

Grant Evans also examines how the government draws on history in order to legitimise itself as the embodiment of national identity. This takes the form of books and textbooks glorifying the advent of a 'new socialist man' in Laos, who has been 'liberated' from the 'obscurantism' and 'exploitation' that characterised the previous periods of colonisation and royal government. Perhaps more importantly, the regime also sought to associate itself with emblems supposed to have an indisputable historical value, notably by reaffirming the status of That Luang as a national monument and creating brochures and statues to establish a symbolic filiation between the late President Kaysone Phomvihane and the most charismatic ancient sovereigns, such as Chao Anou and Fa Ngum – two figures portrayed as having been primarily nationalist.

Already convinced of the need to use economic history to analyse the ideological excesses of collectivisation, as well as of the need to use ethnohistory to understand the construction of ethnicities and the dynamics of interethnic relations, Grant Evans embarked on his last two books as part of a quest to demystify official Lao narratives (Evans 2002a, 2009). It led him to positively reassess the contribution of some prominent figures during the period of the Royal Lao Government adding a deliberately polemical and political historical dimension to his work.

His denunciation of ideological rhetoric, which he exposed by showing that it was contradicted in practice, and his refusal to accept simplified and distorted interpretations of history, made Grant Evans a critical anthropologist and a key actor in the production of a truthful discourse on Laos. Although he had other interests in Asia during his career (Timor, Vietnam, Hong Kong, South China...), his real 'field' of research was Laos, which he examined from different perspectives but also considered as a whole.[24] Having acquired a good knowledge of the Lao language early on, he was able to speak fluently and to read written material that was disseminated through official channels, and he did not shy away from meeting and directly questioning various officials. As an anthropologist, he considered all of those whom he interviewed to be first and foremost his informants, at all levels of the state – up to and including President Kaysone Phomvihane. His uncompromising desire to establish a sincere dialogue and a truthful narrative was only matched by his great eagerness to contribute to opening up the minds of his Lao colleagues – who had hitherto been, as he wrote, 'apprentice ethnographers' following a Vietnamese model from the 1970s – and to training them in new ways of questioning.[25] More generally, he wished to make his work known to a Lao public, even if it meant taking the risk of translating it.[26]

A Volume of 'Post-Anthropological Turn' Field Studies on Laos

Not all of the contributions gathered here are necessarily directly related to the work of Grant Evans, not least because some of the field research on which they are based began before some of his books were published. However, in addition to being the result of prolonged fieldwork, they have all benefited to varying degrees from the openness to theoretical questions that he pioneered in the field of Lao Studies, especially the questions that he dared to ask about the impact of nationalist policies on rural societies, on local cultures, and on the appropriation of history.

24. See his lengthy review of O.W. Wolters, 'Between the global and the local', discussing the heuristic value of the notions of 'cultural area' and 'region/ecumene' and the comparative relevance of studies conducted at different scales (Evans 2002b). On the conception of borders in Southeast Asia, see mainly Thongchai Winichakul 1994, whose pioneering work he greatly appreciated (e.g. Evans 1999: 16), and the stimulating discussion by Alexander Horstmann (2002).

25. See Evans 1999: 160–190.

26. It is worth noting here the decisive and friendly role played by Grant Evans's main publisher, Silkworm Books (Chiang Mai) and its director Trasvin Jittidecharak, who published or distributed almost all of his works, including the risky Lao translation of *A Short History of Laos*.

Photo: Keomany Somvandy-Evans, 2014

Grant Evans and Yves Goudineau, EFEO, Chiang Mai.

Grant Evans's chapter in this volume (Chapter 3), marks an important return to his work in the field of 'Lao Peasant Studies'.[27] Almost 20 years after his initial fieldwork, Grant Evans found that management of the rural economy, which had been marked by the ideology of collectivisation and then by its failure, had largely been delegated to development projects that rely on international aid organisations and consultants. Reasoning in macro-economic terms, these new actors were repeating errors that in some ways mirrored those of the past, through their ignorance of local peasant dynamics. By arbitrarily applying criteria such as 'poverty' and 'inequality', today's so-called experts are simply applying new ideological clichés to rural society. For example, their abstract notion of 'peasant communities' fails to take into account different social roles within families and villages and is not informed by any serious analysis of collective mutual aid. All of this led Grant Evans to regret the decline of theoretical studies on peasant societies and more generally the decline of economic anthropology.

While anthropologists agree that Laos possesses a rare cultural and linguistic diversity, N. J. Enfield reminds us (Chapter 1) how our data concerning this country remains extremely limited in most areas of

27. The material on which this chapter is based was collected during a new survey conducted by Grant Evans in 2004. His initial research on attempts to set up cooperatives among villages in the Vientiane plain dates back to successive visits between 1983 and 1987 (Evans 1990, 1995).

research. Given that this diversity is now increasingly in danger, he notes that there is a real urgency to define a research agenda in Laos, particularly on language and culture. Among the requirements that must guide this agenda are, in addition to funding, the need to recruit and train national field researchers. Regretting the reluctance of some Lao officials to accept local surveys, he, like Grant Evans, makes a strong plea for the necessity for in-depth research that only long fieldwork can provide.

Considering linguistic differences in the context of various socio-cultural environments, Boike Rehbein demonstrates in his chapter (Chapter 2) the co-existence of different 'sociolects' during the history of Laos. These are associated, in particular, with a gulf between the peasant world and that of urban elites. The standardisation of the language that was undertaken after 1975, which was supposed to address this issue, was thwarted by the country's adoption of a market economy in the 1990s. This has led to the emergence of new social 'fields' (in the sense in which Bourdieu uses the term) – technical, commercial, academic, etc. – paving the way for an increased differentiation of sociolects linked to globalisation and generating new linguistic hierarchies.

In this process of differentiation, Lao Buddhism, which can be considered to have its own language, represents a separate socio-culture whose boundaries are analysed by Patrice Ladwig in his chapter (Chapter 4). Adopting a historical perspective, he examines the progressive withdrawal of educational (and sometimes also therapeutic) functions from Buddhist monasteries, a process that began long before the advent of the current political regime. This leads him to analyse the separation and relative autonomy of religious and secular fields under the influence of the Lao nationalist state – which is not, however, as Grant Evans has shown, averse to supporting the recent Buddhist revival movement.

Vanina Bouté's contribution to the book (Chapter 10) offers a diachronic analysis of the transformation of rituals among the Phunoy of Phongsaly, a Tibeto-Burman speaking group that has long been Buddhist but has kept its spirit cults alive. Having done a long fieldwork, in a province held by the Pathet Lao since the 1960s, she could study certain rituals for warding off misfortune. She shows here how the imposition of a supposedly orthodox Buddhism from the outside has led, not to the disappearance of all spirit worship, but to an original reconfiguration of local cultic practices, including a form of cooperation between the various ritual officiants.

In his chapter, which is entitled 'The End of Rituals' (Chapter 9), Guido Sprenger also highlights the flexibility of ritual systems, focusing on the religious practices of the Rmeet of Northern Laos. He shows that in response to changes imposed by the state, notably the marginalisation of spirit cults and the reduction, in kind and number, of sacrifices, the Rmeet have demonstrated agency and cultural creativity in their quest to find functional equivalents (a notion taken from Luhman) that allow them to translate external forces into the language of their ritual system, and thus adapt it from within without having to modify their values or cosmology. Both of these two studies take issue directly with the cultural essentialism of official Lao ethnographic practice.

Based on ethnohistorical research focusing on oral tradition and the local interpretation of archaeological remains, Oliver Évrard and Chiemsisouraj Chanthaphilith, in their chapter (Chapter 8), examine various versions of the myth of the creation of the city of Vieng Phu Kha in Northern Laos (now a district of Luang Nam Tha province). Their research highlights local trans-ethnic dynamics between Tai (Lue, Yuan, Yang) and Austroasiatic (Khmu, Rmeet, Samtao) peoples, which have given rise to numerous shared narratives, including legends of a common ancestry, but also to rituals practiced in common – and still being performed until the 1970s – to honour the guardian spirit of Vieng Phu Kha.

For his part, Yves Goudineau, in Chapter 6, cross-references colonial archive documents with his own ethnographic surveys in Sekong and Saravane to retrace the construction of ethnicity and interethnic relations in Southern Laos over more than a century. Focusing on the specific nature and limits of the process of Lao-isation, he analyses the reasons why this process, as well as that of colonisation, was never able to reach certain Austroasiatic-speaking populations of the Upper Sekong in the Annamese Cordillera, notably the Kantu (or Katu in Vietnam). The history of this particular society, long renowned for its feats of arms in defence of the Ho Chi Minh trail, is emblematic of the transmission and reproduction of a social, spatial and ritual model that has survived, in spite of wars, until recently, even though it is, in many ways, radically opposed to Lao values and at odds with the current norms of Lao national culture.

Focusing on another cultural and socio-political model, among the ethnic Brao of Southern Laos and Northeastern Cambodia, Ian Baird in

Chapter 7 shows how their resilience is intrinsically linked to a certain concept of spatial organisation. In harmony with their beliefs and livelihood requirements, Brao spatial organisation involves the creation of physical borders between social groups, which delineate distinct village territories. This model, which contrasts with the hierarchical structures of Lao and Khmer social space, is typical of egalitarian village societies (in the sense in which Leach [1954] used the word) and its persistence should raise questions about the relationship between territorial organisation and social order.

The production and dissemination of discourses around memory related to the Pathet Lao's revolutionary struggle and its actions during the war remain a preoccupation of the communist nation state. However, the scope of these discourses has increasingly been constrained by the opening up of other information channels and a certain indifference among the younger generation with regard to the origin of the regime. In her chapter (Chapter 5), looking back at the beginnings of the Lao–Vietnamese revolutionary struggle (1945–1949) in the Annamese Cordillera in Southeastern Laos, Vatthana Pholsena juxtaposes facts generally accepted by professional historians with a past mythologised by official narratives and also with the testimony of a Vietnamese veteran settled in Southern Laos. Lao historiography, rather implausibly, places Khamtay Siphandone, former president of the Lao PDR, at the centre of the struggle; however, the testimony she has collected confirms that it was Vietnamese volunteers who were decisive in converting ethnic minorities, the Katu in this case, to the revolutionary cause, on both sides of the border.

Oliver Tappe's chapter (Chapter 11), based on his investigations in Huaphanh, also highlights a complementary aspect of discourses around memory as these are projected by the Party. Working in a region that was especially dear to Grant Evans – where he continued some of Evans' work on the consequences of agrarian change and the dynamics of Tai-isation – Tappe broadens the discussion of the 'politics of ritual and remembrance' with an examination of the quasi-ritual function of visits to the caves of Viengxay, the 'Birthplace of Lao PDR' and with a deconstruction of the locally imposed discourse on the heroic struggle of the valiant multi-ethnic Lao.

It is precisely the invention of a multi-ethnic Lao people and culture that is the topic explored by Yves Goudineau in the concluding chapter of the book, Chapter 12. He notes that the discourse on multi-ethnicity has evolved to accommodate an official acknowledgement of the importance of the cultural heritage of minority groups, and that this discourse has been matched by the government's establishment of what may be described as new cultural 'devices' in the country's provinces. Each ethnic group is now invited to define and negotiate its own 'good traditions', extending the cataloguing work of state ethnography, which is, as discussed above, marked by an openly essentialist perspective. At the same time, folklorised performances in 'cultural villages', which supposedly represent traditions attributed to individual ethnic groups – costumes, dances, songs, etc. – are now organised under the supervision of provincial administrations, with a view to attracting tourists. This official exhibition of multi-ethnicity through imagined (and culturalist) stereotypes is clearly to the detriment of genuine state recognition of the actual specific characteristics – linguistic, social, and ritual – of the 'ethnic minorities'. Although some ethnic groups manage better than others to negotiate the representation of their culture, and some even succeed in earning a small profit from doing so, this does not in any way call into question the political priority of the state, which is the ultimate integration of all the peoples of the country into a national culture based on Lao culture and language.

From Participant Observation to Critical Anthropology

The contributions in this volume are representative of several directions taken over the last two decades by international researchers working on Laos in the fields of social and historical anthropology. However, they do not, of course, cover all the work currently being carried out in this field, even though, when compared to other countries, specialists on Laos remain few in number, as do publications devoted to research done in the country. As this volume is a tribute to Grant Evans, we have focused on authors he knew well and whose work he appreciated to the point of wanting to have it translated into Lao, with a view to contributing to the training of national researchers. Since his demise in 2014, Grant Evans' influence and the avenues he opened up have continued to inspire scholars and provoke discussion.[28] New research subjects and

28. More recent research includes that done by Simon Creak on Lao nationalism through the prism of sport (Creak 2015), Pierre Petit on memory construction and territorial cults in Huaphanh (Petit 2020). See also Holly High's discussion of

new approaches have emerged, but his reflections on field practice and partnership in Laos are still very relevant today.

Among the research perspectives that have undergone recent reorientation is that of the nature of collective identity. There is a need, in Laos, to take into account the transformation of collective identities, whether ethnic, village, religious, etc., which have been fragmented and reconfigured over the past 25 years by the relocation of large numbers of villages and growing individual mobility towards cities. Anthropologists interested in the dynamics of identity in Laos must therefore consider, on the one hand, the conditions under which certain collective identities are resilient; but also, on the other hand, the increased possibility for individuals to embrace a plurality of ways of identifying themselves.

As a result, the relevance of 'local' approaches is also being questioned, particularly studies of 'totalising systems' – houses, villages, communities, etc. – and increasing emphasis is being placed on studies of networks, sectors and trajectories, and on research conducted on the scale of provinces, which takes into account the history of mobility of both social groups and individuals.[29] Some recent surveys have favoured a pragmatic approach to social interactions within a collective,[30] while others have aimed to study the capacity for negotiation and agency on the part of actors such as Lao peasants and ethnic minorities in relation to discourses and practices imposed on them by agents of the Lao state and international consultants. In any case, the ability to conduct detailed studies of social interactions is conditional on in-depth knowledge of the milieux in which they take place, and this can only be gained by extensive immersion in the daily life of communities concerned and a mastery of their spoken languages that is sufficient to allow direct communication with them – in other words, taking into account observations from inside – which once again raises the question of ethnographic fieldwork in a country like Laos.

---

the local relationship with agents of the state and her critique of 'post-socialism' (High 2014, 2021).

29. See, for example, Annabel Vallard's study of the Lao weaving sector in Luang Prabang and beyond (Vallard 2017) and Grégoire Schlemmer's extended surveys on a provincial scale in Phongsaly (Schlemmer 2017).

30. See the work of Rosalie Stolz on everyday lived kinship in a Khmu village (Stolz 2021).

With this in mind, it is necessary to objectively 'situate' both the observer and the actors who are the object of the research. On the one hand, there should be 'participant objectivation' (Bourdieu 2003), that is to say, a requirement for reflexivity, which – far from being a narcissistic reflection by the observer on his or her personal experience (in accordance with an ethical position currently in vogue) – actually questions the social conditions that make his or her work possible in the field. On the other hand, there should also be an evaluation of the margins of choice, negotiation and agency that are available to different actors, taking into account the evolution of the social, economic, cultural and political factors that affect the social groups studied. The late Grant Evans rightly reminded us of this in his study of identities in Southeast Asia: 'Research in mainland Southeast Asia has shown that people participate differentially in different identities and different cultures. Individuals and groups try to make choices as to who they are and how they will act, but they are always constrained socially, culturally, politically and economically. The difficult task of fieldwork is to assess what relative weight to give to each of these factors in an ever-evolving historical situation.' (Evans 2000: 286)

In a recent debate, the very term 'ethnography' has been questioned. This has focused on the etymology of the word, which appears to limit the field to the investigation of ethnic considerations; and on the abuse of the term in the social sciences today. Nowadays, any geographer, political scientist, sociologist, psychologist or economic consultant engaged in carrying out a survey or conducting an interview, however brief, is likely to speak of doing 'ethnographic work'.[31] Used in this manner, the term is no more than a synonym for qualitative data gathering or data collection, which overlooks what rigorous anthropological research entails in terms of fieldwork. Hence, the classic notion of 'participant observation' is preferred by some to the term 'ethnography', because it emphasises a 'relationship' or 'correspondence' to the Other that is free and open and that implies a readiness to listen and learn (Ingold 2014). Such a critique has obvious relevance for official state ethnography,

31. See Tim Ingold 'That's enough about ethnography!' (Ingold 2014), 'Anthropology contra ethnography' (Ingold 2017), and Signe Howell 'Two or three things I love about ethnography' (Howell 2017).

which not only compiles 'ethnic data', but also interprets and controls it for political purposes.

Grant Evans asked what kind of fieldwork was possible with these local collaborators – a question that is still pertinent today and one that also raises questions about the conditions for producing anthropological knowledge in partnership in Laos. Ignoring possible accusations of ethnocentrism, made from the West in a purely demagogic manner by some who claim to be non-judgmental and who generally had never made any real effort to integrate into Lao society or even to give themselves the means to understand it, his response was that we have to help raise the level of competence of our collaborators. This response, which he persistently put into practice, implied to contribute to the training of these partners with whom we had to work, to help them open up to new questioning and above all to develop critical reflection. He wanted to do so in a spirit of local cooperation similar to the training courses set up under the impetus of Professor Chayan Vaddhanaphuti by the Regional Center for Social Science and Sustainable Development (RCSD) of Chiang Mai University, with which he enjoyed collaborating.

No doubt he could have adopted the position defended by Tim Ingold, who considers that anthropology is fundamentally 'critical': 'we must demand the right to speak with voices of our own, and to say what we think on the basis of our inquiries, regardless of whether it accords with the thinking of our interlocutors' (Ingold 2014: 23–24) – a critical implication being a necessary complement to any participant observation.

CHAPTER 1

Language and Culture in Laos

An Agenda for Research

N. J. ENFIELD

For anthropology, a key attraction of Laos is its unusually high degree of human diversity. The problem is that we know little of what defines this diversity. Worse, one of the few things we do know is that this diversity is under threat. This makes the task of anthropologists more urgent than ever. The study of human diversity directly addresses a fundamental question for human science: What are the limits of possibility for human life?

The striking differences between humans and other species are most clearly manifest in the properties of our linguistic and cultural systems. We maintain massively complex symbolic systems, which each individual has to learn over a long period of socialisation, and which differ almost entirely in form and content across thousands of different human groups. The average villager in Laos will know tens of thousands of words and expressions in his or her own language, each of which may differ entirely from the tens of thousands of words and expressions known to the people in the community next door, which will be different again from the next community, even more different from the next, and so on. The same is true for the thousands of local practices, cultural values, and conceptual systems also known to be unique from human group to human group. Each language and culture is in this sense a natural experiment in historical collaborative creation of cultural tradition (Enfield 2005: 192–7). Members of each sociocultural group will conform in following a collectively created pattern of ways of thinking, ways of speaking, ways of doing things and ways of interacting with the environment (Boyd and Richerson 2005). Each linguistic and cultural system can therefore be viewed as a living document of human tradition (Enfield 2006a).

The ethnolinguistic diversity known to exist in Laos makes the country a rich archive for anthropologists of all types. With the current state of the art, the immediate agenda is clear: We need to describe the country's human diversity. Until the empirical data are available, any general discussion of language(s) and culture(s) in Laos is going to be incomplete, or, worse, ill-informed. For now, there is a lack of balance in scholarly attention. The situation in linguistics is indicative: scholars of language in Laos are preoccupied with orthographic prescription in relation to the national language, arguing, for example, about whether written Lao requires a letter 'r' (Institute for Cultural Research 1995; Enfield 1999). Despite the political issues of interest, orthography of the Lao language is just one leaf on a single branch of a single tree in a giant forest of problems for research. We are meanwhile learning next to nothing of the endangered mysteries of language and culture in the country.

Just consider what we do not know about language and culture in Laos.[1] We do not know how many languages are spoken in the country. Existing proposals vary from around 60 to over 100 (see Lao Front for National Construction 2005; Enfield 2005, 2006b), none offering empirical support for the figure cited, or any appreciation at all of the problems associated with answering this question (cf. Hudson 1996: 36). But even if we could state how many languages there are in Laos, this would not get us very far. What are the properties of these languages? What are the words and expressions (numbering in tens of thousands!) that each speaker of each language has to know? What are the grammatical structures? What do the kinship systems look like? How do they differ structurally? How are the languages related to each other, historically and socially? What ethnic importance do the languages have? What sorts of social settings do they inhabit? What are the patterns of language contact and multilingualism? How do children acquire these languages? What degree of cultural knowledge is encoded in the vocabularies and grammatical structures of the languages? What

1. Notwithstanding contributions such as Evans 1999b, 2000, 2003a; Jacq 2002; Sidwell and Jacq 2004; Suksavang Simana and Preisig 1999; Khamluan Sulavan and Costello 1998; Svantesson et al. 1994; Khampeng 1999; Thongphet Kingsada and Shintani (eds) 1999; Wright 2003; Pholsena 2006a; and Rehbein 2007, among others.

kinds of poetry, verse, or song can speakers of these languages produce? What might the languages tell us about the social organisation of the societies in which they are spoken? Or of their mechanisms of face-to-face interaction? Or of the livelihoods of the people (e.g. in the vocabulary of biological classification)? Or of their cognitive analysis of the world in general? Lists of ethnolinguistic distinctions such as the one produced in 2005 by the Lao government (Lao Front for National Construction 2005) are welcome and fascinating (shortcomings, errors and infelicities aside). But they are of little use as reference sources in addressing this list of questions. The reality is that we know little of substance about what defines this country's great human diversity. Hence the pressing need for primary field research.

None of the above questions can be answered quickly or cheaply. Most researchers who visit remote communities do not have the time to collect long-term or in-depth data. From the colonial expeditions of Pavie's time (see Lefèvre-Pontalis 1902) to the helicopter drops by consultants of the last decade or so, short-term research visitors to the uplands of Laos have, by necessity, employed rapid methods of data collection. The relatively superficial results are of great use when nothing else is available. Linguists and ethnographers are grateful for even the sketchiest references to linguistic and ethnographic facts documented by officials of the Pavie mission and similar colonial projects. These are sometimes our only source of word lists and other empirical data on otherwise entirely undocumented languages and cultures. However, for lack of any alternative, there is a risk that such sources will be employed for purposes beyond those for which they were designed.

With appropriate time and resources, in-depth research has a host of virtues and can deliver results that rapid research cannot. It can be broadly systematic, thorough and comprehensive, and can thus represent a significant resource for future researchers and field workers. It can enlist the communities concerned and involve them in ongoing participation, not only in terms of their provision of data, but in their analysis of it, supplying findings that are both significant and comprehensible to the communities themselves. It can feed into the building up of information and analysis, contributing to longer-term cumulative research. With these three properties – comprehensive, participatory, cumulative – research can be responsible, sustainable and of high quality.

The agenda being sketched here entails a number of requirements. One is funding. Researchers need to find and mobilise research funds. Funding bodies need to recognise the importance of field research, and channel research funding into it. As it happens, funding and other kinds of support are available for documentation of linguistic and cultural systems, particularly those most endangered and most implicated in the country's biocultural diversity (Nettle and Romaine 2000; Crystal 2000; Maffi 2005).

A second requirement is people. Willing researchers do not grow on trees, but they do spring from university graduate programs. One of the best kinds of researcher for fieldwork is the humble graduate student. There are great opportunities in Laos for students who would be fieldworkers, not only those based in universities abroad, but also for students and other researchers originating in Laos.

A third requirement is state of the art research methods. There are well-developed tools and techniques for documentation of linguistic and ethnographic material. *(A) Methodological tools:* The dramatic growth of research and other activities being done around the world on endangered biocultural diversity has concentrated on the development of methods that are maximally sensitive to the community's wants and needs (Nettle and Romaine 2000; Grenoble and Whaley [eds] 1998). Findings of these projects are ready to be applied to similar activities in Laos. *(B) Technical tools:* Ethnographic and linguistic research is becoming increasingly sophisticated in its employment of technical resources such as video and sound recording, GPS and computer programmes for data organisation and analysis (e.g. video processing, dictionary/text building, mapping, data processing). *(C) Theoretical tools:* Concerning the relationship between linguistic/cultural diversity and cognitive diversity, much recent progress has been made in the analysis and understanding of relationships such as those between culture and language (Gumperz and Levinson 1996; Enfield 2002; Gentner and Goldin-Meadow [eds] 2003). In addition, there is much recent progress in understanding how linguistic and cultural diversity relates to diversity of livelihoods and lifestyles, particularly as this concerns human interaction with the natural environment (Berlin 1992; Maffi 2005).

Lao people stand to gain from the proposed research agenda. Researchers must strive to impart these tools and techniques to the Lao scholars and field workers who have the chance to be involved in these projects, so that they may carry the work through beyond the confines of limited research programmes. This is part of the desideratum of sustainability in research. But all the resources and expertise in the world will amount to nothing if the relevant authorities lack the political will to approve sustained primary field research in remote communities of Laos. The last two decades have seen willing field workers encounter resistance to their research plans, often when they are offering a good deal of financial, technical, and training resources. These researchers have come from fields as diverse as literature, ethnomusicology, historical and comparative linguistics, ethnobiology, grammatical description and ethnography. Without these projects going ahead, valuable training and resources have been lost to the Lao research community. More generally, research both interesting and important has just not been done.[2]

I have tried to define an agenda for research on language and culture in Laos. The ethnolinguistic diversity characteristic of Laos makes the country a treasure trove for research in human traditions of language, culture and cognition. The key requirement for research to really count is that descriptive and analytical work be conducted in sustained field residence. Now is the time to promote a broad agenda of primary field research in Laos that prioritises the systematic collection of quality empirical data bearing directly on the significant, yet ill-understood, human diversity that this complex country harbours. This will first be a contribution to human science, to documenting the naturally occuring limits on human variation, to figuring out where human groups around the world are alike and where we may (even radically) differ. Second, it will be a sorely needed corrective to the current balance of linguistic and other anthropological research in Laos.

2. There are some signs of emerging opportunities for academic research in Laos, for example through the fast- developing National University of Laos and the National Academy of Social Sciences.

CHAPTER 2

Sociolects, Differentiation and the Integration of Lao

BOIKE REHBEIN

This chapter proposes a socio-linguistic analysis of Lao. I wish to argue that the basic morpho-syntactical and even lexical forms of the Lao language correspond to social frameworks that are rooted in recent Lao history, namely the peasant village, the patrimonial elite, socialism and capitalism. The Buddhist order is, to some degree, a separate framework and has to be studied as such. At the same time, two parallel tendencies within the capitalist framework can be observed. Firstly, there is a differentiation of sociolects. These form part of different sociocultural environments, which have started to multiply with the advent of capitalism and differ especially in vocabulary. Second, and parallel to this differentiation, national integration is taking place. One element of national integration is the emergence of a public sphere with its own variety of language, which is taught to all citizens.

In the first section, I will outline a framework for the interpretation of language use as a sociocultural phenomenon. Language is applied in social contexts that can be analyzed as belonging to different historical layers of a given society. I refer to these layers as sociocultures. The second section summarises the history of those sociocultures that are relevant to understanding contemporary Lao. Then I will try to show that – and how – the nature of contemporary Lao is relevant to the operation of the different sociocultures in Laos. I will focus on terms of address, since these express social hierarchies and thereby the structure of the particular socioculture, although I will also touch on other aspects of language. The sections that follow deal with integration and differentiation, before I go on to discuss the public sphere. The final section deals with the relation of Lao to the Thai language.

Sociocultural Configurations

Any language use is – at least to some degree – a social practice. As such, each linguistic act is, at the same time, both creative and located in a structured universe to which it has to conform in many regards. The use of language has to comply with cultural patterns that must be understood and with social patterns that must be accepted. This relation between existing structures and creative action only partly corresponds to Ferdinand de Saussure's distinction between *langue* and *parole* (or linguistic rules and practice). It is captured more appropriately by Pierre Bourdieu's concept of *habitus,* which relates social structures and practices.

Bourdieu has argued that society can neither be reduced to a timeless structure nor restricted to single face-to-face interactions. Rather, any interaction presupposes structures, while every structure is reinforced or changed in every single interaction. Bourdieu illustrates this with reference to playing games (e. g. Bourdieu and Wacquant 1992: 101). Football and blackjack have different rules, require different skills and different strategies. And someone who is good at football is not necessarily good at blackjack. Interaction in one game is (in most cases) not influenced by the structure of the other game. Bourdieu argues that frameworks of social practices resemble games. He refers to the social frameworks as fields.

With regard to language, Bourdieu's 'field' is reminiscent of Wittgenstein's 'language game' (Wittgenstein 1984: 7). In both, meaning is created in intersubjective processes according to patterns that are unconscious and constantly modified. The main difference between the concept of field and that of language game is the focus on unequal structure. A field is a configuration of positions that are defined in relation to each other by the possibilities of action they allow (Bourdieu and Wacquant 1992: 97). The patterns of action are relative to the field and are subject to struggles and modifications.

Bourdieu's conception of language (and of fields in general) introduces important sociological elements into linguistic enquiry. However, it seems exceedingly reductive. First, it does not tell us anything about the link between grammatical and sociological analysis. Second, it acknowledges only one type of framework for social action – the competitive market. However, not all social frameworks are unequal and not all action aims at retaining or improving one's social position, even though this is often the case. The concept of language game offers a broader horizon.

Wittgenstein argued that the multitude of language games was irreducible. There are 'countless games' (Wittgenstein 1984: 23). Many of them do not have fixed rules that could be reduced to one general model or purpose (ibid.: 43). They simply have a 'family resemblance' (ibid.: 63) to each other, and a certain stability and regularity (ibid.: 207). They are games in progress, with rules and players being modified, changed, replaced and added in the process. Bourdieu frequently cited Wittgenstein and pointed to the similarity between the concepts of field and language game. However, he tried to reduce the purpose of fields to the improvement of one's social position on the field (Bourdieu and Wacquant 1992: 101). It is helpful to interpret some language games from the perspective of the concept of field – but not all.

Fields and language games do not appear out of the blue in an empty space. They are rooted in a social structure, which has a long and complex history. Social structures constantly change, but they are rooted in earlier structures. Social structures, cultures and institutional configurations are relatively persistent. This is true for the entire system of structures, cultures and practices within a given society, which partly persist even after profound transformations of that society. I refer to these persistent systems as *sociocultures* (Rehbein 2007).

Earlier structures, cultures and practices tend to persist because social structures are embodied by acquiring patterns of action in early childhood. As they are embodied, components of society can persist even after profound social change. This is what Bourdieu's concept of *habitus* refers to (Bourdieu 1984). A form of behaviour is acquired and then repeated. With repetition, one adopts a pattern that is put into action when a similar situation arises. Through multiple repetitions the pattern becomes embodied. When conditions change, the embodied patterns do not immediately disappear. This is true for many institutions as well. Think of professions that are organised like guilds in Europe, such as doctors or lawyers. However, many patterns do not change simply because the conditions in which they operate do not change significantly. In Laos, we see both – persistence of *habitus* despite social change; and persistence of older social, political and economic conditions.

Sociocultures

Laos was created as a colony within French Indochina in 1893 and formally became independent in 1954. However, a large part of the country informally continued to be a US colony until independence as a nation state in 1975. Independent Laos was a one-party state under the leadership of a communist party, the Lao People's Revolutionary Party (LPRP), which began to introduce capitalism in 1986, while retaining the same political system. The social, political and economic conditions under quasi-colonial rule before 1975, under quasi-Stalinist rule after 1975 and under capitalism since the mid-1990s differ profoundly from one other. This is reflected in the fact that four sociocultures co-exist – two pre-socialist ones, socialism and capitalism. These are all incorporated into the *habitus* of the people of Laos in the present day. Pre-socialist *habitus* forms persist because at least one third of the population was born before 1975 and almost half of the population were and continue to be subsistence peasants.

Laos is and has been a mosaic of ethnic groups and environments. This mosaic evolved historically through migration and adaptation. Today, most ethnolinguistic groups are scattered over a large territory and have to adapt to different environmental conditions in different places. However, the entire rural population of Laos lives in villages and the majority of the population grew up as peasants. In spite of cultural, social and linguistic differences, all peasants share important elements of their *habitus*. Most people are related to one other within a given village, and the social structure of the village is determined by kinship (Condominas 1962: 2). This means that one's social position improves with age, since old age commands more respect than youth (Jullien 1995: 18). In terms of gender, various configurations exist, ranging from patriarchal to almost matriarchal. Even within an ethnolinguistic group, these relations vary. In addition, people who have special functions, such as healers or village heads, occupy privileged social positions. Apart from gender, all social positions, and hence privileges associated with these, change over an individual's life course. Apart from hierarchies related to age and gender, there are no significant hierarchies within a village, and competition for social positions does not really exist.

Within most villages, a wide variation in lifestyle and behaviour is tolerated; but the basic patterns of behaviour are very similar. One could say that all peasants have a very similar *habitus* (cf. Baumann 2020 for Isan peasants). The peasant socioculture is similar in many regards across ethnic groups as well. It is characterised by a 'subsistence ethic', a term introduced by James Scott (1976). Peasants are not geared toward competition, profit and accumulation but toward having enough until the next harvest. A large surplus of food would rot and a large surplus of other items is useless. Scott identified mutual aid, reinforcing family ties and traditionalism as characteristics of the subsistence ethic. These are key traits of the peasant socioculture.

Villages that are ethnolinguistically different have been interacting for millennia across Southeast Asia. Pottery, metal and salt have been traded over large distances, while forest products, animals and cultivated plants have been traded in the vicinity (Higham 1989). Different environmental conditions resulted in different types of production, which were the basis of trade. Centres of trade and communication developed into towns with an increasing division of labour and with growing hierarchies. Many of the surrounding villages came under the domination of these centres. However, all of the people living in what is now Laos were only fully integrated into larger political structures in the late 20th century. Many villages preserved their political, and often their economic, independence over time because they migrated elsewhere or were too difficult to access in the first place. The result was a mosaic of centres, dependent villages and independent villages without clear territorial demarcations. This structure was called *baan–muang* ('rural centre'–'town/city') (Raendchen and Raendchen 1998). The main character of the relationship between *baan* and *muang* was an exchange of tribute and manpower for security. Loyalties shifted frequently according to the ability of a given centre to guarantee security and stability. Social relations in Laos can best be understood in the framework of the *baan–muang* structure. The structure consisted of some independent *baan*, various dependent *baan*, minor *muang* and a central *muang*. *Baan* and *muang* retained different sociocultures. The relationships between *muang* and *baan* were hierarchical but resembled family relations.

This type of social structure has been called patrimonial (Weber 1972). In Southeast Asia, patrimonialism mainly signified the loyalty of inferiors towards their superior, which was given in exchange for security (Hanks 1975). A superior tried to accumulate as many bonds of loyalty with inferiors as possible, while inferiors tended to look for superiors who could guarantee security. Just as the subsistence ethic characterised the culture of the village, patrimonialism was the prevalent culture of the *muang*.

Much of contemporary Laos came under the domination of the Siamese state, which was also organised as a *muang*, in 1828. In 1893, some of the Lao-speaking *muang* were integrated into the French colonial empire, while others remained with Siam. The French managed to move into Siamese territory but stopped short of integrating all Lao-speaking peoples into their colonial empire. They attempted to codify a national language on the basis of the languages of the former *muang*, to define an orthodox Buddhism, to introduce a bureaucratic administration and to integrate the independent villages. These attempts transformed Laos but were only partly successful.

After the Second World War, the French tried to retain their colonial empire but had to grant independence to Vietnam, Cambodia and Laos in 1954. The United States wanted to preserve French Indochina as a fortress against communism. The Communists were an important force in the independence movements within all three states but were nowhere the strongest power. In Laos, the government was basically formed by a coalition between a conservative faction, the Communists and a neutral group. The neutral group was the strongest faction. The USA insisted on the exclusion of the Communists from government. This led to unrest and eventually resulted in a military coup, backed by the US, in 1960. The coup pushed the neutral group and the Communists out of the government. The Communists withdrew to northeastern Laos, to an area that had been granted to them by the peace settlement of 1954. From there, they organised a revolution, with help from neighbouring north Vietnamese Communists.

There is no doubt that Laos would have remained a *muang*-state with a royal household at its apex, within the borders of a nation state, if the United States had not intervened. Instead, Laos was as heavily bombed as Germany during the Second World War, was contaminated with the pesticide 'agent orange', lost a sizeable part of its population and came under the rule of a communist party (Stuart-Fox 2002 [1996]). During the civil war the towns became centres of capitalism, while the northeast of the country was socialist. In 1975, the Lao People's Revolutionary

Party took over the country, and up to 10% of the population, mostly urban dwellers, left the country.

The overwhelming majority of the Lao population in 1975 were peasants or had been brought up as peasants. They were ruled by a small party leadership, which consisted of intellectuals, workers and peasants. The socialist nation state, which had less than three million inhabitants, had very little infrastructure, basically no industry and a tiny urban population. In the main, it reverted to a peasant economy. Attempts to build a Stalinist or a more moderately socialist economy were unsuccessful (Evans 1990a). This is, arguably, because the structure of Stalinist collectives contradicted the subsistence ethic by which the peasants lived. The peasants were somewhat egalitarian and anti-capitalist but they were not proto-Communists. This was quickly recognised by the party leader, Kaysone Phomvihane (1985, vol. I: 106).

When the Soviet Union began to pull out of Southeast Asia, the Lao leadership introduced capitalism in 1986 and slowly opened up for foreign capital, installed a standardised institutional framework for the market economy and abolished direct state control of business (Rehbein 2007). However, it did not introduce changes to the political system. In the framework of the global system, there was no significant change between the period before 1975, socialism and incipient capitalism. Laos was subject to development policies coming from international organisations as well as from the US (before 1975) and the Soviet Union (from 1975 to 1989). These policies continue to influence the situation nowadays, although they are decreasing in relevance. Their main target is those who live outside global capitalism – in other words, the peasants. Government and aid organisations move upland villages into the valleys, prohibit swidden cultivation, join small villages to marketplaces and improve the infrastructure. At the same time, the peasants have come to consider themselves to be poor. They are aware of the fact that they are viewed as backward and underdeveloped by the rest of the world (Rehbein 2007: 60). Within a few short years the peasants have been transformed from the heroes of the revolution and socialism to a problem group that has to be modernised through development policies and capitalism. In the meantime, capitalism has developed in the towns. Urban districts are considered developed, while districts comprising mainly subsistence peasants rank lowest in official assessments (see e.g. Bountavy Sisouphanthong and Taillard 2000: 147). Peasants with ample good land, especially those who convert to commercial farming, rank in between.

Sociolects and Sociocultures

The sociocultures persisting in contemporary Laotian society can be identified in language use. They are associated with the languages (the sociolects) of the village, the royal court, socialism and the market. The Buddhist order, the *sangha*, has its own language, just as it forms, to a certain degree, a separate socioculture. Each sociolect has its own forms of address, clearly expressing the structure of the socioculture within which it is used; these include kinship terms, terms for hierarchical positions, the term 'comrade' (*sahai*), personal pronouns and Buddhist terms. All of these are in use today within their respective social environments. They refer to specific inequalities and effectively reproduce them linguistically.

In the village, there is no need to use complex definitions in speech, because everything is already defined – culturally, practically and socially. The everyday language of the village is simple and straightforward. To a visitor from the West, the language may come across as impoverished, because many utterances lack a subject and lack grammatical complexity. I would not, however, consider the language of the village as impoverished, as no richness has been lost. I would describe it, rather, as 'interwoven with the situation' (Rehbein and Sayaseng 2004: 13). It is characteristic of Lao (and other East Asian languages) that a one-word utterance is grammatically correct. Semantically, nothing is missing. The meaning is evident from the accompanying situation. When people sit around a meal, and one person says 'Eat!', this would be a correct utterance in English, and it is also correct in a Lao village. It is just that there are many more situations in which simple utterances like this are appropriate in a Lao village, because there are more contexts in which it is clear what is being conveyed. Thus, a one-word utterance is appropriate in many contexts, not just in imperative utterances. It is, I would suggest, not necessary to use nouns, names, polite words and specifications in a context where everyone knows everyone else well.

For an outsider, it is rarely possible to follow intra-village communication, for lack of semantic familiarity. Village language uses considerably more particles and interjections and significantly fewer words of address and appositions than Sila Viravong (1935) and Phoumi Vongvichit (1967) would have considered grammatically correct (cf. Rehbein and Sayaseng 2004: 99). An example would be the utterance *Hue au oei.* This utterance was recorded in the context of a family conversation, and a literal translation into English would be 'Oh take, really.' The first and last words would be analyzed as particles, the second as a verb. In the specific situation in which it was recorded it meant something like: 'Damn, you really should have held onto it!'

In a Western context, we might assert that this everyday language is, in many cases, not 'correct'. In asserting this, we would be referring to norms learnt at school, through the media or from special institutions. But in rural Laos, there is no norm for language use yet, so more or less anything goes. In fact, one might often say that less is more! For there is a – cultural – tradition of saying things, and saying something in a different way might mean that one would not be understood. And there is a – social – order of saying things, and saying something in a different way might mean that one would not be accepted. An elder commands respect and honour, as does a male and anyone with a special role or function. Relative social distance determines the form of address used. The register for forms of address used in the village setting is that of kinship terms. These determine the relationship between individuals, according to age and sex. The register can be extended to relations of honour. In general, one could say that the greater the distance, the more polite utterances have to be. With strangers, a rural Lao will always try to determine the hierarchical relationship between himself/herself and the stranger first, in order to identify the correct form of address to be used. In a remote area it is age that is the primary basis of determining the hierarchical relationship in question; in more hierarchical contexts the bases for determining the nature of the hierarchical relationship include status, function and wealth.

It should be borne in mind, too, that any environment in mainland Southeast Asia is and has always been more or less multiethnic (Izikowitz 1979). In this context, a simple language for interaction between people who are of different ethnicities and different statuses seems to have developed, which limits the need to express hierarchical differences. I call this the language of the market (Rehbein 2007).

The language of the royal court is basically all that is left of the language of the *muang*. A considerable percentage of administrative language originated well before 1975. The language of the royal court has had a profound influence on all forms of polite language, to this day. The court had its own forms of address; there were various registers for different types of hierarchical relations. This hierarchical system was very complex and had the capacity to express the relative social distance between two interacting persons. Characteristic of the language of the royal court are words of politeness and a special sense of euphony. That sense is present in village language as well, albeit not on an everyday basis (Koret 2000).

The Buddhist order, the *sangha*, created its own sociolect. For religious purposes, Pali was often used and the writing system remained close to early variants of Lao with roots in the Mon alphabet (McDaniel 2008). The everyday language within the monastery also differed from that used in other social environments, even though it was usually not Pali. Monks were – and continue to be – required to use a particular vocabulary, including specific forms of address, which are hierarchical. This hierarchical organisation of terms of address extends to the relation between laypersons and members of the Buddhist order. They too must address each other with specific terms reflecting each person's position.

Before French colonial rule was introduced, there was no unified Lao language (Evans 2002a). Several of the principalities (*muang*) spoke languages that were clearly related to what is now described as the Lao language, and had scripts that were similar to what is now the Lao script (Keyes 1995). But none of them was a state in which a codified and officially recognised 'Lao' language was spoken and written. The French not only constructed the nation state of Laos, they also defined a particular language as 'Lao'. A blend of a written form of polite language deriving from the royal court, incorporating elements of Buddhist vocabulary and elements of the language of the market, became the model for what came to be regarded as the 'correct' form of the Lao language. This blend is clearly reflected in the grammars written under colonial rule by Hospitalier (1937), Sila Viravong (1935) and Nginn (1965).

Phoumi Vongvichit, a student of Maha Sila Viravong and one of the leaders of the Lao People's Revolutionary Party, built on the ideas of his teacher. In his book on Lao grammar (Phoumi Vongvichit 1967), he called for a simpler orthography and the removal of Buddhist and royal vocabulary. He was able to enforce his ideas, which appeared to be merely descriptive and not normative, as norms for proper speech when he became minister of education in 1975. He put in motion a language reform, which was based on two main principles: that Lao should be clearly distinct from Thai, and that it should be easy to write. The vocabulary was modified and the infamous letter 'r' sorted out. A specific term of address accompanied the reform, the egalitarian term 'comrade' (*sahai*). The reform was put into practice through the party structure, which was present in every village and controlled all media. The state spread its vision and division of the world into all sections of society through the structures of the Lao People's Revolutionary Party and through education.

Integration

Besides the language – the sociolect – of the village, there were two other important sociolects, which remained distinct for centuries: that of the royal court and that of the monastery (cf. Ladwig 2008). A considerable percentage of administrative and religious language originated well before 1975 and even 1893. The royal court had its own forms of address. There were various registers, for different types of relationships. The best known is the register of *khaphachau-than* (I-you), which persists in modern polite language. This 'courteous' language is one of the roots of modernised polite language. The other root is the language of the market, which was the language used in inter-village communication. Neither of these was a national Lao language. Until French colonial rule, there was no Laos and even less was there a Lao language (Evans 2002, Chapter 2).

Under the French, a national integration of the territory now called Laos took place for the first time. The young nation entered 'modernity' at a slow pace, however (cf. Gay 1995; Stuart-Fox 2002 [1996]). A blend of the written language of the court, Buddhist terms and the language of the market became the model for *the* correct Lao language. This blend is reflected in the grammars by Hospitalier, Maha Sila Viravong and Nginn. One could present this as a case in point proving Bourdieu's claim that the ruling classes use the official language to enforce their own vision and division of the world. For the ruling class in Laos at the time were the French, albeit assisted by Vietnamese and the Lao nobility (Gay 1995). They dominated the emerging market, the administration, and the construction of a Lao identity, aiming to distinguish Laos from Siam. This official language that the French tried to implement as normatively correct was used as a model in Hospitalier's, Sila Viravong's and Nginn's grammars.

After the end of colonial rule and especially after 1975, different forces made themselves felt in the construction of an official language. Laos for the first time became an integrated political entity. Phoumi Vongvichit had the opportunity of seeing the language norms that he had established filter through into the most remote villages in the country. Laos became a socialist peasant society integrated through a single organ, the Lao People's Revolutionary Party, and guided by an egalitarian ideology (Evans 1990a). This posed what proved to be insurmountable theoretical and practical problems, problems that are reflected in Kaysone's writings and in similar problems encountered by other socialist, brother nations.

Over the years, the ruling Lao People's Revolutionary Party strengthened its position to a degree that enabled it to standardise and control language – through national integration, infrastructure, the education system, the media, party structures. Language has come to be subject to rationalisation (Weber 1972) and governmentality (Foucault 1980b). The norms of language use handed down from Maha Sila Viravong through Nginn and Phoumi Vongvichit to the present Ministry of Education have become familiar to a large percentage of the population, through practice (such as watching TV or – though to a much lesser degree – reading newspapers) and learning (especially at school). However, the differentiation of fields and language games renders complete control impossible.

Differentiation

After Gorbachev pulled out of Southeast Asia in 1986, Laos came under economic pressure. The introduction of a market economy meant the development of a somewhat autonomous economic field. The political elite has attempted to control this field through administrative measures. At the same time, many members of the elite are involved in the economic field as agents, especially the military, which is perhaps the biggest enterprise in Laos and the most powerful element within the political elite (cf. Walker 1999: 171). The emergence of a market economy has been coupled with a differentiation of professions, subcultures and fields. Social differentiation is most easily visible in vocabulary. The fields of economics, politics, and law have been subject to international advice and influence. Plenty of loan words have entered these fields. Their sociolects have become ever more technical and less intelligible to outsiders. And the fields themselves have undergone a process of differentiation. This is not conceivable if one attempts to understand what has been happening using only the concept of 'field'; it is only possible to make sense of what has happened by drawing both on Bourdieu's concept of 'field' and Wittgenstein's concept of 'language game'. An electrician does not share the vocabulary of a plumber even though they have a similar social position and act within the same field.

The development of these sociolects is not uniform. Whereas in popular culture, tourism and cross-border trade the influence of Thai is strong, the influence of other languages (not only English but also Pali and Sanskrit) is much greater in other contexts such as politics, law and finance. The academic field is a good example. The university is currently in the process of evolving from a political organ into an entity that is more autonomous. Academic disciplines at Lao institutions of higher education come under pressure from at least two directions. Globalisation links Lao academics to a regional and increasingly to a global discourse, in which they need to participate if they want to be taken seriously in the long run. They also have to react to the increasingly differentiated labour market in a competitive market economy if they want to keep the more promising students (and their own jobs).

University teachers who do not owe their position exclusively to old loyalties are therefore trying to improve their competitiveness. This includes through contributing to the emergence of a technical language within their discipline and increasing their own competency in this language. These technical languages do not differ very much in syntax from polite written language. But there is a need to develop lexical items – mainly nouns – for each specific field of knowledge. These lexical items are imported into the language along with the knowledge itself. The import of these is an active process, however, which is neither one-dimensional nor exclusively determined by power relations. It is strongly reminiscent of the import of Indian terms and institutions in the Middle Ages discussed by Jacques (1979), Wolters (1999), and many others. As in the case of plumbers and electricians, the language import is not restricted to the purpose of constructing the nation state or the struggle for a better social position, as Bourdieu claimed, but it serves practical purposes.

Lao university teachers have participated in courses led by representatives of various intellectual traditions from all parts of the world, but mainly from Japan, Vietnam, Thailand and Sweden. In some cases, teaching has been in English; more often it has been in the respective national language. How are the terms used in these courses rendered in Lao? There seem to be three main options. First, Lao university teachers look for a word in their own intellectual tradition or personal history. Second, Thai textbooks on social sciences are consulted. Third, a term is translated literally. An example of drawing on the first option would be the use of the word *sasana phi* ('spirit religion') to refer to animism; an example of drawing on the option variant would be the use of the word *patithanninyom* for 'positivism'; and an example of drawing on the third option would be the use of the term *thong na* ('rice field') for Bourdieu's 'field'.

Very soon, it will be impossible to trace the ways in which these terms entered Lao academic language. The three terms mentioned in the preceding paragraph could be interpreted as Lao (with partly Indian origins). But they are technical terms linked to the emergence of a Lao academic field. Lao who are not familiar with the social sciences will not be able to understand the language of that field. This is not so much for grammatical reasons; it is mainly because of the differentiation of life-worlds. People do not understand the vocabulary of the social sciences because they are not familiar with their language game, the practice of the field. However, some of the adapted technical terms are re-entering the public sphere. Examples are the terms *kan nyai thin* ('migration') or *pasakone* ('population').

The Public Sphere

The public sphere can be described as the integrated field of symbolic action, which is to a large degree linguistic action. It is a sphere of anonymous encounters, which are rare within the village, the royal court or the monastery. The anonymous language of the public sphere has the same two-fold origin as most practical sociolects: the market and the court. The court was replaced in 1975 by a socialist leadership that had different and partly contradictory linguistic ideals – those that Phoumi Vongvichit prescribed. Since 1986, socialism has been on the decline except in official politics, i.e. in the field of symbolic action on the part of the socialist leadership. The leadership controls the media and most of the public sphere. However, the elite of Laos does not consist exclusively of the socialist leadership any longer. It is only partly different from the elite of the 1960s as described by Joel Halpern (1961). Exiled royalist families are starting to return and are re-entering the elite. They form the spearhead of the other important social group seeking to dominate the public sphere: a group of economically successful families, the members of which have little influence in politics. The economic elite also comprises an upper middle class that is successful but not excessively rich, including technocrats and businessmen. Some of these have even risen into the political leadership, where they have, however, had to yield to the political elite. Furthermore, members of the political elite engage in economics themselves. This all means that the elite is not a homogeneous ruling class holding uniform principles of 'vision and division' of the social world, as Bourdieu implied (Bourdieu 1984: 255). In fact, the ruling class actually pursues inherently contradictory aims: social control through egalitarianism, personal wealth through laissez-faire politics, and the construction of a national identity through evocation of the past.

Social equality is no longer the guiding principle of politics in Laos. Cleavages between rural and urban populations and between the elite and the common people have reappeared. But these do not indicate a straightforward return to pre-socialist times. The main difference between the present and the pre-socialist past is the fact that the country is now politically and economically integrated (Rehbein 2007). That means that control of linguistic norms is at once more effective (because of political integration) and less possible (because of differentiation). Many of Phoumi Vongvichit's grammatical prescriptions have started to erode. The 'r' is being used again, mainly for foreign words but increasingly also for indigenous names and terms. Socialist vocabulary is becoming outdated. Terms that were tabooed after 1975 have started to return. The simplification of orthography does not persist in every field and context.

A market economy calls for an everyday language that is at once very defined and at the same time decontextualised, because the anonymous encounter becomes the rule instead of the exception. The differentiation of social functions and spheres that goes with a market economy also means a differentiation of life-worlds. People do not necessarily share the same semantic horizon, i.e. the same knowledge about a common linguistic topic. Apart from this, they have less time, in a market economy, for linguistic encounters. Everything has to be transacted without much ado – as in the village – and without much shared knowledge – in contrast to the village. Urban language generally seems to have fewer one-word utterances than the language of the village (Rehbein and Sayaseng 2004). Particles, which function as modifiers, such as 'please' or 'also', are more numerous. There is also a different system of address: in rural language, people address each other with kinship terms, while in urban language, personal pronouns have started to become the predominant form of address. This is the register of *khoi-chau-lao* (I-you-he/she). There are three ways in which individuals can address each other: kinship terms, courteous terms, and personal pronouns, of which the last is the most basic. These three alternatives are rooted in the three sociocultures of village, *muang* and capitalism. The socialist form of address is only used within the context of the LPRP.

In addition to the power struggle in the public sphere, the differentiation of fields and the dichotomy between urban and rural life, Laos is also still in a process of national integration vis-à-vis external forces rooted in globalisation and internal forces rooted in ethnic diversity. This process began under French rule and gained momentum after the Lao People's Revolutionary Party consolidated its power. The creation of a national culture – and language – is meant to unite all inhabitants of Laos under the leadership of the Lao government (Evans 1998b). However, close to 50% of the population are not ethnolinguistically Lao and some of them are strongly opposed to the Lao leadership; and the Lao themselves do not have many symbols to distinguish themselves from the Thai, especially Lao living in the Isan region. Language is one of the few ways in which it is possible for Lao to be distinguished from Thai. Phoumi Vongvichit's language reform after 1975 was intended to serve the purpose of distinguishing Lao from Thai. However, many of the elements he eliminated from the Lao language because they did not serve this purpose have started to reappear.

Thai-isation

N. J. Enfield (1999) has commented on the construction of a Lao national language and the current pressure from Thai. He argues that the influence of Thai media and other dynamics rooted in globalisation counter the construction of a Lao national language. His observations are certainly correct as far as the young urban middle class is concerned. However there are differences between what is happening in different social contexts. First, the Lao People's Revolutionary Party still has a powerful hold in the public sphere. This means not only an influence on the media but also on party members. Second, many rural Lao still have no access to most of the new phenomena. I observed in a remote village that even children who had access to a television set preferred playing outside to watching TV because the programmes screened did not mean anything to them. The words used and the things that happened in the programmes did not relate to their daily lives. Furthermore, the Lao People's Revolutionary Party still exerts a strong influence in the countryside, as the village heads are usually party members. Third, town dwellers who have an uncertain position, an underpaid job or no employment tend to be opposed to the urban elite. As part of this opposition they condemn foreign influence. In a survey, all respondents who were poorer than average thought that life in the (imagined) past was better than today (Rehbein 2004). And not all aspects of Thai-isation necessarily extend to the Lao language as a whole. Many technical or subcultural terms will not lead to a Thai-isation of Lao in general. In the previous section, I indicated that the term for 'positivism' (*patithan-ninyom*) in the social sciences has been adapted from Thai textbooks. Even if this term should one day enter the public sphere (which is not likely), it will not be interpreted as a Thai-isation of Lao but as another term of Indian origin. The opposite is the case for the terms that Enfield uses as examples, e.g. Thai *khuat* replacing Lao *kaeo* for 'bottle'.

What is happening among adolescents does seem, in the main, to support Enfield's claim. They tend to oppose the Lao People's Revolutionary Party and to support Thai culture. I even met three young Lao who spoke Thai rather than Lao and who claimed to be Thai. Even this is not a uniform trend, however, as a new Lao youth culture has started to develop, which expresses itself to a large degree in music (Rehbein 2004: 171). There are stars who sing in Lao, try to integrate old Lao melodies, and who are (or used to be) for the most part ordinary young Lao (and not members of the elite). Many young Lao are proud of this music and consider it to be part of their Lao identity, which they regard as distinct from Thai identity. There is also a rise in interest in Lao music and culture among Lao expatriates, both in terms of production and in terms of consumption.

Conclusion

In terms of present-day language use in Laos it would be too simplistic to state that there is a modernising tendency with a strong Thai flavour that is countering a conservative tendency rooted in the nationalist construction of a Lao language. There are, rather, a number of social fields within which various groups interact. These groups may share a linguistic culture; or they may struggle for dominance of their own linguistic culture. What the outcome of these interactions will be is not clear. But in relation to the future of the Lao national language, it is the public sphere that is most important. The public sphere is not just an instrument of symbolic violence, as Bourdieu (1984: 253) claimed, because the interests and the cultures of the ruling classes in Laos are rather heterogeneous. And it cannot be understood without examining the ways in which globalisation is influencing the situation. This is evident in the examples I have given from within the Lao academic field and in relation to Thai-isation. Competition, a struggle to retain or improve one's social position, goes hand-in-hand with globalisation. But it presupposes non-competitive factors rooted in communication, work and culture. The import of technical terms does not only serve the function of 'distinction' (Bourdieu 1984). And the persistence of the language of the village contradicts the notion of a competitive struggle. All of these elements should be viewed as parts of a complex sociocultural configuration that cannot be reduced to one principle.

Any analysis of Lao needs to distinguish between the different dimensions of linguistic hierarchies. Language becomes more anonymous with the move from the village to the city; more polite as society moves away from intimate relationships towards more distant hierarchic relationships; and more abstract as written language becomes more prominent and people move away from solely oral interactions. William Smalley (1994: 52) said something similar with regard to Thai:

> Speakers select among varieties along the social distance dimension according to such factors as formality or intimacy of a situation, the degree of public or private character it has, and the closeness of the relationship between the speakers. A speaker will quickly change from one of these varieties to another in response to ever-changing social situations.

CHAPTER 3

Lao Peasant Studies

Theoretical Review and Perspectives for Anthropology[1]

GRANT EVANS

When it was published, *Lao Peasants Under Socialism* (Evans 1990a) was virtually the only study of the peasantry under the Lao People's Democratic Republic. At that time some work was also available from consultants working with either the United Nations or SIDA, the Swedish aid arm, but even these were few and far between. And in retrospect *Lao Peasants* is unusual because of its immersion in theoretical debates about the peasantry.

Since then, peasant studies has gone into a precipitous decline after what was a 30-year boom. The boom grew out of an attempt to understand firstly the problems of 'underdevelopment', secondly the political upheavals throughout the 'Third World' during and following de-colonisation, and thirdly the role of peasants in revolutionary movements, whether in China, Vietnam or Mozambique. This latter preoccupation was given its clearest expression in Eric Wolf's *Peasant Wars of the Twentieth Century* (1969). In 1973 the *Journal of Peasant Studies* began publishing major theoretical and empirical studies of peasantries, and many other regionally focussed journals carried articles on various aspects of the peasantry. Of course, there were also books that sparked off long debates, such as Jim Scott's *Moral Economy of the Peasant* (1976)

1. The survey on which this research was originally based was completed in September 2004. A report was written afterwards but not published. This chapter was written in 2008 specifically for the book *New Research on Laos* (Goudineau and Lorrillard [eds] 2008) under the title: 'Lao Peasant Studies Today'. We have deleted 'today', which no longer make sense, and reinstated 'Theoretical Review and Perspectives for Anthropology', subtitle omitted at the time, in testimony to Grant Evans's obvious desire for theoretical discussion (editors' note).

or Samuel Popkin's contrasting *The Rational Peasant* (1979).[2] Most of these studies looked at the peasantry within a broad context of capitalist development, and Marxist theories more-or-less held sway. There were few studies of the peasantry under socialism; most were historical and not based on fieldwork because of communist restrictions on research. *Lao Peasants Under Socialism,* as it turned out, was one of the first batch of field studies made of the peasantry under communism during the 1980s.[3]

But as Hegelians say, 'the owl of Minerva only takes flight at dusk', or the fruits of knowledge are only gained in retrospect, and thus much of this effort was in fact commenting on a dying social and cultural formation. Some biting critiques of peasant studies in general have since been penned, such as Kearney's, where he writes: 'the category *peasant,* whatever validity it may once have had, has been outdistanced by contemporary history' (Kearney 1996: 1). His conceptual critique of the category, however, is less convincing than his account of the way rural communities in much of the world today (he focuses on Mexico) are connected into and reproduced by global processes. A more enlightening presentation of the issues is given by the long-time editors of *The Journal of Peasant Studies,* Henry Bernstein and Terry Byres, in the introductory essay to a journal, the title of which in itself marks the shift in perspective: *From Peasant Studies to Agrarian Change* (2001). Yet for Southeast Asia the most important overview has been that by R. E. Elson, *The End of the Peasantry in Southeast Asia* (1997), which provides a wonderfully clear statement of the political, economic, and social and cultural forces which ensured 'that the peasantry, gradually from the early twentieth century, and from the mid-century on at an accelerating rate, has been radically reconstituted, through its own agency and that of broader forces of change, into a series of more modern categories of social formation. The world of Southeast Asia is no longer a world dominated by peasants and peasant modes of life' (ibid.: 241)

Yet Laos (and perhaps Myanmar) remains dominated by peasants and peasant modes of life. Laos' geographical location and its recent political history ensured that the forces which swept across Southeast

2. My contributions to this debate were Evans 1986 and 1987.
3. The other studies that come to mind are: for China, Siu 1989 and Potter and Potter 1990; for Romania, Verdery 1991; for Hungary, Hann 1980; and, for Vietnam, Wiergersma 1988.

Asia have only lately arrived there. Hence the processes leading to the end of the peasantry in Laos have only started to gather steam in the 90s.

Sociologists, geographers, rural economists, and anthropologists flooded into Laos at the same time. Yet to date relatively little research has been published as either articles or as books. Restrictions on research meant that many studies are done under the cover of aid work, by consultants, and this work is discussed at length in the second half of this essay. I argue that the decline of the peasantry globally has deleteriously affected studies of the peasantry in Laos. Much of the knowledge that was accumulated by students of peasant societies is now ignored, and economic anthropology has been side-lined.[4] Therefore, in the pages below I try to point out the real world consequences of this. But lack of theoretical clarity also has implications for the study of history.

Historical Studies

Whatever the debates about the peasantry today, few people dispute the role of the peasantry in pre-modern Laos. Yet there has been relatively little discussion among historians of Laos about the social and economic relations they entered into in the past. Indeed until Yoshiyuki Masuhara's recent *Economic History of the Lao Lan Xang Kingdom* (2003) there had been no serious attempt to write an economic history of pre- modern Laos. Most other histories focus on political events. My *Short History of Laos* (Evans 2002a) is no exception to the rule, but it does provide a sketch of the socio-economic situation in the Lan Xang Kingdom.

While Buddhism was instrumental in creating a unified kingdom, Lan Xang faced serious material constraints to its ability to rival the other Tai kingdoms, especially the one emerging in Ayudhya. Based in the valley plains of the north, the peasantry continued to combine paddy and dry rice cultivation producing small surpluses and supporting populations much less dense than was possible on the Vientiane plain, or further south. For this reason, as the kingdom grew, so the capital naturally gravitated south towards Vientiane. But even when the kingdom was relocated, there is little evidence that the state ever sponsored irrigation as a way of augmenting its economic surplus. The construc-

4. It seems reasonable to speculate that, in an era of triumphalist capitalism following the fall of communism, a body of work that argues for the rationality of other economic systems would fall into disfavour and be overwhelmed by the current fetishism of 'the market'.

tion of dams and irrigation associations was left to local communities. The relatively small surpluses restricted the taxes and *corvée* that could be levied on the peasantry and therefore also the scale of public works that could be carried out, whether it be building roads or major temple complexes and cities. The other main source of revenue was trade in forest products such as sticklac, cardamom or beeswax, which were supplied primarily by minorities who remained in the mountains, some still as hunter-gatherers. This economic inter-dependence underpinned the ritual relations the Lan Xang court enacted with the surrounding Kha. Indicative of the relative weakness of the central king's power was that, unlike the king at Ayudhya, he could not monopolise trade in these goods. Another source of revenue, of course, was war and plunder and the capture of slaves to augment the population under the kingdom's control. While each new addition to the kingdom added to the tribute sent to the central court, the flows were not great by comparison with neighbouring kingdoms (ibid.: 12–13).

If this was in fact the basic structural condition of the Lan Xang kingdom, it nevertheless tells us relatively little about the actual dynamics of the kingdom at any particular period.

Masuhara (2003) divides the peasantry into the familiar categories of *phrai*, peasants who owe annual labour dues to an overlord, and *that*, a slave-like peasantry controlled by an overlord. We know from studies in Thai history that the fluctuations in the relative numbers of these two categories of peasants played an important role in the consolidation, or not, of centralised power.[5] And despite Masuhara's excellent work we still know relatively little about this in the context of Lao history.

Volker Grabowsky (2001) has provided a very interesting outline of the social organisation of the Lue of Chiang Khaeng, the core area of which was on the Muang Sing plain in Luang Nam Tha. He points out that different villages were connected to different groups of the aristocracy, and that different groups had varying *corvée* obligations, including the Kha. He also points out the importance of the latter's labour during harvesting of lowland rice, a situation that one no doubt found all the way down to Luang Prabang. Similar studies of the other Lao principalities would be very useful and enlightening.

5. In the Siamese kingdoms these two groups also had many sub-classifications. See e.g. Terwiel 1983.

An important question that could be taken up by modern researchers is the extent of paddy cultivation associated with the Luang Prabang kingdom in the past. Such research could presumably take several routes: looking at the yields and extent of paddy cultivation in the 20th century for which we have reasonable data; looking at the distribution of old established villages; and archaeological investigations, perhaps guided by areal photography. This at least would start to give us some idea of the type of manpower that could have been mobilised for war or building infrastructure. Similar studies could be done on the Vientiane plain.

Such research would certainly provide a better framework within which to tackle some recent issues that have emerged in historical studies of Laos, in particular the importance of internal and foreign trade. In fact, Masuhara's book mainly focuses on trade and is important for its systematisation of the data we have on trade in the Lan Xang period. Ann Maxwell Hill has also written an important book on trade in this region and its varying importance for the kingdoms of Lanna and Lan Xang. Like other writers before her she notes the importance of trade for the Luang Prabang court. But she goes a step further, saying that:

> Lao peasants themselves were characterised as more dependent on river trade than rice cultivation, work that was left to Khmu labourers or slaves [...] Luang Prabang's economy was based on trade, beginning at its foundations with the forest products bartered from the Khmu, collected by Lao commoners, and sold to intermediaries, Lao and foreigners, who supplied markets outside the Lao kingdom.
> (Hill 1998: 88–89)

Chiang Mai, on the other hand, was

> [...] strongly centralised and agriculturally based, a configuration of small rice-growing valleys with tribute relations with the centre. While ruling families in both cases were involved in trade, the role of long-distance trade was differently institutionalised. In Luang Prabang, the court's agricultural revenues appeared to be less significant than was income from trade [...] The Chiang Mai court had more land and people at its disposal than did Luang Prabang.
> (ibid.: 91)

Her characterisation of the courts in Luang Prabang and Chiang Mai is, I believe, broadly accurate. However, what should we make of her claim that 'Lao peasants' were mainly traders? (And if so, why call them 'peasants'?) She offers only anecdotal evidence of French travellers to give substance to this claim. And, even if trade was important, how big were the agricultural revenues she refers to in passing?

Andrew Walker – in a unique ethnography of traders in northern Laos in the 1990s, which came out at the same time as Hill's study – seems to suggest something similar in his chapter on historical trade and its regulation in the region. He argues that those of us who have studied Lao peasants have not paid sufficient attention to the role of trade for their livelihood. Although he does not in fact demonstrate how this alleged lack actually compromises our studies, I certainly agree with him that a good study of peasant marketing in Laos is well overdue.

In the historical context he disputes my characterisation of the Lao social formation as a 'tributary mode of production [...] a form of social organisation in which surpluses are extracted from the subordinate population by political rather than economic mechanisms' (Evans 1990a: 30, cited by Walker 1999: 27). But Walker does not ask who, precisely, this subordinate population is. Clearly the peasantry formed an important and large part, but there was also a hierarchy of individuals in official positions, and craftsmen and traders who were divided into local traders and foreign traders. To finance itself the state used political power to extract surpluses from subordinate groups either in the form of *corvée* or taxes. This says nothing about the role of trade amongst the peasantry, or among those farmers who fell outside the state's control. How the state financed itself, and the role of trade, both generally and among the peasantry, are distinct issues that Walker confuses.

Maybe this is because he did not grasp that the precise aim of Eric Wolf in *Europe and the People Without History* (1982), from whom I borrowed the concept of the tributary mode of production, was to critique the idea of self-sufficient villages or cultures.[6]

6. Walker has read Wolf, but does he understand him? As a supposed critique of Wolf's views of the role of merchants, he writes (Walker 1999: 29): 'my argument is that the pre-colonial states of northern Laos actively and enthusiastically supplemented their tributary income with direct and indirect revenue from trade and that, in some cases, tributary and mercantile institutions were closely interlinked'. Compare this with Wolf: 'If tributary relationships and mercantile activity have long existed side by side, often to their mutual benefit, such mutualism also entailed conflicts.' (1982: 84) What Wolf is interested is in the implications of these conflicts for the distribution of power in pre-modern states.

Maybe the confusion involves deeper issues that have been debated in economic anthropology for many years – a difference between those who recognise the 'embeddedness' of economies, and those who adopt a neo-classical economic position that only sees undifferentiated economic exchanges regardless of social structure.[7] I shall return to these issues.

The relocation of the Lan Xang court from Luang Prabang to Vientiane was an attempt to emulate the 'Chiang Mai model' through gaining access to wider swathes of agricultural land. A larger peasantry could be supported on the Vientiane plain and down along both sides of the Mekong River. Naturally, this meant that trade played a less central role in the support of the Vientiane-based Lan Xang state, although it remained critical for the principality of Luang Prabang. It also enabled a greater concentration of tributary power, which was why Vientiane-based kings are associated with Lan Xang's glory days. All the same, we need better studies of the kingdom's social and economic structure under, for example, King Surinyavongsa (1637–1695), in order to try to understand its dynamics.

But let us return to Hill's claim that Lao 'peasants' were mainly engaged in trade and not rice production. This raises many complicated theoretical and empirical issues. For instance, in a pre-modern kingdom does it matter what ethnicity your peasantry is? Surely, the key issue is first and foremost the social relations entered into by the peasantry, regardless of ethnicity. Most pre-modern kingdoms (at least in this part of the world) were multi-ethnic. What the marking of Lao ethnicity may indicate in the case of Laos is the degree to which a certain population came under the political and cultural sway of the state. Hill in fact commits the opposite error to that allegedly committed by those who emphasise tribute from the peasantry (according to Walker) – namely, there is no discussion of the economic role of the lowland rice-growing peasantry and its contribution to the state's coffers. Admittedly, the actual size of this peasantry is open to debate, as is the potential surplus it could produce, and obviously it was not sufficient to maintain a major pre-modern state. But one might argue that however large the lowland

7. In the language of this debate the former are known are 'substantivists' and the latter as 'formalists'. For an introduction to the key issues see Plattner 1989.

peasantry was, it was a crucial pre-condition for the formation of the Luang Prabang state, regardless of the importance of trade for the latter.

The composition of peasant villages is also an important avenue for research. Grabowsky's study of Muang Sing indicates that there were lowland 'minority' villages incorporated within the compass of the pre-modern state, and this was true in Luang Prabang too. There were also 'mixed' villages. At the edge of the state's reach and into a zone of fluctuating state influence there were obviously many more such villages, and beyond that the peasantry faded into what Wolf calls kin-based modes of production. Presumably, as the reach of the state waxed and waned, some groups moved in and out of peasant status. Much later, in the 1930s, anthropologist Karl Izikowitz documents this frontier zone when he writes about the 'penetration' of small groups of Lao merchants and handicraftsmen into areas populated by Khmu and Lamet peoples, and the establishment of often ethnically mixed villages at the mouth of tributaries to the Mekong River (Izikowitz 1979 [1951]: 27–29). The main item traded with the Lao merchants was rice, but trade fluctuated, and as Izikowitz writes 'during recent years trade has been poor, and the Lao had been obliged to change over to agriculture in order to exist' (ibid.: 28).[8] Masuhara (2003: 143–5) remarks on the importance of rice produced by the upland 'Lao Theung'[9] for the maintenance of Luang Prabang historically, and indeed up into the 20th century. He also points out, in contrast to others, that most Lao were also engaged in rice growing but that the latter could always make up for any shortages through trade with the uplanders. Many of these upland farmers were historically beyond the direct control of the state or any overlord, but surpluses were gleaned for the state by taxing the upland-lowland traders.

The penetration of Tai and Lao groups into areas dominated by other groups clearly fascinated Izikowitz and he devoted two important essays to the process (1962, 1969). The issue has also been addressed by Condominas (1990), by me (Evans 1999b) and by Évrard (2003). This though is a process with a long history, and these relatively modern studies can give us some indications of the processes in the historical past.

8. At that time the introduction of motorboats and access to rice from Siam was changing the direction of trade (Izikowitz 1979 [1951]: 311).

9. Masuhara uses this 20th century category uncritically, whereas the historical category would have been 'Kha', which was used to signify subordinate populations who were not necessarily marked ethnically.

It is interesting that although Izikowitz's book *Lamet* (1979 [1951]) is subtitled *Hill Peasants in French Indochina*, he refers to them on the opening page of his introduction as a 'tribe'. I have discussed the problems of this concept elsewhere (Evans 1999a: 175–6), but essentially what it signifies is a form of social organisation without a state, or perhaps it would be better phrased in our context as 'beyond the state'. Interestingly the upland Tai have historically been referred to as 'tribal Tai', and although this designation has never been theorised it would also appear to draw its meaning from the idea that these peoples never formed a state. The Sip Song Chu Tai, which encompassed parts of the provinces of Huaphanh, Son La and Lai Chau in the past, is probably best conceptualised as a kind of segmentary chieftainship, rather than as a state. In a chieftainship the surpluses that flow up towards the chiefly lineages are largely redistributed, rather than accumulated as they are in a state.

So, a central feature of Lao history has been attempts by the lowland states to control and incorporate culturally distinct peoples beyond their reach – a process that accelerated with the formation of the first modern state under colonialism, and which is continuing today as the state carries out the large-scale resettlement of upland groups. A key difference between the pre-modern state and the present is that the modern state is consciously committed to the cultural conversion of the minorities – regardless of proclamations of 'multi-ethnicity'.

The social relations entered into by peasants changed over historical time. The pre-modern peasantry lived in prebendal domains (to use the taxonomy of Wolf 1966: 51–52), where an overlord was sanctioned to collect tribute from the peasantry, take a share, and pass the rest onto the central sovereign's treasury. Lao peasants were not tenants, but held land by customary right associated with particular villages. By the mid-19th century, however, the number of Lao peasants living in prebendal domains had shrunk dramatically as a result of the destruction of the Vientiane kingdom and the Phuan principality, and the contraction of the state's power in both Luang Prabang and in Champassak. Many former peasant villages existed independently of any state and were indistinguishable from so-called 'tribes'. French colonialism set about bringing these villages back under the aegis of the state as a free landowning peasantry, which was then subject to a fairly light tax in kind (*corvée*) or in cash. Later, during most of the Royal Lao Government period, taxes were rarely collected because the state was maintained by foreign aid. The most serious challenge to the freeholding peasantry was the ill-fated collectivisation programme launched by the Lao PDR in 1978, and effectively shelved by the mid-1980s. Today, land allocation and registration is encroaching on what many peasants consider to be their natural rights.

The relationship of the peasantry to the state and the classes sustained by the state has fluctuated, both in the pre-modern period and up to the present, and these variations should be documented. For example, after Randy Ireson (one of the best essayists on the Lao peasantry) pointed out that my argument on village cooperation in *Lao Peasants* did not take into account variations between the north and south of the country (R.W. Ireson 1992), I was prompted to make some historical speculations in an introduction to the re-issue of the book in 1995:

> [...] [Ireson] points out that in the south labour exchange tends to follow principles of generalized reciprocity across the whole village, while in the north principles of strict reciprocity are more common and apply to a narrower group of people. In both cases this works to distribute labour effectively, to inhibit stratification and to provide a form of baseline insurance for families in difficulty. His explanation for these differences is ecological. In the north peasants farm in upland valleys and combine paddy with swiddens, while in the southern plains paddy predominates and market access is greater, and these differences have implications for labour distribution and exchange. Ecology is clearly an important variable when considering variations in patterns of exchange. Reading his article also caused me to wonder whether there are also historical variables, and whether the prevalence of strict reciprocity among many northern villages is also related to the formation of villages by refugees. The history of the north is one of wars and peasant displacement since the sacking of Vientiane by the Thai in 1829, the later destruction of the Phuan state, and then wars at various times in the twentieth century. The coming together of refugees, many of whom are strangers, to form new villages may also have contributed to the predominance of strict reciprocity in the north. These speculations call for good social or ethno histories of the Lao peasantry.
> (Evans 1995a: XXV–XXVI)

No doubt many other features of peasant social organisation and cultural practice could be subject to the same historical scrutiny.

The Peasantry and French Colonialism

Almost every aspect of French colonialism in Laos remains understudied, including the impact of colonialism on Lao rural society. An important exception is Geoffrey Gunn's *Rebellion in Laos: Peasant and Politics in a Colonial Backwater* (1990). But as is apparent from the title, his study is a paradigmatic example of the Marxisant analyses of the peasantry produced during the heyday of peasant studies. Gunn writes:

> The thesis of this work holds that even in the most remote village of a colonial backwater, peasant behaviour was influenced from the outset of the imperialist encounter, as much by the laws of capitalism (unequal exchange and surplus accumulation) as by the transformations engendered by the imposition of the colonial bureaucratic state. (1990: 4)

Gunn draws heavily on the framework of Murray's study *The Development of Capitalism in Colonial Indochina (1870–1940)* (Murray 1981), which primarily looks at Vietnam, while Gunn shifts the focus to Laos to demonstrate that the 'colonial state project' there was also to establish the conditions for capitalist development. Yet despite some colonial fantasies about great wealth, the pickings were slim. They were largely confined to a tin mine, some logging, some trade in forest products, and state subsidised transport, although Gunn wants to suggest that their impact was deeper: 'while certain structures upheld the surface quality of tradition, in fact these structures were to a large extent penetrated by the laws of motion of capitalist production' (Gunn 1990: 30).

The French promoted the growing of opium in Laos and Gunn is quite right to point out the importance of opium revenue for French colonialism. Of course it had an important impact on the upland economy in northern Laos, but did it transform the highlanders who grew opium into 'cash crop opium farmers' as Gunn claims (ibid.: 46)? Unfortunately, he provides little on-the-ground evidence for this. Studies of the Hmong highland economy indicate that it was not totally dependent for its reproduction on outside commercial trade, as Gunn's thesis would have it. One would like to know how this wealth was used inside Hmong society? Did it lead to social stratification, inflation of bride-wealth, and so on? For example, the father of a well-known Hmong leader during the RLG period, Touby Lyfoung, used opium revenue to hire a Vietnamese teacher to teach his sons French in the 1920s and thereby ensured their future standing inside the colonial political structure. What is really needed is a less politically motivated study of the impact of opium on upland societies both in the past and present.

Gunn also provides the most comprehensive picture to date of colonial state impositions on the Lao population. Yet, despite the intentions of the author the picture that emerges is of a relatively *ad hoc* and inefficient system, though more efficient than pre-modern dynastic states. His main conclusion would seem to disarm his stronger claims: 'The colonial state project [in Laos] was almost coterminous with road building.' (ibid.: 55) The French impact on rural Laos in fact appears to have been very uneven. The political stability it brought no doubt encouraged rural trade, but it had relatively little impact on basic social relations in the villages.

Entitled 'The Non-Rebellion of the Lao', part two of Gunn's book gives away its political agenda. Why is this even a relevant issue unless one assumes that peasant should naturally revolt against colonialism? Gunn wishes to argue that they were 'exploited' economically by colonialism but is not at all convincing. The highland revolts that occurred during the colonial period, among the Hmong in the north and the Loven centred on the Boloven Plateau in the south, are also supposed to be reactions to economic exploitation by colonial capitalism. Yet what is clear even from the material presented by Gunn is that the main motive for all of these revolts was political. The French intervention disturbed pre-existing alliances and power structures and the revolts were attempts to re-order them (see Goudineau, this volume Chapter 6). That they took on a millennial cast is hardly unusual for a colonial situation, or indeed any situation where the spread of the influence of the modern state upsets traditional relations.[10] Official communist histories inside Laos today take a position not so different from Gunn in seeing these revolts as proto-nationalist and revolutionary, rather than perhaps being 'reactionary'. More theoretical clarity and more rigorous empirical work needs to be done on these issues.

The Peasant Economy

Those who approach economies as undifferentiated exchange systems are uninterested in the concept of a peasant economy as a distinct form

10. In neighbouring Thailand at the same time, millennial revolts were occurring in the northeast in reaction to the expansion of the modern state. See Keyes 1977.

of economic organisation. Economic anthropology, on the other hand, has tried to show how particular forms of economic action are embedded in specific social, cultural and indeed political forms, and therefore are not amenable to a single economic theory.

Some anthropologists, such as Bowie (1992) in 'Unravelling the myth of the subsistence economy', an influential essay on 19th-century northern Thailand, seem to believe that a peasant economy is autarchic – a proposition which she easily disproves by pointing out the importance of trade for the economy in general in the north. But any serious consideration of the anthropological literature on the peasantry (which she does not provide) would make it clear that peasants are part of larger political, cultural and economic networks. One might say, they are non-autarchic by definition. She gives some important empirical data, but what she and others like her do not show is how trade articulates with the peasant economy.[11]

Yet one important feature of peasant society is its high level of self-provisioning (often glossed as 'subsistence'). So, for example, Izikowitz writes of the Lamet:

> It is undoubtedly true that the Lamet produce the greatest part of their food, their houses, and many implements. But in order to manage their life of production, they are dependent on a number of necessities that they cannot produce themselves, and therefore these commodities must be obtained by means of trade with other tribes. (1979: 309)

One of these necessities was steel axes. But, for instance, how did the trade in axes affect the peasant economy? A classic anthropological essay by Lauriston Sharp, 'Steel axes for stone-age Australians', used the penetration of steel axes into aboriginal communities as the 'epitome of the increasing quantity of European goods and implements received by the aboriginals and of their general influence on the native culture' (1987 [1951]: 397). Significantly, this technological innovation produced little economic change, simply giving the aboriginals more leisure time. But the flood of axes into the society through the missionaries and other whites upset fictive kinship relationships between trading partners, and upset gender relations, among many other things. So, it is reasonable to ask, what impact did the trade in steel axes have on the Lamet? Izikowitz

11. Like Walker she confuses the importance of trade for the state with the importance of trade for the peasants.

does not say, and so perhaps it was insignificant. But a key question for any anthropologist studying trade is, how and at what point does engagement in outside trade begin to transform village social relations?

One of the many virtues of Izikowitz's study is that he also inquires into the broader motivations for Lamet economic action, which he finds are in fact associated with prestige (e.g. acquiring a bronze drum) and marriage alliances, not a search for profit. Thus:

> Wealth is accumulated in the form of buffaloes, bronze drums and other articles of luxury, and these things are exchanged on entering into matrimony [...] there seems to be a division of articles into masculine and feminine categories. The men often contribute with buffaloes, bronze drums and gongs, in the matter of bride price, while women bring silks, clothes and jewels, and perhaps a pig on some occasions, as dowry. (Izikowitz 1979: 316)

Izikowitz also points out that the 'gendered' nature of economic action reserves important economic rights for women.[12] Here we are in the unmistakeable presence of an economy that is motivated along very specific cultural lines, and is not amendable to explication by any general economic theory.

Opium cultivation in the highlands also drew the Hmong into wider circuits of exchange. However, even though they used Khmu wage labourers in their fields, they accumulated wealth for marriage exchanges, not capital accumulation *per se.*[13] In an essay on Buddhism and economic action in Laos (Evans 1993a), I proposed that an important motivation for economic action among Lao peasants was the acquiring of merit, which had the spin-off effect of redistributing wealth in such a way that it reproduced village solidarity. The essay looked at how collectivisation threatened this economic practice, and at how the government's programme could not mobilise this peasant motivation to its own ends.

A central feature of my critique of collectivisation in *Lao Peasants Under Socialism* (Evans 1995a) was based on a particular understanding of how the peasant economy operated. Of course, a central part of its critique was aimed at the conventional communist understanding of class stratification among the peasantry. The notion that independent peasants were incipient capitalists who would grow in strength and

12. This contrasts with the picture painted by Carol Ireson (1996: 91–2).

13. See my remarks on the Hmong in Evans 1990b: 54.

come to oppose the regime was a key motivation for collectivisation. The most convincing body of theory marshalled against this argument was by A.V. Chayanov (1888–1939). Peasants were not spontaneous capitalists, he argued, because the categories of the capitalist economy were simply inappropriate to the peasant economy (see, for example Chayanov 1986: 68–9). Its basic unit was the household, whose dual role as a producer and consumer unit involved it in production mainly for use rather than exchange.

The structure and activity of the peasant farm pivots on production of use-values, as distinct from the generalised production of exchange-values typical of capitalism. This determines farm use of land, labour and investment. Because the peasant farm does not need to turn a profit and at a minimum only has to feed its labourers and dependents, it can run at a 'loss', and in this respect it can have a competitive edge over capitalist farms (ibid.: 89, 236). What is so striking about Chayanov's formulation is that it proposes a diametrically opposite result to that of classical Marxism.

The last chapter of Chayanov's book *Theory of Peasant Economy*, 'Peasant farm organisation' (1986 [1925, 1966]), offers a unique model of social differentiation among the peasantry. Referring to Russia, he argues that while some social class differentiation was observable in the countryside, the underlying reason for the heterogeneity of the peasant farms was demographic: 'in the depths of the peasantry takes place a series of very complex and tangled demographic processes' (Chayanov 1986 [1925, 1966]: 246). The various strands of this tangled process entailed some families dying out, others migrating, or families dividing into several independent farms. Very small farms were the ones which completely broke down, and the occupants would migrate in search of better territory or to the towns. Among the larger and older farms at the other end of the scale, 'more than half of them reached full maturity and broke down into a number of new farms' (ibid.: 247). The general pattern, he maintains, is the rising and falling sizes of particular farms: 'Before us are two powerful currents. One in which the young, undivided farms with small sown area mainly participate, is rising, expanding the volume of its farms under pressure of family growth. The other is declining, largely due to the dividing of old, complex families.' (ibid.: 248) In this model the peasantry is seen to experience considerable social mobility, but if we choose to look at the balance of respective currents 'we get a picture of complete static calm' (ibid.: 249).

The relevance of Chayanov's demographic model of peasant differentiation or mobility to the peasantry in the late 20th century was questioned by one of his main defenders, Teodor Shanin, who writes: 'demographic determinants act relatively slowly compared with the current trends of social transformations. The growing complexity, heterogeneity, and changeability of contemporary agriculture and of the peasant ways to make ends meet would make this demographically related model very limited as against the factors which do not enter it: state policies and markets for goods and labour (now worldwide), new agricultural techniques, the extra-village cartelisation of supply, demand, and credit, or the social construction of new needs' (Shanin 1986: 2–3). Shanin does not question the capacity of peasants to survive in the face of capitalist development, but he suggests that the main determinants of peasant mobility and economic effort are today no longer demographic. However, Shanin does acknowledge that the less developed a society is, the more salient is the demographic model. In an economy and society like Laos, where the peasant natural economy predominates, Chayanov's observations retain their force.

The Lao natural economy has largely survived up to the present because firstly, under French colonialism, agrarian social relations remained largely unchanged except for the expansion of the reach of the state. Then under the Royal Lao Government attempts to promote economic development in the countryside were thwarted by war. Communist tendencies towards economic autarchy and the state's attempt to control all internal and external trade, combined with a policy of collectivisation, in fact reinforced the natural economy during the first decade of the Lao PDR. Only in the past 20 years or so has this begun to change. The socialist economic system has been abandoned, and we can observe changes in the Lao countryside today that are similar to developments in other developing capitalist countries in Southeast Asia.

Commercial farming of coffee has expanded in the south, and timber plantations are being established along with other forms of commercial farming. New forms of technology have spread rapidly, such as 'iron buffaloes', new rice seed varieties, and irrigation systems fed by mechanical pumps. Commerce has expanded swiftly throughout the country, and road building has assisted its spread.[14] The commercial value of land has grown dramatically, especially near towns, and while some farmers have benefited from this, others have been swindled.

Yet the reality of Lao agriculture, as both the government and aid agencies continually remind us, is that it remains relatively undeveloped despite the fact that in the past 20 years massive amounts of foreign aid have poured into the sector. Nevertheless, we can probably say that Laos has now begun its irreversible march towards the end of the peasantry. In the meantime, however, we find conditions in Laos that provide anthropologists and others with a final glimpse of a traditional peasant way of life.

The Theoretical Poverty of Consultants

In the wake of foreign aid came a phalanx of consultants, including rural sociologists and anthropologists. My reading of dozens of reports produced by these consultants has convinced me that peasant studies has barely touched them, and that an understanding of basic issues in economic anthropology is completely lacking.[15]

The mantra of foreign aid in the last decade has been the eradication of rural poverty, and Lao newspapers are filled on a weekly basis with articles concerning the struggle against poverty. This emphasis follows the Millennium Goals of the UN and other international agencies, such as the Asian Development Bank (ADB). Laos, a heavily aid-dependent country, is constrained to follow these externally generated campaigns.[16] By internationally-determined criteria, Laos is considered one of the poorest countries in Asia, a 'fact' which is repeated in almost every foreign journalist's report and every foreign aid report. Yet, those who work in the country see very little of the kind of desperate poverty that one

14. See, for example, Trankell's 1993 study.

15. In 1998, I carried out a review of consultant reports on poverty in Laos for the FAO. In 2004, I reviewed a Japan Foundation for Poverty Reduction project for upland small-scale irrigation areas.

16. In response to these internationally-generated pressures, the Lao have tried to construct 'objective' statistical criteria for poverty measurement. One major study on poverty by the Asian Development Bank, the Lao State Planning Committee and the National Statistical Centre, *Participatory Poverty Assessment in the Lao PDR* (Asian Development Bank et al. 2001), does attempt a critique of this approach, and tries to develop a contextually sensitive analysis of poverty – one that looks, for example, at ethnicity as a key variable.

finds in other Asian countries, who by these internationally-generated criteria are considered less poor than Laos. As one Luang Prabang villager in the Houay Lor area said to me in June 2004, 'We are not really poor. But we're poor in the sense that if we want to buy something we just can't go out and get it.'

In Lao villages there is a very small stratum of people who are universally considered desperately poor. However, their poverty is not systemic. That is, they are usually widows or women with young children whose husbands have left them, or disabled people, or old people with no relatives. For example, in June 2004 in Ban Hin Houa Seua, a Hmong village in Muang Xaysomboun, there were nine people identified by the villagers as being in this category. They rely in part on the charity of the villagers, and the latter would like to be relieved of that burden and have approached the district administration for help. Social welfare for the very poor, however, is hardly known in Laos. One could also add people who are poor because of alcoholism or drug addiction. These individual pathologies are found the world over. However, among minorities in Laos it has also been observed that alcoholism and drug addiction rise during and after resettlement, due to social and cultural disorientation.[17]

It is easy to see that the campaign against poverty in the rural areas of Laos, sponsored firstly by international aid organisations and consequently by the Lao government, is based on theoretical premises derived from India or Latin America, for example, where there is a long history of class inequality in the countryside and a long history of commercial farming. This is simply not true in Laos, where the campaign against poverty has produced a rather invidious situation in which villages have been asked to categorise their population into various strata of poor – the prevalent categories seem to be those who have enough, the medium poor and the very poor. In practice such categories are arbitrary and problematic, generating two paradoxical results: on the one hand it is in the interests of all villagers to present themselves as poor to international agencies in order to attract aid, and on the other hand they are confronted with the problematic task of categorising themselves in ways which highlight relative social status in the village. No one really wants to be typecast as 'poor' relative to fellow villagers – it is a matter of *kiat saksi*, or dignity. Consequently, these categories are generated arbitrar-

17. See Asian Development Bank et al. (2001: 50) and Cohen 2000.

ily for external consumption. But while the villagers may have a good reason for producing vague categories, this is not true for the consultants themselves, who demonstrably are unable to create anything more coherent because of their theoretical lack of understanding of peasant economy and society.

The villagers' criteria for being poor are those pertinent to a natural economy. That is, where 'poverty' is primarily measured by whether people have enough to eat or not.[18] Degrees of rice self-sufficiency play a major role for most groups because for most of them rice is a staple. But such an economy also depends on many other food inputs, gathered from forests and produced in gardens, fished from rivers and streams, and raised as livestock of various kinds. These factors are generally poorly enumerated in most studies of 'poverty' in rural Laos. Rice, however, is a prestige food and this is reflected in upland preferences even when greater attention to the production and consumption of maize and tuber crops, for example, would increase food security in remote areas. Reported rice shortages of up to four months may in fact be deceptive and various factors, according to one important study, 'may make it more attractive for the family to produce and store rice for 8–10 months only, rather than having large surpluses' (Roder et al. 1996: 406). Commercial development in the countryside of Laos is very uneven, but villagers are increasingly engaged in market exchanges which contribute to their well-being. Indeed the above study predicts that with improved market access 'upland farmers will become more dependent on rice produced in lowland environments' (a reversal of the historical trends we observed earlier). But, it remarks, there remains a strong demand for upland varieties to be 'sold at premium prices' (ibid.: 407).

The growing interaction of rural villagers with a wider world, not only via the market but also via mass media, has made them aware of their relative poverty. In other words, they now have sources of comparison previously unavailable to them and this, combined with a widely advertised government programme to combat 'poverty', makes

18. *The Participatory Poverty Assessment* claims that this idea of 'enough' is characteristic of lowland Lao peasants, but not of highlanders, who are described as 'maximisers', a concept which is not, unfortunately, fully explained. But if true, one would expect that these 'maximisers' feel the subjective impact of relative poverty more than those who consider themselves to have 'enough'. See Asian Development Bank et al. 2001: 6.

them increasingly aware of what they do not have. This is an important factor in their perception and presentation of their own poverty.

But there are deeper issues to be considered. Consultant documents are replete with terms like 'equity', which are presumably founded on some concept of equality. The actual meanings of these terms are never made clear because they are so deeply entrenched in international aid rhetoric (i.e. a highly conventionalised use of language which is rarely queried). But what do such terms, even concepts, mean in the context of village society? In no consultant document that I have looked at can one find a theory of peasant economy or society which would support, or give meaning to these rhetorical terms.

What is 'equality' or 'inequality' in Lao peasant society? As I argued in *Lao Peasants under Socialism and Post-Socialism*, one finds no real long-term inequalities within Lao rural villages. This is because a key dynamic of the village economy is the domestic cycle of household groups, which means that over time there is a wave-like undulation of family fortunes. Invariably, newly-wedded people with immature children have relatively few resources, but they acquire them through inheritance and as their children's labour enters the peasant economy. A snapshot of a village will reveal families in different stages of this domestic cycle. Thus someone who appears 'poor' in the snapshot would appear better off in a snapshot taken further on in the cycle. Similarly, a family at the height of its use of labour and land will appear well-off, but will appear in a later snapshot as a diminished entity when land and labour are dispersed through inheritance and through children beginning their own domestic groups.

Most so-called poverty measurements in Lao villages operate with a static snapshot model of the society, rather than the more dynamic one proposed above. If this latter model is accepted, then it is reasonable to treat villages as poor, rather than using the invidious strategy of trying to enumerate which *individual villagers* are poorer than others. After all, 'poor' young married couples are connected to 'the rich' in the village by ties of kinship and other bonds, which are also sources of village solidarity.

Thus, one can conclude that almost all consultant studies are based on an incorrect understanding of the dynamics of Lao peasant society. Of course, one can argue as the *Participatory Poverty Assessment* study does (Asian Development Bank et al 2001: 17), that in the past decade inequalities have increased within Lao society as a whole, and indeed between provinces. But so far, except perhaps in the areas where production has become most commercialised, this has not had much effect on the dynamics of individual peasant villages, and certainly not in the more remote areas. Where land use has been monopolised at the expense of villagers in Laos it has most often been a result of land being taken over by outsiders, in particular for logging.[19] This makes all villagers poorer, but it is not a result of internal village social differentiation.

There are wealth and resource differences found within villages, but rarely can we talk of a 'rich group' dominating the affairs of a village. Visible signs of wealth differences are obvious in some villages, such as brick houses for some families. In Ban Hin Houa Seua, mentioned above, this is largely an outcome of the wealth of overseas Hmong relatives and the remittances they can afford. Others have opportunities because of the success of a relative in the bureaucracy, or more rarely business in a rural town or city. Others have the bad luck to be farming on bad soil. And there are those people who are poorer than others because, as the villagers will readily say, they are 'lazy'– a commonly used indigenous category usually passed over in embarrassed silence by consultants and academics.

The main poverty differences one can observe in Laos are between villages, not within villages, and these differences are not the result of the dynamics of the peasant social structure itself. Poverty is a direct outcome of outside intervention in the workings of these societies, in particular the government's policy of re-locating upland minorities in the lowlands – a policy which has been conducted at various levels of intensity since 1975, but especially in the past 10 or so years. These facts are obscured by the methodology adopted by consultants who emphasize differentiation within the peasant social structure (which as I have argued is relatively minor and not structural at a village level).

The Lao Government justifies its relocation programme by claiming that swidden agriculture is ecologically destructive. This debate on upland swidden cultivation has been going on for years in Laos, and strong arguments have been put forward to show which systems are

19. For example, see the case discussed in 'Making money from trees? Commercial tree plantations in Lao PDR', *Watershed* 9(3), March–June, 2004.

viable and which are not.[20] Land re-allocation policies conducted in the past decade seem to have largely ignored these debates, and allocation has made what were viable systems unviable by restricting access to certain uplands. This has forced people to shorten fallows, causing yields to fall, thus further impoverishing them. As one study on the ongoing land titling and allocation notes of those carrying out the project 'field staff make a direct association between land allocation and the program of shifting cultivation reduction, i.e. the purpose in allocating land is to reduce the area of land under swidden farming. The principle of sustainable land allocations seems to be less important [...] Restoring forests is an admirable objective, but if it is done at the expense of sustainable agricultural production systems, it will lead to long term livelihood problems.'[21] In fact, the drive to bring upland societies firmly within the compass of the state is the fundamental cause of this blindness to reasoned economic and ecological arguments.

The Rural Community

But the lack of preparedness of rural sociologists and anthropologists is also evident in the use of the ubiquitous but rarely scrutinised category, 'community'. Well-established villages have very clear ideas about who belongs and who does not belong to their village community. By being in such a defined community one is bound by customarily established rights and obligations, which can be referred to as the 'moral economy' of the village.[22] The rules of this moral economy do not apply, by and large, beyond that defined community. Such village communities establish their collective identity through adherence to and participation in rituals associated with a Buddhist temple – if they are lowland Lao – or *phi ban* ['village spirit'] celebrations, which are also common among other ethnic groups. Celebrations for ancestral spirits in, for example, Tai Daeng or Khmu villages, may even see the village sealed off for the day – a clear definition of who is part of the community. Among Hmong, lineage and ancestral rituals help to define their moral community, and

20. The most exhaustive study of this population relocation programme to date is Goudineau ed. 1997a. On swidden cultivation see Roder 1997.

21. Lao Consulting Group of the Ministry of Finance 2002: 11. See also Asian Development Bank et al. 2001: 62–66, 88–90, and Vandergeest 2003.

22. In Lao this could be translated as ເສດຖະກິດ ຢູ່ໄຕ້ ສິນທຳໆ. The classic statement is in Scott 1976.

so on.[23] In the past, upland Tai villages came together in larger ritual communities for *phi muang* ['spirit of the muang'] celebrations. These, however, disappeared with the revolution. Kinship networks are also dense in these rural villages, and have their own criss-crossing ritual forms.[24]

It is within such a community that transactions for collective endeavours mainly take place, such as labour exchange, house building, temple maintenance, traditional irrigation maintenance, and so on.[25] Not surprisingly, these moral economies generate ideologies which value mutual help and cooperation highly because it is fundamental to the system. In the countryside people readily speak, usually rhetorically, about the value of 'solidarity' and 'mutual help'. However, it would be a grave mistake to assume that such commitments easily transcend a clearly defined community, or are applied indiscriminately internally (to do so was a fundamental misunderstanding during the collectivisation programme in Laos from 1976 to 86. See Chapter 6 of Evans 1990a). Indeed, reckonings are made of reciprocity, usually scaled according to kinship distance. Everyone has an acute eye for 'free riders' (i.e. people who do not reciprocate), who are always a problem in systems of mutual assistance, and such people are usually spurned, primarily by others refusing to enter into reciprocal transactions with them, and perhaps finally branded as 'lazy'.[26]

In consultant documents, and in the speeches of local officials, one can find simplistic appeals to 'community', 'solidarity' and 'mutual help', 'because we are all Lao!' Of course, no villager is going to contradict

23. In Ban Hin Houa Seua a significant number of the Hmong are Christians, and they have a well established church. For some, therefore, this involves negotiation between traditional and Christian beliefs. One Christian explained that when the Hmong moved there several people died in quick succession and the elders therefore made offerings to the *phi* ('spirits') of the Hin Houa Seua ('tiger head rock'). He did not attend the rituals, but he remarked that they were effective as the deaths stopped soon after.

24. *The Participatory Poverty Assessment* makes the important point that upland societies are less village-focused than Lao or Tai peoples, among whom time is distributed equally between their fields and the village (Asian Development Bank et al. 2001: 85). This oscillation would influence the dynamics of their moral economy. As long as they rely on the uplands, resettling these people near or in lowland villages is unlikely to change this dynamic.

25. A good study is by C. Ireson (1996). This article refers mainly to ethnic Lao villages.

26. Officials are inclined to use 'lazy' differently, usually as a way of characterising peasant resistance to top-down schemes.

such statements in the abstract, for indeed on the surface the rhetoric is compatible with their basic viewpoint. However 'the nation' is the most abstract community these villagers belong to (if indeed they do see themselves as belonging to such an entity), and it is a long way from the very concrete village communities they live in from day to day. The practical concerns of their everyday commitments override these wider claims to allegiance.

Such broad appeals, however, often obscure quite distinct communities. Thus in the case of my recent investigation of 'community' projects for improving upland small-scale irrigation I found well-established lowland Lao villages (in one case hundreds of years old), or well-established upland Tai villages, into which other communities, usually of a different ethnicity too, have been recently introduced either as adjacent villages or in some cases made part of an already established village. So, for example, in Luang Prabang in the Houay Lor scheme there is the Lao village of Ban Nakhone, which was apparently established in the 17th century. In 1986 it seems some Khmu were encouraged by the government to settle nearby at Ban Viengkham. It is into this latter village that some 50 families of Hmong were resettled in 1999, expanding the village by half. In another project area, also in Luang Prabang, the village of Pha Deng was established in 1958 by Tai Yuan, disrupted by the war and established in its present position in 1973, and Pha Vieng in 1975 by Khmu. Both villages now formally contain a substantial portion of Hmong, who were encouraged to come down to these villages in 2002, partly as a result of a campaign against opium growing. In reality the Hmong are concentrated in an area between the two villages, informally called Ban Kok Muang.[27] Even if they were Lao or Tai integration would still be problematic. For example, Ban Muang Soum in Muang Saysomboune was compelled by the administration of the special region to accept five households (seven families) of Tai Daeng migrants from Huaphanh province.[28] The ancestors of Ban Muang Soum are also Tai

27. *The Participatory Poverty Assessment* report also noted that despite being formally integrated into villages, most resettled minorities remained as distinct communities within them (Asian Development Bank et al. 2001: 18, fn.1).

28. Population pressure on the available paddy is leading to spontaneous migration. Apparently Tai Daeng migrants can now be found as far afield as Xayaboury. These migrants to Saysomboune were led to understand that the head of the Special Region, who is from Muang Xieng Kho in Huaphanh, had said there was

Daeng from Huaphanh, but they settled where they are nearly 100 years ago and have subsequently become ethnic Lao through their adherence to Buddhism. It is clear that although these households have been placed under the village administration, they have not by that fact become part of the community. It is clear that from the villagers' point of view that the regional administration that must find and prepare suitable land for them, not the village.

In fact most local areas or *muang* in Laos, especially in the highlands, have complex profiles and are made up of culturally distinct communities. This is the basic reality. Obviously all these communities prefer harmonious and amiable mutual relations, and will express their desire to work together to solve problems. Nevertheless their primary commitment is to their own village and its interests.

In some cases, the *muang* claims the right to distribute irrigated land rights, but this is strongly resisted by communities who consider these rights to have been claimed already by themselves. Communities with strong ideas of their rights have caused disputes during land allocation exercises. A study prepared for SIDA writes:

> Especially contentious were situations involving old long-established villages whose boundaries with neighbouring villages were already well-defined. Here local District Agriculture and Forestry Office officials had arbitrarily drawn new lines which created problems as villages were affected by gains and losses causing continuous dissatisfaction and conflict. Demarcations between old and new villages have been even worse as the new villages are almost always perceived as infringing on the territory and livelihood of the old village, and during altercations new villagers would invariably respond by saying they did not want to be here, but were placed here by the government.
> (Chamberlain and Panh 2002: 32)

In some cases villagers who have paddy land are being encouraged to allow those without paddy land to use this land during the dry season. There is, however, considerable reluctance to do this both because of the uncertainties that farmers have about future yields, and perhaps

plenty of land there for poorer Tai farmers. No doubt this was a rumour that may have grown out of a casual remark. But the fact that dozens of families responded is indicative of the volatility of the upland system in some areas. Other spontaneous migrations across long distances have been observed, such as Hmong from Xieng Khouang to Luang Nam Tha.

uncertainties about whether such multiple use would compromise their claims to such land. One Khmu man insisted to me in June 2004 that those without paddy should be allowed to use the land if it was unused. I asked if any land would be rented. 'No way, in this area!' he replied, and his appeal was to a moral idea that people have a right to use land which is not being used. In other areas of Laos rent is common and communities have adjusted to this, and no doubt more remote villages will have to adjust to it in the future.

Common Property Resources[29]

Rather than talking abstractly about 'community participation' it is it is more appropriate to try to understand the different types of collective action and property found in rural areas of Laos.

The traditional irrigation schemes maintained by specific groups of farmers throughout Laos are good examples of common property resources.[30] Most of these are village-based and are therefore anchored within the village moral economy, which has its own informal mechanisms for disciplining water users. Where irrigation systems are expanded to include other communities, then any higher form of organisation would have to be cognisant of the forms of organisation of these basic communities, especially if they involve different ethnic groups.

In Huaphanh most paddy land is still held and managed collectively. My discussions with local officials in Viengxay indicate that there are no immediate plans to change this situation in the government's land use and allocation exercise. The functioning moral economy of these villages, it seems, would resist a change to individual titles. Khmu villages manage common river and fish areas. Some villages also hold common resources in timber stands jointly with their respective *muang*.

The land use and allocation project has revealed some complex commonly-managed upland systems among the Hmong. A Hmong village in Luang Prabang province provides an intriguing glimpse of the possibilities for upland farming:

> Upland agricultural land areas in the village are divided into large blocks of land of about 100 hectares in which all families cultivate land for two years. There are three such large blocks of land in the village, the other

29. See Feeny et al. 1990.

30. See R.W. Ireson 1995.

> two being secondary forest fallow. These are rotated in a modified fallow system every two years that enables a five-year recovery period before the first fields are cultivated again. This block rotation is helping villages maintain rice productivity. The system provides for flexible family field allocations each year, depending on family requirements.
> (Chamberlain and Panh 2002: 19–20)

Chamberlain and Panh remark that the Hmong families are reluctant to accept outsider allocation of land parcels because it would diminish the system's flexibility (ibid.).

My point in the preceding sections is that an understanding of the nature of the peasant economy and its possible transformations is not just an academic question, but has real world implications, whether for collectivisation or campaigns against poverty. Unfortunately, few anthropologists or rural sociologists working in Laos seem theoretically prepared for this.

Gender Studies

Carol Ireson's *Field, Forest, and Family* (1996) is the only substantial study of gender relations among the Lao peasantry to date. The book, which is full of detail on rural livelihoods, attempts a comparison between ethnic Lao, Khmu and Hmong women. Ireson, a feminist sociologist, is interested in measuring power:

> *Power*, as used in this analysis, refers to the ability to exert control over self, others, and/or valued resources in economic, political, religious, domestic, or other social arenas. Other social criteria, like ethnicity, social class, and religion, combine with gender to shape the overall stratification system of a society. (ibid.: 4)

These are among the 'battery of indicators' used to ascertain 'women's power' in Lao society (ibid.).

Ethnic Lao women, she says, have more power than either Khmu or Hmong women:

> The strength of ethnic Lao women centers on their key economic roles. Women control the production and distribution of some of the goods they produce, and women who care for their ageing parents receive the major portion of their family inheritance. Woman have traditionally held the family purse strings and, while not the sole financial decision makers, have shared this role with their husbands. (ibid.: 60)

By comparison, only some Khmu and Hmong 'women are able to exercise control in some aspects of their lives' (ibid.: 88).

One of the real strengths of Carol Ireson's study is its inter-ethnic comparisons. However, it is compromised by the imbalance in strength between her data on ethnic Lao and the relatively scattered data she has on the two other groups, where she relies much more on secondary sources. Ireson also attempts to chart how government policies have affected women since 1975, and examines the role of the Lao Women's Union under the Lao PDR, all of which is very valuable. The focus on women, however, vitiates her analysis of gender relations, though her response might be that she is just righting the current imbalance that focuses on men.[31]

The unargued premise in studies like Ireson's is a modern conception of equality, by which the social relations of all other societies are measured and evaluated. Also, there is an individualistic bias in most studies and reports, whereby individuals are seen as the main actors in rural Lao society.

One could argue, however, that the prime cognitive unit of rural men and women is their own family and that they are concerned that benefits flow 'equally' to the family regardless of whether those benefits are channelled to the family by men or women. Indeed, in rural Laos one's primary identity is tied up with the family, with individual identities, male or female, being largely subordinate to family demands.

One can plausibly argue that women primarily conceptualise themselves as mothers, wives or daughters, rather than as 'women', and that men conceptualise themselves primarily as fathers, husbands and sons, rather than as 'men'. In other words their perception of gender is relational rather than individuated. Indeed, one could argue that there is no cultural space for unconnected persons within rural society. The cognitive organisation of men's and women's lives speaks of their interdependence, and that is expressed in the division of everyday manual work, and social and cultural work too. Culturally the coming together of men and women is therefore both necessary and 'natural'; and it is often asserted by both men and women that men should play a dominant role in society.

31. The book that Ireson wrote with Moreno-Black (Ireson-Doolittle and Moreno-Black 2004) does not add anything substantial to our understanding of rural society, although it is a more accessible introduction to many issues.

This cognitive organisation of the world is a kind of ideal statement about how things should be, and therefore is a statement of cultural order. In practice, however, one sees men doing 'women's work' and women doing 'men's work' in the villages, out of necessity if nothing else. Development, of course, may produce a more individualistic cognitive framework, but that has to be demonstrated through research.

Hmong society is invariably cited as an example of patriarchal control of family resources, where men supposedly have control over 'all' decisions. Ireson veers close to this when she says that the 'subordination' of 'Hmong women is not complete' (1996: 88), but by implication is almost 'complete'. Needless to say, concrete evidence for such assertions are rarely forthcoming, and rarely is it considered that this is an ideal cognitive model of the society readily enunciated by its members. Jan Ovesen is one of the few researchers who has been prepared to argue that:

> The position of women among the Hmong, like the case in so many other tribal societies, is not so much one of inferiority as it is a reflection of the fundamental social difference and complementarity between the two sexes. The practical application of this principle of complementarity (rather than 'inequality') may be seen in the sexual division of labour.'
> (Ovesen 1995: 73).[32]

Furthermore, age is as salient as gender, and older women, whose place is made secure in society through their sons, have a venerated role in such societies. Of course, they do not conform to the cultural norms of lowland Lao society, and certainly not to the norms of female emancipation proclaimed in international documents premised on modern individualism. But surely it would be counter-productive to imagine that they do.

Much is made of the burden of women's work in Lao rural society, and it is indeed great. Unfortunately, once again, detailed studies of this issue are lacking, but those that do exist do not show a dramatic gender imbalance. However, it seems that men's workload may have been lightened by technological innovations, such as the prevalence of 'iron buffaloes' for ploughing which speed up the work and make it less tiring, or

32. Ireson is only prepared to concede that the ethnic Lao value gender complementarity rather than opposition (Ireson 1996: 101).

the rapid expansion of tin roofing which makes house maintenance less demanding on male labour. The pounding of rice, invariably women's work, can and has been lightened by mechanised mills. The reason why women's work remains heavy is because of their primary responsibility for domestic work, and labour saving technologies in this sphere are few and far between in rural Laos. But even in the most highly educated industrial societies, where there are conscious attempts to allocate domestic work to men, domestic work remains largely in the hands of women and means that they often work longer hours than husbands, especially if they are in the paid workforce.[33]

It would not be an exaggeration to say that almost every aid project in Laos has a compulsory gender 'component' and a 'gender document' to go with it. Yet, besides the important work of Ireson we have no other substantial studies of gender relations in rural Laos, regardless of ethnicity. Consequently these aid documents simply spew out the clichés and verities demanded by the international aid 'community' without advancing our knowledge or understanding of the issues one iota.

Peasants in a Wider World

An interesting feature of Izikowitz's early study is not only his documentation of local trade and exchanges, but also the way in which remote peasants had been and were being touched by the world economy. The Lamet had to get iron from outside, but no doubt they were unaware that it came from countries as far away as Sweden, and indeed Izikowitz (1979: 313) was surprised to make this discovery.[34] But research in recent decades has shown just how far the tentacles of trade reached historically and its varying impact on local societies.

The transformation of the peasantry is not just an economic issue, however. Obviously an important threshold is reached in the transformation of peasant societies when the conditions of the family farm's reproduction begin to become more dependent on various inputs and interchanges with the market. However, as Wolf (1966: 96–106) made clear many years ago, surpluses are not only required for payment to

33. For the USA, see Flanagan 2004.

34. Some foundries in Sweden had deliberately not modernised so that they could cater to this trade in a less pure form of iron. This is a lovely illustration of the complex feedback effects one can find in the international system.

superordinate classes and institutions, but are also crucial for the representation of the family within the peasant community through outlays for the cultural reproduction of the community, such as the earning of merit by Lao peasants mentioned earlier. A second key shift in peasant society occurs when individuals begin to orient themselves, culturally, away from their immediate community and towards a wider world. One might argue that it is at this point that peasant society begins to die.

The spread of a national education system has, of course, been an important instrument in this process, as has the formation of a national army that recruits from among the rural population. Each of these institutions draws individuals into a wider community and teaches them to identify with it. In the last 30–40 years there has also been a revolution in mass communications, with access to newspapers, radios and television becoming widespread. The speed with which TV dishes have appeared in remote areas in the 1990s in Laos was nothing short of astounding. Roads too have increased mobility. While it was common in the 1950s, even close to Vientiane, to find villagers who had never visited the capital, now villagers travel far and wide across the country. From the 1990s onwards, thousands of villagers have begun to travel internationally in search of work, mainly to Thailand but also further afield. Much of this labour migration is illegal, but migrant labour is also being organised in much the same way as one has seen with Thai farmers. So far, however, there has been little research on this in Laos.[35] But as this phenomenon develops – as it will – we will begin to see in Laos conditions observed earlier in Southeast Asia, as summarised by Elson:

> [. . .] the village was in the process of becoming just a place to live rather than a rural settlement where farmers interests enjoyed some general degree of broad acceptance. Villagers, in other words, were becoming citizens of a much wider community than their own settlements, and many of their connections with that world were of greater importance than those they had in common with their neighbours close by.
> (Elson 1997: 226)

Studies of the Thai peasantry have demonstrated the diverse impact of the wider world on peasant communities. The excellent study of two northeastern villages by Formoso and his co-researchers (Formoso [ed.] 1997) has shown the differential adaptations to the modern economy

35. But see Inthasone Phetsiriseng 2003.

and to modern society by one village dependent on labour migration, and by another dependent on a state-sponsored irrigation project. In one case (the village dependent on labour migration) the consequences were more traumatic and drastic than the other, but both witnessed significant cultural re-orientations.[36] Another excellent study of agricultural change, in the Chao Phraya delta, demonstrates that smallholder agriculture has survived much better than one may have expected, but the editors observe a 'decrease of the social and psychological distance between the village and Bangkok's factories and way of life' (Molle and Thipawal [eds] 2003: 21). Niti Pawakapan (2002) has written a lovely overview of decades of changes in people's cultural and material life in a small town in north-western Chiang Mai province. And there have been some excellent studies of the social and cultural impact of overseas labour migration, such as Mary Beth Mills (1999). There are no equivalent studies for Laos.

Final observations

The decline of peasant studies coincided with a shift in focus and emphasis within the social sciences. Social class, in particular the working class, fell out of favour as an 'agent' of change, as did attention to the peasants as a 'class' elsewhere. What might be termed 'materialist' research strategies (e.g. political economy) were eclipsed by 'culturalist' ones – the so-called 'cultural turn' in the social sciences– which stressed the contingencies and constructedness of subjectivity, meaning, and perception. In Laos this has manifested itself mainly in studies of ethnic minorities and their identity, such as the work of Proschan (1997), Pholsena (2002), Évrard (2003), and perhaps a mixture of the two strategies in Evans (1999b). All the same, there are no subsequent in-depth dedicated studies of aspects of peasant culture, such as religious practices. A 'substitute' materialist strategy has been created by a seemingly ever-expanding programme of research into ecological issues, a list of which would be too long (but see for example, Thapa 1998).[37] And

36. Also, in relation to the northeast of Thailand, Shinichi Shigetomi and al. (2004) provide a clear study of how kinship roles and expectations have changed as the economy has been transformed.

37. Mention should be made of the uncategorizable study by Laurent Chazée (1998) on agrarian systems in Laos. This provides a wealth of data on a wide range of issues relating to rural Laos, but as far as I can tell it is theoretically aimless.

this has been accompanied by a journal based in Bangkok dedicated to environmental issues, *Watershed,* which regularly runs critical articles on Laos. However, these studies appear to have little interest in questions of peasant social structure.

To understand the momentous social and cultural changes which lay ahead for the peasantry of Laos, we will need to combine the knowledge generated by both of these approaches with the achievements of a now neglected economic anthropology. The peasantry as a social formation may be entering its terminal phase in Laos, but there is still much to be learned about the Lao peasant's way of life.

CHAPTER 4

The Genesis and Demarcation of the Religious Field

Monasteries, State Schools and the Secular Sphere in Lao Buddhism[1]

PATRICE LADWIG

While I was a teacher at the only Buddhist College in Vientiane from 2004 to 2005, and lived for some months in one of the largest monasteries of the city, I was struck by the social and regional backgrounds of my fellow monks and novices. The monastery had 60 members, and none of us was originally from Vientiane; and, with the exception of myself, all were sons of rather poor peasants from deep rural areas. The questionnaires and small statistical survey I carried out revealed that the villages they came from belonged to the weakest regions of Laos, from the point of view of infrastructure. This was confirmed during an interview with Sisuk,[2] a man in his early 60s and one of the headmasters of Vat Ong Toe College, the highest institution for Buddhist education in Laos:

> The Buddhist College is primarily an institution that cares for the sons of the poorest of the poor from rural areas. Every peasant family that has

1. This research was conducted, particularly in Vientiane, between 2003 and 2007, with funding from the German Academic Exchange Service (DAAD) and the University of Cambridge. Grant Evans, as a reviewer, generously advised and supported me on this article and suggested that I add a piece on post-revolutionary Laos. I unfortunately could not do so before his death, but some additional perspectives regarding the changing roles of monks as 'intellectuals' can be found in Ladwig (2013), and a wider contextualisation with reference to Lao Buddhism under colonialism is elaborated in Ladwig (2018).

2. All personal names have been changed.

> a bit of money sends one of its children to the new colleges in Vientiane, and our pupils are the ones who cannot afford to do this. In the past, monastic education was held in high esteem, and monks were respected teachers. The value of monastic education has declined, and now it is only an option for a small group in society.

In Laos and Thailand, a career in the monastic order (*sangha*) has often been an option for social upward mobility (Wyatt 1966), but the basic framework for this mobility seems to have changed. Sisuk's concerns were also shared by many of the monks and the laypeople I worked with in Vientiane; there was a general feeling that – despite the resurgence of Lao Buddhism[3] – Buddhist education was in decline, and that it did not have the value that it had had when they were young. In the past, as some older laypeople asserted, the monastery was one of the few places where one could receive a basic education, even as a layperson. Before the expansion of the state school system in the Vientiane area in the 1950s and 60s, monastic education was highly esteemed and children and novices were often taught together in the temple by a monk acting as a teacher. Over the last 50 years, state schools have progressively taken over the roles of temple schools and Buddhist education has become a specialised subfield for novices and monks. Despite the fact that the Buddhist schools in urban areas are currently flooded with novices from the provinces,[4] the business colleges and private schools, all founded in the last 10 years in the course of the economic reform policy of the communist government, are obviously much more attractive to most pupils. Although Lao novices and monks today also learn according to secular curricula, monastic education primarily serves the rural poor, and has little value in comparison to a certificate from a business school. How can we explain this shift from a system of public education with the temple at its centre to a state school system in which Buddhist education has become a specialised option for the rural poor? Seen from a historical

3. When I speak of Lao Buddhism as a general category, I mean the (post)colonial 'mainstream Buddhism' that is to be found in the current national boundaries of the Lao PDR. I shall focus on Vientiane and its surroundings and Buddhism as practised by ethnic Lao. I will occasionally make comparative references to the Isan region today located in Thailand, but will not discuss the wide variation within Buddhism among ethnic minorities.

4. See, for example, Holt's excellent description (2009: 186) of the lives of novices in Luang Prabang in the present day.

perspective, are we dealing here with an effect of modernisation, differentiation and even secularisation? Intuitively one is tempted to argue that the communist revolution of 1975 provides the major framework of explanation. However, I think that we have to employ a *longue durée* perspective that reaches back to colonial period, as the major changes had already taken place before 1975.

This chapter explores differentiation in relation to a specific aspect of Lao Buddhism, namely the transformations of the temple-based education system that served novices, monks and laypeople. I argue that by looking at the history of this sector over the course of approximately 70 years (1900–1975) we can partially reconstruct the genealogy of the category of religion (Asad 1993) and its relationship with the secular world. I am interested in the boundaries of the religious field, and in its genesis in the context of a process of functional differentiation.[5] I will not focus here on the 'privatisation of belief' (Casanova 1994), new religious subjectivities and the potential decline or resurgence of belief in contemporary Laos (cf. Rehbein 2009b). Instead I shall, intentionally, avoid looking at questions of agency and will limit myself to the history of the larger structural and institutional features that have evolved in the Buddhist education system in the Vientiane area. I will mainly draw on Bourdieu's notion of the 'field' and its boundaries (1991; 2000: 10), and only in passing will I touch on the rules and forms of capital usually associated with his sociology of religion (Rey 2007: 82). By looking at the boundaries of the religious field and its interaction with the bureaucratic field of the state and its educational apparatus, I shall discuss the gradual marginalisation of the role of the *sangha* in public education in the Vientiane area. By using histories and ethnographies of Lao Buddhism from the colonial and early postcolonial period, I will outline the way in which the temple-based education system for monks and laypeople developed and a state school system was created.

5. There is little agreement about what (functional) differentiation actually means in the context of the various branches of sociology, despite the fact that it was one of the key concepts of the discipline from the very beginning. The essence of the concept, however, can be said to be an argument that all the functions within a system come to be ascribed to a particular location within that system, through division of labour. See Nassehi (2004) and Tyrell (2008) for discussion and clarification of this point. I should say that it is my exegesis of Bourdieu that is the basis of my own use of the concept.

Through the establishment of modern state institutions such as the school, I would argue that monks lost one of their principal tasks in their communities. They now teach only other members of the *sangha* and have a more restricted sphere of responsibility. I would say that what we see here is not secularisation as part of an overall process of the decline of religion, or with secularism as an explicit political or ideological project (Asad 2003: 21). Instead, I think we are witnessing a redefinition of the religious field that is intrinsically linked to the expansion of the influence of the state, through the enlargement of a public school system. I see this a process of functional differentiation that has caused the separation and demarcation of the religious field and has at the same time created a sphere that, in an institutional sense, can be described as secular (Casanova 2006).

Differentiation and the Religious Field: The Lao Temple as Public School

Looking at the few ethnographic accounts we have of Lao Buddhism from the late 1950s and 1960s, it becomes clear that the tasks of temples and the role of monks implied more than what today would be described as 'religious'. The temple took on a variety of roles, stood at the centre of social space and was a hub for a number of social relations in Lao peasant society. Condominas' (1998) elaborate study of Lao Buddhism in the late 1950s understands the temple in Marcel Mauss's sense, as a sort of 'total social fact'. On the back cover of Condominas' study we read:

> A Lao village community does not really come into existence without its *vat*, its monastery, which carries its name and gives it its name. At the centre of social space the temple fulfils multiple functions and is at the same time school, town hall, festival location, a place of care for ill people and suffering souls, shelter for travellers, and a location for flirting games and match making.

Yoneo Ishii says something very similar about the role of monks and that of temples in the rural areas of 'pre-modern' Thailand. He divides 'secular' from 'religious' uses of the temple; but he also proposes that monks held positions that were similar to those of intellectuals, as they were considered to be 'more knowledgeable than laypeople' (1986: 27). Other accounts report that until World War II public education and what was then considered schooling were largely in the hands of monks (Tambiah 1968; Taillard 1974); traditional health care was provided by monks or by traditional healers who often got their training in monasteries (Pottier 2007: 123). Moreover, monks played an important role in local village law and conflict resolution (Koret 1996: 12), and in earlier periods they even held important political positions, as Grabowsky (2007) has shown for Luang Prabang. As I will explore further below, little of this has remained in the current period. The position of the temple and that of monks are today very different one. Are the accounts of Condominas, Ishi and others then based on an over-holistic image of a 'Buddhist society'? Is their romanticising, even orientalist, image of Lao Buddhism, if it is valid at all, only valid in relation to the 'pre-modern' period? In a recent roundup of current discussions of secularisation, Fennella Cannell (2010: 96) attests that there is 'a tendency of classic secularisation theory to exaggerate the contrast between a relatively stable European past where religion was a single moral universe and a fragmented, unstable present'. Transferring this to Laos, are these transformations outcomes of processes of secularisation, social differentiation, modernisation and modern fragmentation? Or do we as researchers simply construct this opposition, projecting it into a stable past? Before coming back to a concrete historical analysis, let me briefly explore the relationship between modernisation and religion in the thought of the founding fathers of sociology, and specifically of Bourdieu.

The idea of a homogenous and predetermined development towards modernity with Euro-American characteristics has been heavily contested (Mitchell 2000; Rehbein this volume, Chapter 2). Many social scientists now speak of 'multiple modernities' (Eisenstadt 2000).[6] However, despite criticism of the deterministic views of Durkheim and Weber on social evolution and the decline of religion, current

6. The dualisms at the basis of the construct of modernity, such as the contrast between 'traditional' and 'modern societies' and between *Gemeinschaft* and *Gesellschaft*, have been debunked as too general and are part of what James Ferguson calls a 'modernisation myth' (1999: 13–17). The focus is today very often on the hybrid constellations and the contradictions that have emerged through modernisation. Although it is important that the social sciences critically question main concepts such as modernity, it is also crucial to mention that modernity has for a long time been and still is a powerful narrative in countries like Laos. The omnipresence of notions of development (Lao: *patthana*) and prosperity (*chaloen*) in postcolonial Laos demonstrate this.

theories of secularisation and secularism still 'circle constantly around the problem of the relation of religion to modernity' (Cannell 2010: 86). In Bourdieu's theory of differentiation we encounter a similar argument about religion and modernity. He argues that pre-modern societies are not differentiated into fields, which suggests a somewhat generalised and problematic view of social evolution.[7] The notion of the field plays a constitutive role in his theory of differentiation, as these are presented as the primary outcome of this process (1998: 148). According to this view, modernisation is marked by the emergence of various fields (the economy, arts, religion, law), which then constitute relatively autonomous entities that have their own rules, forms of capital and actors. It is interesting to note that he first developed his notion of field through a critical reading of Weber's work on religion. In *The Genesis and Structure of the Religious Field* (1991), Bourdieu gives us a theoretical macro-analysis of the development of world religions. He postulates that through socio-economic development and urbanisation, society becomes increasingly marked by division of labour and social differentiation. This in turn leads to a systematisation of religion, the evolution of an expert culture and the delineation of a border around the religious field. The idea is that in pre-urban and pre-modern societies religion was all-pervasive and did not constitute its own field; it is the increasing specialisation of religious leaders in an urban context that leads to the genesis of the field of religion. The emergence of a field is not regarded as the decomposition of something that was 'whole' before, which then falls apart or disappears, but is to be understood as a process of separation and secession (Kneer 2004: 28–39), leading to a certain

7. Rehbein (2007) has applied the notion of the field to the study of contemporary Laos, and makes the critical remark that Bourdieu does not give us any hints regarding 'how a society could have looked like before the differentiation of fields' (Rehbein 2009a: 103). Bourdieu's notion of the field is, indeed, far from being consistent and it evolved over his career. For different examples of how he defined the field, see Bourdieu 2000: 10; 1996. Generally speaking, fields may be understood as structured spaces that are organised around actors who have specific types of capital. They are arenas of production, circulation, knowledge or status. As they do in the religious field (Bourdieu 1991), actors in other fields struggle to accumulate different kinds of capital. For field theory in general and specifically the genealogy of Bourdieu's notion of it, see Martin 2003. I will here only use a limited definition of the field and not refer to habitus and other core components usually associated with Bourdieu's theory. I will focus on the borders of the field and its genesis.

autonomy of the field. In one of Bourdieu's earlier essays on Algeria, he also discusses the dissolution of the religious field with increasing differentiation within society (Bourdieu 1979: 69). However, Bourdieu is not arguing that this leads to an overall secularisation and disappearance of religion; his argument is that it leads to a change in the border around the religious field. It is nevertheless the case that Bourdieu, like other sociologists of modernisation before him, believes that religion on an institutional level comes to be marginalised through differentiation. In this vein, Dianteill (2004: 82) states that it is Bourdieu's 'conviction that religion is a declining institution in differentiated societies'. This Weber-inspired focus on institutions has rightly been labelled a 'unidimensional' view, in that it fails to address questions of bricolage religion or of beliefs outside of institutions (Furseth 2009: 102). However, this focus on institutions and the borders of the religious field are my main interest in the Lao case and I will only in passing look at changing forms of capital and changes in the players in the field ('agency').

Bourdieu (1991: 5–6) explicitly states that an analysis of social differentiation and the emergence of the religious field must be carried out in a historical context; we must look at its historical genesis and structure. Theories of differentiation thus always imply 'historical deduction' (Russo 2009: 69; see also Tyrell 2008: 130). In order to analyze the changing role of the monastery and monks in this process, I will first give a short historical overview of the development of the school system in Laos. In doing this it is important to distinguish the monastic education given by monks for monks from the wider role of monks in teaching laypeople. The two systems are dependent on each other, however, and I will first of all focus on schools that were also teaching laypeople, with monks as teachers located in the temple. I will then outline the process of differentiation in which temple schools became institutions for religious specialists only.

Looking at the history of Lao Buddhism in the Vientiane region, it is clear that its institutions were already considerably weakened through the numerous wars that had occurred before the arrival of the French in 1893. Most temples had been destroyed, and Vientiane's population had been drastically reduced. However, French colonial politics supported a Lao Buddhist revival with the aim of fostering Lao nationalism (Ivarsson 2008: 93). The reconstruction of temples and relic shrines, and more importantly the founding of schools for monks represented a central way in which French colonial politics influenced Lao Buddhism. Nevertheless, in many fields these revitalisation effects were quite limited (McDaniel 2008: 42). Due to the marginal role of Laos within French Indochina – it was a 'colonial backwater', as Gunn (1990) has described it – Laos received very little colonial revenue and very little in the way of infrastructural projects. The marginality of Laos in Indochina can be seen as one of the reasons for the fact that Buddhist temples often continued to fulfil their traditional roles, especially in terms of schooling. There were practically no other schools. In Vientiane there was only the Lycée Pavie (founded in 1921), whose main role was to educate the children of the Lao and Vietnamese colonial upper classes (Pathamavong 1955: 94). Its curriculum was entirely in French, and was 'largely irrelevant to the needs and life-styles of the vast majority of the rural population' (Ireson 1994: n.p.). Basic literacy could in early colonial Laos only be acquired either by attending a monastery school as a child or by actually becoming a monk or a novice.

Pathammavong (1955: 77–85) describes the Lao temple-based education system in detail, but his highly romantised account does not differentiate between laity and monks. One of the best descriptions we have of 'traditional schooling' for the laity comes from Tambiah, who worked in a region inhabited by ethnic Lao in Thailand, close to the Lao border. He reports that lessons usually took place in the open courtyard, and that it was mainly boys who attended, although some girls also did:

> At the turn of the century the village school was situated in the old temple (which was later abandoned). The temple had an abbot, called *acharn* (teacher) Wangthong and two or three other monks. It was the abbot alone who taught the children, sometimes helped by a layman (an ex-monk). The teaching was voluntary and the abbot received no pay from the government [....] There were no grades, no examinations, and no child studied for more than two years. What the children were taught was the rudiments of reading, writing and arithmetic.
> (Tambiah 1968: 94–96).

Phoutong (1973: 126) describes the Buddhist monastery as being, in Laos, '[...] the centre of religious, professional, social and moral education [...] Here the pupils receive their first rudimentary training in education. They learn reading and writing, arts and the sciences with the help of technical treaties of the traditional system of education.' As in the school described by Tambiah, writing was taught in Lao, usually using various local writing systems (*akson tham*) that are only rarely used by monks today. The subjects taught in the monastery were in our modern sense not only religious; the teaching was, as Kourilsky (2006: 31) describes it, 'multidisciplinary'. Colonial education officials clearly saw monasteries as being at the centre of the Lao education system, and the early colonial regime tried to expand that system. In 1907, a few years after the establishment of the French protectorate in 1893, the colonial administration began to encourage the establishment of primary schools in temples.[8] Publicly-funded higher education institutes in which monks were the teachers, called *écoles normales des bonzes*, were established in 1909 in Vientiane (and subsequently in Luang Prabang, Pakse and Savannakhet), in order to strengthen the underdeveloped colonial school system (Kourilsky 2006: 32). Chagnon and Rumpf (1982: 164) suggest that the French colonial government did not institute a large-scale educational system until 1939. In this year, a plan for a network of primary and secondary schools was decided upon, but it was soon abandoned because of the major disruptions caused by the onset of World War II. Pathammavong's (1955: 92) statistics show that numbers of pupils attending primary and secondary schools started to rise sharply only after 1947. Even with the independence of Laos after the Second World War, most teachers were in fact Buddhist monks. Despite some efforts by the state to build a new school system, the consequence was that 'resources for adult education remained solely the province of temple based educational systems, and much of the activity in the rural government schools duplicated that of traditional temple schools' (Bernhard-Johnston 1993: 147). In the 1950s, in the rural areas of Laos, and even around Vientiane, there were no state institutions and the tasks these were supposed to fulfil were in the hands of villagers themselves.

8. McDaniel (2008: 38), in contrast, asserts that the 'The French did not base their secular or Catholic educational institutions on local monastic models, nor did they invest in the maintenance of monastic schooling.' I would argue, rather, that due to the marginality of Laos as a colony those colonial efforts to establish schools that did take place were relatively unsystematic, and that they may therefore have simply gone unnoticed. They also had a very limited impact in comparison to the reforms advanced in Vietnam.

I asked at the beginning of this chapter if the representation of the temple as a total social institution is based on an orientalist, over-holistic view of Lao Buddhism before modernisation. To say that the temple had a role as a public school is not necessarily a romanticisation. However deficient and limited in reach the institutions of Buddhism may have been at that time, monks were often the only teachers available and the temple was, in fact, also the school. One can argue that, at least from an institutional perspective, there was little differentiation between the religious and the secular field. Buddhism was not omnipresent in all spheres of Lao life, but at least in relation to the educational and institutional spheres there was no significant differentiation of domains. Before the arrival of a state school system, the school was located in the temple. Even when efforts began on the part of the colonial regime to establish schooling, the educational field, the religious field and the bureaucratic field of the state were hardly differentiated at all, and were not autonomous one from another.

However, I also mentioned that theories of functional differentiation and secularisation often contrast the image of a stable religious past with today's situation, when society is fragmented and differentiated into fields. However, differentiation and secularisation are gradual, incomplete processes that take place, asynchronically, on different levels.[9] What on the structural, institutional level may not be visible – here, the fact that school and temple appear to have been a single institution – may be obvious in other areas. Despite the fact that the temple continued to be the public school for a long time, the contents of the curricula did change. Ivarsson (1999: 77–78) reports for the early colonial period that 'while Vientiane in this sense was revived as a secular educational centre for Laotian monks, this was not linked with religious education as in the past'. In his view, Vientiane became the centre for monks carrying out 'secular studies', and pagoda schools were used 'as a means to diffuse secular education' (ibid.). Unfortunately, Ivarsson does not specify what was actually secular about these schools. Justin McDaniel (2008), in his excellent study on Buddhist monastic education in Laos

9. See Schober's study of the Buddhist education system in Burma under colonialism. She draws together theories of modernity and the impact of colonialism on the monastic educational system, but points out that this is not 'a continuous narrative that distinguishes between modernity and tradition, secularism and religion, rationalism and Buddhist cosmology' (2007: 67).

and Thailand, presents a slightly different picture of this development. For him, there are significant continuities to be found *within* the monastic education system. Although he recognises the changes that occurred in the curricula due to the engagement of several EFEO (École française d'Extrême-Orient) scholars (2008: 42–51), he argues persuasively that the methods of teaching and most of the contents actually changed surprisingly little over one hundred years: 'In fact, "Western" influence, in practice and theory, seems to have bypassed monastic educational practice.' (ibid.: 38) While I largely agree with McDaniel in relation to the inner workings of the monastic education system, I would argue that there was less continuity in relation to the social value of this education and the overall significance of the temple as an educational institution for the laity. Social recognition of the value of a monastic education changed, and it came to be regarded as useful in different ways. This transformation began during the colonial era, when the elite 'seems to have absorbed certain French anti-clerical attitudes' (Halpern 1964: 23). This had an impact on relations between that elite and the monastic community, the *sangha*:

> Under colonial rule, the elites began to claim national leadership for themselves, while the members of the *sangha* were denied a socio-political role. Particularly frustrating for this latter group was the devaluation and diminution of monastic education in urban society, which may have led to a fall in the general level of literacy under the French.
> (Thant and Vokes cited in Rehbein 2007: 101).

While the value of monastic education itself was already diminishing under colonial rule, the role that monks took on as teachers in schools was still crucial. According to Gunn (1999: 38) and Schneider (2000: 51) the majority of Lao pupils went to monastery schools until World War II. However, what was already happening in relation to the content and recognition of this form of education came, a few years later, to affect the institutional structure of schooling.

Establishing a State-School System without Monks

The establishment of a state school system has to seen as one of the most crucial parts of efforts to 'develop' a country, and is often intrinsically bound up with a powerful vision of modernity and the nation state. The establishment of a national school system is often the precondition for anchoring a specific vision of the world in the population, instilling discipline, spreading nationalism, creating the conditions and know-how for a new economic order and giving citizens of a country a sense of belonging to a wider imagined national community.[10] In this sense the school is the 'prime institutional state' apparatus, as Althusser (1977: 151) has described it. In and around Vientiane in the 1950s and 1960s we see concerted efforts to establish such an educational apparatus. From the 1950s onwards, Laos received a massive influx of foreign aid, sustaining a technocratically-oriented state apparatus, ideologically and financially maintained by the USAID (Castle 1993). With postcolonial Laos effectively being split into two fluctuating zones until 1975 – one part administered by the Royal Lao Government (RLG), and one, the 'liberated zone', under the control of the communist movement, the Pathet Lao – the United State's politics of containment also supported the building of a state school system. There were efforts to expand the zone of influence of what had been a relatively decentralised state apparatus, and to modernise the country in order to contain the advancement of the communist forces. This was in the context of the fact that the PL had been more advanced in promoting basic education in the provinces under their control and was thereby putting the RLG on the spot.[11]

With this expansion of state institutions, the role of monks as teachers in temple schools changed rapidly. Taillard (1974: 149) gives us detailed information on the development of the Lao school system for the postcolonial period: 'The monks played a crucial role in that evolution until 1950, the moment when the Lao government took power concerning all affairs of primary education. They represented 878 out of a total of 1172 teachers.' With 75% of all teachers being monks, most pupils were exposed to monks on a regular, if not on a daily, basis; and the schools remained in the temples. In the following years, we see

10. For a discussion of the iconographic strategies of building Lao nationalism and the specific writing of history advanced in post-revolutionary Laos, see Tappe's excellent study (2008).

11. The history of education in the northern provinces (mainly Huaphanh and Phongsaly) that were already under control of the communist forces from the beginning of the 1950s has to be seen as separate development. Here, the Pathet Lao put a stronger emphasis on the establishment of primary and secondary schools, which has been described in detail by Langer (1971). During the height of the American bombardments monks also taught in 'forest schools' in the liberated zone (Ladwig 2009).

concerted efforts to further expand the state school system. Due to staff shortages, the government initiated a new training programme in 1953, with a teacher training college preparing future teachers for their careers in 3–6 months courses and 300 new posts being created. Taillard gives us the concrete numbers for this development:

> The number of monk teachers begins to drop after that. According to the UNESCO report from the year 1956–1957, their number was not more than 220 out of 1686 teachers. At the end of the 1950s, the monastery schools disappear from the statistics and are replaced by the Community Centres for Rural Education, where monks continue to teach, but their number drops rapidly.
> (Taillard 1974: 149)

However, the plans to create a 'secular' education system were not immediately successful and many of the schools had no teachers. The Bousquet reform of 1962 once again tried to integrate monks into the state-schooling system. Due to a shortage of staff and capital, the resources that were ready at hand – the personnel and infrastructure of the *sangha* – were used as a pragmatic interim solution. In the following years, the government introduced evening alphabetisation classes and more rural education centres. The efforts to integrate temples into this system were only short lived, and there was a clear preference for a separation of temple and school as institutions. Taillard sums up the end of this development as follows:

> For the year 1971–72 the situation presents itself as follows: the number of primary school teachers was 6084, and there were 1021 teachers in the Community Centres for Rural Education. In the latter group, we find the number of monks varying between 9 and 14. *One can therefore say that the monks have definitely lost their educational function.* Not only the monks have lost their role in education, but moreover the schools have left the temple. In the whole of Laos, only 9% of the schools are situated in the temple (all Community Centres for Rural Education). For the Vientiane region, the development is even more advanced because the number doesn't even reach 4%. School and temple are spatially dissociated from each other.
> (Taillard 1974: 149–150; my emphasis)

Barber (1974: 48), speaking of villages around Vientiane and looking at an evolving urban Buddhism, states that this process 'effectively removed one of the *wat*'s [temple] principal functions'. On a general level we witness here a dramatic change in the role of monks in Lao society and a demarcation of school and temple as institutions. In the course of 25 years their significance as public school teachers was reduced to almost nil. The state entered the villages via the school, which now acted as a mediator between the political urban centre and the rural periphery, bringing the state into the village. Althusser's (1977: 157) statement about this institutional shift in Europe is very appropriate in describing this situation: 'In fact the church has been replaced today in its role as the dominant ideological state apparatus by the school.' Monastic education did not become irrelevant, but was increasingly limited to a specific social field and was now largely provided by monks for other members of the *sangha*.

The situation that I have described in relation to the school system is also true, to some degree, of the healthcare system in Laos. Monks were very often practitioners of medicine and traditional healthcare was either in the hands of monks or was at least based on their knowledge, as Pottier (2007) has shown in his seminal study. There are parallels with the 'outsourcing' of monks in the school system, as Keyes (1990: 180) notes in relation to health care among the Lao in Thailand: 'In the past twenty years [...] dramatic change has been brought about by relatively easy access to western medication [...] The increasing irrelevance of religious belief for some aspects of life in Thai–Lao villages is indicative of a growing separation between religious and secular spheres of meaning.' In his recent study of Lao Buddhism, John Holt also looks briefly at the superseding of monks in public education, and then adds that the '*wat*'s marginalisation was also abetted by the provision of more health care centres, which displaced the monk's function as a primary dispenser of traditional medicines' (Holt 2009: 159). Hospitals and doctors have now taken over the roles of temples and monks.

The rather macro-historical perspective that I have employed in looking at what happened in schooling and health care might appear to imply that monks were passive victims of these developments. Putting their agency and reactions towards these developments in a historical perspective is, due to the shortage of sources, a difficult one, but three examples come to my mind that elucidate what happened. One is the fact that after 1959, several 'Buddhist Youth Schools' were founded in Vientiane (McDaniel 2008: 53–56) and 'Buddhist Morality' was introduced as a school subject in the 1960s. Moreover, monks started to teach laypeople *vipassana* meditation on an institutionally organised basis in a few Vientiane temples.[12] I think that these developments partially compensated for the marginalisation described above. Monks continue to have a role in the modern world. They continue to teach laypeople on a personal basis, and in some temples in Vientiane monks still plant herbs and practise traditional medicine. However, it is also important to be aware of the fact that the scope and nature of these activities has changed. There has not been a radical exclusion of religion through an intentional secular ideology, but there has been a process that has created new practices in the religious field. Through this process a new hierarchy has come into being in the relationship between the religious field and the state.

The State's Hierarchisation of Fields and the Secular Sphere

There are several explanations for the significant changes that I have outlined in relation to education and healthcare. Schooling and healthcare are two of the state's key mechanisms of social regulation, and these could not be left in the hands of the monks on their own. New forms of knowledge had to be transmitted, and neither the number nor the qualifications of the monks was deemed adequate for this. Trained experts (i.e. teachers and doctors) were needed in order to build up a modernised system that would be appropriate for a rapidly-growing population; monks, who were regarded as 'peasant intellectuals', were only of limited use for the state. Moreover, in order to reach out to the non-Buddhist ethnic minorities both schooling and healthcare had to extend beyond

12. The creation of a Buddhist youth organisation and the activities in Sunday schools for children included Buddhist plays. Both entertainment and the teaching of ethics were central here. McDaniel (2008: 55) mentions that 'these activities were completely foreign to traditional Lao monastic education'. The arrival of 'Buddhist modernism' (McMahan 2008) in Laos was indeed something new, and a largely urban phenomenon. The teaching of meditation on a broader basis has been identified as one of the major changes that have occurred in Theravada Buddhism and in 'protestant Buddhism' (Gombrich and Obeyesekere 1988: 202). See also Cook (2010) for similar developments in Thailand. The Lao efforts, however, were rather short lived. After the revolution, all of these activities were prohibited; the schools were closed down. Only in recent years have similar types of activities begun, slowly, to hesitantly re-emerge (Ladwig 2008).

the areas in which monks were active. With a non-Buddhist population of approximately 40%, the question of a secular agenda of the state suddenly became crucial.[13] In the context of a more Foucauldian perspective one could argue that 'schooling in itself has been a disciplinary response to the need to manage growing populations; within the progressively discriminating space of the schoolroom the productive regulation of large numbers of pupils also required new methodologies' (Deacon 2006: 181). Health is also part of the state's project to manage its population, for 'medicine is a bio-political strategy' (Foucault 1994: 210). Although the new systems of schooling and healthcare remained far from perfect, the state (via a multiplicity of agents) definitely rearranged social practices and made the role of monks as teachers and healthcare practitioners for the laity largely redundant. There has been a significant decrease in the number of monks in Laos since the 1950s, and this may well be connected to this process of functional differentiation, which has led to their marginalisation.[14]

I believe that the spatial separation of temple and school and the outsourcing of teaching and health care through a modern division of labour advanced by the state are congruent with the emergence of a distinct religious field. By taking away certain responsibilities and roles from the monastery, monks became responsible only for matters that are 'religious' in the modern sense (rituals, blessings, teaching other members of the *sangha*, etc.). For Bourdieu (1991: 6–7) the autonomy of the religious field is demonstrated by the fact that the production of religious knowledge largely happens with reference to esoteric, specialised teachings that exclude the laity. Although this is another problematic generalisation deriving from Bourdieu's Weber-inspired reading of

13. Charles Taylor (2007: 210) sees a direct link between the rise of the nation-state and the emergence of the secular sphere. In order to make citizenship the primary principle, different identities built on gender, class, ethnicity and religion have to be replaced by a unifying experience. Secularism is an important part of this replacement (Asad 2003: 5).

14. For the number of monks in Laos, see the rather unreliable and fluctuating figures given by Bechert (1967) and Zago (1972). I rely here on the numbers given by Halpern (1964, Table 1): 17,000 monks and novices in the whole of Laos for 1957 in an overall population of about 2 million (= 0.85%). The relative decline becomes apparent when looking at the current statistics (Khampeuy Vannosopha 2003): 20,000 monks and novices in an overall population of 6.5 million (= 0.30%).

world religions, we can indeed observe a specialisation of teaching in the *sangha* after the differentiation of public and monastic schooling. However, one also has to acknowledge that fields continue to overlap and that there are many exceptions and hybrids to be found, even in contemporary Laos.

When we look at the dissociation of school and temple – or rather the process that has led to the school leaving the temple and inhabiting a new space – in relation to Bourdieu's theory of differentiation and fields, we observe two interconnected processes: the actual genesis of a religious field and a simultaneous process of demarcation of the borders of this field. Bourdieu (1984: 226) also asserts that the field's boundaries are variable and depend upon the power relationship within and between fields, which fades over distance like a magnetic force (Bourdieu 1996). The effects of the field cease where its rules are not valid any longer. The further we move away from the centre of the field, the less its rules are operative. Earlier in the chapter I presented data that related to the emerging boundaries of a distinct religious field. I will now take a closer look at the changing structures of fields and their content in the specific historical constellation in Laos, which will enable us to better understand the reasons for the emergence and delineation of the religious field.

If we take Tambiah's account of the development of public schooling in the Isan region of Thailand as being valid in the area in and around Vientiane too, we can extend our analysis and look at further reasons for the dissociation of the religious field from the emerging educational sector of the state. Tambiah (1968: 96) reports that 'in 1966 the school was moved for the first time into a building of its own and a fourth teacher was appointed. The teachers are now salaried; the syllabus and curriculum are controlled on a national level; and the medium of instruction is Thai alone.' The payment of the teacher by the state, the implementation of state curricula and the teaching of an official Lao script were also major points in the development of the Lao state school system. These led to the creation of a national educational space and a linked ideology. It is very clear that it was the state and its bureaucratic field that was the driving force in implementing a school system and replacing monks and the temple. In the context of the political situation in Laos in the 1960s, we must also remember that these developments took place in a time when Pathet Lao intrusion into the rural areas of Laos was advancing fast. Halpern (1964: 16) remarks that in '1959 infiltration proceeded to the point where Lao government officials were made unwelcome even in the villages in the district of Vientiane'. As mentioned before, the Pathet Lao promoted mass schooling in the zones under their control from early on, and was by comparison with the Royal Lao Government was much more advanced in this sector. The 'development' and 'modernisation' of the rural regions around Vientiane were regarded as a means of inoculating the population against communism and of getting a foot into the villages of the Vientiane plain, which were still quite isolated. Asad (2003: 13) asserts that in order to understand the secular we have to understand that 'modernity is a project – or rather a series of interlinked projects – that certain people in power seek to achieve'. The central Lao government can be assumed to be these 'certain people in power'; and it was eager to promote 'modern' state institutions like the school in order to secure its influence.

Bourdieu (1994: 1), discussing the genesis and the structure of the bureaucratic field, states 'that one of the major powers of the state is to produce and impose (especially through the school system) categories of thought'. New and more efficient players had to occupy the educational sector, replacing monasteries and monks. Functional differentiation is also a process of reshuffling the hierarchy of fields. Some fields are privileged; society is a hierarchically structured space in which a multitude of actors are active, competing for resources and influence (Kneer 2004: 40). Fields emerge through differentiation and in a process whereby resources in demand are distributed and redistributed; and for Bourdieu (1994: 4–5), the state becomes a holder of 'metacapital' centralising different fields. In the Lao case, the state authorities intended to enter the villages via secular institutions, not the temple. Taillard (1979) has examined the relationship of state bureaucrats with the villagers and has shown that teachers took over some tasks that had befor been reserved for monks. The school took over the role of giving children names (which had traditionally been based on astrological calculations); and, even more importantly, it took over the organisation and implementation of festivals (*boun*). The festivals were still marketed with a religious vocabulary, but largely profited state institutions and their employees in the context of election and mobilisation campaigns. Thus the actors and specific rules of the religious field were transformed, and with them the boundaries of the field itself. Bourdieu postulates that there are two processes at work when religions are exposed to differentiation: one of increasing differentiation of the religious field, and one of dissolution. We see here '[...] two conditions of the religious field; two conditions of the boundary of the religious field', which are the consequence '[...] of the transformations of the borders of the religious field and that of other fields' (Bourdieu 1987: 120). Thus, in Laos, we have on the one hand a delineation of the field (the monastery became more religious in the narrow sense of the term); but on the other hand we also have a partial dissolution of religion (religious tasks are taken over by the state and taken to a new field).

I would, finally, like to link up this analysis of the religious field with recent discussions of theories of secularisation. Talal Asad (2003: 182) has written extensively on the topic, and he proposes that 'the principle of structural differentiation – according to which religion, economy, education, and science are located in autonomous social spaces – no longer holds'. When we take these spaces to be isolated fields, it is impossible to disagree with this. But when we sharpen our analysis and focus, for example, on institutional issues as I have done, I am inclined to agree with José Casanova, who responded to Talal Asad's statement above with these words:

> I argued that the core component of the theory of secularisation was conceptualized as a process of functional differentiation and emancipation of secular spheres – primarily the modern state, the capitalist market economy and modern science – from the religious sphere and the concomitant differentiation and specialisation of religion within its own newly found religious sphere. I argued that this was still the defensible core of the theory of secularisation.
> (Casanova 2006: 12–13)

A secular sphere is not something that is 'free' of religion, but a space where religion has been assigned a different position. Teachers may still imbue pupils with Buddhist morality, but being taught by a monk or a state employee is, I believe, still something fundamentally different. Again coming back to the notion of the field, I think it is reasonable to argue that the emergence and the transformation of the boundaries of the religious field are a consequence of this process of functional differentiation. This should not be understood as a process in which the religious field, or the secular sphere, become isolated, but rather as a gradual and incomplete chain of events. In this context, Bourdieu's understanding of differentiation as a gradual process of an evolving autonomy with varying degrees of connectivity between fields is important. For him, fields are only 'relatively autonomous' (Bourdieu 1991: 5). By contrast with Luhmann's analysis, Bourdieu's fields are neither self-referential and autopoetic subsystems of modern society (Luhmann 1985: 14; 1977: 224), nor are they located in autonomous social spaces, as Asad suggests in the quotation above. They do have increased autonomy, but can only be understood in relation to other fields and their shifting borders. The boundaries between the secular and the religious may still be very fuzzy, but the centres of gravity they evolve around drift apart.

Conclusion

I have in this chapter explored a historical perspective on one aspect of institutional Lao Buddhism and its educational functions. I have looked at length at the colonial period in order to present the workings of the 'traditional' temple schooling system, but I have also referred to this as the beginning of a series of transformations. I then referred to the dissociation of public school and temple schooling as a process of differentiation in the course of which the religious field emerged and was delineated from other fields, especially the field of the state. I argued that in the course of 25 years the monastery and monks were dispossessed of one of their principal functions, which were progressively taken over by the state. Today the temple and the monks are active in a more restricted sphere that can – after this separation has occurred – be labelled the religious field. I do not want to propose that there was an intentional secular agenda at work in Laos' postcolonial modernisation. Modernisation is rarely a unilinear process and does not follow a single logic, but is, rather, a 'complex rearrangement of social practices driven by a series of different and intersecting logics' (Mitchell 2000: 14). I have simply suggested that the modernisation process created secular state institutions, and that this simultaneously created and relocated the boundaries of the religious field. In this context, secularisation and religion have entered a paradoxical process of production that Asad described as follows:

> Although religion is regarded as alien to the secular, the latter is also seen to have generated religion [...] thus the insistence on a sharp separation between the religious and the secular goes with the paradoxical claim that the latter continually produces the former.
> (Asad 2003: 193)

With reference to Bourdieu's theory of the field and its autonomy, we might add that at least in the Lao case, and given the institutional focus I have developed, the separation of the religious and the secular is not necessarily marked by their being 'alien' to each other, but by an increasing (but never complete) autonomy of fields that can be characterised as 'secular' and 'religious'. What is important, however, is to understand the reasons that have driven this process. I have argued that the state had a political interest in increasing its reach through establishing a school system, in order to curtail the influence of the communist Pathet Lao and to promote nationalism.

I have not discussed the potential consequences of this, however, or made a more thorough exploration of the secular in terms of belief or subjectivity; I have (rather conventionally) remained on a level of analysis that Charles Taylor (2007: 423) labels 'Secularity I', in describing the retreat of religion from various public spaces like politics, science, art and the market. It has not been my project to examine what Taylor calls Secularity II (the decline in belief and practice) or Secularity III (the change in the conditions of belief). In order to analyse those, it would be necessary to take a more detailed look at the post-revolutionary and current state of affairs within Lao religious politics. This is another story – though it is, of course, intrinsically related. Grant Evans (1998b: 67) has, for example, spoken of a 'Re-Buddhisation' of Lao society in the current period of reformed socialism. I completely agree with this standpoint. However, I believe that any analysis of the resurgence of Buddhist state ritualism, and of the general Buddhisation of Lao society, must take into account the pre-revolutionary history of the religious field. Although Buddhism was substantially transformed and 'politicised' after 1975 (Stuart-Fox and Bucknell 1982), the institutional changes that occurred before the revolution are perhaps of equal importance. In other words, Secularity II and III can only be explored on the light of Secularity I.

CHAPTER 5

The Early Years of the Lao Revolution (1945-1949)

Between History, Myth and Experience[1]

VATTHANA PHOLSENA

Following the surrender of the Japanese on 15 August 1945, and as the French army instigated their return to Indochina, the political situation in Laos was confusing and precarious. In 1945, the country proclaimed its independence twice within the space of a few months and experienced the abdication of its king under the pressure from an emancipated Lao elite. In addition, it lived through the threat of a Vietnamese-led communist takeover in 1945–6, then witnessed the narrow escape of its newly-independent government to Thailand in 1946, under French fire, followed by the eventual return in 1949 of most nationalist leaders. Laos became a constitutional monarchy and an Associated State within the French Union on July 19, 1949. It seemed, therefore, that by the late 1940s the Lao polity had reverted to its pre-

1. This chapter originated in a workshop that I organised in January 2004 in Singapore with the support of the Asia Research Institute (National University of Singapore). The inspiration for the analytical structure of this chapter is drawn from the three approaches – event, experience, myth – that Paul A. Cohen (1997) applies in an illuminating fashion in his study of the Boxer uprising in China. Cohen explains his framework as follows:

   > Experiencers of the past are *incapable* of knowing the past that historians know, and mythologisers of the past, although sharing with historians the advantage of afterknowledge, are *uninterested* in knowing the past as its makers experienced it. In other words, although the lines separating these three ways of knowing the past are not always clear (historians do, as we are well aware, engage in mythologisation, and the makers of the past are entirely capable, after the fact, of turning their own experiences into history), as ways of knowing they are analytically distinct. (2003: 105, emphasis in the original)

war status as a component of French Indochina. Appearances were deeply misleading, though, as the French army was caught up in a costly, prolonged war that only delayed the end of the colonial presence in the region. (The Royal Lao Government gained its sovereignty in October 1953.) During the five years between 1945 and 1949 an embryonic Lao communist movement emerged along the Vietnamese border under the sponsorship of the Vietnamese Communists (Viet Minh).

There is little doubt that the events that took place in 1945–49 had a formative influence on the history of Laos. These years witnessed the crystallisation of the two forces – royalist–nationalist on the one hand and communist on the other – that would determine the fate of the country in years to come. The same period saw the establishment of revolutionary bases in highly strategic areas, which were to have a decisive influence on the course of the First (1945–54) and especially the Second (1964–75) Indochina Wars, when they spearheaded the communist presence on the future 'Ho Chi Minh Trail' (a complex network of tracks, roads and rivers that ran through eastern Laos, the central highlands of Vietnam, and eastern Cambodia). However, important aspects of this period have remained in the shadows, in particular in the hinterlands of the region formerly known as Indochina.

The significance of the Central Highlands to the Vietnamese revolutionaries – and also to the French and later on the Americans – has been highlighted.[2] These mountainous areas of Vietnam were seen as being of crucial strategic importance for the control of Indochina. Of equal importance to the communist strategy – both Vietnamese and Lao – was the upland region of central–southern Laos, adjacent to the Central Highlands and a Viet-Minh stronghold during the First Indochina War (Christie 2000: *supra* note 2, 94). The history of the hinterlands of Indochina straddling the Lao–Vietnamese border during that conflict is arguably the least studied aspect of this turbulent period.[3] Paul Langer and Joseph Zasloff, two of the most prominent scholars on wartime Laos, readily admitted this gap in their 1970 study of the relationship between the Vietnamese and Lao communist movements. They noted, rather pessimistically, that:

2. See, for instance, Fall 1966; Hickey 1982; McLeod 1999; Christie 2000; Salemink 2003; and Prados 1999.

3. However, see Engelbert 2004.

> [...] the other side to the story of the Lao revolution, which was centred in the east, probably will never be fully documented. Actually, however, it was more important for the development of the Lao communist movement than were the activities of Souphanouvong [the Lao prince famously known for joining the Vietnamese revolutionary side after 1945]'.
> (Langer and Zasloff 1970: 37)

This chapter seeks to partially unravel the period between 1945 and 1949 in those areas in south-eastern Laos. The narrative of this period unfolds differently depending on the narrator.[4] My aim is not only to present the different sides of 'this story', that is, to expose the different points of view that different people have of events depending on their position in relation to those events. I am equally, if not more, interested in analyzing different 'ways of knowing the past'.[5] 'The story' as narrated by historians is a careful reconstruction of a chain of events based on a close and critical examination of documents. While their accounts may emphasise the role of certain individuals or the importance of certain events to varying degrees, they all share a commonality: they explain the past in retrospect. Historians know the outcome of events and moreover can place them within a wider temporal and spatial context.

The first section of this chapter will focus on the historically-reconstructed past of the revolution in south-eastern Laos in the aftermath of the Second World War, encompassing the persons and events – and the structural narrative that links them together – that historians have deemed worth saving from oblivion. There exists another version of this 'story' which is less concerned with the past itself than with the use of it. By re-interpreting the past with little consideration for (non-partisan) historians' reconstruction work or the experienced past, this narrative seeks to achieve political and historical legitimacy. It is this narrative that I cover in the first section of this chapter. The chapter also explores a process of mythologisation in official Lao-language historical studies, in particular the present-day regime's efforts to portray former President Khamtay Siphandone as the liberator of southern Laos.

4. Two other versions of the events in the aftermath of the Second World War will not be discussed in this paper: the nationalist (i.e. non-communist) and revolutionary Lao historiographies. The differing versions of the events of 1945 are analysed in an insightful manner in Lockhart 2003.

5. I borrow the phrase from Cohen 1997, *supra* note 1.

Yet another version of 'the story', and one that is commonly overlooked, is the one that is experienced by its most immediate participants, that is, the experience of reality as narrated by those who lived it, which does not always take the form of a coherently designed narrative. I have constructed the final part of the chapter around the memories of a former Vietnamese war veteran who was among the first Viet Minh fighters to penetrate the highlands of southern Laos in 1948. It is an analytically distinct way of knowing the past, based on the study of original experience of events, at once both fixed, and – unconsciously or consciously – transmuted in the narrator's mind over the years. I will return to this paradox in the last section.

The Lao Revolution: From Independence to Protectorate

On 9 March 1945, the Japanese interned what remained of the French colonial administration in Indochina and incited the rulers of Cambodia, Laos and Vietnam to proclaim their countries' independence under Japanese patronage. Laos was thus proclaimed an independent kingdom on 8 April by King Sisavangvong. A few months later, the return of the first French troops to Lao soil after the capitulation of the Japanese forces on 27 August led to an open conflict between the King and the Viceroy, Prince Phetsarath. The King, replying to the latter's demand that the King reaffirm the unity of Laos, informed him instead of the abrogation of the country's declaration of independence and its return to the status of French protectorate. Sisavangvong viewed the compromise as Laos' best protection against foreign threats, in particular from the Chinese Nationalist occupation army in the north and the Viet Minh's activities among the overseas Vietnamese (Việt Kiều) communities in the country's urban areas (Evans 2002a: 84).

On 15 September, Prince Phetsarath nonetheless went ahead and proclaimed the independence of Laos again, along with the amalgamation of all the country's provinces (and thus the fusion of the separate regional authorities of Luang Prabang, Vientiane and Champassak). However, the position of the Prince and his supporters soon became untenable with the reoccupation of the country by French troops, and the King dismissed him from his posts as Prime Minister and Viceroy on 10 October. Less than a week after Phetsarath's dismissal, on 14 October, a motley coalition led by the Lao Issara ('Free Laos'), which eventually embraced all the existing Lao anti-colonial nationalist movements, set up a provisional government in Vientiane with Phanya Khammao as Prime Minister-cum-foreign minister. Two governments were therefore established in Laos in the aftermath of World War II: one in Luang Prabang, which was pro-French and headed by the King, and the other in Vientiane, which was led by the Lao Issara and sought independence.

On 21 March 1946, at Thakhek in central Laos, the Lao Issara forces (with support from the Viet Minh) were decisively defeated by the French, and the leaders of the Vientiane regime fled to Thailand. On 23 April, Sisavangvong was crowned King of Laos once more, having earlier been deposed by the Issara government; the following day, French forces entered Vientiane. A constitution was promulgated on 11 May, and Laos became a constitutional monarchy within the French Union. The Issara refugees in Bangkok carried on their activities as a Lao government-in-exile, but some members began to support a compromise solution, especially after late 1947, when the right-wing Thai leader Phibun Songkhram returned to power following a coup and imposed severe constraints on anti-colonial activities on Thai soil.[6] Fundamentally conservative and anti-revolutionary, these Lao Issara members regarded the French as their best option for safeguarding the stability of Laos against the communist threat (Christie 2001: 117; Lockhart 2003: 154). In consequence, a division of opinion gradually appeared within the ranks of the movement over the issue of whether to cooperate with the French.[7] Phetsarath and his brothers began to

6. See Murashima 2015. A *coup d'état* in November 1947 in Bangkok ousted the government of Pridi Phanomyong and his Seri Thai ('Free Thai') allies from power. The rise to power of Phibun Songkram, the new strongman of Thailand, heralded the beginning of the end for communist support networks outside Indochina in Southeast Asia, especially in north-eastern Thailand, although it took two more major events before the Vietnamese re-oriented their war operations eastward – namely the rapidly increasing American involvement in Thailand and the Chinese Communist victory of 1949. For more details on the Vietnamese Communists' military strategy and operations at the regional level in Laos and Cambodia during that period, see the very informative article by Christopher E. Goscha (2003a).

7. However, divisions within the Lao Issara leadership were more complex than a binary opposition between supporters of a French solution and anti-French opponents. As Murashima explains: 'The thinking of the Lao leadership about the future course of Laos fell into three groups: 1) those who argued to stay under France, 2) those who argued for merging with or joining in a federation with Thailand, and 3) those who called for a greater Laos.' (Murashima 2015: 144)

drift apart; he adopted a wait-and-see policy that led him to a ten-year exile. (He eventually returned home in 1957 to become Viceroy again, only to die a few months later.) Most Issara leaders, including Souvanna Phouma, returned to Vientiane when the government-in-exile officially declared itself dissolved on 24 October 1949.

By this point Souphanouvong had made clear his refusal to accept the new political direction in Vientiane and was expelled from the Lao Issara movement on 15 May 1949 (Murashima 2015: 176). Over the previous two years, he had tried to persuade the Lao Issara to join the Viet Minh, whose fear of a Lao–French *rapprochement* had led them to throw their weight behind this particular Prince, who publicised his allegiance to the cause of the anti-French struggle in Thailand and Vietnam widely (Deuve 1999: 246–247). On 30 October 1945, the Lao Issara and the Viet Minh had signed a military agreement aimed at building up a 'Lao liberation army'. Phetsarath and other non-communist nationalist leaders very reluctantly accepted this military collaboration, given the absence of a strong Lao resistance army and because of the presence in their country of hundreds of Việt Kiều under Viet Minh command. Souphanouvong, by contrast, willingly declared that 'the independence of Laos [was] inseparable from that of the Vietnamese' (Goscha 1999: 148, 151).[8] In September he had travelled to Hanoi, where he had met Hồ Chí Minh and other Vietnamese leaders and, at Hồ's suggestion, had agreed to form a Lao–Vietnamese military force. This unwilling coalition between communist and non-communist nationalists was short-lived, however. Meanwhile, far from the cities with their power struggles and the atmosphere of confusion that marred Lao politics between 1945 and 1949, the evolution of the Lao communist movement marched on in the eastern regions along the Vietnamese border.

The Early Years of the Lao Revolution in South-Eastern Laos: Historical Reconstitution and Myth-Making Narration

By late 1947, it became evident that the war between the French army and the Việt Minh was going to be a prolonged conflict. Furthermore, north-eastern Thailand, as a base for Viet Minh activities, was no longer a viable option with Phibun's increasingly anti-communist policies, hence the new strategy of reopening an Indochinese front – this time, how-

8. See also Brown and Zasloff 1986: 28–33.

ever, in eastern Laos. (Goscha 1999: 340) The Viet Minh consequently began to support clandestine resistance movements in the following year inside French-controlled Cambodia and Laos. (Furuta 1992: 147; Rathie 2017) There is a study, entitled 'History of the Revolution in Sekong Province, 1945–1975', that provides interesting details of the Vietnamese incursions into south-eastern Laos in 1948.[9] According to this, in April 1948 Phạm Văn Đồng, the Indochinese Communist Party (ICP) and Democratic Republic of Vietnam (DRV) representative to Nam Trung Bộ (south-central Vietnam) formed an armed unit on the Lao–Vietnamese border. This unit, led by Hoàng Tang, was composed of Vietnamese volunteers and propaganda cadres. The group was based in Tà Ngo (Quảng Nam province), from whence it was dispatched a month later to south-eastern Laos with the mission to build revolutionary bases from Tchavane, the district town of Dakchung, to Ban Phon in Lamam (the westernmost district of present-day Sekong province).

Another of the unit's tasks was to support the Lao Issara group led by Som Manovieng (a Việt Kiều from Pakse in Champassak) which had recently returned from Thailand and crossed through Laos to the Interwar Zone (Liên Khu) V, where the group arrived in July 1948. Som was carrying a letter from Souphanouvong to Phạm Văn Đồng in which the Prince requested further Vietnamese assistance for the Issara in southern Laos. The main outcome was the creation by Interwar Zone V of a 'Special Zone' (Khu Đặc Biệt), with its headquarters in Quảng Nam. The Lao–Vietnamese armed forces in the 'Special Zone' appear to have been rather small in number at that time, amounting to only three armed units: an Issara group under the command of Khamsen and Thavone, another composed of Việt Kiều soldiers and a third led by Hoàng Tang, in addition to 19 communist cadres. Towards the end of 1948, these forces were increased through the creation of two Lao–Vietnamese armed units.[10]

9. Khambay Nyundalat 2000–2002 [1991]: 21. Many thanks to Khambay Nyundalat for sharing the unpublished manuscript of this document with me. It was written by a Vietnamese scholar and completed in 1991. Khambay translated the entire manuscript from Vietnamese into Lao and rewrote parts of it (I do not know which ones, however) in 2000–2002. Sekong used to be part of the Eastern Province (Khwaeng Tavaen-ok) until it was detached in 1984 to form a province of its own.

10. Khambay Nyundalat 1991: 22–3. See also Goscha (1999: 343; 2003a: 35). Interwar Zone V coordinated activities in the Central Highlands (Tây Nguyên) and in the lowland central region from Đà Nẵng to Nha Trang (Ang 2002: 165).

Between late 1948 and early 1949, organisation of the revolutionary bases in southern Indochina was stepped up. In February 1949, a Lao Issara delegation travelled to Vietnam to formally solicit more aid, including assistance in the creation of a unified resistance zone in southern Laos. Interwar Zone V authorities and the Lao leaders subsequently agreed on several other measures. First, in March 1949 a 'Lower Lao Zone' ('Khu Hạ Lào') was created to replace the 'Special Zone', with Khamtay Siphandone as its President, Sithon Kommadan its military commander and Som Manovieng as head of the administrative committee. Second, a resistance committee was formed in Central Vietnam – the 'Lower Lao Cadres Committee' ('Ban Cán Sự Hạ Lào'), headed by Nguyễn Chính Cầu – which was to operate in close collaboration with the resistance zone in southern Laos. Finally, a fully-fledged joint Lao–Vietnamese armed force was established, with Sithon as its commander and Đoàn Huyên as his deputy.[11]

What is clearly evident in these events is the close Vietnamese supervision of their Lao allies' activities, which was inseparable from their determination to strengthen their position on the western front. Several factors incited the Vietnamese to intensify their efforts in building up military forces and revolutionary bases in Laos (and Cambodia). First, in developing close military and political collaboration with the local communist movement in southern Laos, the Việt Minh were creating a buffer zone intended to protect their western flank from French attack and to facilitate their troops' intervention in Laos. The safety of, and access to, these sanctuaries outside Vietnam remained a constant imperative throughout the war and was key to the Việt Minh's military survival and final victory. Second, as in Cambodia it was viewed as essential for the ICP to expand its membership in Laos and train local cadres so that they could lead the struggle side-by-side with the Vietnamese and carry out a genuine Indochinese revolution.[12] Finally, the establishment of the People's Republic of China (PRC) in October 1949, followed shortly afterward by the new Beijing regime's formal diplomatic recognition of the Democratic Republic of Vietnam in January 1950, removed Vietnamese

11. Goscha (2003a: 36); Khambay Nyundalat 2000–2002 [1991]: *supra*, pp 24–25.

12. However, 'Lao-ising' or 'de-Vietnamising' the core of Lao radicalism proved to be an uphill task; according to a report submitted to the Second Congress of the ICP in early 1951, of the 2,091 Party members in Laos only 81 were Lao, the rest ethnic Vietnamese (Goscha 1999: 344). See also Furuta (1992: 151–153).

security concerns on their northern frontier. As a result, they were able to concentrate their efforts on building revolutionary bases, structures, and cadres on their western front.

The Past Mythologised

The following section applies another analytical approach to the narration of the Lao revolution: the use of the past to accommodate the needs of the present, specifically the political and historical legitimation of Khamtay Siphandone (who recently retired as President of the Lao People's Democratic Republic) and, at a broader level, of the Lao leadership in the early years of the anti-colonial struggle in the hinterlands of Indochina. Official histories are known to change from time to time, and state-sponsored Lao historiography is no exception. Christopher Goscha has shown that Lao studies on the revolution written in the 1990s placed great emphasis on Vietnamese aid and the bilateral 'special relationship'. In addition, he argues that the 'making of a common [revolutionary] past' has also been the task of Vietnamese historians, who have sought to legitimise their Party's influence over the Lao revolution by emphasising the idea of Indochinese communist solidarity and 'proletarian internationalism' (2003b: 289). This was particularly the case after Hanoi's overthrow of the Khmer Rouge regime in 1979, which tore these concepts down in a dramatic fashion, at least as far as the relationship between the Vietnamese and Cambodian communist movements was concerned. However, Goscha (2003b: 292) also predicted (correctly) that the Lao and Vietnamese historiographies would not continue to advance the same version of their countries' recent past indefinitely, contending that 'Vietnamese should not be shocked or hurt or bitter when Laos decides to take its own, more independent path towards writing the past'.

In this regard, the publication of *Pavat Khet Tai Lao* (Narrative of the Southern Zone of Laos) on the occasion of former President Khamtay's 80th birthday in 2004 is worth noting, for two reasons. Firstly, the book contains a section on the activities of early anti-colonial groups in southern Laos in the period 1947–49; and secondly, it clearly diverges from the official historiography concerning the Lao–Vietnamese wartime relationship. While paying the conventional tributes and paeans to communist solidarity and brotherhood, it enhances the stature of the

Lao revolutionary leaders but also – and in a less orthodox manner – at times describes their strategy and policies as being in disagreement with those of their Vietnamese counterparts. In other words, the Lao leadership, particularly Khamtay, is portrayed as having taken charge of the revolutionary struggle in southern Laos with greater autonomy *vis-à-vis* the ICP than one might expect.[13] *Pavat Khet Tai Lao* thus differs to some extent from other officially-sanctioned narratives, such as the account published in 1993 of the three 'Iron Men of Thakhek' (Souphanouvong, Singkapo Sikhotchunnamali and a Vietnamese officer). This book (Duangsai 1993) not only stresses the prominent role of these two Lao revolutionaries in the anti-French struggle while ignoring the existence of non-communist Issara leaders; it also places great emphasis on the participation of Việt Kiều leaders and communities in revolutionary activities in the southern towns of Savannakhet and Thakhek in 1945–6. (Lockhart 2003: 144)

The sudden change of political leadership in Thailand in November 1947 forced the Lao Issara forces there to go underground, and its members took odd jobs in order to earn a living and to escape from Phibun's anti-communist crackdown. According to the *Pavat Khet Tai Lao*, in the face of the deteriorating situation in north-eastern Thailand Souphanouvong met with Nguyễn Đức Quý, the DRV representative in Bangkok, to discuss the dispatch of an Issara vanguard armed unit to Interwar Zone V. Their mission was to meet the Vietnamese authorities there and request their assistance in building up resistance bases along the border in southeastern Laos. It transpires that this vanguard unit was the group led by Som Manovieng, who had delivered Souphanouvong's letter to Phạm Văn Đồng in July 1948. The book notes that the trip was conceived and prepared in coordination with the Việt Kiều 'Association' (*Samakhom*) in the northeastern Thai town of Ubon Ratchathani. The armed unit under Som's command, assisted by a Vietnamese cadre, departed in May 1948. It was composed of members of a unit called 'Sainyachakkapat' together with 'overseas Vietnamese brothers' from north-eastern Thailand.[14]

13. *Pavat Khet Tai Lao* [Narrative of Southern Laos] (2004), State Printing Press, Vientiane.

14. Som Manovieng was a leader of the first unified anti-French resistance groups in southern Laos. Initially (in 1945) it included 50 'young Lao and foreign patriotic Vietnamese brothers', and was carrying out its activities in the southern province

Upon their arrival in Interwar Zone V, the Lao Issara members received political training in accordance with the ICP's plan to 'indigenise' the Lao communist movement. It was not until October 1948 that the Issara soldiers returned to Laos, where they joined with Vietnamese troops from Interwar Zone V to engage in propaganda and recruitment activities in Dakpam, Daklu and Dakchung on the borderlands between Laos and Vietnam. They soon expanded their field of action to the provinces of Attapeu (Muang Sansay, Kao and May) and Saravane (Muang Thateng). In early 1949, according to this account, Souphanouvong, concerned by anti-communist repression in north-eastern Thailand, decided to send Khamtay to Interwar Zone V in order to solicit more aid from the Vietnamese. Khamtay was accompanied by the rest of the Sainyachakkapat unit and by the 'foreign Vietnamese' under the command of Sithon Kommadam, who was himself assisted by a Vietnamese cadre (*Pavat Khet Tai Lao* 2004: 20–21).[15]

The overall chain of events as related in the *Pavat Khet Tai Lao* generally corroborates accounts found elsewhere (Langer and Zasloff 1970; Goscha 1999, 2003a). What is of particular interest in this most recent historiography, however, are the missing – or, more precisely, the silenced – elements. The political demise of Pridi Phanomyong and his Seri Thai allies (who played an essential albeit indirect role in the protection and consolidation of Vietnamese revolutionary networks in north-eastern Thailand), in tandem with the rise of Phibun's military regime, which was less sympathetic to the Indochinese liberation movement, threatened the Lao Issara organisation in Thailand (Murashima

of Champassak along the Thai border. It expanded to over 100 members after the inclusion of 30 men from the 'Samsen Thai' unit sent by Phoun Sipaseuth from Savannakhet, and the remnants of the 'Sainyasetthathirath' group (including Isan people) led by Thao Bounkhon, which was disbanded in late 1946 due to its exactions against the local population. In May 1946, during a ceremony that took place in Ban Don, in Ubon province, the armed unit was named 'Sainyachakkapat' by Souphanouvong, then Defense Minister of the Issara government, and placed under the command of Sithon Kommadam (*Pavat Khet Tai Lao*, pp 18–19). All three of these units bore the names of great kings from the early centuries of Lao history.

15. The narrative of these events is found in *ibid.*, pp 20–21. Strangely, the book dates these episodes a year earlier – e.g. May 1947 instead of May 1948, early 1948 instead of early 1949 – which is illogical, since the coup in Thailand which convinced the Lao resistance leaders to request help from the Vietnamese occurred in November 1947.

2015: 166–167). Other plausible reasons for Souphanouvong to seek Vietnamese aid (twice in a very short period of time) were the fragmentation of the Issara exile group in Bangkok and his own pro-Vietnamese proclivities. The *Pavat Khet Tai Lao* is mute on that subject, though; nor is there is any mention of the non-communist nationalist leaders, especially Phetsarath and Souvanna Phouma.

MacAlister Brown and Joseph Zasloff noted in 1986 that '[a]n official history of the Communist Party of Laos treats the Lao Issara movement with condescension', quoting a 1976 *Bulletin* from the KPL (*Khaosan Pathet Lao*, the official news service), which effectively condemned the members of the Lao Issara for having been 'born from the petty-bourgeoisie who knew nothing about the laws of social development and the obsoleteness of the bourgeoisie' (Brown and Zasloff 1986: 35). In the aftermath of the communist takeover in 1975, those words were hardly surprising, yet thirty years later the distribution of 'good' and 'bad' roles within the Lao nationalist movement remains. 'The true patriots [within the Lao Issara government-in-exile] under the leadership of Prince Souphanouvong returned to the country to join the resistance', writes a recent military history book, 'while the capitalists and a certain number of royals and leaders whose interests were linked with the French returned to Vientiane to surrender.' (Ai Souliyasaeng et al. 2004: 104–105) There is no condemnation of the Lao Issara movement *per se*, only of those among its members who were not truly 'patriotic', i.e. the non-communist nationalists.

Vietnam's own strategic interest in developing a revolutionary platform in eastern Laos is likewise completely omitted from the narrative, which suggests that armed forces and bases were developed there primarily upon the initiative of the Lao leaders, and that it was in the name of Indochinese communist solidarity that the Lao requested Vietnamese assistance to pursue their goals. The text therefore carefully avoids any reference to the prodigious Vietnamese sponsorship of the Lao movement during this period. Although the latter were crucially dependent on Vietnamese support for political and military training, logistics and materials, the *Pavat* is keen to show that the Lao leaders somehow remained in charge. The decision to create the south-eastern 'Special Zone' in early 1949, for instance, is said to have originated with the Lao Issara:

> Comrade Khamtay Siphandone informed his Vietnamese counterparts of the Lao Issara's decision to create a resistance zone in southern Laos, with Comrade Sithon Kommadam as its military commander, comrade Som Manovieng its administrative chief, both under the overall command of [Khamtay], representative of the Lao Issara government. (*Pavat Khet Tai Lao*, p. 23)

This version of events contradicts some of the Vietnamese sources. General Võ Nguyên Giáp's memoirs recall that in 1948 Som, on behalf of the Lao Issara, and Phạm Văn Đồng 'entirely agreed to coordinate their activities in southern Laos [*vùng Hạ Lào*, "lower Lao zone"]' and that Đồng 'continued negotiations' with Khamtay and Sithon on 'how the Vietnamese would help strengthen joint resistance activities in lower Laos' (Goscha 1999: 343–365; Goscha 2003a: 35–36).[16] It is reasonable to believe that at the very least the Lao Issara leaders would not have taken their decision unilaterally without prior consultation with the Vietnamese.

The most remarkable example of this post-war 'Laocisation' of the revolution is the portrayal of Khamtay as having a leading role in the anti-French struggle in southern Laos. The *Pavat*'s introduction clearly depicts him as the liberator of that region, claiming for instance that 'under [his] intelligent and wise leadership, the southern resistance committee was created in early 1948, and under his command, the multi-ethnic southern population mounted resistance against the French colonialists'.[17] In contrast, one of the better-known Lao-language texts, *Pavatsat Lao* [History of Laos], published in 2000, is far less expansive on Khamtay's anti-colonial actions, which are subsumed among the heroic war deeds of other leading revolutionaries (Souneth Phothisane and Nousai Phoummachan 2000: 742–744).

In this regard, one of Khamtay's strategic military decisions, developed at length in *Pavat Khet Tai Lao*, merits closer consideration. The development of revolutionary bases on the Lao side of the border regions was seen as imperative by Vietnamese military commanders.

16. See also Goscha (2003a: 35–36.) 'The *Khu Hạ Lào* consisted of Champassak, Salawan [sic] and Attapeu provinces...The Vietnamese involved in its creation were Phạm Văn Đồng, Nguyễn Đình Bình (special delegate from the "Western Laotian Cadres Committee"), and Nguyễn Thế Lâm (Acting Commander of Interwar Zone V)' (Goscha 1999: 142).

17. *Pavat Khet Tai Lao*, p. 4.

According to the text, however, this priority was not shared by the Lao leaders, particularly Khamtay. As a matter of fact, during his discussions with the Vietnamese concerning the creation of a resistance zone in southern Laos, he is said to have expressed his 'firm opinion that the establishment of a resistance zone in the mountain areas along the Lao–Vietnamese borders was not achievable'. Khamtay is said to have believed that the plains were more suitable for building up revolutionary forces so as to 'rapidly defeat the aggressor enemy', since they were more populated and people and materials would thus be 'readily available'. Also, the resistance could 'not possibly be isolated, neither surrounded nor destroyed'. *The Pavat Khet Tai Lao* book notes the disagreement on this issue between the two groups. Confronted with this difference of views, Khamtay negotiated with the Vietnamese to reach a solution, for his concern was 'to intensify the struggle in southern Laos to the same level as in the other zones [which the Communists had penetrated] in the country and other battles in Indochina'.[18]

It is worth reproducing Khamtay's explanation of his strategic standpoint as reported in *Pavat Khet Tai Lao*:

> To the east of the provinces of Saravane and Attapeu was a mountain region difficult to reach, and although it was located behind the Vietnamese Interwar Zone V, it was sparsely inhabited and the population lived far from one another and in great need. The conditions were lacking to build up bases and develop forces that could support our resistance movement. More importantly, if we did not hurry or move on, the enemy would have gained in strength and cut us off in these mountain areas. Besides, our armed forces, both Lao and Vietnamese, were still weak and our field of action vast. If we moved, we would leave our rear base and subsequently run the risk of having our line of communication and supply cut off by the enemy.
> (*Pavat Khet Tai Lao* 2004: 28)

As a result of Khamtay's analysis, he and the Vietnamese reached a 'unanimous' agreement that endorsed the movement of the troops to the plains behind the enemy line. 'In spite of their own problems in various battlefields', the Interwar Zone V authorities subsequently increased the number of Vietnamese volunteers and cadres by 20 'to mobilise

18. *Pavat Khet Tai Lao*, pp 24–25 (suitability of plains) and p. 27 (disagreement and negotiation with Vietnamese, emphasis added).

and build the political base', as well as providing two more armed units (Units 200 and 44), 'both trained to fight behind enemy lines'. In the meantime, Interwar Zone V pulled back its troops for them to rest and be re-supplied with weapons and food before launching operations behind French lines (*Pavat Khet Tai Lao* 2004: 28).[19]

The years between 1948 and 1950 arguably formed a crucial period during which the ICP and the Lao movement created and developed their strategic bases within the regions along the Lao–Vietnamese border from north to south. It is not implausible that Khamtay wanted to expand their military operations to the plains and asked for more forces in southern Laos, but this strategic move could not have gone ahead without prior Vietnamese approval. This historiography may also be explained by the authors' intention to show that anti-colonial struggle in Laos was not limited to border zones, but in fact encompassed the whole country and thus involved a much larger share of the population, including those living in the plains. On the other hand, Vietnamese motives appear nowhere in the picture, even though they played a more prominent part than the text is willing to concede. This understatement of the Vietnamese role may represent not only a desire to preserve the façade of an Indochinese communist brotherhood and dismiss the accusations of (forced) Vietnamese occupation of eastern Laos, but also, and perhaps more importantly, to retain control over the narrative of the Lao revolutionary movement's own destiny.

Another – lesser known – side of the story of the First Indochina War, which is by and large silenced in *Pavat Khet Tai Lao* and has only recently emerged in historical studies on the conflict, continued to develop during these years. In the mountains and forests of Laos, the Vietnamese and a few Lao relentlessly pursued their campaign of recruiting and building up revolutionary bases among the local populations, making contacts and progressively adjusting themselves to an unfamiliar environment. It was often a thankless task; nonetheless, in Jean Deuve's somehow prophetic words, 'the fate of Laos was shaped in that manner, along the rivers, during those Lao–Vietminh discussions and meetings, in those villages, forests and mountains in the hinterlands'.[20] The follow-

19. Both quotations are from *ibid.*, p 28.

20. 'Le destin du Laos se forge ainsi, le long du fleuve, dans ces conciliabules and ces réunions lao-vietminh, dans ces villages, ces forêts et ces montagnes de l'intérieur.'

ing section examines this side of the revolutionary story, as experienced by its most immediate participants.

The Experienced Past

In an illuminating article, Christopher Goscha unravels the complex Vietnamese motivations in exporting communism to Laos and Cambodia in the aftermath of the Second World War. As we have seen in the sections above, in 1948 the Vietnamese-led ICP decided to launch a new policy of building up bases and military activities in these countries. While strategic factors played a crucial part in this decision, they were not its sole determinants; the Vietnamese were also – and perhaps even more decisively – driven by ideological and cultural impetus. Goscha argues that:

> Just as the Chinese felt it was their 'internationalist duty' to assist the Koreans and the Vietnamese against the French and the Americans, so too did the Vietnamese consider it their international obligation to bring communism to Laos and to Cambodia and to fight for their 'liberation' from French colonialism as part of a wider worldwide communist struggle against imperialism.
> (Goscha 2004: 152)

Vietnamese Communists felt a sense of belonging to a wider internationalist movement and believed they ought to play a role in spreading the revolution, hence their anxiety and determination to demonstrate and gain acceptance for their internationalist credentials, most importantly among the Soviets and Chinese. In truth, they 'saw themselves on the cutting edge of a superior revolutionary civilisation running from Moscow to eastern South East Asia by way of China' (Goscha 2004: 151).

It is with heightened fascination that one reads Goscha's comments on the memoirs of Vietnamese war veterans who, armed with such a profound faith, carried out this 'internationalist mission' inside their neighbouring countries. The accounts of their political activities in southern Laos and north-eastern Cambodia in the late 1940s and 1950s forcefully reveal 'the degree to which these Communists believed in their missions in Laos, the righteousness of the cause, its legitimacy and their duty to spread the revolutionary word there' (Goscha 2004:

(Deuve 1999: 248)

153).[21] The harsh living conditions and sometimes hostile environment in an unknown land were matched by the depth of their commitment and determination, as revealed in their published recollections. What is particularly fascinating is the highland population's encounter with these communist 'missionaries', who possessed their own version of the *mission civilisatrice* targeting the mountain areas of Indochina. As Goscha notes:

> The Vietnamese admit today that their aim was to bring modernity to these backward peoples, to change their habits and customs in favour of what they saw as superior ones. The discourse of modernity was an important tool in the Vietnamese bid to win over converts and gain the trust of the Laotians (and Cambodians). (2004: 156–157)

The following account – collected on the 'Lao side' – complements Goscha's analysis.

Until we were told his country of origin, it was hard to guess that the tanned old man who spoke fluent Lao with an occasional trace of an accent was a Vietnamese-born Lao citizen. Originally from Hội An, Quảng Nam province, Bonyeun first came to Laos as a 'volunteer' (*asasamak*) in 1948 and never left. He married a Lao woman and now lives in Sekong town, a few hundred metres away from the provincial government office. In his mid-seventies when we met him, he still vividly recalled his years of 'revolutionary struggle' in Laos.[22] My colleagues and I were seated in his recently-built concrete two-storey house, which was almost bare except for a few chairs and a low table. His wife was also present, seated quietly on the floor in the background; she said only a few words during the interview, and only when directly addressed.

21. Goscha 2004: 153. Particularly important are the memoirs by Nguyễn Chính Cầu and Đoàn Huyên, two long-standing and high-ranking political and military advisers in Laos. Cầu was the head of the Resistance Committee in Trung Bộ (Central Vietnam), the sister organisation to the resistance committee in southern Laos, while Huyên served as Sithon Kommadam's deputy commander (Khambay Nyundalat 2000–2002 [1991]: 24–5).

22. I was then part of a team involved in a research project funded by the Toyota Foundation, which aimed to collect the life stories of former revolutionaries noted for their 'heroic' actions during the Indochina Wars. Sekong was one of the three provinces, together with Savannakhet and Saravane, that the team visited in 2003 and 2004. Our visit to Mr. Bonyeun took place in December 2003; all quotations are from this interview.

Like many young people of his age, including his own friends, Bonyeun joined the Vietnamese youth movement (*khabuankan saonum Vietnam*) in 1945 during the euphoric moments of the August Revolution. Then 17 years old, he enlisted in an army unit that was soon deployed to defend urban areas against the return of the French a year later. He candidly admitted that he merely followed his friends and was not very aware of the events that were going on at that time; he only knew that they were exciting times of which he wanted to be part. After his first experience of fighting, he decided he would continue the revolutionary struggle and subsequently bade farewell to his mother during his last visit to his village. In July 1948, his provincial/rural army unit (*kongphan tamluat khwaeng*) received an order from Phạm Văn Đồng, the DRV representative in southern Trung Bộ. The latter had just received a letter from 'President Souphanouvong and Khamtay', who 'went and gave it to him directly by hand in the Interwar Zone V'. Bonyeun heard from his friends that apparently 'the Lao were asking the Vietnamese for aid'.

His unit was ordered to establish a section of armed soldiers and a propaganda unit; the latter had nine members including himself, constituting a 'special armed propaganda unit' (*noei khosana pakop avut phiset*), with the clear mission 'to move [their] activities from Vietnam to the Lao–Vietnamese border'. They did not immediately cross into Laos, however. Their first and foremost priority was to 'neutralise' (*kam*) the influence of a very important Katu leader (holding the Lao titles of Chao Lam or Chao Khwaeng under the colonial system) on the Vietnamese side, who apparently was in control of the whole region bordering the district of Dakchung (in present-day Sekong) and whom the Vietnamese had been trying desperately and unsuccessfully to 'control'. Bonyeun and his comrades began by offering the chief and his followers salt, sugar, rice, 'all sorts of stuff and gifts, whatever he asked for'. The highland leader remained unimpressed, however, and in fact manifested signs of great suspicion, if not hostility, towards them. Fiercely anti-French, he believed that these Vietnamese soldiers were working for the former rulers and therefore did not trust their anti-colonial propaganda.

The highland population to whom the French gave the name 'Katu' (see Goudineau this volume, Chapter 6) were traditionally feared by the lowland Vietnamese, who used to set up armed groups to protect themselves against the highlanders' attacks on their settlements. These raids did not stop when the French began to 'penetrate' the interior of Quảng Nam, prompting the creation in 1904 of a military post at An Điêm (inland from Hội An) to protect Vietnamese villages along the Bung River. It took nearly ten years for the French authorities to 'pacify' the area, which finally quietened down in 1913 and remained quiescent for a long period of about 20 years (Le Pichon 1938: 360). A series of Katu attacks erupted again in 1936, however, coinciding with the expansion of the French economic and physical presence in the Central Highlands through the construction of roads aimed at accelerating the occupation and control of the 'hinterlands'.[23] Another military post had been established the previous year at Bến Giang, as it had been planned that Route 14 would reach the coastal towns of Hội An and Đà Nẵng (Tourane) by passing through Katu country. In an effort to stabilise the region and to prevent the unrest from spreading, the post at An Điêm was replaced by another one at Bến Hiển (or Pi-Karum) in 1937, located further northwest in the interior on strategic high ground near the confluence of the Con and Se Kalum Rivers, which was a crossroads of important trade routes. At the same time Poste 6, situated on a plateau commanding a view of the Giang, Cái and Bung River valleys, replaced the fort at Bến Giang (Le Pichon 1938: 361).[24]

The peace finally established in the area was fragile and hollow. J. Le Pichon, a commander with the local militia (Garde Indigène de l'Annam), who authored an influential study on the Katu published in 1938, himself expressed doubts over the long-term ability of the French to rule (for him, 'to protect') the 'Katu race' in the face of the

23. This policy was known as the 'oilspot method' (*tâche d'huile*). It 'combined military repression of the rebellion with the political and social organisation of the region [...] First a fort would be constructed in a strategic site in the fractious region, from which the surrounding population(s) would be militarily pacified. Then the infrastructure would be developed – roads, military posts and supervised markets constructed. When this area was entirely controlled, a neighboring area would be pacified. Thus, this "structural pacification" would spread like an oil spot. The political leadership in the area would be more or less respected, if the local leaders would formally submit to French authority.' (Salemink 2003: 63)

24. Le Pichon notes (1938: 359) that part of this region was inhabited by an ethnic group which he refers to as 'Dié'; this would seem to be the Mon-Khmer-speaking minority now known as 'Gié', officially classified together with another group as 'Gié-Triêng' (Đặng Nghiêm Vạn, Chu Thái Sơn and Lưu Hùng et al. 1986: 121).

immense task that the colonial rulers hoped to accomplish, namely to bring progress and 'civilisation' to the mountain regions of Indochina and their inhabitants (Le Pichon 1938: 402–403). The campaigns of repression against the Katu in the early 20th century, and again in 1936–38, together with the labour *corvée* and heavy colonial taxes, must have left bitter memories among the highlanders. It was therefore hardly surprising in this context that the Katu leader manifested hostile reactions to Bonyeun and his comrades, who were probably perceived as representing yet another form of invasion.

After weeks of trying to persuade the tribal chief of their good intentions, the Vietnamese began to feel increasingly frustrated. They were at a loss and simply did not know what to do, and they could not afford a more forceful approach for fear of angering the chief and thus risking an attack on their unit. They had set up camp near the village and continued to exchange food and other items with its inhabitants, but, despite these continuous interactions, they did not make any noticeable progress until they decided to change their strategy. The young son of the Katu leader was growing increasingly close to them and frequently came to their camp, in spite of his father's disapproval; he eventually ended up sharing their daily meals. The Vietnamese volunteers consequently decided to get closer to the village, hoping that their friendship with the chief's son would help smooth the process; as the leader of Bonyeun's unit put it, 'if we can't control the father, we at least have the son on our side'.

Their calculations proved correct: the son was allowed to spend more time with the Vietnamese soldiers, who willingly looked after him, and their relationship with the villagers subsequently grew warmer, particularly as they learnt some of the Katu language. They eventually succeeded in getting physical access to the village and, more importantly, to the interiors of the houses. From then on, they helped the villagers in all their work, including carrying water, building houses and feeding animals. Bonyeun and his fellows provided the villagers with water when they returned from the *hai* (swidden rice fields), for instance. By integrating themselves into the village's daily life, they eventually won the Katu chief's confidence; his support proved to be extremely valuable for their propaganda work. His undisputed authority over approximately 20 villages greatly eased their task; he had only to issue an order to the chiefs from the neighbouring villages for them to gather.

During the meetings that Bonyeun and his comrades had with the chiefs, he told us that the 'solidarity and mutual support between the Viet Loum and the Viet Theung[25] against the French' were emphasised, and that the final victory of the Vietnamese revolution, which would 'bring about equality among every people [i.e. ethnic group] in Vietnam', was promoted. It is uncertain whether the Katu villagers and their chiefs had heard of the Congress of the Southern National Minorities held under Party auspices in Pleiku two years earlier (in April 1946); or, if they had, whether they would have felt connected with it. It is more probable that the Vietnamese cadres had been made aware of Hồ Chí Minh's speech, which was read during this meeting. This stressed the brotherly relationship between the 'Kinh majority people and minorities', 'all Viet-Nam's children' (Ho Chi Minh 1967: 164). The ethnic policy of the Vietnamese Communists was not merely a by-product of their war strategy; the policy of 'national' equality and unity was also very much influenced by Lenin's own prescriptions. For example, in 1934, the External Bureau of the ICP warned the Laos Section (which at that time would have been almost certainly composed exclusively of Việt Kiều) to remember Lenin's strategy of encouraging full liberation for ethnic minorities and of fighting against 'regional, patriotic, or chauvinist ideology, since Communism recognises only the class struggle, not the struggle of races' (Brown and Zasloff 1986: 15).

There is little doubt that the cadres had been taught these principles before travelling to the highlands. However, like the conversions to Catholicism attributed to French missionaries in the 19th century among the peoples of the Central Highlands, 'conversions' to (socialist) modernity were also carried out through concrete actions resulting in practical benefits.[26] In *History of the Revolution in Sekong Province*

25. The ethnic groups of Laos are often informally divided into three broad categories: Lao Lum (lowland Lao and some other Tai-speaking groups), Lao Theung (Mon-Khmer-speakers living at higher altitudes) and Lao Sung (minorities inhabiting the highest altitudes, mainly Hmong and Yao). Vietnamese, on the other hand, generally make a two-way distinction between Kinh (lowland ethnic Vietnamese) and Thượng (highlanders). Bonyeun's terminology seems to reflect a fusion of the two sets of classifications.

26. Oscar Salemink notes that 'the attraction of the Catholic religion did not lie in its theological qualities, but rather in the practical advantages offered to new converts in economic and political fields. Already the former Governor-General De Lanessan noted in his *Les missions et leur protectorat* [written in 1907] that con-

(Khambay Nyundalat 2002–2002 [1991], it is stressed that one of the first priorities of the Revolution was 'for the population to have enough food' (*ibid.*: 38), which explained the participation of Lao and Vietnamese cadres and soldiers in agricultural work such as the clearing of fields and the protection of harvests by installing traps and chasing away elephants. An episode narrated in the *History of the Revolution in Sekong Province* highlights the Vietnamese Communists' early economic support to the upland population. As a consequence of the blockade imposed by the Royal Lao Government on the distribution and trade of staples into the zones deemed to be under communist control, their inhabitants began to face a serious shortage of salt by the early 1950s. To alleviate the situation, the Communists decided to organise groups of hundreds of people led by district cadres, protected by soldiers and supplied with food and medicine, to travel to Interwar Zone V in Vietnam and bring back salt that would be distributed to 'every household in the Eastern Zone of Laos'. According to the *History of the Revolution in Sekong Province*, this action greatly contributed to the popularity of the Vietnamese revolutionaries among the highland population.[27]

Such an operation also shows the impressive logistical capacity and political authority that the Vietnamese revolutionaries managed to achieve only a few years after their first incursions into the hinterlands of Laos. The Communists, in their way, pacified the upland areas not through sheer military force but by shifting political authority within highland societies. For instance, they played the role of mediator in conflicts between villages, mostly involving land and water usage. They would call representatives of the respective villages to a neutral location, usually the district town in Muang Dakchung, and oversee the discussions for several days until an agreement was reached. The *History of the Revolution in Sekong Province* praises the Party's promotion of mutual

versions were more often than not economically motivated, and tended to disjoin individuals from their family and community, resulting in great social tensions.' (Salemink 2003: 57)

27. Khambay Nyundalat 2000–2002 [1991]: 38–39. The marketing of salt was a state monopoly in French Indochina; during the Japanese occupation, annual production of salt reached almost 250,000 tonnes (249,128 tonnes, in 1945) in order to meet the increasing needs of Japan's war efforts. See Le Manh Hung 2004: 29, 166; my thanks to Tobias Rettig for pointing out this reference to me.

support among the highland population and with the ethnic Lao and Vietnamese revolutionary personnel.[28]

The Vietnamese cadres' accounts detailed in Goscha's article have much in common with Bonyeun's own recollections. One of the cadres explains, for instance, that they targeted the families of headmen, considering them as 'good, having the confidence of the village'; their support would thus be 'advantageous to the work of winning over the support of the people'. Like Bonyeun and his companions, these Vietnamese cadres immersed themselves in the life of the upland village. As Goscha explains it, 'cadres sent westwards and into the highlands were expected to live with the villagers if need be, to work in the fields with them and even to marry into their families'. Their commitment was so deep that he readily compares the Vietnamese volunteers to Catholic missionaries: 'Their capacity to live for years in remote areas of Laos and Cambodia, working laboriously and often fruitlessly for the international faith, also parallels the diffusion of Catholicism.' (Goscha 2004: 156)

It is difficult to tell whether Bonyeun was consciously motivated by an equally intense mission to spread the 'new revolutionary civilisation'. He pioneered the communist venture in the Lao–Vietnamese border areas in the late 1940s, and while his narration undoubtedly reveals extremely enthusiastic sentiments (the old man repeated the word *sanuk* several times, which can be translated as 'fun'[29]), it also reflects enduring memories of hardship and uncertainty. Overall it took Bonyeun and his comrades approximately nine months to achieve their mission, which began in August 1948 and was not completed until April 1949. As he recalled, 'it was far from easy in the beginning for Vietnam to establish itself in that frontier region on the Vietnamese side. We had to work our way hard. But we had the energy, we were enthusiastic.' In 1957, the American anthropologist Gerald Hickey travelled to Katu country. An overnight stay in a Katu village called A-To was enough to make him realise that the Vietnamese Communists had 'already' been spreading their anti-colonial propaganda, and had even rallied some of the villagers to their cause.[30]

28. Khambay Nyundalat 2000–2002 [1991]: 45–47.

29. Intriguingly, Bonyeun used the Thai term for 'fun'; however, it should be pointed out that this term is widely known in Laos.

30. A somewhat unsettled Hickey (2002: 73, 75) wrote that 'talking through Mr. Phuong, the chief expressed dissatisfaction at having "Frenchmen" in the village, saying the "Viet Minh" would not like it. He noted there were Viet Minh in the for-

The next stage, after turning the Vietnamese side of the border into a Viet Minh-friendly zone, was to 'spread over' into Laos, starting from Dakchung and Tariuy, now the easternmost district of Sekong. The cadres' task was made easier by their newly-acquired experience among highland villagers and, more importantly, their knowledge of the Katu language, since the local population on the two sides of the border belonged to the same ethnic group. On the Lao side they faced another type of obstacle, however: the French anti-Viet Minh propaganda that had been spread among the highland population (suggesting that the French were aware as early as 1947–8 of Viet Minh incursions into the Lao borderlands). The 'Keo' (a derogatory Lao term for ethnic Vietnamese) had been portrayed as ruthless killers and demonised: 'they were told that the Keo had long teeth [and] the villagers believed that!' The mission's early days in Laos were therefore difficult, as the population was unreceptive. In many cases there were only elderly people in the villages, as most of the young people had left. Bonyeun and his comrades applied the same strategy of sharing the villagers' life that they had used on the Vietnamese side. According to him, they gradually managed to project another image to the local population, one that was different from the one disseminated by the French. The villagers subsequently began to change their minds and to believe that 'these people were not as the French told them after all!'

After successfully 'recruiting' the local population in that area, Bonyeun and his comrades continued their route downwards to the plains and the Sekong River. Their mission accomplished on both sides of the border, they were on their way back home to Vietnam. Their problems were not over, though; one of the men fell ill and died a week later. They could not find their way back to the border and wandered in the forests for several weeks, losing one more companion in unclear circumstances during a return journey that turned into an ordeal. They rapidly ran out of water and survived on forest fruits. Not wanting to steal from the villagers, they left money behind every time they took some food. When they finally reached Tà Ngo in Vietnam, they had lost three of their comrades.

---

est, adding that his brother, who "had gone north" [presumably North Vietnam] was now with them.'

At times the encounters between upland villagers and the Vietnamese Communists could be rough and tense. Some 'volunteers' were reported to have been aggressive, behaving violently towards the population and forcing them to comply with their orders. Some instances of excessive control and supervision over the harvests were also noted by the Party leadership, with some villagers even coerced into giving their paddy fields to Vietnamese cadres. The religious beliefs and practices of the local population were sometimes violated, and there were cases of theft, which were denounced and subsequently punished by the communist authorities.[31] However, such instances of incorrect behaviour are presented in the manuscript as the work of 'bad apples', a few isolated cases which were successfully rectified. In the early years of communist penetration into the highlands of Laos and Vietnam it seems that the communist cadres were careful, or at least tried not to violate the villages' taboos. This was often difficult. For example, as Bonyeun recalls, in the villages of the Taliang and Triuy 'brothers' where he lived it was strictly forbidden to sweep the interiors of the houses, as it was believed that any cleaning would chase away the house's protecting spirits. 'It was very hard; whatever you did, it was wrong (*phit*)!' They nonetheless managed to teach some notions of hygiene to the villagers, especially to the young people, who were the most receptive; but they would often clash with elderly people, who disliked this intrusion into their traditional lifestyle and would vehemently express their opposition.

Like the Catholic missionaries, these Vietnamese volunteers began by observing their new environment and gathering knowledge about the local culture through direct contacts with the villagers – the classical anthropological method of 'participant observation' – before attempting to interfere with customs, religious beliefs and practices. They adopted a gradual approach. In one instance they convinced the villagers that they should inflict a lighter punishment, in the form of a smaller fine, on someone who had violated a custom. They persuaded them that instead of a buffalo, the offender should only need to give a piglet or another 'smaller animal with four legs'. Young people were the primary group targeted, as they were often more willing to listen to the cadres' suggestions. In another instance, the cadres encouraged a group of young people to eat venison during the field-clearing season, which broke a

31. Khambay Nyundalat 2000–2002 [1991]: 47–48.

strict taboo in in the local culture. Violating this taboo was believed to lead to deadly nightmares, but when none of these occurred the young people decided to abandon this custom.

Eventually, as noted in *History of the Revolution in Sekong Province*, 'the young people no longer cut their teeth or pierced their ears or wore silver or brass rings around their necks or wrists; the women/girls were now wearing [Lao?] skirts and shirts. And families were eating and drinking in good hygienic conditions.' The 'civilising' campaigns gradually became more systematic and even institutionalised. From 1954 onwards, each time a village 'decided' to abandon its 'absurd beliefs', a finely tuned ceremony was set up in the presence of communist representatives from the district and provincial levels and under the supervision of a master of ceremonies whose task was to officially register the event. Most interestingly, a picture of Prince Souphanouvong was displayed during the ceremony, which seems to have endorsed the transfer of political and spiritual allegiances from a local system of belief to a secular and national political authority.[32]

His experience of life in the highland area was radical for Bonyeun, who was, as he put it, 'from the city'. The process of immersion was truly total: 'We had to do everything like the people. We had to become the people'. They allowed their skin to become tanned so that it went 'from white to dark'; they pierced their ears; and they grew their hair longer, whenever necessary. If they did not do this, he said, 'you were not able to be part of the people (*khao pasason*)'. It was the 'Party's instruction' to live with the people, like the people. The biggest problem for him, and many others, was the food. He still retained vivid mental pictures of it: 'the dried meat was swarming with maggots. I could not eat. But our superiors were keeping an eye on us. We had to comply with the Party's instructions. We had to eat with the villagers. Several of my friends got discouraged (*sia kamlangchai*) as a consequence and were sent back.' The taking in of alien food may be viewed as the ultimate test of integration – the penetration of one's body by foreign elements – that helped the Vietnamese volunteers to grow closer to the local inhabitants when they were finally able to overcome their gastronomic repulsion. After that, Bonyeun recalls, 'I got pretty much used to life in the village.' He

32. For an account of these developments see Khambay Nyundalat 2000–2002 [1991]: 41–44.

had passed the test by accepting the highland 'forest' food into his Kinh lowland body. His transformation was complete, both on the outside (dark skin, long hair, etc.) and on the inside.

During the interview with him, Bonyeun stopped short of describing the minority peoples as 'backward'; the only mildly derogatory word he used to describe them, after some hesitation, was 'rural', as opposed to himself as 'urban' (which is not quite true since his parents were farmers). Years of ideological correctness certainly guided his careful vocabulary, as did, most probably, the presence of ranking officials of ethnic minority origins (one was Katu, another Makong) in the room during the interview. However, there was another, deeper reason for the way in which Bonyeun spoke about the area in which he now lived: the fact that he had fallen in love with a Taliang woman in one of the upland villages in which he was staying, and made the unusual request to stay on there, despite an order for him to return to Vietnam. In consequence, he went 'native' more than he had ever probably expected he would when he first crossed the border into Laos in 1949 at the age of 21, eventually becoming 'one of them'. The account of his life in Laos – over 20 years of it in highland villages (Triu and Taliang) in Dakchung – offers a fascinating picture of a man 'going native', struggling along the way and ultimately being transformed by his extraordinary experience.

Conclusion

Except for the studies by Langer and Zasloff, Deuve, Goscha, Rathie and the state-sponsored Vietnamese and Lao historiographies, the events that occurred in eastern Laos have been little studied. The past experienced by Bounyeun, shared with us during that evening by drawing on his reservoir of memories, is one way of knowing the past in these areas. The war veteran remembers the past as something that happened to him; the narrative of a reality experienced is analytically different from a historically reconstituted past. Bounyeun was not back-reading the past; he lived again his intimate experience of the war through his story-telling. Certainly, a human experience is already being processed and analysed in the person's mind as soon as it has occurred. An original experience rarely keeps its 'pristine' form. Yet Bounyeun's narrative and the testimonies found in Goscha's article allow us to understand better what went on in these people's minds, opening a window on to their feelings, thoughts and motivations, which often go unnoticed in historically reconstituted works. In contrast, *Pavat Khet Tai Lao* is an extreme example of historiographers' common indifference towards experienced past. The booklet has one specific and openly declared agenda: the legitimation of Khamtay Siphandone's status as the liberator of southern Laos. The myth-in-construction has a degree of plausibility, though: as we have repeatedly seen throughout this paper, the history of the First Indochina War in the border regions remains relatively understudied. The main concern, however, is not whether the myth is believable; rather, those involved in this historiographical project should ask whether today's Lao people actually care about it.

CHAPTER 6

The Anthropology of Southern Laos and the Origin of the Kantu Issue[1]

YVES GOUDINEAU

In the Lao imagination, the Upper Sekong region has always represented a sort of horizon, like a vanishing point towards which all the 'lines of flight' of southern Laos converge, literally and figuratively. The colonial power, for its part, had long been fixated on the peoples of this region, which was considered to be the last bastion of rebellion that needed to be eliminated. This part of the Annamese Cordillera had rarely been penetrated and was also believed to be the repository of archaic traditions, supposedly holding key elements to understanding local indigenous culture before 'Lao-isation'. Amongst the peoples occupying this region, the Kantu (now officially called Katu in Laos as in Vietnam) have been given a particularly emblematic status, up to now, the origin of which we will try to understand here.

Representations of the South

There are various ways to geographically define the area that can be considered southern Laos. The easiest way is to consider the Mekong as a kind of natural lateral coordinate. It can be said – given that the Lao provinces are located almost exclusively on the left bank of the river – that the south is defined on this axis as lying between the Khemmarat rapids and the Khone waterfalls, if the province of Savannakhet is included. If the latter is excluded, it is the area between the confluents

1. This text benefited from extended discussion with the late Grant Evans, when we went to Aix-en-Provence together and worked at the Colonial Archives (ANOM), and from generous positive comments from Martin Stuart-Fox (2010).

of the Se Done river (in Saravane) and of the Sekong river (in Stung Treng, a province in Cambodia, which was long a Lao *muang*). On the other hand, 'southern Laos' can also refer to a political division. The central administration and the press now usually refer to the 'southern provinces'. Colonisation divided the territory into North/Central/South (later replaced by Upper and Lower Laos), and for almost two centuries, the history of southern Laos was associated with the history of the principality, or *muang*, of Champassak.

However, ultimately such attempts to define southern Laos geographically or geopolitically are trumped by the fact that southern Laos exists above all in the minds of the Lao people. In this context, it refers to images, attitudes, sets of values, to what anthropology calls representations of otherness, which seem to be based on the widely shared idea that southern Laos is not really, or not completely, 'Lao-ised'. For an inhabitant of Vientiane or Luang Prabang, people from Attapeu, Saravane or Sekong do not only have an accent and their own culinary practices; they also live in dangerous regions, and are even considered slightly dangerous themselves. Lao living in the southern provinces share these biased opinions, but they attribute them differently: for them, the dangerous horizon is towards the east. The cultural frontier becomes more pronounced as you leave the Mekong for the interior of the provinces. The inhabitants of Pakse, Champassak and Khong, all towns located on the Mekong, are still in some ways within the Lao cultural orbit; but the nearer you get to the foothills of the Annamese Cordillera, the more unfamiliar the territory becomes to the Lao.

For Lao who live in the south themselves, some of the southern provinces are said to be less safe than others. A Lao official from Pakse would not happily accept an appointment to work in Sekong or Attapeu, and if he did accept it, this would certainly be a source of anxiety for his family. In each of these provinces, the mountain districts are the most feared. In 1993, when I first lived in Saravane and was working in the remote mountainous districts of Ta Oi and Samui, my Lao neighbours constantly gave me friendly but precautionary warnings. Most of them, who had arrived after the war from Khong Sedone, a lowland region bordering the Mekong, had endless stories, each one more frightening than the other, about the Ta Oi or Pacoh villagers among whom I was doing fieldwork and spending weeks at a time: one should not touch their food because they could surreptitiously add *van*, a poisonous root which makes buffalo skin grow in your stomach, resulting in a horrible death; one should also avoid any open argument with them because they were allied with powerful evil spirits; and so forth. However, none of these informants, most of whom were government officials, had ever been as far as these not-so-distant mountains delimiting the horizon around Saravane. They only knew the little groups coming to the local markets, crossing the town furtively before dawn in single file and leaving early to return to their villages, generally several days away on foot.

On the eve of the 21st century, entire districts of Saravane, Attapeu and the majority of the province of Sekong remained, in the eyes of Lao officials, on the outskirts of 'national culture' and required special and repeated efforts from provincial authorities to hasten their integration. This exceptionally long-lasting state of marginality with regard to national development is not unrelated to the fact that 'Lao-isation' seems to have stopped at the first foothills of the cordillera and never took hold any further afield on a long term basis – despite years of conflicts and wars during which the uplands were forcibly opened and subjected to heavy military traffic. This situation contrasts with that in the north of the country where, although there are several small regions occupied by non-Lao ethnic groups, Lao-Tai economic and cultural infiltration has long been evident, be it through the influence of the Lao or of various Tai groups (Lue, Tai Dam, Tai Yuan, etc.), and this has resulted in regular exchanges between the diverse local populations.

By contrast, the eastern part of the southern provinces seems to be one of the rare examples, and probably the last, of a marginal area inherited from an important Lao *muang* – Champassak – that has never really been integrated. The only geographical factor that may be relevant to this, a particularly rugged terrain, is not sufficiently significant to explain the durability of this non-integration; it is, therefore, useful to trace the history of the aborted penetration of this area, starting with the formation of the *muang*, followed by the colonial period and then the war.

The Thwarted Logic of the *Muang*

The *Annals of Champassak*, local chronicles translated and annotated by Charles Archaimbault as *L'histoire de Campasak*, point out that, unlike the great 'chiefdoms' of the north, Luang Prabang and Vientiane, this principality was not established very long ago (Archaimbault 1961: 546). It was only at the beginning of the 18th century that Prince Soi Sisamut gave Champassak the status of *muang* and organised its administration. Before him, Phra Khru, a historico-legendary Buddhist monk from Vientiane who is considered to have been the spiritual founder of the principality, was said to have created 'lands of pagodas' beyond Champassak. But Archaimbault remarks that 'as these religious centres were isolated, they formed monads only united by the memory of their founder and the reason for their foundation: propagation of the faith'. All around, the country was still inhabited by the 'Kha' (savage people and potential slaves) to which both the *Annals of Champassak* and the *Annals of Attapeu* attribute various names, rarely using current ethnonyms, with the notable exception of 'Suei'. The Suei represented the aboriginals in all the important rituals of the principality, even though they were the most 'Lao-ised' of the Kha, being both rice growers and Buddhists.

Whereas Phra Khru is primarily viewed as the guardian of pagodas and stupa, Soi Sisamut is considered to have established the framework of officialdom and to have set up a network of small dependencies, each governed by a vassal. At the end of his reign, the principality was made up of ten vassal *muang* located around the Mekong valley, from Stung Treng in the south to Yasothon in the north-west, thus including certain regions that are today part of Cambodia and others located on the Khorat Plateau in Thailand. Attapeu and Saravane (then called Muang Mane) represented the most advanced points of Lao expansion to the east. Archaimbault notes that the eastern frontier was thought to stretch as far as the mountains, but that its boundaries 'must have been very imprecise as the texts [to describe them] refer to "*nang*" trees (*dipterocarpaceae*) which served as frontier posts' (Archaimbault 1961: 587).

However imprecise or allegorical these local chronicles may have been, it is interesting to note that, in the minds of Lao writers and probably in reality, Buddhism comes first and administration second in the process of creating a new *muang*. As settlement progressed, monasteries and stupa helped to anchor Lao villages, giving them an identity and protecting them in little-known territories. Those designated to take charge of sanctuaries were also often amongst the first vassals chosen by the prince of Champassak. They were responsible for 'applying codified law overriding regional customs and introducing a more stable legal structure'. According to the Siamese versions of the chronicles, Soi Sisamut not only increased the number of administrative centres; he also undertook to develop a local economy by minting a currency whose value was recognised throughout the region, and established a 'sensibly calculated' tax. He understood the importance of basing the legitimacy of his power on rituals that were carried out throughout the principality and instituted 'rites of first tillage and the expulsion of plagues' (Archaimbault 1961 : 553).[2]

However, the 10-*muang* structure established by Soi Sisamut did not even last a century. Coming under Siamese control from the beginning of the 19th century, after having long been under its influence, Champassak became an official vassal of Bangkok in 1827 following the failure of Chao Anou's attempt to conquer the Khorat Plateau. This resulted in the complete fragmentation of the principality. And even though it kept control over a few ancient *muang* and created new minor ones, it had to resign itself to the fact that many of its most important and strategically located *muang*, such as Khong or Saravane, were placed directly under Siamese sovereignty. According to the chronicles, from 1841 onwards the Siamese officers 'went to watch over the defiles on the Annamite border' (Archaimbault 1961: 556). This was followed by many major relocations. Wanting to remove the local populations from the influence of the Hue court, to which some of them paid tribute, the Siamese moved entire villages, mainly Phu Tai ones. They took them to Khemmarat on the right bank of the Mekong, and around Champassak, from the Se Bang Hieng and Sepone valleys, making this natural corridor, which was now largely depopulated, a sort of buffer region with Annam.[3]

These large movements of population added to the confusion already brought about by the multiplication of small administrative centres, some of which were still controlled by Champassak, while others were directly ruled by Siam. In the middle of the 19th century, the principality was therefore completely fragmented and its sovereign, who had only nominal power, was obliged to refer constantly to the Siamese authorities in Ubon Ratchathani or Bangkok. For this reason, it can be said

2. Ch. Archaimbault suggests that the New Year and the 'Boat Race' rituals, of which he describes Champassak's specificities for modern times, already existed (1961, 1972: *passim*).

3. See Nguyên Thê Anh 1997.

that the *muang* Champassak only benefited from a very brief period of stability during the golden age of its first years under Chao Soi Sisamut, and thereafter was never really in a position to take autonomous decisions. Being the most southerly of the Lao principalities– a sort of final stage, in space and time, of the territorial extension of the Lao following on their advances down the Nam Ou and the Mekong (Stung Treng, a dependency of Champassak, being the ultimate point) – the logic of the *muang* could never be fully instituted.

This thwarted destiny of the *muang* of Champassak – which Archaimbault likes to psychoanalyse in his writings (1971, 1972) – meant that the increase of its territory remained limited and that it had a similarly limited cultural impact. Every Lao-Tai *muang* was built with 'savage' margins inhabited by peoples described as 'Kha', margins that were symbolically and politically integral parts of its construction. It had then to control and reduce these margins with a view to their gradual integration, as was the case in all the large principalities of the Indochinese peninsula.[4] In this respect, the remaining 'margins' of Champassak, occupying the largest part of what was considered its territory, appear to have preserved a unique character and position in regional history, to this very day (Map 6.1).

The Boundaries of 'Lao Country' from the French Perspective

This was the situation found by the first French observers who, between 1865 and 1890, were appointed to carry out various exploratory missions. Some of these were political, in preparation for military and administrative colonisation, such as the Doudart de Lagrée Commission, the Harmand missions and the Pavie Mission. Others, such as that of Etienne Aymonier, were of a more commercial nature, representative of colonial entrepreneurship. Their descriptions of Champassak and of the southern Lao towns concur. Francis Garnier (1873: 336) depicted Bassak, the capital, as a line of little houses dotted along the river, perched on high banks. Jules Harmand (1994 [1887]: 25) referred to a large Lao village; Aymonier (2003 [1885]: 45), six years later, described it as having 500–600 'huts', this number being an estimate based on the fact that it had 13 pagodas. They considered the eastern towns, Saravane and Attapeu, to be the most distant Lao positions in 'Kha' territory. While Saravane still seemed to reflect Lao cultural values, farming a fer-

4. For a discussion of this, see Turton 2000.

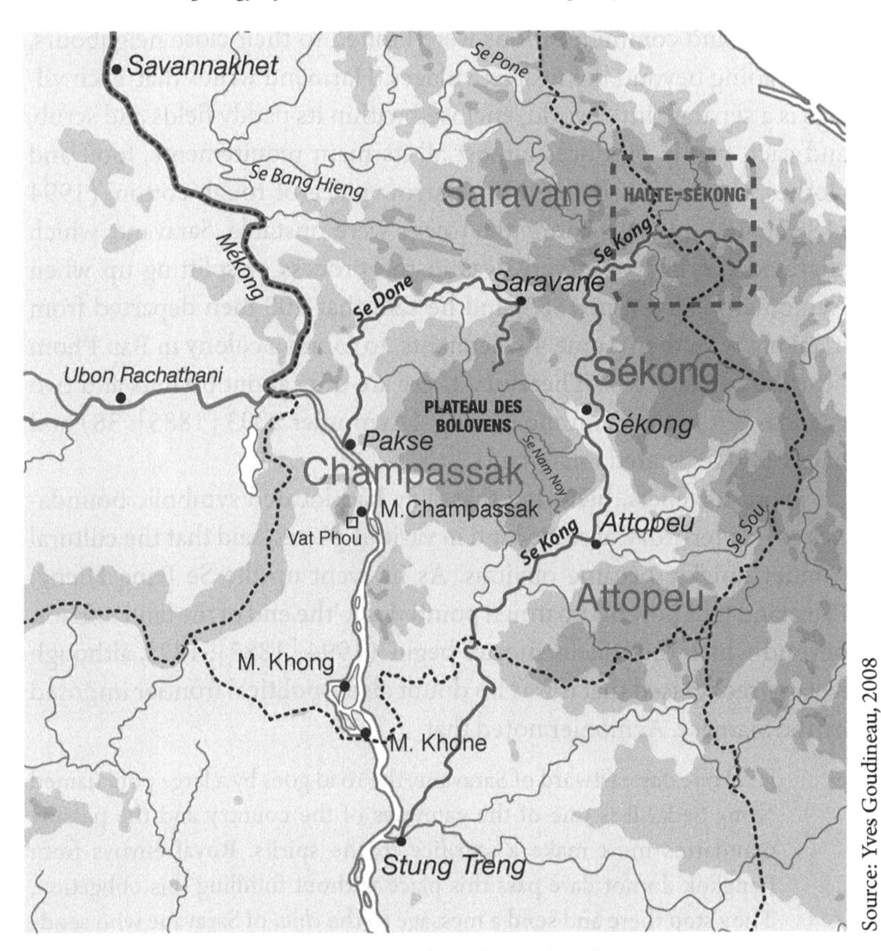

Map 6.1: Southern Laos from Champassak to the Upper Sekong.

tile plain and owning several monasteries, including one with a beautiful library, Attapeu was a pioneering border town. It was very 'mixed' and only had two pagodas for more than 300 dwellings, Aymonier tells us. He also says that its residents were mainly traders and boatmen, hardly cultivating rice at all.

All of these authors noted that the Lao had not advanced far into the region. There were hardly any villages along the Sekong and none at all upstream after Attapeu. There were paddy fields along the Se Done and further north on the banks of the Se Bang Hieng, but they did not necessarily belong to Lao villages, as the Suei or the displaced Phu Tai were also rice growers. The dwellings in villages in this area were very widely dispersed and communications were limited to their close neighbours, rarely going beyond the nearest villages. Harmand writes that 'each village is a separate little world, enclosed within its paddy fields and scrub, and each family produces almost all its main requirements, food and clothes, these often being just a narrow piece of rough cotton' (1994 [1887]: 181). Furthermore, the towns were unstable. Saravane, which charmed the first observers, was in the process of splitting up when Aymonier visited it in 1883, and he said that 200 men departed from it, taking with them some 40 elephants, to found a colony in Ban Phom near the Se Nam Noi. Therefore 'there are only about 60 huts and two pagodas left in the Saravane Muang' (Aymonier 2003 [1885]: 38) and barely 600 registered inhabitants.

These travellers, believing that they had located symbolic boundaries of Lao territory of some kind in various places, said that the cultural frontier quickly became obvious. As he went up the Se Bang Hieng, Harmand tells how his boatmen pointed out 'the end of the land of Laos, beyond which the Kha territories begin' (1994 [1887]: 182), although he later recognised that it was no doubt also a political frontier imposed by the Siamese. Aymonier noted that

> [...] one day eastward of Saravane, the road goes by a large pool named Nong Seda. It is one of the gateways of the country and the passing mandarins must make a sacrifice to the spirits. Royal envoys from Bangkok do not dare pass this place without fulfilling this obligation. They stop there and send a message to the *chau* of Saravane who sends them an ox or a buffalo to sacrifice.
> (Aymonier 2003 [1885]: 38)

This indicates that even prosperous Lao settlements such as Saravane were still felt to be incursions into potentially hostile territories. Generally speaking, 'the entire left bank of the Mekong, from La-khôn to Stung-Treng, is close to being completely wild', Harmand says (1994 [1887]: 25). Coming from Annam, in the opposite direction, Malglaive (2000 [1902]: 167) came across many different peoples, ranging from the most uncivilised to the most 'Lao-ised', Ta Oi, Kha Luong, Phu Tai, Suei, etc., before finally reaching the real 'Laotian' settlements – those that had stayed close to the Mekong or colonised the fertile regions of the Se Done valley, often with the help of the Suei people, who were partially subservient.

In general, French authors tended to insist, sometimes to the point of caricature, on the political, moral and cultural weakness of the Lao, resulting from their observations in the south of the country. All of them were also very ironic about the modest pageantry of the Prince of Champassak and his very simple palace, compared to the court of Luang Prabang, and more especially his total political dependence on Siamese commissioners (*khaluong*). According to them, the Lao did not 'rule' the region: not only did they barely control it, but their cultural influence was minimal, geographically limited and likely to be precarious in the longer term. The incapacity to rule on the part of Champassak became one of the arguments put forward to justify the direct administration of southern Laos by the colonial authorities from 1893 onwards.

The Foundation of Colonial Ethnicity in Southern Laos

The sharp downturn in the slave trade throughout the region, together with the very formal Republican declaration about equality between 'races' has often been presented in colonial literature as marking the beginning of the French presence in Southern Laos. Explorers, the forerunners of colonisation, all reported with great disgust the 'Kha hunts' carried out by the Lao or Tai 'mandarins' (Harmand 1994 [1887]: 38).[5] Attapeu, Stung-Treng and Bassak were denounced as being important trading centres from which convoys of slaves left for Khorat, Bangkok or Phnom Penh. The whole region appeared to be affected by this trade, which led to relations between ethnic groups that were often violent and to villages grouping together or fortifying themselves for defence. For French observers slavery was the main political and social scourge of southern Laos, together with Siamese occupation, which was regarded as undermining any local authority, condemning the area to a sort of general anomie.

The Lao and the Siamese sometimes obtained their supplies directly by raiding Kha villages, an excuse for festive escapades involving up to 150 men. But not all villages could be attacked. Aymonier (2003 [1885]: 54) indicates that as long as they paid tribute, 'obedient savages' could not be abducted and taken away, otherwise their captors were punished by law. Nevertheless, they could be imprisoned for debt, a practice

5. For a description of the preparation of an expedition by the prince of Champassak's brother, see Aymonier 2003 [1885]: 62.

that was tolerated by the colonial administration. Paying taxes meant protection. However, as these expeditions were not common and never ventured far afield, regular trade functioned effectively, mainly through fixed trading posts. The Kha people were themselves both hunted and hunters, acting mainly as intermediaries. Transactions involving the sale of captured people were carried out exclusively on the Lao or Cambodian side of the Annamese Cordillera, but Vietnamese peasants were often captured on the other side of it. Malglaive (2000 [1902]: 153) reported that certain large Kha villages, such as A-Roc, in the heart of the cordillera, were veritable hubs for this type of trafficking.

Although Siam had decided to put a stop to slavery in Laos even before French colonial rule, the French seemed to have made a more determined effort to accomplish this. However, this 'French peace', when it was brought to the different ethnic groups, did not make relations with them any easier. Jean-Jacques Dauplay, who was in charge as administrator-commissioner in Saravane for a long time, wrote ironically:

> [...] as for the Kha, whom we have just liberated and invited to come and savour with us the heady joys of Freedom (*Liberté*), it is only logical and natural to expect them to be infinitely grateful to us and celebrate every day, to the sound of the *khene*, the beauty of the immortal principles of 1793.[6]
> (Dauplay 1929: 57)

Instead of this, he remarked that they were manifestly very wary and even hostile, precisely because of the abolition of slavery, in which many ultimately had an interest even though they also suffered from it. This observation also features in Dauplay's explanation of the first phase of the Boloven Plateau rebellion, which he had put down with great force, in relation to the fact that the Loven (also called ethnic Boloven), who were at the heart of the revolt, were major sellers of slaves to the Lao. Slavery, whilst providing a frequent reminder of the moral work accomplished by colonisation, was long used by the French administration as an analytical grid to interpret the economy, inter-ethnic relations and, in many ways, all the social dynamics specific to southern Laos.

Although it was promoted in theory, it proved very difficult to implement a true policy of 'racial equality'; and this was partly attributed also

6. 1793 refers to the adopion in that year of the first 'Constitution of the Republic' following the French Revolution.

to slavery. Still, during the colonial period recurrent other reasons were given for the difficulty of achieving racial equality. These included the idea of a 'mixing' of races on the one hand, and a 'crumbling' of ethnic groups on the other. The first was interpreted in terms of physical anthropology, which was very much in vogue at the time and was regularly used by administrators, while the second was interpreted in terms of a sort of political sociology. However, reports often referred to the supposed impurity of the 'Lao race' in the south of the country. Even the first observers, notably Harmand, continually spoke with some contempt of the Lao for being 'interbred with Kha blood', including those in official positions. Many decades later, the administrators still saw this as one of the reasons for a sort of moral defect of the race, distinguishing them from other Lao-Tai: 'they are lazier, less skillful, more open to superstitions, and from their frequent contacts with the Kha, they seem to have retained a little of each of the inferior traits of the mountain inhabitants', which, amongst other things, resulted in the fact that 'in all the province, there is not one well-built [Lao] village'.[7] The idea seems to have been that although this racial mixing was longstanding, the recent practice of slavery, and notably of slavery for debt where the dependant was integrated into family life, would have further accentuated the opportunities for and varieties of interbreeding.

Thus, not only was southern Laos regarded as not being completely 'Lao-ised'; it was also believed that the Lao from the south had wild blood in their veins. It is clear, therefore, that this cliché, which, as we have seen, is still very prevalent, has its roots in the past. Archaimbault saw it as one of the ideological foundations of the Lao 'chiefdom' of Champassak and the reason for the large number of specific rituals there. He demonstrated that in the cosmogony of the south, in contrast with that of Luang Prabang, the Lao and aboriginal races were interbred from the outset, the Lao only being differentiated by choice, appointed by the envoys of the gods to guard the territory. In his opinion, this original interbreeding had an impact on the entire future of the principality, reflecting a veritable trauma of the collective psyche (Archaimbault 1961: 523; 1972). This fundamental collective impurity is mentioned in several historico-legendary stories – notably the one about Nang Malong,

7. M. Vitry, report n°130 on Saravane province, 1911, Archives Outre-Mer, Laos D2, ANOM (Vitry, 1911).

a princess bearing the child of a Kha chieftain – and is exorcised during many of the purification rituals to which the 'aborigines' (in this instance the Suei) are solemnly associated. There is an underlying sentiment that the southern Lao had been in some way contaminated by the unbridled sexuality of the Kha, a claim made again by Chao Boun Oum, the last Prince of Champassak, at the end of the 1960s, in a spicy appendix to Archaimbault's *The New Year Ceremony at Basac* (1971).

In this way, Archaimbault provides a sort of erudite foundation for the statements of French administrators in Southern Laos who, for over 50 years, maintained that they were surrounded exclusively by races in an advanced state of deculturation. On the one hand, the southern Lao were regarded as representing a sort of sub-culture, far removed from the refinement of the north, and even inferior in many ways to the Phu Tai who had been moved from the Sepone basin. There were constant references to the fact that they only occupied a small portion of the territory (Vitry 1911: 8). On the other hand, most of the Kha ethnic groups, especially those that had acknowledged their submission, were considered to be 'degenerate' as they were all 'Lao-ised' to a certain degree, even though it was common to mention the alleged freedom of morals still said to prevail amongst them. The fragmentation of groups was seen as the reason for being unable to rely on any particular ethnic group to implement the 'civilising' project of the colonising power effectively. In reality, the local French commissioners and government officials were very dependent on the Lao elite, whilst at the same time expressing considerable contempt and distrust of them and always ready to blame them for their difficulties in dealing with the various local ethnic groups.

Faced with the lack of any group considered capable of sharing the moral responsibility for colonial development, it was taken for granted that the only authority that should prevail in the south of the country was French. The colonial authorities therefore tried, in the name of racial equality, to systematically break down any hierarchical relationships other than those required by the newly-established law. However, there had long been interdependent relationships between groups in the south, distinct from those of direct servitude. The Suei worked in the paddy fields of the Lao and sometimes of the Phu Tai; the Lao exerted power over the Boloven, resulting in a dominant relationship linked to the sale of cardamom and ramie; the Boloven exerted a similar power over the Nya Heun, their immediate neighbours, and employed the Ta Oi as seasonal workers; the Alak provided woven materials and jewels to the Nya Heun, with exchange relationships between them that were often stormy; etc. The colonial administration, which appointed village heads (*pho ban*) and district heads (*nai kong*), who all had, in theory, the same abilities and powers whatever their origin, showed a refusal to recognise these often long-standing relationships of economic and cultural dependence and demonstrated, on the contrary, a desire to abolish any sort of 'ethnic' hierarchy between groups. Within the framework of the colonial state, all groups became, in principle, equal.

The Subdued and the Rebels: The Dynamics of Flight

The ideal of a law that would be the same for the whole population was, at the outset, a strict application of the concept of a modern Republican state, based on the idea of a homogenous area with a single administrative network – although it was readily admitted that colonial rule could result in significant exceptions to this ideal. The chronicles of Champassak and Attapeu show that this concept was profoundly different from the way in which the *muang* were set up and governed. The geography reflected in the structure of *muang* is remarkably non-homogenous, as it is made up of places with no connections between them, each primarily defined by its spiritual character (monastery, sanctuary, etc.) and by links – either individual or collective – maintained in different ways between one village and another, with the heart of the *muang* being the princely family and its vassals. Here again, as noted above, the organisation supposedly set up by Soi Sisamut in Champassak is only mentioned in the Siamese version of the chronicle. This is very significant: anticipating French organisation, and in order to be able to oppose it diplomatically when the borders were being negotiated between the colonial powers in the Indochinese peninsula, the Siamese, inspired by certain European state principles (Thongchai 1994), drew up maps and set down some basic military and administrative principles for the southern Lao territory up to the borders of Annam. They also carried out the first population census and tried to set up mandatory labour service and a system of taxation.

In order to be more efficient than the Siamese, the French colonial power sought to set up a more rational system of taxation and labour service, as well as more systematic control of the territories and the population. In 1912, Vitry, the Commissioner of Saravane, making a sort of disillusioned assessment of French will in the drafting of these new policies, compared them with the Siamese occupation, and noted the extent to which one provoked the overall hostility of the population whereas the other was ultimately well accepted: 'The Siamese administration kept on all the Lao authorities that were in office when they arrived' and 'taxes were not heavy, only necessitating the payment of four ticals per person registered. The *Chaumuong* [provincial heads], moreover, concealed a large number of people, thereby reducing their overall burden. No taxes, no special rights, no labour services, only this capitation.'[8] Furthermore, except for part of the Boloven Plateau, which paid an annual tribute, 'all of the mountainous region had retained its full independence'. He added: 'I have never heard a Laotian complain about this occupation, on the contrary; by the way, the people often talk about it to make a comparison with the current situation.'

Pressurised by the central administration, the main task of the provincial colonial officials, with the help of Lao collaborators – who were regularly accused of corruption and of ruining French policies (especially the *Chaomuang*, provincial heads and the *Lamkha*, intermediaries and interpreters) – was to impose a per capita tax, payable in cash, and to make sure that a specified number of obligatory labour service days was imposed on every able-bodied man, so that they would take part in government construction projects. Labour service was particularly unpopular, seen by all to be a new form of subjugation invented by the French for their own benefit to replace slavery. Moreover, contrary to the great principles put forward about racial equality, the tax rate and the number of days of obligatory service varied according to 'ethnic category', creating even more of a sense of injustice; an initial distinction between 'Laotians' and 'Kha' was later made more complex, to the extent of creating five different categories of taxpayer in 1940 (Gunn 1990: 52). Economic discrimination was also added, as those who wished to avoid the labour service days could 'buy them back' in cash without fulfilling them, and only well-to-do villagers already partially integrated into the colonial economy could afford to do this.

8. Vitry, report on the situation of the province on the 31st of May 1912. Saravane Province, AOM, Résidence supérieure du Laos, E7 (Vitry 1912).

The most frequent response to the increased taxation and to the obligatory labour days for 'public' construction works, mainly road building, which was regarded as only benefitting the occupying power, was either not to register or to flee, in other words insubordination. Although, soon after the arrival of the French, some Lao or Phu Tai people left the region for the right bank of the Mekong and migrated to Siam, it was mainly large numbers of Kha who decided to avoid the census and practice a strategy of flight. From this point of view, the entire colonial history of southern Laos can be viewed as a succession of advances and retreats in the submission process or, on the flip side of the same phenomenon, in terms of the dynamics of rebellion. [9] Colonial officials who were urged to continually increase the number of people registered on the population rolls in order to increase the province's revenues had neither the means nor often the inclination to carry out this task. In Saravane in 1938, for example, the colonial administration, apart from two French officials, only had some 80 riflemen from the 'indigenous guard' for the whole province, which was actually more than in some previous years (Colonna 1938). Controlling the whole territory, two-thirds of which was mountainous, was a major challenge for them.

All colonial power is imposed and maintained by force, but this force can rarely be exercised permanently. It was their capacity to intervene with superior technology (notably firepower), even if they did not necessarily react very quickly, that enabled the French to govern vast areas and to be feared despite having with them very few men. For half a century, colonial political action in Saravane and Attapeu was limited to a number of sporadic and often disorganised expeditions that aimed to quell the 'independent Kha'. These were sometimes preventive actions in the form of annual 'tours' by administrator–commissioners (postponed, some years, when an administrator's mission allowance had not been paid in advance). Visiting different regions and following different itineraries, they were accompanied by militia and attempted to win over villages and encourage them to 'register' and swear allegiance to the colonial authorities. An oath was taken by the heads of 'obedient'

9. This may of course be reminiscent of James C. Scott's thesis on ethnic groups 'fleeing the state' (Scott 2009), although this text was first published in French before his book was circulated, and the historical dynamics of the peoples studied here ultimately do not fully confirm his analysis.

villages and districts (*tasseng*), who were then officially registered as 'submitted'. This was followed by solemn ceremonies, often including the sacrifice of a buffalo, organised in the provincial capital or in certain military posts. Another form of intervention was to send heavily armed militia to punish those rebellious villages considered too 'turbulent' or to try to subdue whole regions that were still dissident.

In any event, the usual reaction, when confronted with representatives of the colonial power, was to flee. Families either fled into the forest when the administrator arrived, this often resulting in the latter setting fire to certain houses in retaliation, or entire villages moved to faraway valleys to avoid repression. Carried out with the aim of staying away from any foreign incursion these migrations – in a way voluntary but under pressure – meant that colonial authorities were totally unable to control the mountainous districts of southern Laos for any length of time. Villages or areas that were declared to be under French control one year, following a visit from the commissioner or a section of the 'indigenous guard', were a year or two later considered to be dissident. The map of 'subdued' Kha and 'independent' Kha was continually changing, as were the declarations of the administrators in their annual reports in relation to the extension, progression or reduction of dissident areas.

The Boloven Plateau rebellion, which lasted from 1901 to 1936 with periods of calm and periods of uprising, was particularly representative of this situation. Much has been said about the causes of the rebellion: rejection of taxes and labour days, rejection of the intrusion of colonial trade, changes imposed by colonial rule to traditional structures of authority and exchange relationships, a messianic cult movement, proto-nationalist contestation, etc.[10] These reasons are not mutually exclusive and there was undoubtedly a combination of different causes, given that the various protagonists, over a 30-year period, did not all have the same motivations.[11] Anyway, this rebellion is still the best illustration of this attitude of rejection towards any territorial incursion or occupation by outsiders and of the tactical and strategic dynamics of flight. The inca-

10. See Moppert 1981 and Gunn 1990.

11. Particular mention should be made of Ong Kommadan, who led resistance to the French until 1936, and who devised a Khom script to legitimise his symbolic authority, both political and religious, over the so-called Khom people as a whole, supposed to include all the various Mon-Khmer peoples in the region (Moppert 1981: 53–54, Gunn 1990: 117–118, Sidwell 2008: 24).

pacity of the colonial power to put an end to it in a sustainable way was all the more significant given that it was dealing with largely 'Lao-ised' populations on the Boloven Plateau.

The continual risk of insecurity created by rebellion prevented any economic development of the plateau region such as had probably been planned, or dreamed of, in the early years of colonisation.

Ultimately, then, despite their desire to rule over an area that they had mapped out with considerable precision, the French colonial authorities only ever had partial control over the provinces of southern Laos. French control, like that of the Lao and the Siamese before them, was mainly limited to the valleys of the Se Done and the Lower Sekong. Beyond this area, their influence was only sporadic and temporary and had to be continually reasserted. Amongst the territories said to have remained 'independent', a special mention must be made of 'the left bank of the Sekong' or 'Upper Sekong', which is constantly referred to in all the administrative reports as an inaccessible stronghold, the domain of the 'Kha Tou' and a refuge for all rebels, particularly the Boloven insurrectionists, etc. This area, which remained a sort of rather large blank spot on the colonial map during the entire period of French rule, was to be the subject of many fantasies on the part of administrators. In 1938, at the end of his report on the province of Saravane, commissioner Colonna announced, following the deployment of a large detachment of riflemen and militiamen to the area, 'the submission of the Kha peoples living in the Upper Sekong and Upper Sepone region (Alak, Kantou, Pacoh)' and the creation of a permanent look-out post manned by Sedang riflemen (Colonna 1938: 88). He concluded, his duty done: 'There is no longer any part of the territory in this province that is not under the control of the French administration.' One year later, this area was once again considered to be in 'open armed rebellion' (Inspection des Colonies 1938–1939: C. 290); and two years later, the outpost no longer existed.

Ethnography of the Boloven

Knowledge of the people living in an area was one of the main principles of good colonial administration, prior to becoming the subject of specifically scientific surveys (Goudineau this volume, Introduction). From 1895 to the 1970s, the ethnography of Southern Laos only concerned the groups living in the Boloven Plateau and its surrounds. This meant that studies were only carried out on peoples who were not only 'subdued' but who had also formerly been dependant on the Lao and were therefore considered to be more or less 'Lao-ised'. Administrators tended to list and discuss the different groups in an order that went from more 'subdued' to less 'subdued' in reports, published writings, monographs and articles: first came the Boloven (or Loven, Laven, Jirru), then the Nya Heun, the Alak, the Oi, the Kaseng, the Lave (or Love, Brao) etc.[12] The Suei can sometimes be found at the beginning of this list, presented as being so close to the Lao (Buddhists, rice growers, Lao-type villages and clothes, perfectly bilingual, etc.) that they are of no interest to the authors (they are 'ex-Kha', says Dauplay) and are often barely mentioned. At the other end of the scale, the Ta Oi, whose submission is sometimes announced only to be denied later, represent savagery in the controlled areas where some of them were seasonal workers on the cardamom or ramie plantations. They were mentioned for their sacrificial practices, which were often presented in sensationalist terms.[13] Further east, in the Upper Sekong region, the Nge, the Pacoh, the Kantou and the Talieng are named but represent the unknown.

Southern Laos did not have any administrators, officers or missionaries with a real passion for ethnography like Father J. Kemlin and Paul Guilleminet in Kontum or Colonel Bonifacy in Tonkin. The desire to know the different ethnic groups in the region was mainly motivated by a utilitarian concern to identify the 'exploitable' parts of the country as well as its inhabitants who could possibly be requisitioned.

The reason for the fact that the ethnic Boloven, or Loven (identified today as Jru'), were systematically listed first is that they were considered to be more 'evolved', being more prosperous – cultivating and selling cardamom, ramie, tobacco, ginger and owning large herds of cattle and domesticated elephants – and therefore also more open to monetary transactions. Most importantly, they lived on the plateau of the same name, and it was important to understand the different trade routes that crossed the plateau, as these were central to the regional economy and the dynamics of contacts between peoples. Indeed, it is from the 'centre'

12. See Lavallée 1901; Baudenne 1913; Dauplay 1929; Colonna 1938; Fraisse 1951.

13. See, for example, Dauplay 1914.

constituted by the Boloven that the topographical, economic and cultural positioning of the other ethnic groups was conceived.

The Nya Heun, living in the southern foothills of the plateau in the valley of Se Nam Noi, commanding the route to Attapeu, were presented as being dependant on the Loven, and were thus seen as economically and culturally inferior to them. The Alak, who occupied the foothills in the east, provided a link between the plateau and the territories and peoples of the Upper Sekong. They exchanged woven materials and jewellery for domestic animals, but were not very 'Lao-ised' or integrated into the local economy. They represented the partly subjugated edge of the 'rebellious' area. The Oi, more 'Lao-ised' and fairly prosperous (certain administrators also mentioned the Sou in their immediate vicinity), were the rice-growers of Attapeu, as the Suei were in Saravane, cultivating, for the Lao, a small plain in the Sekong valley that stretched to the foothills of the plateau. The Lave (Brao), although somewhat marginal, ensured the transition with the Cambodian hinterland, whilst the Kaseng were considered to be useful intermediaries for Lao merchants. Other groups were also sometimes mentioned: Tieus, Cheng, Veh, Halang, etc.; but they were considered to play only a very minor role, being on the outskirts of the sphere of Lao influence.

This representation of Southern Laos, centred on the Boloven Plateau and treating the plateau as a sort of topological operator of economic and cultural differentiation, was one shared by all French colonial observers and administrators and also by some ethnographers. However, it is quite clear that it was very different in many ways from the Lao representation of their own penetration of the region and their view of its history. For them, the issue has always been the upper reaches of the two main waterways that bypass the Boloven Plateau, the Se Done in the north and the Sekong in the south. By making the plateau the centre of gravity of the south and the heart of its economic development, the colonial project resulted in the political and economic marginalisation of the two local bridgeheads of Lao civilisation – Saravane on the Se Done and Attapeu on the Sekong. In fact, there were regular requests in administrative reports to be allowed to abandon these small regional capitals developed from Lao *muang* for new locations on the plateau (Thateng, Dasia, Paksong, etc.) and to set up provincial services there. Reflecting the same attitude, the new roads built across the plateau considerably modified the commercial routes held by the Lao, as well as the exchanges they had with the diverse Kha peoples, and also disrupted relations between these peoples themselves. In the light of this, it is not surprising that the Boloven Plateau, the centre of colonial organisation, was the departure point for a regional rebellion that associated the Lao with the Loven or the Alak.[14]

The categorisation – based on the Loven – of the various ethnic groups according to their level of economic development raises the question of their links with one another and therefore also of interethnic relationships around the Boloven Plateau. These interethnic relationships were, moreover, soon to be further developed, paradoxically, through the obligatory labour days (the *corvées*) that brought together villagers from different origins, with the unanticipated effect of fostering certain coalitions between distant villages. Even if it were generally accepted by colonial ethnography that there were only two 'races' in the South, on the one hand the Lao, and on the other the Kha (all speaking Mon-Khmer or Austroasiatic languages), it remained to be explained what could have caused among the latter so many cultural variations between the different groups or 'peoples'. The only explanation for this diversity appeared to be the greater or lesser dependency of the Kha populations on the Lao.

This explanation was reluctantly put forward because, as we have seen, the southern Lao, particularly those of Attapeu or Saravane, were considered to be irremediably decadent, both because of their restricted capacity to spread Lao culture in the past and because of their poor current influence. Even if this decadence was accelerated by French colonisation, observers liked to point out that in several ways, such as the quality of village dwellings and weaving, the Kha demonstrated great cultural superiority.[15]

In spite of their biased viewpoints, these colonial observations nonetheless helps us to understand how in southern Laos the mainspring of ethnicity was linked to the 'Lao-isation' process, and demonstrates that this process was much clearer here than in the north of the country, where successive phases of migration from China have complicated, or even completely blurred, cultural interactions. The 'Lao-isation' of the

14. See also Moppert 1981; Gunn 1990.

15. See for exemple, Baudenne 1913: 260–261.

south was not a uniform process that could be traced and assessed in degrees, depending on how far it had progressed in one place or another, but was a complex dynamic that has resulted in many different configurations, from which later 'ethnic groups' have emerged. This dynamic was doubtless partly the result of coercive actions by the Lao (particularly evident in the case of the Suei) but it was also the result of the acceptance or refusal of local peoples to embrace Lao-isation.[16] Thus, the Loven adopted Lao-type dwellings and clothes and spoke Lao, but few at the time were Buddhist[17] – Loven Buddhists became much more numerous later – and they practised *na* (rice cultivation in small flooded fields in flat areas). The Oi are rice growers and have dwellings similar to those of the Lao, but they are not Buddhists; the Suei are very similar to the Lao, but they have kept their language, etc. Through a complex dynamic, each local group developed its own original cultural profile, although it is obviously impossible to clearly identify, in each instance, why certain traits were borrowed and others rejected. The important thing is to note that while no village in the Boloven region has been completely assimilated, all have been affected by the 'Lao-isation' process, if only through trading, the Lao having retained control of the heads of local trade networks (and acting at that time as intermediaries with Chinese merchants). Moreover, most ethnonyms in use in the area have been inherited from the Lao, even if they do not come from the Lao language. This is true whether they have stood the test of time (Suei, Loven, Lave, Nya Heun, Alak, etc.) or not (Sou, Kaseng, Veh, Tieu, etc.).

In relation to possible economic cooperation, the most 'Lao-ised' amongst the Kha were said to have intellectual and moral virtues superior to others (more open, more hardworking, etc.); they were also the most obedient, paying their taxes regularly and either fulfilling or buying up their obligatory labour days. But on the other hand they were frequently considered to have lost much of the genius of their race that the 'independent' groups, particularly those on the left bank of the Upper Sekong, were said to embody to the highest degree. In 1930–1931, the crossing of the Annamese Cordillera by the geologist

16. On 'Lao-isation' or 'Tai-isation' as having generated differentiated identity processes across Laos or the region, see Evans 1991, 1999b, 2000 and Évrard 2007, 2019.

17. To my knowledge no-one observed at that time there were already 'pioneer Buddhist temples' in Boloven villages (Sprenger 2017a: 113).

Josué-H. Hoffet – the first crossing made since 1900 to the 'rebel Moi hinterland of Tourane' – to reach the Upper Sekong on the Lao side, had confirmed the existence of a specific culture in this region, considered to have inherited very ancient traditions (Hoffet 1933). One of its most striking characteristics, apart from carrying out ceremonial sacrifices, was a circular village layout in most villages. This layout could also be found in the Boloven region in the past, and A. Baudenne had already drawn attention to it in 1913, but it was falling into disuse and was progressively being replaced by a village structure based on dwellings built in straight lines on either side of a street, following the Lao model. André Fraisse witnessed these morphological changes, linked to a conversion to Buddhism, in an Alak village in 1944 (Fraisse 1951). While efforts were made to pinpoint anything that might distinguish the Kha from the Lao, notably their social organisation (marriage rules) and their beliefs (concerning death), the general impression remained that one was faced with worlds in an advanced state of cultural disintegration. But it was considered enough to provide general, superficial information on each ethnic group as a whole. It was not until the 1950s that interest in the study of particular villages started to grow, and it was the end of the 1960s before any real field studies with an explicit scientific purpose were carried out in the Boloven region.[18]

To this day, the only village monograph for Southern Laos is the one by Barbara Wall (1975) on the Nya Heun, following her seven-month stay in 1967. Of classic layout (with chapters organised by topic: technology, economy, social organisation, religion, and so on) the monograph describes village life, at that time very disrupted by the war, showing its coherent nature but without presenting it as based on a model opposed to Lao culture. The author also describes the economic and 'diplomatic' relationships of the Nya Heun with the Lao (and with Westerners) as well as with their Loven, Alak and Oi neighbours, providing the first reliable analysis of longstanding interethnic relations in this region studied *in situ*.

Soon afterwards, claiming to follow the perspective opened up by Fredrik Barth, which was new at that time, Bernard Hours (1973)

18. Among recent studies conducted on the Boloven Plateau and in Attapeu, see Ladwig 2016 and Sprenger 2017a, 2017b. On the need for field research in Laos and the beginning of the official recognition of 'minority cultures' under pressure from UNESCO, see Goudineau 2003.

became specifically interested in inter-ethnicity studied in the Boloven context. Taking up – in turn – the issue of a regional opposition between two models or 'types of ethnic organisation', the Lao model and the 'mountain' model, he tries to analyse this in the context of displaced villages along the road from Pakse to Paksong. Combining a rather innovative approach in terms of social relationships with another that was clearly based on culturalism, his study struggled to deal with the very heterogeneous nature of the regrouped villagers under consideration, and is weakened by a rather sketchy ethnography.

The ethnographic work of Jacqueline Matras-Troubetzkoy (1983, 1992) among the Brou (or Brao – Lave in Laos – Baird 2020), although conducted from the northeast of Cambodia, appears in retrospect to provide a pertinent contribution to the anthropology of Southern Laos. This is because she carried out the first research, from both a functional and a symbolic point of view, into spatial organisation resulting from the circular pattern of Brou villages, with a communal house in the centre. Her analysis provides support for the idea that this 'circular' model, the extension of which is described by Hoffet, can be regarded as being in opposition to both Khmer and Lao notions of inhabited space.[19] The decline of this spatial model in the Boloven region has often been presented as a patent symptom of the degeneration of Kha populations under the pressure of 'Lao-isation', whilst *a fortiori* its survival and spread in the villages of Upper Sekong have been presented as proof both of the social vitality and of the cultural conservatism of the populations that remained on the margins and unsubdued (Map 6.2, page 155).

The Horizon of the Upper Sekong

These territories – which ultimately became a sort of blind spot in the colonial field of vision from whence unknown danger could appear at any time (and would regularly appear until the Indochinese war period) – had, in fact, long been visited. Although it is impossible to know for sure whether the Lao had never ventured in these remote highlands before the colonial era, the Siamese did go and it is certain that even before the beginning of colonisation, Captain Malglaive (2000 [1902]) from the Pavie Mission carried out two reconnaissance missions, in 1890–1891 and again in 1893. Thereafter, one of his colleagues, Prosper

19. On this point, also see Ian Baird's contribution to this volume (Chapter 7).

Odend'hal, returned to seek a route joining Hue and Tourane (Danang) with Saravane and Attapeu (Odend'hal 1894). His quest having remained unfulfilled, some 40 years later, the official pretext for the Hoffet mission across the Annamese Cordillera would again be to identify a transverse route between central Annam and Southern Laos other than the northern route through the Ai-Lao pass (already explored by J. Harmand since 1877). In the interval between Odend'hal's and Hoffet's missions there were some visits by Saravane *commissaires*, as evidenced by a few reports found in the archives. These included tours by Humann and Rémy, the first two men to occupy this position between 1897 and 1900, who went every year to the villages of the Upper Sekong, of the Selanong or of the Upper Sepone.[20]

Despite the fact that the region was vast, it appears that both the explorers and the *commissaire* only ever travelled through these areas for about ten days. They were often obliged to stay outside the villages because many of the villagers fled before they arrived, as mentioned above, or the village was declared 'closed' (*diang* or *kalam*). This particularly irritated these colonial administrators, who had come to make the villagers submit to their authority. They were usually accompanied by a troop of 15 to 40 armed militiamen and they did not hesitate to use force (for instance, burning down villages or sending troops to find the villagers who had fled) whenever they considered this to be necessary. After 1901 and the beginning of the 'Kha revolt' in the south of the country, whose leaders were suspected of having sought refuge on the left bank of the Upper Sekong, these missions were interrupted or appear to have become very irregular. Apart from a few notes, most not very detailed, written by the successive administrators in Saravane on one or two short operations to maintain order, there are no more available accounts of visits until the end of the 1930s.

In fact, the first detailed account from the 1930s is Hoffet's article published in 1933 about the 'Moïs' of the Annamese Cordillera between Tourane (today Danang) and the Boloven Plateau. His text is accompanied by a tentative mapping of the various 'unsubdued' tribes – some described as 'very wild' – which appear to occupy most of the region (Map 6.2). Then there is a series of reports made following two

20. File : « Bas-Laos, Commissariat du Gouvernement de Saravane, Rapports de tournée », AOM, Rés. Sup. Laos, E7.

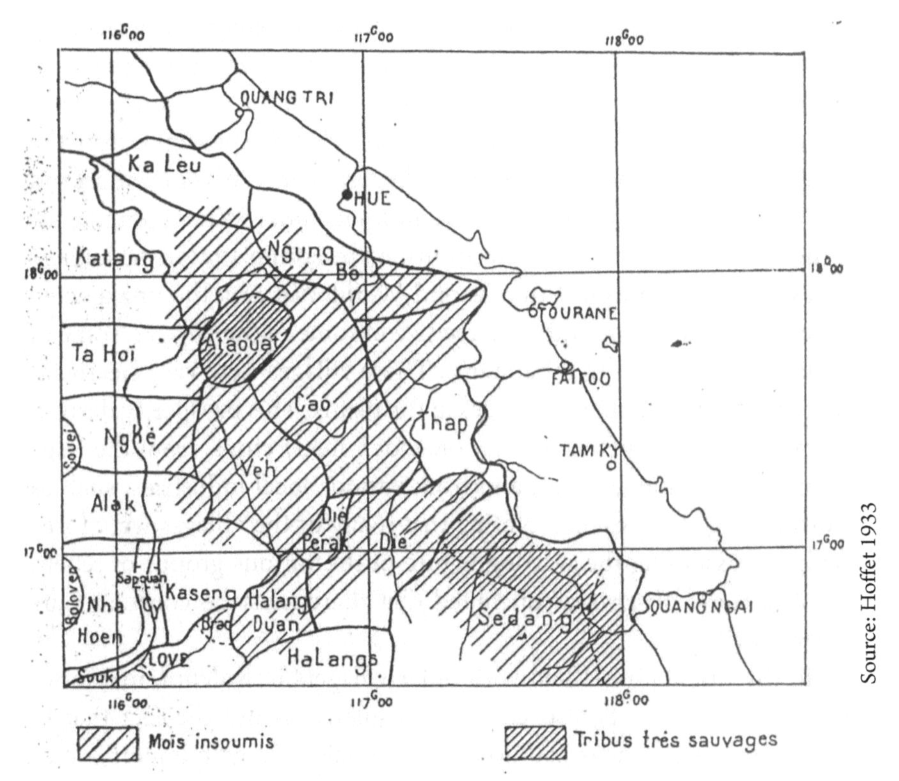

Source: Hoffet 1933

Map 6.2: The Upper Sekong: 'unsubdued Moïs' and 'very wild tribes'

major repressive campaigns, one in 1936 to track down Kommadam, the last leader of the Boloven rebellion,[21] and the other in 1939, with the support of aircraft, marking the final (and fruitless) intervention of colonial forces in the Upper Sekong.[22] From the early 1940s, the region was considered to be under the influence of the Viet Minh (Salemink 2003: 111) and soon became one of its first bases in Central Vietnam and Southern Laos, before becoming one of the strategic nodes along the Ho Chi Minh trail. Because of this, it was one of the most heavily-bombed areas during the 'American war'.[23]

21. See the report by 'Chef de bataillon' Nyo on the organisation of the recently subdued zone between Sekong and the Annam frontier, January–March 1936 (private documentation), and see Nyo 1937.

22. *Report following the events of the Upper Sekong. Politics of interaction in the Saravane province: rebellion of Kha groups in the Upper Sekong delegation*, March 1939, AOM, Indochina N.F., c. 290 (see Inspection des Colonies 1938–1939).

23. See Hickey 2002: 73–74.

What emerges from the old written records extending over the half-century before the region became involved in the 20-year international war is astonishingly coherent and coincides with the testimonies that I collected in the 1990s in Kaleum, a district in Sekong province, from the oldest villagers amongst whom I was living, mainly in Vel Kandon and Vel A-Rô (*vel* meaning 'village' in Kantu, see *infra*). What immediately struck Odend'hal and was then confirmed by administrators or soldiers crossing the region until the Second World War was the unexpected density of settlements and the large size of some of the villages, some of which had hundreds of inhabitants. These villages were very clearly far more prosperous than the villages in the plains. This prosperity derived from the growing of various *hai* (swidden field) crops, from the large numbers of buffaloes kept, and from various local industries, such as ironworking and weaving. Noting that many of the villages were fortified, and assuming the warring nature of the various groups of rebels, most of these observers concluded that there must be constant wars between villages.

In the discussions I had with older villagers in Kaleum, memories of abundant harvests also came up regularly, as did the fact that in their youth the villages had domestic animals in large numbers – buffaloes, oxen and pigs – which allowed them to organise collective sacrifices every year. The comparison between their lives then and the precariousness of their situation in the 1990s made them particularly bitter. Their descriptions of the most important villages in the region (A-Roc, Kandon, A-Ling, A-Vac, A-Rô, etc.) are of what appear to have been, even in the 1930s, equivalent to 'town-villages'. These were often the result of regroupings and were constituted in direct connection with satellite villages comprising dozens of long houses. This meant that the total population, depending on the year, amounted to several hundred inhabitants, even as many as 500 in certain villages. It is worth noting that, in the view of these older informants, the defensive nature of the agglomerations at that time was more the result of the continual threat from the surrounding colonial presence than of rivalry amongst villages. On the contrary, there was a sort of arrangement between them, taking turns to harbour Boloven rebel leaders who made regular visits to the area, most notably Kommadam, and also coordinating their involvement in the rebel movement.

From the perspective of the Upper Sekong itself, the isolation of the region seemed relative. Even though it was protected by difficult terrain made up of small, steep-sided and differently oriented valleys, frequently described by all observers as being extremely difficult to cross, the people of the area were aware of the permanent latent danger represented by the colonial efforts, however irregular, to penetrate the territory. Moreover, the idea conveyed by the colonial administrators that the peoples of the Upper Sekong were in a state of marginality and deliberate isolation must also be revised, as it is clear that they had long been involved in commercial exchanges of a regional scope. As mentioned above, certain villages had in the past been important nodes in the slave trade between Annam and Laos, and the testimonies that I gathered confirmed that villagers from the area had long frequented markets on the Vietnamese side,[24] which are closer by several days than the Laotian markets. In 1998 it took only two days on foot to go from Vel A-Rô, where I was living, to A-Luoi on the Vietnamese side, but five days to reach Sekong or Saravane on the Laotian side. Throughout the whole of this part of the Annamese Cordillera, traditional barter relationships linked most of the villages together, either directly or indirectly, which also ultimately led – via a sequence of steps – to trade relations with the Lao and the Vietnamese.

The Emergence of the Kantu

Here, as in the Boloven Plateau, it seems that the dynamics of ethnicity – in the very heart of the massif – were inextricably linked to the various positions held by different villages within networks of relationships. Around the Boloven, the 'Lao-isation' process appears, as we have seen, to have been determinant in the creation of various different 'ethnic groups'. But in the case of the Upper Sekong valley, its opening towards the eastern side and its contacts with Vietnamese culture, even though these were through a series of intermediaries, meant that these dynamics were more complex. Without going into a detailed analysis of the ways in which relations were progressively established between villages – which can be reconstructed for sub-regions within the whole – and bearing in mind that the whole region remains remarkably homogenous

24. See also Le Pichon 1938: 364.

with regard to the proximity of cultural practices and of languages,[25] it is clear that specific social, economic and geographical 'positions' held by particular villages are likely to have had an effect on the progressive formation of separate groups and of the generation of ethnonyms supposed to identify them.

We have already seen that on the Laos side the people called Alak lived in villages located in the eastern foothills of the Boloven Plateau and in the lowlands created by the Sekong just below the first real escarpments. These were the villages at the lowest altitudes within the Annamese Cordillera and the only ones to trade directly both with the Lao and with the peoples of the Boloven region. They were also the only villages that were directly affected, if marginally, by 'Lao-isation', and more so by Buddhism which never penetrated any higher than this in the valley of the Upper Sekong. Last in a sort of chain bringing down forest products, woven materials and forged objects from upriver, they were in immediate contact with the villages controlling the upper section of the Sekong that was still navigable. This part of the river was inhabited by a prosperous group called the Nge (or Ngkriang). Their prosperity was based on swidden farming, as well as on the fact that they acted as boatmen and intermediaries for the remote hill villages. Those who occupied the far-away territories in the northeast, who had the largest villages, were described as Kantu (and as Talieng, more to the east and further away from the river).

On the Vietnamese side too, certain positions seem to have been established quite a long time ago in the system of local relations. The Brou (now called Makong in Laos) had been subject to the most Vietnamese influence. All those who were fairly mobile and lived in small villages were called Ta Oi. They ensured a good flow of products between Vietnam and the Sekong valley, or even beyond. These products, including jars, gongs, cauldrons and jewellery, were essential symbolic goods for village ceremonies, notably for weddings. The Pacoh (Pako), who were close to the Ta Oi but located in the Upper Sepone, seem to have been distinguished because they were organised in more structured lineages with very long houses, and in particular because their prosperity came from raising and selling buffaloes – animals required for major sacrifices

25. Most of the Upper Sekong languages belong to the Katuic sub-branch of the Austroasiatic family (Ferlus 1974; Diffloth and Zide 1992; Sidwell 2005).

and at the heart of all important ceremonies. The Ta Oi and Pacoh had traditional bartering relations with the Nge and Kantu on both banks of the Sekong.

The massif at the heart of this mountainous area was described by colonial administrators and cartographers as the 'Ataouat' massif. It had a supposed height of 2,500 metres and was long regarded by the French as the highest point in this part of Indochina.[26] Unlike the Boloven Plateau, it amounted to a true natural barrier. Therefore, notwithstanding the existence of a few identified passes that were very difficult to cross, no road could be plotted through it. Trading was carried out by going around this mountainous area rather than across it, from the northeast – from the Ta Oi Plateau opening on to Vietnam – to the southwest, where it rejoins the Sekong valley and Laos, avoiding the highest points of the Ataouat.

The various 'ethnic groups' mentioned above occupied specific positions in the exchange process. However, the peoples living in the heart of the Ataouat are both the least known and the most difficult to place in the system of relations. They were often said to 'secure' this system, as their villages were considered to be the most powerful in the region, and appeared to ensure its defence.[27] At the same time, their real identity remained unclear for the colonial authorities. In fact, no one was able to establish what were the boundaries of the area, which came to be called 'Kantu country'. The Kantu identity that emerged is mainly made up of what is not known, leaving much to the imagination. In fact, the region that came to be associated to the ethnonym Kantu (or Katu) would long be defined indirectly, in comparison with and in opposition to other better identified areas; and for several decades, the name had an existence that was quite independent from the people to whom it was supposed to refer.

The history of ethnonyms is often conjectural and questionable, even though the origins of some of them can be traced.[28] However, it

26. The name 'Ataouat' almost disappeared from Vietnamese and Laotian maps after 1975. The highest peak in the southern part of the Annamese cordillera that appears on current maps is the Ngoc Linh with 2,598 meters.

27. According to Nyo: 'The Kantous, totally unpenetrated and unknown, living in big and numerous villages, are the most independent, the wildest and the most unfriendly.'(Report of the 16th of March 1936, 2). See Nyo 1937.

28. See, for example, Proschan 1997 and Đặng Nghiêm Van 1998.

was undoubtedly Jean Le Pichon's illustrated opuscule on *The Blood Hunters* that finally popularised the name Katu.[29] Le Pichon was a 'principal guard' (a sub-officer) in the indigenous guard posted at Bến Hiền, near the unsubdued area in Annam. He attributed the original use of the ethnonym Katu to one of his predecessors, Sogny, who in 1913 was, according to Le Pichon, the first to 'assert that these Moï are an original race with a common dialect' (Le Pichon 1938: 360).

However, long before this, ever since the Pavie Mission and the reports from Malglaive (2000 [1902]) and Odend'hal (1894) the most distant villages in the cordillera on the Laotian side had regularly been referred to as Kontu, Kon-Tou, Kantu, Kan-Tou, Kha Tous, or Tou, with a total lack of precision.[30] In fact, in several Katuic languages of this region the term *tuu* means 'top' – the top of a tree or the upper reaches of a river – with *kh'* possibly indicating a direction.[31] Although the hypothesis that this is the origin of the term cannot be formally verified, more than a century later, it is not impossible that the first Western observers, accompanied by Vietnamese or Lao guides who hardly spoke these languages at all, mistook for an ethnic group name what was merely a designation used to provide a vague description – here, perhaps, 'those who are higher', or 'towards up there'.[32]

Uncertainty about this ethnonym proved to be amazingly long-lived.[33] Although it is difficult to know where names such as Alak, Ngè, and Ta Oi (as well as the various other versions of these that exist) come from, after being in use for at least a century as exonyms they currently

29. 'Les chasseurs de sang' was published as a special issue of the *Bulletin des Amis du Vieux Hué* in 1938 (Le Pichon 1938).

30. A-Roc, for instance, was described as a Kontu or a Talieng 'big village' depending on whether one reads Malglaive or Odend'hal.

31. Personal communication from Michel Ferlus.

32. Le Pichon notes this, but does not draw conclusions, as he wants to believe in the value of the ethnonym. 'Ka-tu means wild. During my tours, I had the following kinds of conversations with the Moï people I met: "Where do you come from?" – "We are men (*mo'nui*) from such-and-such a village." – "Do you know the Katu?" – "Yes, those are the people living up there in the mountains." And up in the mountains, I was shown other mountains of the Lao side. I did not, however, conclude that the savages did not exist in the region!' (1938: 363).

33. It should also be remembered that until very recently linguists had still not precisely defined the extent of the area, which lies between Vietnam and Laos, that is inhabited by Katu or Kantu – or by people speaking dialectal variations of the language spoken by Katu/Kantu.

tend to be used as autonyms by the villagers concerned. Things were, until recently, different in relation to usage of the term Kantu. Even in the 1990s, the inhabitants of the Upper Sekong referred to themselves only by the name of their villages. As mentioned above, many of these villages had been, before the wars, very large, equivalent in size to towns, and were well known centres in the region. 'It appears that we are now Katu,' an old man said doubtfully to me in Vel A-Rô (Kaleum), adding that this was an invention of the Americans taken up by the Vietnamese, then in turn by the Lao. As far as he was concerned, repeating – and reversing – the answer given to Le Pichon 60 years before, the 'Katu' were in Vietnam; in Laos, there were certainly some 'Kantu' but they were quite far away, near the Vietnamese border.

Without relying on a purely geographical determinism that we know to be irrelevant in explaining long-term variation, it is tempting to go back to the comparison between the Boloven Plateau and the Ataouat Massif, as the two emblematic places in Southern Laos where social differentiations have been the most often framed in terms of ethnicity by different observers. During the colonial period, and still to a certain extent today in some Lao representations of the 'Lao Theung' ethnic groups, the Loven and the Kantu are thought of in a sort of symmetrical opposition. The Loven were deemed to be more 'evolved', easily accessible because they lived in the centre of the plateau, and linked to a multitude of trading circuits, but they were also considered to be degenerate and to have lost a large part of their cultural identity, which made them unworthy of interest.

The Kantu, in contrast, who were little known, misidentified and 'independent', and who lived in the heart of the Ataouat in the most inaccessible areas, came to represent a sort of racial purity linked to their role as guardians of an ancient cultural model as yet untouched. From Odend'hal in 1893 to Nyo in 1936, who came with the intention of breaking down their last strongholds, onwards, colonial observers extol the richness of their villages and the authenticity of their customs, attributing this to their capacity to resist 'contacts'[34], whilst at the same time condemning their intellectual and economic conservatism, which was deemed to make them both dangerous and unsuitable for participa-

34. Odend'hal wrote that 'the richest tribes are those who, protected in the highlands, have never been visited by any stranger' (1894: 148).

tion in any development projects. Even more prestige on them was later heaped by Le Pichon in his account, with numerous supporting photos, which presented the Katu – without any relevant evidence – as the last head-hunters in Indochina – 'more intelligent, but alas! far more bloodthirsty.'

In formal terms, it is interesting to note that the Kantou / Loven relationship can be understood through a grid of hierarchical inversions, depending on the values put forward: on the one hand, an ethnic group that has retained its cultural integrity but is backward and dangerous / on the other, an ethnic group that is evolved and open to contact, but culturally degenerate. In many respects, the anthropology of Southern Laos will long remain caught up in these representations and in this tension of values, first formulated in the colonial discourse.

Epilogue: The Memory of the Circle

I have discussed elsewhere the circumstances in which any anthropologist coming to investigate the villages of the Kaleum District (Sekong) in the 1990s could, if he was not careful, easily fall victim to what Lévi-Strauss referred to as 'the archaic illusion' (Goudineau 1997). Despite the decades of war, the daily bombings, the defoliant spraying and the destruction of all inhabited dwellings in the region by US Air Force napalm bombs, there were traditional-looking villages with a communal house in the centre on the banks of the Sekong, corresponding with descriptions from the past. Further up the river there were other villages, also perfectly circular but much larger, and which resembled, both in size and in terms of the quality of their longhouses, the defensive 'town–villages' described by past commentators (Figure 6.1).

In this region, where one would have thought that the war would have erased everything, ancient toponyms and the same ethnonyms as before were still found, generally in use and accepted. It was also striking that villagers, when referring to the name of their village, were more likely to use the vernacular term *vel* instead of the Lao word *ban* – thus speaking of Vel Bac, Vel A-Rô, Vel Tavang, and Vel Kandon, for instance. This is significant, when one takes into account the fact that in the Katu language the word *vel*, which means 'village', also means 'circle', as it does in several Austroasiatic languages. Inter-ethnic relations also broadly corresponded to the analysis given above, as some traditional exchanges

Photo: Y. Goudineau, 1996

Figure 6.1: Vel A-Rô, Kaleum. → Colour version on page 379.

had started up again on both sides of the Sekong. This was all the more remarkable because it was in marked contrast with the situation in the district of Ta Oi (Saravane province), on the right bank of the Sekong, where I conducted my first investigations and where the villages, which appeared to be strictly controlled by the district authorities, had undergone profound and very obvious transformations.

Yet in Kaleum, too, everything had changed in the period during and after the war. The fighting had brought about new inter-ethnic relationships and the region had been 'opened up' – even 'gutted' – by the conflict. In the post-war period, new types of villages sprang up everywhere around paddy fields on poor soils in some of the not-too-remote lowlands, following either Lao or Vietnamese models. Large numbers of local villagers, who had joined the ranks of the Pathet Lao or of the North Vietnamese army (the Vietcong, for the Americans), were obliged to take part in post-war development projects initiated by the revolutionary government.[35] However, following the departure of Vietnamese advisors from Laos, and taking advantage of the creation of the province of Sekong, which was promulgated in 1984 as a 'Lao Theung province' (Austroasiatic *de facto*),

35. See also Vatthana Pholsena's contribution in this volume (Chapter 5).

most of them went back to their old territories and rebuilt traditional village 'circles' (Goudineau 2001).

What meaning should be attributed to their return not only to the land of their forefathers, but also to the former village model? This question will only be considered here in relation to the issues related of the anthropology of Southern Laos developed above; the economic and political reasons that were often given to me by the villagers will need to be the subject of a separate analysis. The new villages were rebuilt on a very regular pattern, far superior to the rather vague layout of the old villages, I was told. Moreover, the renewed practice of large collective ritual sacrifices in several villages, which I had observed and participated in between 1995 and 1999 and which was often linked to the construction of the village communal house in the centre of the circle, added a cosmological dimension to the functional characteristics relating to the circular morphology of the habitat (Goudineau 2000a).[36] Despite a 30-year hiatus, the memory of the circle had been preserved by the ancestors, and it was they, I have often been told, who then guided their living descendants and oversaw the construction of the new villages (Figure 6.2).

The interesting question here is less why the model – a very ancient one in the region, according to certain archaeologists – was passed on; it is, rather, the way in which it was 'updated' and what the effects of this may turn out to be.[37] The fact that Upper Sekong villagers who were once very involved in the war are still well represented in the army is significant here. It is with a sort of historical consciousness and in the context of a national framework that, this time, they have affirmed their identity through the almost perfect actualisation of a 'model' in a way that would delight any structural anthropologist (Goudineau 2009). This model, perpetuated by a number of Austroasiatic societies, appears to be the

36. Since this text was first written and published, some studies have been carried out on the Vietnamese side aiming at reconstructing the social morphology and cosmological structure of a 'traditional' Katu village (Luu Hung 2007; Arhem K. 2010; Arhem N. 2015). Recovering an ancient model was a task made all the more difficult by the fact that these villages were deeply and durably 'Vietnamised' after 1975, although the development of tourism led to the reconstruction of a few stereotyped communal houses in the 2000s under the leadership of the provincial authorities, according to a model largely inspired by Le Pichon's photos.

37. See also Bloch 1989.

Photo: Y. Goudineau, 1995

Figure 6.2: Ritual in Vel Kandon, Kaleum. → Colour version on page 379.

most obvious and visible expression of an ideology that is in competition with – although progressively marginalised by – 'Lao-isation'.

In Kaleum the updating of this model was also an expression of the desire of many Kantu villages to remain out of reach of provincial administrative control and of future development plans, as they did in the past. Starting in the mid-1990s, the Lao government's response to this has been to move large numbers of villages and resettle them down on the plains (Goudineau 1997 [ed.], 2000b).[38] In their new locations, the structure of their villages is imposed on them and conforms to 'national culture'. This usually means that their villages are not circular – as if to deliberately sever the last Southern Laos ideological 'line of flight' and appease the Lao imagination – as Archaimbault would have said.

38. On the fate of a Kantu village relocated in the lowlands and an analysis of the desire on the part of some villagers to move and integrate into 'modernity', see Holly High's study of a 'socialist model village' (High 2021); and on the creation of 'cultural villages' in Sekong, see Goudineau, this volume (Chapter 12).

CHAPTER 7

The Case of the Brao

Revisiting Physical Borders, Ethnic Identities and Spatial and Social Organisation in the Hinterlands of Southern Laos and Northeastern Cambodia[1]

IAN G. BAIRD

Thongchai Winichakul's *Siam Mapped: A History of the Geo-Body of a Nation* (1994) has had a significant influence on the ways in which Southeast Asian scholars view concepts of spatial organisation and physical borders in the region. He tells us how the creation of national borders, as espoused by the British and French colonial powers at the end of the 19th century, was quite foreign to Siamese rulers, and he skilfully demonstrates the socially constructed nature of space and the importance of physical geographical borders.[2] Thongchai shows the power of map-making in defining national borders and creating the 'geo-body of the nation', as he describes it; and he points to the importance of discourses related to the geo-body of Siam in modern nation-building. He points out that we should never assume that pre-colonial spatial concepts in Southeast Asia were always the same as those of Europeans. Thongchai's overall argument is important and worthy of careful consideration. Moreover, his writings are useful in that they make us question spatial ordering, and its crucial role in social organisation.

1. I would like to thank Philippe Le Billon, Martin Stuart-Fox and Kennon Breazeale for comments provided on an early draft of this chapter. However, I take full responsibility for any errors or weaknesses that remain.

2. The terms 'physical geographical border' and 'physical border' refer to physical borders or boundaries between countries or other social groups at a more localised level. They do not refer to the type of social or ethnic boundaries that exist between ethnic groups as referred to by Fredrik Barth (1969), although these social boundaries certainly do affect the way physical borders are created and maintained.

However, Thongchai's thesis, as it relates to the creation of physical national borders, has sometimes led to over-generalisations, especially in relation to considering concepts of borders used at local levels, and by peoples in peripheral areas with different ethnic identities. Although the topic of Thongchai's book did not relate directly to local physical borders, in arguing against assuming that boundary concepts in Siam were the same as those of the European powers he appears to have contributed to the adoption of certain ideas about the nature of physical borders during pre-colonial times. These conclusions deserve to be carefully unpackaged and deconstructed. The purpose of this chapter is to show, using ethnographic data from a particular ethnic group from southern Laos and northeastern Cambodia, the Brao, that, despite the fact that many Southeast Asian scholars have apparently accepted that the concept of strict physical borders did not exist in pre-colonial Southeast Asia, there is strong evidence to suggest that local-level physical borders have long been important. These concepts are related to particular systems of social organisation, including rituals and taboos associated with animist traditions that are manifested through particular practices associated with local livelihoods, including swidden agriculture. It is also important to consider scale and not to assume that what might be true at one scale of analysis (national) is necessarily applicable at a different scale (local).

However, before continuing it seems appropriate to absolve Thongchai of much of the responsibility for the over-generalisations to which his work has at times contributed. In fact, in *Siam Mapped* Thongchai does not suggest that his example from Siam should be applied to other countries in Southeast Asia. He mainly focuses on the Siamese monarchy at the end of the 19th century and the early 20th century, and on the understanding of boundaries at a time when Europeans were dividing up the region territorially. Nor does he claim to have any detailed understanding of local concepts of physical boundaries, either in Siam or in other parts of the region, although he does touch on the issue briefly. While the spatiality of peripheral groups of people from different ethnic groups was not specifically addressed in *Siam Mapped*, it is worth pointing out that Thongchai has more recently shown increased interest in these groups and their marginal histories (Thongchai Winichakul 2000, 2002).

Trying to avoid an essentialised view of ethnic identities, this chapter argues that while concepts of physical borders in Southeast Asia were undoubtedly different from those of Europeans in pre-colonial times, they did exist prior to the arrival of Europeans, at least amongst peripheral groups like the Brao, and probably also among lowland groups. However, physical borders tended to be created and utilised in ways different from those advocated by the British and the French at the end of the 19th century. In essence, this chapter argues for a more complex and context-specific way of considering the role of physical borders and other spatial concepts in Southeast Asia. The concepts of spatial organisation adhered to by dominant lowland groups like the Lao, the Khmer and the Siamese (Thai) are not the only ones that differed from those of Western colonial powers. Rather, ethnographic data about the Brao people of southern Laos and northeastern Cambodia clearly indicate that their pre-colonial conceptions of spatial organisation differed considerably from those of both the lowlanders and of Europeans. It is this third way of conceptualising space and borders, and the implications it has in relation to livelihoods and land and resource tenure arrangements, that is of particular interest to me here.

The next section of this chapter considers the influence of *Siam Mapped* on how Southeast Asian scholars view concepts of spatial organisation and physical borders, and also presents some of the critiques of Thongchai's thesis. Since this chapter provides ethnographic data from one particular 'ethnic group', the Brao, a brief overview of ethnic identities is then provided, including some specific examples from parts of southern Laos and northeastern Cambodia, in order to illustrate the flexible and fluid way in which ethnicity is often applied. A general overview of the Brao ethnic group is then presented, followed by a detailed description of the Brao spatial concept of *huntre*, which is key to this chapter. Some of the ways in which the Brao apply the concept of *huntre* in relation to their social organisation and livelihoods are presented, and the implications of these findings are discussed. Finally, some concluding remarks are provided.

The Influence of *Siam Mapped*

It is clear that Thongchai's work has contributed significantly to convincing many scholars that there were no clear physical borders anywhere in Southeast Asia prior to European colonialism (see Duara Prasenjit 1995; Jerndal and Rigg 1998; Horstmann 2002; Fox 2002; Keyes 2002;

Ludden 2003; Wadley 2003; Chiengthong Jameree 2003). For example, Prasenjit Duara, in a book review of *Siam Mapped,* stated that:

> The geo-body makes claims to areas, peoples, and cultures that are in fact historically unverifiable because these people did not associate sovereignty with territorial boundedness.
> (Duara 1995: 478)

Duara states later in the same review that:

> Historically in the kingdoms of Southeast Asia, as in other parts of the world, territorial boundaries as lines of demarcation were nonexistent. Rather, there were shifting boundaries and zones, occupied often by petty rulers and tributaries subject to the authority of two or more overlords.
> (ibid: 478)

Charles Keyes (2002), in a Presidential Address to the Association of Asian Studies about identities in China, Viet Nam and Thailand, said, in a similar vein, that he was persuaded by the arguments of those who see well-defined borders as concomitant to the creation of modern nation-states. Reed Wadley (2003), in writing about Indonesia, stated that indigenous states in Southeast Asia were highly fluid territorially during pre-colonial times and thus did not possess fixed borders. Jerndal and Rigg (1998) pointed out that historians of Southeast Asia have gone to great lengths to emphasise that kingdoms in Southeast Asia were not interested in the control of land *per se* during pre-colonial times. Land was abundant, while people were scarce and valuable (see for example, Stuart-Fox 1997). All these authors cite Thongchai's work, among that of others, to back up their positions.

However, Thongchai's work has been criticised. Deborah Tooker (1996), for example, attempted to up-end Thongchai's perspective by examining local views of space, control and potency with reference to the Akha of Thailand and Burma. She pointed out that historians of early Southeast Asia have essentially only been able to speculate about the views of local and peripheral peoples, as almost all their source material originates from elites. Moreover, she has emphasised that focusing purely on the centre tends to over-stress the elitist, hegemonic perspective at the expense of the local. Her work resonates with discussions in the social sciences concerning the inherent political nature of space, and the cultural construction of spatial realities through practice (Lefebvre

1974; Foucault 1980a; Harvey 1990; Gupta and Ferguson 1992). Tooker (1996) argues that the Akha use spatial signs differently depending on the context, and that the Akha are not replicating the centre of the mandala polity. However, it seems that she has not significantly altered the way in which scholars see the production and reproduction of space in the region (Jerndal and Rigg 1998).

Duara, although quite sympathetic to Thongchai's overall argument, has also cautioned that:

> Winichakul tends to present this territorial conception of the nation as established fact, even naturalised, and uncontested. And yet, in most nations around the world, there are also alternative conceptions of nationhood that, if they do not contest, certainly produce some tensions with the territorial conception.
> (Duara 1995: 479)

Duara (ibid.) mentions race, ethnicity and religion as possible origins of 'extraterritorial identities' and, while acknowledging that Thongchai does touch on this issue in the last few pages of his book, Duara ultimately believes that Thongchai's treatment of this was carried out 'all too fleetingly'. This echoes the main criticism of Thongchai's work by Kevin Hewison (1995: 160), who stated that: '[Thongchai] privileges elite perspectives, saying little about "the people" and how they might have conceived of nations, borders, etc.' Horstmann (2002) has called on scholars to concentrate more on the cultural complexity of borderland communities and not just on the invented entities of the nation-states. This is certainly a very important point – and one that is crucial for my own arguments here.

Probably the most important critique of Thongchai came from the late Gehan Wijeyewardene (1991), who considers Thongchai's PhD dissertation, which would later be published as *Siam Mapped*. Although Thongchai emphasised history, Wijeyewardene criticised Thongchai's argument as relativistic, and felt that Thongchai's identification of the field of discourse appeared to deny historical events. Wijeyewardene took the view that however provisional a statement about the past or the present, its value lies in how closely it approximates to what was, or is, actually the case. He pointed to the fact that while Thongchai argued that ethnic, linguistic and cultural identities were not relevant to the pre-19th century situation, Edmund Leach (1954) clearly demonstrated otherwise by pointing to the connection between ecology, linguistics, religion and ethnic identities in Burma.

Wijeyewardene disagreed with Thongchai's idea of traditional frontiers in the region, especially with regard to the nature of the concepts of domain and boundary. He mentioned one of Thongchai's examples, Chiang Saen in northern Thailand, and attempted to refute Thongchai's idea that because feudal rulers accepted settlers, there were no borders. He also stated, in relation to northern Thailand, that while the term *wiang* (fortified settlement) was used to describe city centres in pre-colonial times, there is definite evidence that boundaries separating areas also existed in the first half of the 19th century. He pointed to the existence of spirit shrines located at the highest points of roads, showing how their locations almost always coincided with provincial boundaries in northern Thailand. He also drew attention to the fact that major watercourses were seen by feudal powers as borders in the 19th century. Thongchai had argued that the idea of physical boundaries was alien or only partially applied before European influence; while Wijeyewardene accepted that unbounded political units did exist, he felt that against this must be placed the very definite and fundamental notions of boundary, both spatial and categorical.

Wijeyewardene stressed that taboo is fundamentally associated with boundaries in northern Thailand, and therefore argued that it is not true that 'boundaries', including territorial ones, were alien to Siamese understandings of space during the pre-colonial era. For example, he claimed that village boundaries were ritually marked, and that village sacrifices often required fencing to prohibit strangers from entering. Wijeyewardene agreed with Thongchai that space was ritual, but he thought that it did not mean that it was merely a 'point field' of identified shrines.

Wijeyewardene proposed that the difference between his views and those of Thongchai was mainly a matter of viewpoint. While sympathetic to Thongchai's ideas about the kingdom of Siam and its boundaries, and also agreeing that mapping was very significant for ethnography and nation building, Wijeyewardene felt that traditional notions of borders were more complicated and better defined than Thongchai seemed to appreciate at the time he wrote *Siam Mapped*. This last point in particular fits with the position adopted here. However, some remained sceptical.

For example, a number of years ago Peter Vandergeest wrote that Gehan Wijeyewardene had provided 'an unconvincing criticism of what he believes is the denial of history in the semiotic approaches represented by Thongchai Winichakul's dissertation *Siam Mapped*' (Vandergeest 1993: 207).

Andrew Walker is much more sympathetic to Wijeyewardene's arguments than Vandergeest. In his 1999 book *The Legend of the Golden Boat: Regulation, Trade and Traders in the Borderlands of Laos, Thailand, China and Burma*, Walker engaged with Thongchai regarding the issue of pre-colonial territoriality, pointing out that according to the centre-oriented mandala models that Thongchai (1994) and others have discussed, pre-colonial polities had no clearly defined boundaries or borders in their peripheral zones, and social structures in peripheral areas were seen as replicas of the centre, but on a smaller scale. 'The borderlands, it seems, were the zone of ambiguity, flexibility and nonchalance, well outside the historical trajectories of the region's main powers.' (Walker 1999: 7) However, Walker later claimed that while Thongchai had rightly identified territorial ambiguity as being characteristic of the region in the decades prior to European colonial rule, this did not arise out of nonchalance, as Thongchai claimed, but rather due to spatial competition. Walker also provided some examples from northwestern Laos that indicated, in much the same way as the examples that Wijeyewardene (1991) had given, that boundary markers, including natural boundaries like waterways, were used in pre-colonial times, and territorial disputes did occur during that period. He suggested that Thongchai might have overstated the rupture that existed between pre-colonial and colonial ideas about territoriality. Walker pointed out that:

> When the French negotiated the colonial boundaries on the upper-Mekong, their motives were similar to the territorial demarcators who preceded them: they wanted to secure access to strategically important territory that would facilitate their control of trade and natural resources. (Walker 1999: 44)

There is also other evidence to suggest that the concept of physical borders was not as unheard of during pre-colonial times as Thongchai has suggested, even within lowland societies in the region. For example, Michel Lorrillard's 1995 doctoral thesis has about three dozen examples from the 16th and early 17th centuries of instances in which adjacent towns, villages and monasteries created fixed boundaries once they came into proximity with each other (Lorrillard 1995). In addition, the Dutchman Gerrit van Wuysthoff (1669) found, in 1642, a sign halfway across Khong Island written in Lao and Khmer that stated that the site was the boundary between two kingdoms. There are also examples of inscriptions marking the Khmer–Siamese boundary in around 1585 (Cushman 2000), and the Lao–Siamese boundary in around 1563 (see Lorrillard 1995). In addition, pre-colonial geographical texts from Lanna specify boundary limits in each direction for Nan (Kennon Breazeale, personal communication, November 2005). Mayoury and Pheuiphanh Ngaosyvathn have argued that Lan Xang always had well defined frontiers specified by listing the *muang* comprising the territory wheel (*kong din*) of the kingdom, although determining the frontiers between neighbouring mandalas is somewhat problematic (Stuart-Fox 1998). Breazeale also recorded an instance in which a resource dispute between two ethnic Lao inhabited villages occurred in pre-colonial times, and in this case both parties accepted a stream in a forest as the boundary between the two communities (Kennon Breazeale, personal communication, November 2005). Finally, the royal court of Thailand has discovered some pre-colonial Siamese maps that may indicate that the Siamese did, in fact, have more of an understanding of physical borders than Thongchai gave them credit for, although research on these maps has not yet been completed (Jonathan Rigg, personal communication, October 2005).

Having laid out Thongchai's main arguments, and critiques of his work, it is now time to turn to an article by Jefferson Fox (2002) that clearly demonstrates some of the dangers of applying Thongchai's ideas about the lack of firm boundaries at vastly different scales and in very different analytical contexts, in relation to ethnic groups with very different livelihood and socio-cultural circumstances from those that Thongchai considered in *Siam Mapped*. Fox's article is, suitably, entitled 'Siam mapped and mapping in Cambodia: Boundaries, sovereignty and indigenous conceptions of space.' Like Thongchai, but in the context of a discussion focused on ethnic Kreung people (a Brao sub-group) in Ratanakiri Province, northeastern Cambodia, Fox believes that indigenous conceptions of space have been overwhelmed by the need to have a location that can be recognised by political power. His overall thesis is valuable, but I have misgivings about some of the details of his analysis. My own work with the Brao and Kreung of Ratanakiri, which began in 1995, clearly indicates that these groups have long recognised physical borders between community lands (see Baird et al. 1996). While these borders are often not recognised by the state, and do not serve the purposes of promoting state control over territory and state simplification of and control over resources (see Vandergeest 1996; Scott 1998; Peluso and Vandergeest 2001 for examples of how state territorialisation occurs), they are, nonetheless, important in relation to taboos and the spiritual life of the Brao, just as Wijeyewardene (1991) and Walker (1999) pointed out in the context of northern Thailand and northwestern Laos.

Fox's empirical findings are largely in line with my own, but the influences of Thongchai and others appear to finally lead him to come to what seem to me to be erroneous conclusions. Initially, he says that:

> While villagers [...] have a clear sense of ancestral lands, specific boundaries between two hamlets were not traditionally required unless the cultivation areas from the two hamlets met one another. Villagers believe that if they farm on the other side of another hamlet's swidden fields and hence have to cross those fields frequently, the spirits will be unhappy and cause misfortune or death. When a hamlet's swidden fields are adjacent to those of another hamlet, village elders may meet to decide the boundaries. But in most cases the physical location of the swiddens and the taboos against crossing each other's field for cultivation define the limits of cultivation.
> (Fox 2002: 69)

However, my research indicates that Brao elders almost always establish clear boundaries for swidden cultivation between communities once swiddens from two hamlets get close enough to each other to pose a potential risk of taboos being broken by swidden fields overlapping. Considering that Fox appeared to be on the right track in revealing the complexity of spatial concepts, it is surprising that he later claimed, in line with Thongchai's thesis, and apparently contradicting his earlier findings, that 'Hamlets did not have a common border connecting them with other hamlets, let alone a line dividing the realms of the two hamlets' (Fox 2002: 72).

Fox apparently did not conduct detailed investigations regarding this spatial taboo, which is called *huntre*[3] in Brao. However, *huntre* is important for the Brao. It is an indigenous concept of space that differs both from what Thongchai describes for pre-colonial Siam and from colonial and post-colonial concepts of space. I now turn to the ethnic Brao people of southern Laos and northeast Cambodia, the spatial concept of *huntre*, and its role in the creation of physical borders. I will demonstrate that the existence of this fundamental concept of physical borders for the Brao clearly indicates that Thongchai's example from Siam is not directly applicable throughout mainland Southeast Asia, due to different socio-political and cultural contexts and livelihoods, and that it is also different from European colonial ideas promoted in the 19th and early 20th centuries about maps, physical borders and property tenure.

Ethnic Identities

Before attempting to describe what can nominally be referred to as the ethnic 'Brao' people, it is useful to touch on the very fluid and flexible nature of 'ethnic identities' in Laos, and throughout mainland Southeast Asia, in order not to contribute to the myth of firm and well-defined ethnic identities in the region. In Laos, ethno-linguistic traits have largely been used as a basis for establishing ethnic identities, in the literature (Chamberlain et al. 1995; Lao Front for National Construction 2005). Ethno-linguistic classifications can be extremely useful in determining communication and sometimes socio-cultural links between peoples throughout history, and should never be underestimated by researchers working on ethnicity or identity issues in the region. However, my experiences with the Brao and other diverse Austroasiatic language speakers in southern Laos clearly indicate that the concept of particular, large ethnic groups, with common ethnonyms based largely on linguistic similarities, is a relatively new one for the region, and is certainly not adequate for considering questions of ethnicity or identity in Laos or for classifying the peoples of the country into different ethnic groups and sub-groups. In Laos groups with very different linguistic dialects

3. *Huntre* is a term used by all Brao subgroups, but some Brao also use the term *tung kup* in relation to the concept *huntre*. *Tung kup* refers to incorrect spatial ordering that results in *huntre*, which then causes illness or misfortune.

are sometimes referred to using the same ethnic group name. A good example of this can be found amongst the so-called Katu or Kantu ethnic group of Kaleum District, Sekong Province (see, in this book, Y. Goudineau's contribution).

On the other hand, some peoples whose linguistic dialects are quite similar and who can easily understand each other's respective dialects have adopted different ethnic identities and labels. One example relates to the Triang (Talieng[4]) and the Banneng people of Dak Cheung District, also in Sekong. When ethnic Triang district government officials tried to convince the Banneng people who inhabit three villages to recognise themselves as Triang, one village leader reportedly said: 'There are now over 1,000 Banneng people, and that should be enough for the government to classify us as our own separate ethnic group.'

Another good example of the confusion surrounding ethnic identities in Laos relates to the Kaseng, a recognised ethnic group in southern Laos since the colonial period (see for example, Bourotte 1955; Lebar et al. 1964; Chamberlain et al. 1995). When visiting Sekong Province in 2004 to investigate ethnic issues, officials from the provincial Lao Front for National Construction told me that there used to be 14 ethnic groups in the Sekong, but that one had disappeared – the Kaseng. Since the Kaseng were previously believed to inhabit southeastern parts of Sekong in present-day Dak Cheung District, it was initially thought – after no villages in the district were identified as being Kaseng during an ethnic group census of the province – that the Kaseng people must have moved to Attapeu Province. However, when the officials from Sekong went to Attapeu, officials there told them that they had not been able to identify any villages in the province populated by ethnic Kaseng people either! However, in both Sekong and Attapeu officials were able to identify individuals who claimed to be Kaseng living in the provincial capitals. So what happened to the Kaseng in the villages? Considering that in 1962 it was estimated that there were 4,000 Kaseng in southern Laos (Lafont 1962, cited in Lebar et al. 1964), the population was too large to have simply vanished.

4. Triang is the term that people in this ethnic group presently use to describe themselves in their own language, while Talieng is what they are called in the Lao language.

In early 2005, the mystery of the missing Kaseng was finally solved when a number of ethnic Harak (Alak[5]) and Triang people explained – during a workshop about ethnicity in Sekong – that there never really was an ethnic group called the Kaseng. Instead, the term was applied during the period of Siamese domination to people who participated in a particular loyalty oath-taking ceremony. At this ceremony, some ethnic Harak and Triang men put the tips of their swords into sacred water and swore to submit themselves to the influence of the Siamese. This sacred water was called *nam sep nam seng* in Lao, and so some of those who participated in the ceremony came to be referred to as Kaseng, and the label stuck for many decades. However, more recently those people from the villages previously known as Kaseng have chosen to call themselves Triang and Harak. This explains why no Kaseng villages can be found, and why there are still individuals who claim to be Kaseng living in the provincial capitals of Attapeu and Sekong. These people left their villages of origin long ago, before those villages changed their identities from Kaseng to Harak or Triang, and so have retained the ethnic identity of Kaseng even though most people from their villages of origin have long abandoned the label. We can see from this example that while ethnonyms do not in themselves constitute identities, they are meaningful for understanding ethnic identities, especially when members of labelled groups adopt them, as was once the case with the Kaseng.

The term Triang as an ethnonym appears to be of relatively recent origin, apparently coming into use during the French colonial period. According to Somphavanh Xainyavong et al. (2003), Triang originates from the term *tring*, which means 'listen' in their language. This is apparently what people told each other to do when the French came to visit them, and the term stuck and changed slightly. The Triang are unaware of an earlier ethnonym for themselves, and Somphavanh et al. speculated that they have either forgotten the earlier term due to not having a written language, or perhaps did not have an ethnonym for themselves before then.

There have also been critiques of the strict use of ethno-linguistic classification based on ethnographic studies from other parts of Laos. For example, Grant Evans in his book *Laos: Culture and Society* (1999a)

5. Harak is the term that people in this ethnic group use to describe themselves in their own language, while Alak is what they are called in the Lao language.

shows how fluid ethnic identities are in northern Laos. Frank Proschan's (1997) approach is particularly useful for understanding the issue of ethnicity in Laos. He put it well when he stated that:

> Because they designate such complex sociocultural situations, ethnic naming-systems are not likely to resemble the neat classificatory schemas that ethnoscientists and structural anthropologists have described for flora and fauna, kinship, color terms, or cultural artifacts [...] no classification of ethnic groups really satisfies such a definition.
> (ibid.: 93)

However, Proschan has also pointed out that there are times when people in Laos choose to adopt ethnic identities based on both primordial or essentialising characteristics and situational or flexible concepts (ibid.).

Oscar Salemink's work in the central highlands of Vietnam has also indicated that essentialised concepts of ethnicity – as understood by most people of European descent, even today – were largely foreign to the peoples of the region in pre-colonial times, and that colonial administrators, explorers, military officers, missionaries and even anthropologists have contributed to the creation of ethnic identities along the Annamite chain (Salemink 2003).

I have even noticed how my own work with the Brao in Laos has affected their ethnic identities and has caused some to refer to themselves as Brao, whereas they previously identified themselves as 'Lave'. Local ideas in different parts of Laos clearly differ from the ideas of those who espouse strict adherence to ethno-linguistic classification systems as the basis for defining ethnicity. I concur with Leif Jonsson's statement, referring to the peoples of Ratanakiri Province, northeast Cambodia, adjacent to Laos' Attapeu Province, that:

> Social organisation among uplanders is not along ethnic lines. At the present, there is no supra-village organisation, and a high degree of household autonomy within villages. Household and village organisation suggests some gradations between extreme household autonomy and extreme lineage/village monopoly in ritual. These gradations relate to historical and political economic factors, and do not fall neatly along ethnic lines.
> (Jonsson 1997: 546)

It should therefore come as little surprise that while the Lao Front for National Construction, which is responsible for ethnic classification questions in Laos, largely bases its official ethnic classifications on ethno-linguistic characteristics, they also recognise the principle that no ethnic classification should be applied to any group of people without that group agreeing that the name be applied to them (Lao Front for National Construction 2005). In other words, while they see ethno-linguistics as the most 'scientific' way of doing ethnic classification, they also implicitly recognise the practical reality of ethnic identities in Laos – that they are socially constructed and that it should never be assumed that ethnic labels based on ethno-linguistic classifications will always be accepted by the people to whom the ethnonyms are being applied.

The Brao

Ethnic Identities

As with other ethnic groups in Laos and the region, there has long been considerable uncertainty regarding the ethnic classification of peoples sometimes referred to as 'Brao'.[6] In Laos, for example, in June 1911 an unauthored French language monograph about the history of Attapeu Province identified one Brao-associated ethnic group that is no longer recognised either by scholars or by those who are termed Brao nowadays. These people were said to live in the upper Xe Xou River basin and were referred to by the author of the monograph as 'Breugards'. They were described as being half ethnic Halang from Kon Tum (in the Central Highlands of Vietnam) and half ethnic Love (Brao) (Anonymous 1911).

Lao people have historically referred to the Brao using many pejorative terms, including Lave (Love), Kha Lave, Kha Kheo Hian, Kha Kheo Tat and Kha Sam Kha, just to name a few. Today the term Lave continues to be commonly used, and while most people in this ethnic group prefer to be called Brao, which is the name they most frequently apply to themselves in their own language, some people from Champasak and Attapeu Provinces have fully internalised the label Lave, and insist that they are Lave and not Brao!

In northeastern Cambodia, with specific reference to the Brao, Leif Jonsson (1997: 549) correctly comments that: 'In local usage, "Brao",

6. These people mainly prefer to be called Brao (sometimes spelt Brou, Braou, Preu, Proue, Prov, Brau or Blao) but are also referred to using other terms. Apart from pejoratives, they are also, in Laos and Cambodia, called by the general terms Lao Theung and Son Phao, and Chun Chiet and Khmer Leu respectively.

"Krung" and "Kravet" are rather interchangeable references, and there is no consistent pattern in their use.' My own experience is very much in accordance with this statement (see for example Baird 2000). Jonsson (1997: 549) also stated, as a follow up, that: 'Broad similarities and interconnections do not imply any overarching organisation or an ethnic consciousness among these people.' In fact, many of the people in Ratanakiri Province who call themselves 'Kreung'[7] today referred to themselves exclusively as 'Brao' in the past. For example, this was true in 1966–1967 in the Ratanakiri village where Jacqueline Matras-Guin conducted her field research. In fact, Matras never heard anyone in the village identity themselves as Kreung (Jacqueline Matras-Guin, personal communication, October 2005) even though people from the same village where she worked mainly refer to themselves as Kreung today. Moreover, Captain Cupet (1998 [1891]) recorded the people from Kalai village in present-day Ratanakiri to be ethnic Brao, as did Henri Maitre (1912) and Jacqueline Matras-Troubetzkoy (1983), when they passed through the village in 1890, 1910 and 1967 respectively. However, the people of Kalai are today almost exclusively recognised as being ethnic Kreung (Ironside and Baird 2003).

The Brao-to-Kreung identity switch seems to be related to the large numbers of ethnic Brao people who fled in 1975 from northern Ratanakiri to Attapeu in southern Laos and to the central highlands of Vietnam due to the draconian policies of the Khmer Rouge. Therefore the term Brao became synonymous with traitor (Jonsson 1997). It quickly became convenient for many of those Brao who were not able to flee the Khmer Rouge to abandon the label Brao and replace it with the label 'Kreung', which did not come with the negative baggage associated with 'Brao'. The term stuck, and it continues to be in widespread use now, long after the Khmer Rouge's demise. However, the situation is probably more complex than this, as some Brao have also adopted the label 'Kreung' because their language dialect is more similiar to Kreung than to the dialects of other peoples in the north of Ratanakiri Province who call themselves Brao.

7. The term *kreung* also refers to a particular type of mature forest with large trees in the Brao language, and thus historically the term denoted the habitat in which these Brao people lived.

The Brao People

Despite the confusion surrounding ethnic classification amongst the Brao, if one includes the various so-called Brao sub-groups, including the Kavet, Kreung, Lun, Brao Tanap and Amba in Cambodia, and the Kavet, Hamong, Jree and Kanying in Laos,[8] there are over 50,000 people included in what is today known as the 'Brao ethnic group',[9] including between 19,000 (Chazée 1999) and 23,000 (Johnstone 1993) in southern Laos; between 26,606 (Asian Development Bank 2002) and 28,134 (Helmers and Wallgren 2002) in northeastern Cambodia; between 202 (Vu Dinh Loi 2001) and 1,600 (Evans 1995b) in central Vietnam; 90 in the United States; and five in France (Grimes 1996). Although the people belonging to the various Brao sub-groups speak somewhat different dialects of what is recognised by linguists to be a single language (Gerard Diffloth, personal communication, 2000), they can communicate with each other pretty well, each using their respective dialects.

The Brao people mainly inhabit areas that lie approximately south of the Xekaman River in Attapeu Province, southern Laos; west of the Lao–Vietnamese border and the Cambodian–Vietnamese border; east of the Sekong River in southern Laos and northeastern Cambodia; and north of an area not far south of Banlung town, the capital of Ratanakiri Province. There is also reportedly one ethnic Brao village in Kon Tum Province, central Vietnam (Loi 2001), and there are some Brao villages situated in Champasak Province, southern Laos, to the west of the Sekong River (personal observation); but the people from those communities are believed to have originated from areas east of the Sekong River (see map overleaf).

For the most part, the Brao have their own particular animist-oriented belief systems, and while some from Ratanakiri Province have recently converted to Christianity, almost all the Brao in Laos have retained animist beliefs. However, some Brao in Laos and Cambodia are increasingly adopting Buddhism, which is itself mixed with various animist beliefs and practices. The animists believe in a wide variety of spirits, including those associated with houses, ancestors, forests, water

8. In Laos the Brao subgroups are all commonly referred to as Lave.

9. Most recent estimates indicate that there are probably closer to 55,000 ethnic Brao people in Laos, Cambodia and Vietnam combined, these increases being largely a result of high birth rates amongst the Brao.

Source: Ian G. Baird, 2008

Map 7.1: Areas inhabited by the Brao in southern Laos and northeastern Cambodia

bodies and other things in nature, and when ill they frequently offer domestic animal sacrifices in order to appease the unhappy spirits that are believed to be causing the illness. Chickens and pigs are frequently sacrificed, while buffaloes are sacrificed more rarely. Rice beer is almost invariably consumed when sacrifices are conducted (Baird 2003).

Although over history the Brao have certainly had some contact with neighbouring ethnic groups, including the ethnic Lao and the Siamese, their location in remote mountainous areas in the southeastern-most periphery of Laos and the northeastern-most corner of Cambodia left most of them relatively 'independent' from French, Lao, Siamese and Khmer control. In fact, French administrators only visited most Brao villages for the first time well into the 20th century, and many of the Brao who did pay taxes to the French administration remained quite independent throughout the colonial period; their egalitarian ideas made submission difficult for them. 'Khmerisation' attempts focused on the Brao in Ratanakiri and Stung Treng Provinces of Cambodia did not begin until the Sihanouk government initiated them after 1958. Moreover, due to the poorly-conceived nature of these programmes and the rise of the Khmer Rouge in northeastern Cambodia in the 1960s, these efforts were generally short-lived and most failed (Ironside and Baird 2003). In Laos, many Brao communities were disrupted and forced to move around between 1964 and 1973 due to the aerial bombardment of the Ho Chi Minh trail, but prior to the 1960s most lived in upland areas with little contact with ethnic Lao lowlanders, and were largely self-sufficient, although they traded for salt with lowlanders and with other ethnic groups for clothing, jars and gongs.

Livelihoods

The Brao are primarily rotational swidden agriculturalists, although some have recently adopted lowland wet rice paddy cultivation as their main means of producing rice (Ironside and Baird 2003). This is especially the case for those in Attapeu and Champasak Provinces in southern Laos. The Brao in Attapeu are also facing widespread internal resettlement to lowland areas and along major roads, with the associated promotion of lowland paddy agriculture (see Baird and Shoemaker 2005). Government officials working with the Brao of northeastern Cambodia have also been promoting lowland paddy cultivation (Baird 2000; Ironside and Baird 2003). The swidden agriculture practiced by the Brao is spatially quite different from lowland rice cultivation, as it is a more extensive agricultural system that requires intermittent fallow periods in order to achieve sustainability over long periods. As will become clear, this system of agriculture is one of the key factors that has influenced the development of certain types of social organisation, spatial concepts and physical borders amongst the Brao.

The Brao have long relied heavily on fishing and hunting for birds, reptiles, amphibians and small mammals, as well as collecting non-timber forest products (NTFPs) for subsistence and income generation. Some important NTFPs in terms of generating income are *Dipterocarpus* wood resin and malva nuts (Bottomley 2002; Baird and Dearden 2003; Baird 2003), but there are many others that are used on a daily basis (Baird et al. 1996; Baird 2000).

Huntre – A Brao Concept of Spatial Organisation

What is Huntre *and how does it Work?*

Huntre is a general Brao language term used to refer to a number of different spatial taboos that are very significant for the way in which the Brao are organised socially and spatially. *Huntre* relates to situations where social order, as defined spatially, does not follow a certain system believed to be correct by the Brao. *Huntre* can be manifested in more than one manner, and the best way to illustrate the meaning of the term, which cannot be easily translated into English, is through providing some examples of how it is applied in daily life.

The first example involves the positioning of walking paths in relation to different settlements and villages and places like rivers, streams or swidden fields. It is taboo, or *huntre,* to use a path to reach regularly-visited locations if it passes directly through other settlements, villages or swidden fields belonging to different villages. If people want to reach

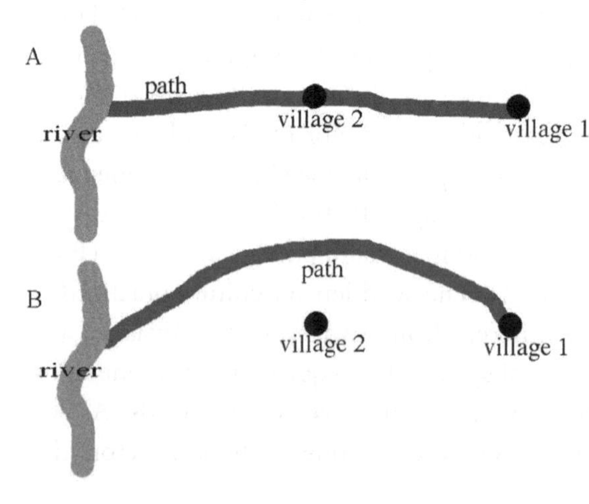

Figure 7.1: An example of a path-related situation where a *huntre* taboo has been broken (A), and another example where *huntre* has not been broken (B). The latter is what the Brao normally prefer.

those locations on a regular basis, they must make different paths that bypass the other villages (see Figure 7.1).

A second example relates to the positioning of swidden fields and fallows. The Brao rotate their swidden fields, often moving them annually or biannually in one direction up one side of a river or stream until they reach the extent of the village's territory. They then cross the stream and move in the opposite direction downstream (see Ironside and Baird 2003; Baird 2003). For this reason, it is *huntre* to place a recent swidden fallow between two active swidden fields owned by the same family (see Figure 7.2), especially if there is a path that crosses through the fallow swidden connecting the two active swiddens. Misfortune that might result from not obeying this spatial taboo could come in the form of becoming seriously ill, being accidentally cut with a bush knife while working in a field, or being bitten by a poisonous snake or stung by a scorpion. Therefore, this spatial concept greatly influences the organisation of Brao swidden fields, as one of the main goals of locating swiddens in a particular way is to prevent *huntre* situations from arising. When *huntre* occurs, the Brao often conduct animist rituals particular to the situation in order to appease the spirits. This usually involves sacrificing a chicken or pig and drinking a jar of rice beer.

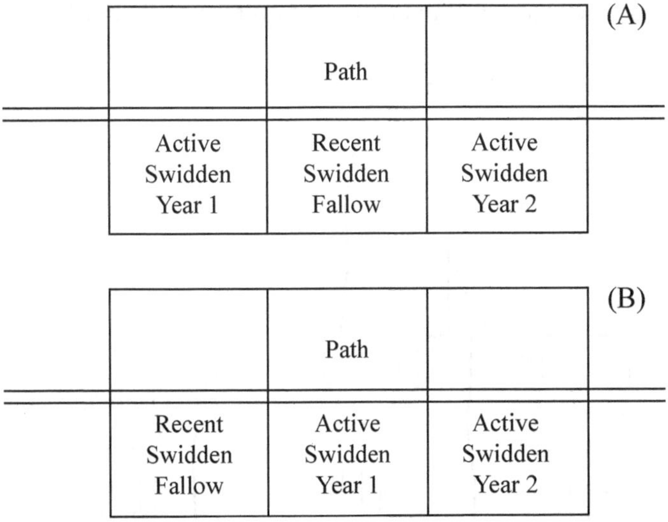

Figure 7.2: An example of swidden fields being situated spatially so that a *huntre* taboo is broken (A), and another example where *huntre* is not broken (B). The latter is what the Brao normally prefer.

The importance of *huntre* to the spatial organisation of the Brao, and probably to that of most of their neighbours who also cultivate swiddens, fits well with the idea of creating physical borders between particular social groups of swidden cultivators who want to ensure that their respective swidden fields do not cross each other. As described by Baird et al. (1996), specific physical borders between these communities or villages are commonly based on practical need, especially when the swidden fields of one community begin to approach the swidden fields of another. When a border is regarded as necessary to prevent *huntre*, the leaders of the two communities meet and come to a mutual agreement regarding where the village border between them should be located. Natural markers like streams, ponds, hills, and large rocks are generally used to define these quite specific physical boundaries. People from the two communities are allowed to situate their swidden fields almost right up to the edges of their community's boundary, provided that a small patch of forest separates their swiddens from those of the adjacent community (Figure 7.3). However, it was probably not unusual for the Brao to maintain physical borders in certain directions and no borders at all in others, when neighbouring communities were far enough away that there was no practical reason for establishing such borders. Baird et al. (ibid.) found, for example, that an ethnic Kreung village in Taveng District, Ratanakiri, had quite specific borders to their

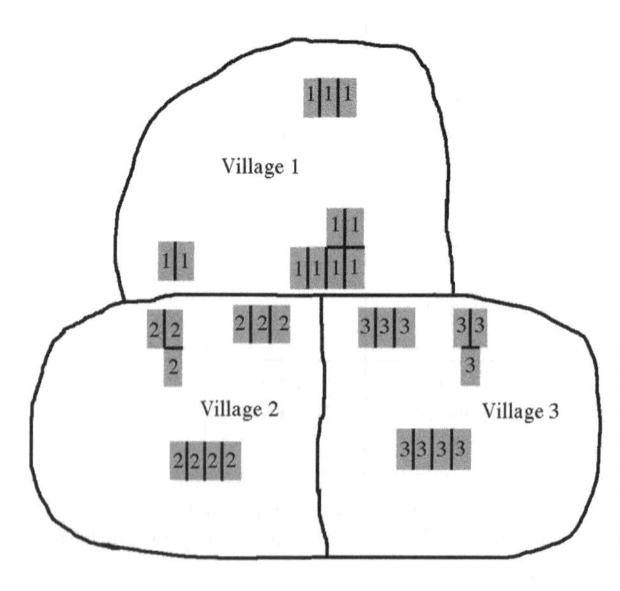

Figure 7.3: A situation where three Brao village territories are separated by physical borders in order to avoid *huntre* taboos due to swidden fields crossing over one another.

east, west and south, but did not have any border in that direction, since there were no nearby communities to the north. There are also a large number of other types of spatial taboos that, if violated, are believed to result in *huntre,* illness and misfortune amongst the Brao, but there is not enough space here to describe them.

Reconstructing History

It is never an easy matter to know how people thought in pre-colonial times, especially when evidence is largely based on interviews with people over half a century after the end of French colonial rule. Memory and associated narratives are always influenced by politics and shifting identities (see, for example, Pholsena 2003, 2004). However, it is evident for a number of reasons that *huntre* is a concept with pre-colonial origins. Firstly, elderly Brao people are much more familiar with the concept than younger people, and while it could be argued that these were the people who were the most influenced by colonial ways, since they were born during the colonial period, the reality is that many remote Brao villages were not greatly influenced on a day-to-day basis by the French, whose main goals were to maintain security and collect taxes. Most Brao communities in southern Laos and northeastern Cambodia were also relatively independent well into the 20th century. Secondly, people living in more remote areas near other peoples with similar ethnic identities are generally more aware of the concept than people from more 'Lao-ised' and 'Khmer-ised' villages. Thirdly, this concept does not resemble any of the spatial ideas used by any of the dominant lowland peoples in the region, be it the Khmer, Vietnamese, Lao or Thai (Siamese).

In the 19th century and early 20th century, when most Brao villages were still considered to be nominally independent – a period that one old Kavet man described to me as being 'the time when each village was a country' – there were frequent armed conflicts between different village communities, with people from similar ethno-linguistic backgrounds sometimes aligning themselves with each other, but also sometimes collaborating with groups of people with quite different linguistic backgrounds, in order to fight against people with the same linguistic backgrounds as themselves. During this period the physical borders between communities were particularly important, and were, as Captain Cupet of the Pavie Mission reported in the late 19th century (1998), rarely violated, due to the risk of causing serious conflicts between villages. More recently, however, after the slave trade declined in the late 19th and early 20th centuries, possibilities for crossing these borders for hunting and fishing, if not for swidden agriculture, probably became more frequent, especially between allied villages.

I have also heard of cases amongst the Brao in which neighbouring villagers received permission to make their swidden fields near the borders with their territories but on the territories of neighbouring villages. In these cases, swiddens were still not allowed to cross over the host community's swiddens, in order to prevent *huntre*, but neighbouring villages were allowed to 'borrow' land from the host community to make swiddens. Sometimes this borrowing took place at no cost, but in other cases the arrangement appears to have been more like land renting, as those temporarily occupying another community's land for swidden agricultural purposes were expected to provide their hosts with a certain amount of unhusked rice (measured in back baskets). The guests were also required to offer the host community a jar of rice beer and to provide a chicken to be sacrificed to the host community's spirits.

Jacqueline Matras-Troubetzkoy has probably written more about the spatial organisation of the Brao[10] than anyone else, focusing on the ways in which houses, villages and swidden fields are spatially organised. For example, she showed how Brao villages have historically been organised with a circular pattern of house distribution (Matras-Troubetzkoy 1975). She also provided a detailed description of how swidden fields are sometimes divided up between different cooperating families (Matras-Troubetzkoy 1983). At the village level, spatial organisation follows a sort of mandala model, in which communal houses are located at the centre and houses are situated in a circle around these areas (Matras-Troubetzkoy 1975). Gates are often built to designate the immediate boundary between the domain of village spirits and those of forest spirits (Baird 2003). In many ways, this situation mirrors the one described for the Akha by Tooker (1996). However, for this chapter the focus is on the broader village territory scale of spatial organisation, rather than the household or village-proper. Although Jacqueline Matras-Guin was well aware of some of the taboos associated with *huntre* during the time

10. She calls them the Brou.

of her research in Ratanakiri in the 1960s, she never wrote about the concept, and she has acknowledged that she was not aware of the term or of the full dimensions of its application at the time of her research with the Brao (Matras-Guin, personal communication, October 2005).

Unfortunately, this complex way of organising space, including settlements, paths and swidden fields, is not considered in most development planning, either by Lao or Cambodian government agencies or by international aid agencies. In many cases, modern land-use planning has overwhelmed these indigenous concepts of spatial organisation. Firstly, people thinking in terms of either lowland or colonial models have rarely looked for different systems. Secondly, the scale of modern land-use planning is generally much greater than the scale of land-use planning by the Brao, who have historically managed their resources at the village level. Thirdly, modern development planning has tended to emphasise private or state-controlled property rather than common property.

Brao Social and Spatial Organisation

It is useful to begin this section with a quote from Captain Cupet (1891), a French military officer working with the famous Pavie Mission to Laos in the late 19th century. Captain Cupet, as part of his duties, was amongst the first Frenchmen to reach the relatively unknown and nominally independent region presently included within the boundaries of Ratanakiri Province, northeastern Cambodia. Although colonial accounts should certainly never be taken at face value, referring to comments made by early explorers like Cupet can be revealing. Responding to claims that the people of the area he visited were nomadic, Cupet stated that:

> Nowhere have I found any [highlanders] that are at all nomadic, as they are generally believed to be. Besides, even if they wanted to move around, they could not do so except within a short radius. As a consequence of secular fighting, the inhabitants' territory has been divided up between the villages. Each of these has won a corner, in which it billets itself and which truly belongs to it. Simple verbal agreements and traditions limit the public domain. Within it the inhabitants mark out their fields as they see fit, fish and hunt as they please. The smallest incursion into neighbouring territory brings about a conflict because nothing safeguards collective property among them. The different peoples are, consequently, more or less immobilised where they are established. Despite the forces working against autonomy, resulting

> from their way of living, from their social organisation and from the deep-rooted, continual fighting, a great number of them have preserved their independence almost entirely until today.
> (Cupet 1998 [1891]: 147–148)

The key to understanding Brao concepts of space appears to be not assuming that physical boundaries did not exist, nor accepting that boundary concepts were applied in the same ways as Europeans did. What is required is a more complex and flexible approach to defining spatial organisation. Brao boundaries are very important for regulating where swidden fields can be located, as well as other land and resource tenure issues. Livelihoods have undoubtedly played an important role in the application of concepts of spatial organisation. Thus, there has certainly been considerable variation in the ways in which borders have been applied and in how strictly they have been enforced over space and time. For example, for hunting or fishing, Fox (2002) is probably right in believing that borders were sometimes breached, either with permission or otherwise. In some cases, the Brao have demonstrated that these types of boundaries do not always apply to other non-swidden agriculture livelihood activities like collecting wild fruit, which in most cases does not require the recognition of strict physical borders, at least today. This indicates that tenure arrangements are complex and fluid, and that whereas physical boundaries may exist for one livelihood activity, they cannot be assumed to apply to others. In this regard, Fox (ibid.) is correct to cite Vandergeest and Peluso (1995: 415) in stating that, as in present-day Thailand, local property rights and tenure arrangements amongst the Kreung 'continue to comprise complex bundles of overlapping, hierarchical rights and claims'. Baird and Dearden (2003) have also emphasised the importance of considering the various types of land and resource tenure arrangements used by the Brao in the context of protected area management.

Ultimately, concepts of physical boundaries are closely linked with the socio-political systems of organisation adopted by different peoples, as Tooker (1996) has emphasised. Or, in other words, all boundaries are socially constructed, and so boundaries are likely to depend a great deal on who creates them (Horstmann 2002). Those adopted by Europeans and the lowland Lao differ from those of the Brao. It is worth noting that other SE Asian groups who live in upland areas have, like the Brao, also developed quite definite physical borders between communities. Cramb and Wills (1990) have shown, for example, how the Iban people of Sarawak in Malaysia, who have local institutions and land and resource tenure arrangements centred on particular longhouses, appear to have developed quite strict physical borders during pre-colonial periods to separate different longhouse groups and to ensure social stability and organisation (Cramb and Wills 1990).

Since systems of spatial organisation appear to be intricately linked with the particular livelihoods and socio-political and cultural systems adopted by particular peoples, be it the Lao, the Akha, the Iban or the Brao, it is not surprising that the systems of spatial organisation adopted by these groups vary. While the Lao had, historically, a hierarchical (and matrilineal) socio-political and cultural system, the Brao, Akha and Iban all lived in relatively egalitarian societies. Historically, there does not appear to have been any hierarchy beyond the village level amongst the Iban, Akha or Brao (Cramb and Wills; Tooker 1996; Baird 2003).

The Brao have organised themselves around a particular type of bilateral kinship system. When a couple marries, they generally move into the house belonging to the parents of the bride. Depending on the family, and the particular traditions of certain Brao subgroups, a couple will tend to reside in the bride's parents' house for between two and seven (or more) years. Then, after appropriate rituals are performed, the couple moves into the groom's parents' house, where they are expected to live for an equal number of years. In the Jree subgroup, for example, a couple will usually spend seven years with the bride's parents, followed by seven years with the groom's parents, and then the couple will either continue to live with the groom's parents or will establish themselves as a separate household. However, for most other Brao subgroups in Laos and Cambodia, a couples will generally spend three or four years with the bride's parents, the same amount of time with the groom's parents, and then they will move back to the bride's parents' house. This cycle may continue, or a couple may either decide to stay with the parents of one member of the couple, usually the groom's, or they may choose to establish a separate household. However, the Brao tend to be pragmatic, and particular situations can lead to differences from the pattern of movements described above. For example, if the parents of either the bride or the groom have passed away, a couple may decide to simply move into the house of the remaining parents and either stay there permanently or eventually branch off as a separate household.

It is very important to note that Brao social organisation has, historically, necessitated the safeguarding of communal property rather than of private property. When a couple moves from one household to another, whether within the same village or to a different one, they give up tenure to whatever land they may have been farming and replace it by gaining access to new land associated with the family and community that they are joining. Thus, the land tenure situation of individual families is quite fluid, since couples frequently change residence, at least in the early years of their marriage. The Brao social system has always provided flexible systems that allow the amount of land farmed within a particular community to fluctuate based on the movement of labour back and forth between households, in the fashion just described. This system does not fit well with the retention of private property; but private property does not, in fact, fit well with swidden agriculture and the need for long fallows to help ensure fertility and good harvests. Instead, communities have protected their communal rights over particular territories, which have included active swiddens, forests at various stages of fallow and other areas which are determined, for either spiritual or practical reasons, to be unsuitable for swidden agriculture (see Baird 2000). This maintenance of communal tenure is ensured through a particular spatial organisation based on *huntre* and the associated maintenance of quite specific physical borders with other similar social groups. It is therefore not surprising that many Kreung communities in Ratanakiri Province are advocating for the protection of communal land rights (NGO Forum on Cambodia 2004).

The ethnic Lao, in contrast, have quite different social and livelihood systems that are based on relatively fixed wet rice cultivation and matrilineal social organisation, neither of which fit well with the frequent family movements of the Brao. While boundaries within cultivated areas, particularly between wet rice fields belonging to different households, are important among the Lao, they do not practise swidden agriculture or use the forest for other purposes nearly as much as a group like the Brao. Outside the areas that they cultivate, therefore, the Lao have tended to rely on rather blurred frontiers, rather than on precise physical borders. For the Lao of pre-colonial times, there were probably fewer practical reasons for setting up such borders. For them, the mandala concept of social and spatial organisation made more sense. However, it is probably true, as Wijeyewardene (1991) and Walker (1999) have argued, that a sense of territoriality existed in pre-colonial times, even among lowland groups.

One theoretical point that deserves further investigation relates to the fact that lowland societies like the Lao and the Khmer have long relied on hierarchal social arrangements to control populations and maintain social order, whereas the Brao – and probably other more egalitarian groups with no hierarchy beyond the village level – have relied on spatial control at the territorial level, including physical borders, in order to maintain social order.[11]

Changing Concepts of Spatial Organisation

Concepts of spatial organisation are never stagnant, as they are linked with social organisation, which is in constant flux due to various factors. The increasing prevalence of maps is undoubtedly having a great deal of influence on how people view spatial organisation and territoriality in Asia (Ludden 2003). Thus, it should come as little surprise that indigenous concepts of spatial organisation, such as *huntre* among the Brao, are susceptible to the same types of cultural integration and change as other socio-cultural aspects. For example, my investigations in Pathoumphone District of Champasak Province, southern Laos, indicate that the concept of *huntre* is no longer relevant to most Brao people there, even for those who can still speak Brao. It appears that these people have already undergone a significant degree of what could be called, following Georges Condominas (1990), 'Lao-isation'. In many cases, interviewed Brao elders were not even aware of the term *huntre* or how it is applied. Instead, they have fully adopted most, if not all, of the spatial concepts commonly held by ethnic Lao people living near them. They have even abandoned the bilateral kinship system of the Brao. However, the concept of *huntre* is still relevant in places where Brao culture and livelihoods are more intact, such as in Phou Vong District, Attapeu Province, which is the heart of Brao culture in southern Laos, and amongst the Brao, and the Kavet and Kreung sub-groups, in Ratanakiri and Stung Treng Provinces in northeastern Cambodia. There, the concept is still well understood, even by young people, but

11. I am indebted to Philippe Le Billon for helping me to develop this idea.

modern forms of spatial organisation are undoubtedly threatening to alter the concept there as well.

Differences in Spatial Organisation

Thongchai's arguments about mapping and the socially constructed nature of space are important. He correctly reminds us not to blindly assume that spatial concepts have always been as colonial and post-colonial states have defined and redefined them, or that they will never change. However, the Brao live in a context with quite different livelihoods and socio-political and cultural organisation. As mentioned earlier, the context with which Thongchai was concerned was at the level of nation state, while the Brao context is at the level of the village, which is quite a different spatial scale. This point is important.

It would also be incorrect to assume that people from different places and ethnic groups have the same spatial concepts, and the same ideas associated with physical borders, as their social organisation is different, and this is critical for the development of spatial concepts. Furthermore, as Wijeyewardene (1991) has correctly pointed out, taboos are often crucial to spatial concepts in the region, and the taboos of the Brao in Cambodia and Laos are certainly not the same as those of the Siamese, the Khmer or the Lao. It is also certain that concepts of spatial organisation also shift in space and time. Finally, it would be foolish to discard the idea that physical boundaries did not exist for the Brao in pre-colonial times, but it would be equally foolish to assume that they always existed, or more importantly, that they were always similar to or the same as European boundaries at the time. Thongchai's book represents an important scholarly contribution, but it provides only a partial perspective, and it tends towards overgeneralisation. Like Wijeyewardene (1991), Tooker (1996) and Walker (1999), I advocate a more complex and contextualised approach to looking at spatial and social organisation in Southeast Asia. This scepticism is in the true spirit of Thongchai's work, but without producing and legitimising new essentialising concepts of space such as the ones that Thongchai seeks to liberate us from.

Conclusion

Using ethnographic information about the Brao people and other peoples from southern Laos and northeastern Cambodia, I have tried to demonstrate the flexible and fluid nature of ethnic identities in the region. Most importantly, I propose that the Brao, and probably other ethnic groups in the region, including lowlanders, have since pre-colonial times had relatively clear concepts of physical borders at the local level, although this has not been properly appreciated by Asian scholars, probably due to their focus on lowland principalities and kingdoms.

The point of this chapter is not to entirely refute the major findings included in Thongchai's *Siam Mapped*, but rather to point out the dangers of taking his findings about the creation of the national borders of Siam and applying them to local concepts of physical borders in Southeast Asia, especially when it comes to people from different ethnic groups with different forms of livelihood and different socio-political and cultural organisation.

In addition, the ethnographic data presented here about the Brao indicate that it is incorrect to present the spatial concepts of people in mainland Southeast Asia simply in terms of the dichotomy between pre-colonial and colonial time periods. As Newman and Paasi (1998) have noted, boundaries are part of the discursive landscape of social power, control and governance, which extends itself throughout society and which is produced and reproduced through various social and cultural practices. Thus, ethnicity and associated social organisation are important when it comes to spatial concepts. Moreover, it is clear that the livelihoods of the Brao, as swidden cultivators and gatherers of forest products, have been central to the fact that the Brao may well, as has been argued here, have placed more importance, historically, on territories and physical borders than their lowland neighbours. These livelihoods have, arguably, had a significant role in the development of the particular type of egalitarian social system that the Brao have adopted. Just as the livelihood and social organisation of the Brao differ from those of others, the Brao had spatial concepts that coincided neither with those of Tai-language speaking groups in pre-colonial times nor with those introduced to the region by Western colonial powers. Thus, the data suggest that it is important not to assume that different ethnic groups in Laos or other countries in Southeast Asia live by the same spatial norms. There are probably other conceptual frameworks related to space that include similar concepts to the Brao concept of *huntre* in Laos and the wider region, among other upland peoples who practice swidden agriculture and for whom forest resources are important. However, the overpowering influence of Western ideas about space, and growing trends that are leading to a globalisation of space and a harmonisation of what were in the past different forms of social organisation and a different concept of space, even in relatively remote parts of southern Laos, mean that it is likely that many aspects of Brao spatial organisation will change along with the systems of social organisation that are fundamentally linked with them.

Paradoxically, this critique of Thongchai actually builds on his original thesis, by encouraging us not to assume that spatial organisation is always the same, while at the same time cautioning against over-applying one of his major conclusions – that which relates to the lack of physical geographical borders during pre-colonial times.

CHAPTER 8

The Ruins, the 'Barbarians' and the Foreign Princess

Heritage, Orality and Transethnic Imaginary in Northern Laos

OLIVIER ÉVRARD AND
CHANTHAPHILITH CHIEMSISOURAJ

As in many other remote areas in Northern Laos, the origin of the ruins and material scattered around the small town of Vieng Phu Kha[1] is the subject of questions and speculation among historians and local people alike. Because of the scarcity of written sources, historians recognise that if 'the historical importance of Vieng Phu Kha is well attested [...]', particularly in documents from the nineteenth century, '[...] this *müang* is probably one of those which, in Laos, still conceals the most mysteries' (Lorrillard 2008: 134). As for the local populations, they attribute the origin of the ruins to invaders who came either from the Burmese banks of the Mekong (Man, Ngiu), or from Chinese regions (Ho), or even from northern Thailand (Yuan) without, however, placing them in a well-defined chronological framework. This imprecision is not simply due to the scarcity of written documents or to the absence of a very extensive genealogical memory among local people, most of whom are Tai (Yuan, Lue) or Mon-Khmer (Khmu, Rmeet,[2]

1. The toponym Vieng Phu Kha refers to one of the five districts of the current province of Luang Nam Tha (north-western Laos), as well as to the small town that forms its geographical and administrative centre by grouping together three villages: Ban Thiao, Ban Dong Vieng and Ban Mai. The last two were created in 1974 while Ban Thiao claims an older origin.
2. The name is usually written 'Lamet' but it is the Lao-ised version of their autonym Rmeet.

Samtao) speakers. It is mostly the result of the chronic instability that this region has experienced and of the numerous population displacements carried out over the last few centuries by the regional powers' armies and, since 1975, by the communist regime in Laos.

However, there is still, today, a wealth of oral literature relating to the foundation of the town of Phu Kha and explaining the origin of its name. The fact that this has been neglected by historians until now is no doubt explained by the difficulties encountered in carrying out field surveys in this region over the last few decades. It is probably also a consequence of the lack of credit generally given by historians to oral sources and the difficulties associated with their interpretation without a solid ethnographic background.

This chapter presents the results of ethnohistorical research undertaken between 2009 and 2012 in several villages within Vieng Phu Kha district.[3] It analyses the various versions that exist of the original myth of the ancient walled town; and then goes on to analyse the descriptions provided by Khmu, Tai Lue and Samtao villagers of a ritual they performed regularly until the early 1970s for the guardian spirit of the locality. My aim is to supplement Lao 'official' history, which is somewhat deficient, using oral sources (a much-needed effort everywhere in Laos) and also to understand how the inhabitants relate the present to the past. More broadly, I wish to bring to light an imaginary common to both Tai and Mon-Khmer populations in this region and to contribute to building a transethnic (as opposed to an interethnic) approach to understanding cultural dynamics.

The Origin of Vieng Phu Kha: Two Legends

Covered by vegetation and scattered on the foothills, the ruins of the Vieng Phu Kha Plateau are difficult to access and not all of them have been identified or even precisely located so far. On the western and northern perimeters of the present township, there are a number of relatively small stupa, most of which are isolated from each other. A site known as Vat Bo Kung on the top of a small hill is now covered by vegetation; while another site a little further north, known as Vat

3. The surveys were part of a project funded by the National Research Agency entitled *Sedentarity around the Mekong*, which was carried out in partnership with the National Academy of Social Sciences of Laos and the Faculty of Social Sciences of Chiang Mai University.

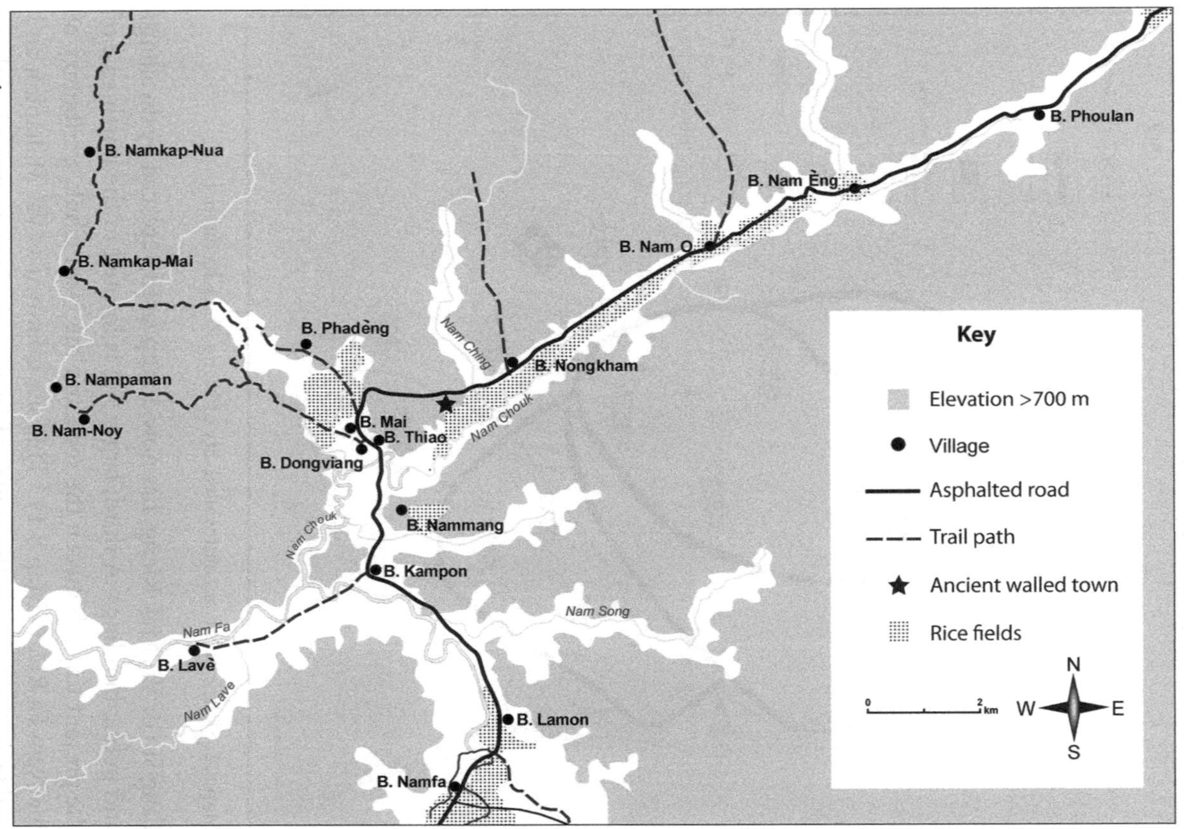

Source: Évrard, 2011

Map 8.1: Centre of Vieng Phu Kha district, Luang Nam Tha Province, Laos.

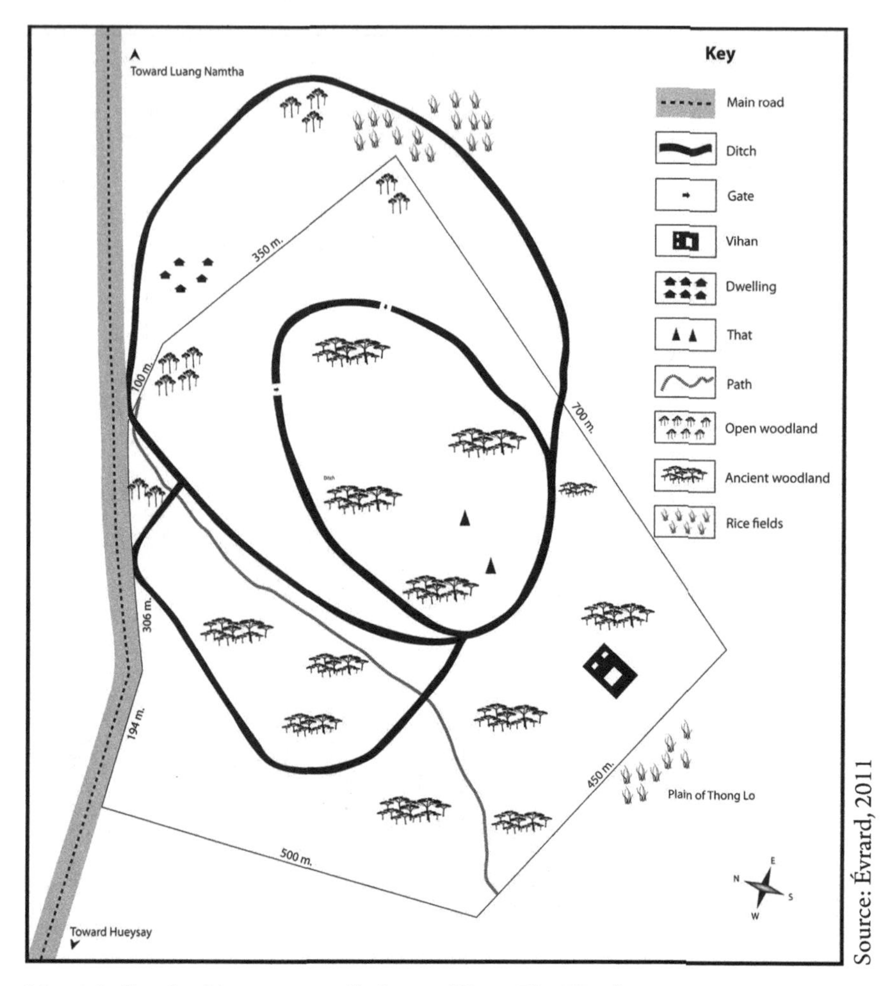

Map 8.2: Sketch of the ancient walled city of Vieng Phu Kha district.

Fang Sin or Vat Mak Kiang, has now disappeared, replaced by dwellings and public buildings. A third, larger site is located to the north-east of the present town, between the road and the Nam Chuk, a tributary of the Nam Fa River (Map 8.1).[4] This site is known as Vat Mahaphot and oral tradition has it as the centre of an ancient town organised in three concentric circles, 'the first for the monks, the second for the soldiers and the third for the craftsmen'.[5] Three circular ditches can be seen here,

4. Other remains of religious buildings are said to exist a few kilometres further south, along the Nam Fa River, but also northwards towards Muang Long.
5. *Vieng* means a village or a group of villages protected by a fortification, usually a circular moat flooded with water connected to a main stream nearby.

as well as the remains of ramparts and brick buildings with religious functions, probably including an assembly hall (*vihan*). The remains cover, in total, an area of more than 40 hectares (Map 8.2). On the north side, the ditches are adjacent to the main road and face a cliff known as Pha Huak, clearly constituting a kind of strategic barrier to control the main track and access to the rice fields. On the east side, the ditches run along the Nam Ching, a small tributary of the Nam Chuk that is used to irrigate the neighbouring rice fields. On the south side, the hill on which the site is situated overlooks the plain of the Nam Chuk, where there are a number of ovens, one of which has several chimneys, within 100 metres of the ditches. Some of the ovens have been damaged by the recent expansion of rice fields on the plain. This part of the site is known as Thong Lo, (*thong*: flat place; *lo*: wheel, turn, roll, turn) and is said to be a former bronze drum-making site, although the remains found nearby tend rather to suggest artisanal production of pottery, ceramics and glassware.[6]

Oral tradition attributes a leading role to the Khmu populations (formerly known, together with the enslaved populations of the valleys, as Kha) in the foundation of the town of Vieng Phu Kha, a role recognised by the Tai populations and which is supposedly at the origin of the toponym. Nevertheless, there are divergent views on this matter. One relatively minor issue is rooted in the linguistic puns that are possible due to the monosyllabic and tonal languages spoken in the region. Depending on the height of the initial consonant and the associated tone, *phu* can mean 'mountain' (ພູ /p^{h}ú:/) or 'person' (ຜູ້ /p^{h}ü:/); while *pu* (ປູ່ /pū:/) refers to the paternal grandfather.[7] Similarly, the word *kha* can, depending on the height of the initial consonant and the associated tone, refer to the populations formerly enslaved by the Tai and more widely all those living outside the *muang* in its mountainous dependencies (ຂ້າ /k^{h}ä:/); or it can be part of a word that refers to a grass with a green and

6. For a discussion of traces of ancient metallurgy and oral traditions related to bronze drum-making among neighbouring Rmeet and Khmu highlanders of Northern Laos, see Évrard et al 2016.

7. In Lao, the letter ພ transcribes an aspirated sound labia (/p^{h}/) and the letter ປ an unaspirated sound labia (/p/). But in Tai Yuan and Tai Lue the letter ພ in Lao is pronounced as an unaspirated sound labia (/p/, i.e. as the ປ in Lao). The Tai Lue or Tai Yuan pronunciation thus allows the confusion between 'phou' and 'pou' on which the second of the two mythical frames mentioned below is based.

red top that is commonly called 'straw grass' (ຫຍ້າຄາ /ɲȁ:kʰá:/, *Imperata cylindrica*). It is the latter meaning that was adopted by the Lao State and used in the transcription of the toponym. Vieng Phu Kha thus became the 'town of the straw grass mountain' (ວຽງພູຄາ /wíaŋpʰú:kʰá:/), a choice that avoids any pejorative connotation for some inhabitants but contradicts what oral tradition relates.[8]

A second, and more serious, difficulty lies in the fact that there are two intertwined mythical frameworks within which the role of the town may be understood. The first makes Vieng Phu Kha a fortified town (*vieng*)[9] built by foreigners (Man or Ngiu or Ho or Yuan, depending on the version) and then placed, after their departure, under the control of the mountain populations, in gratitude for the help they had given to those who had built the town – hence the name 'town of the Kha' or 'town of the barbarians' (ວຽງຜູ້ຂ້າ /wíaŋpʰȕ:kʰȁ:/). The second mythical framework attributes a central role to a female character of Tai origin who, through her alliance with a local hero, succeeds in convincing the mountain people to settle on the plain and build a town there. The full toponym then becomes Vieng Pu Kha Ya Tai (ວຽງປູ່ຂ້າ ຍ່າໄທ /wíaŋpū:kʰȁ:ɲā:tʰay/), which means 'town of the Kha paternal grandfather and Tai paternal grandmother' or 'town of the Kha and Tai ancestors'. The first mythical framework is more related to Khmu oral tradition, while the latter appears more frequently in stories told by Tai Lue storytellers.[10] It is in the context of this deliberately simplifying

8. The official transcription adopted by the Lao State gives the toponym the same meaning as that associated with Doi Phu Kha (ดอยภูคา) in Nan province, Thailand, thus introducing, certainly erroneously, the idea of a historical relationship between the two toponyms. In any case, nothing in the oral traditions of the two regions supports such a hypothesis for the time being.

9. In the absence of serious archaeological research, it is difficult for the moment to know the extent and nature of these fortifications. Only the three circular ditches are clearly visible today

10. The differences in meaning between the three toponyms are based on clearly differentiated lexemes in terms of both writing and pronunciation in standard Lao: opposition between ພູ /phú:/ 'mountain', ຜູ້ /phȕ:/ 'person' and ປູ່ /pū:/ 'paternal grandfather' on the one hand, and between ຄາ /khá:/ 'straw grass' and ຂ້າ /khȁ:/ 'wild, from a mountain tribe, from the kha ethnic group' on the other. But what is true in standard Lao writing and pronunciation is not necessarily true at the level of local speech and it is possible, even probable, that the passage from one lexeme to the other can be explained by local particularities in terms of phonetics and tonal systems. Thus Volker Grabowsky (personal communication September

perspective that I present the following two versions of the myth. The first was provided in 2008 by Tao Rot Vongpassuk, an inhabitant of Ban Phu Lan, a Khmu village (moved to the valley in 1985) that occupies a special place in local mythology.

> A procession arrived from China[11] with a total of 3,000 people from different ethnic groups led by a leader named Chao Muen Sin.[12] All these men stopped at the place where the town is today. They dug canals, built ramparts, installed the *muang* and then left for Chiang Mai. But before establishing the *muang* here, they had to face three fierce beasts: a snake, a wild elephant and a tiger, which were manifestations of the spirit of the place. Chao Muen Sin called for volunteers to kill them, promising a reward. Two men volunteered, Saen Khunkuen, a villager from Phu Lan, and Muen Klao Klao[13], a villager from Kon

2011) points out to me that if in Lao, the letter ພ transcribes an aspirated deaf lip (/ph/) and the letter ປ an unaspirated deaf lip (/p/), in Tai yuan and in Tai read the letter corresponding to ພ Lao is pronounced as an unaspirated deaf lip (/p/, i.e. as the ປ Lao). The pronunciation in tai lue as in tai yuan thus allows the equivalence between /phu:/ and /pu:/ in the passage from /phú:/ (mountain) to /pū:/ (paternal grandfather). Furthermore, Michel Ferlus (personal communication October 2011) made the following remarks to me: it appears that Viang P(h)or Kha was originally a Yuan toponym. Karl Gustav Izikowitz (Lamet, Hill Peasants in French Indochina) notes 'Viang Pou Kha' (map p. 11); he also places great emphasis on the Yuan influence in the region (Izikowitz 2001). The toponym ວຽງພູຄາ / víaŋphú:khá:/ 'city of the mountain of straw grass' seems to be the Lao translation of the Yuan expression, a correct translation both in terms of meaning and phoneme equivalence. The toponym ວຽງຜູ້ຂ້າ /víaŋphù:khà:/ 'city of the Kha' seems to be the Khmu's interpretation of the Lao expression. Only an examination of the tonal system of Lao in this region and of the Khmu khuaen in question (all the Khmu dialects in the region have two tones) would make it possible to say whether this interpretation is due to a misidentification of tones when passing from one language to another, or whether it is due to popular etymology. And in the toponym ວຽງປູ່ຂ້າຍ່າໄທ /víaŋpū:khà:ɲā:tháj/ 'quoted from the paternal grandfather Kha and the paternal grandmother Tai', the first three syllables could very well represent the Yuan pronunciation phonetically noted in Lao script. Here again, to be sure, it would be necessary to be able to compare the Lao tonal system of this region with that of Yuan. I would like to thank Volker Grabowsky and Michel Ferlus for providing me with these comments as well as Gérard Fouquet for helping me to write this footnote.

11. Another rather similar version collected in the village of Nongkham mentions the arrival of 'Ho people'.
12. The name is pronounced Cao Muen Chin by the Khmu Khuaen and by the Lue, but Cao Muen Sin by the Lao.
13. The Tai languages do not have the consonant group 'kl' but the storyteller here was of Khmu origin.

> Talong.[14] They killed the elephant by cutting off its trunk with two swords that they had forged themselves and used as scissors: deprived of its trunk, the elephant ended up dying of hunger. Then they killed the snake by using a bamboo around which the animal wrapped itself, thus becoming an easy prey for the two hunters. Finally, they killed the tiger, which was attracted by the smell of the snake's blood. This gave them the right to ask for a reward. Muen Klao Klao asked for a gold necklace that went around his neck three times. This was a ruse and proof of his greed, for he had a goitre. Sen Khunkuen first asked for an elephant but was unable to lift it. Then he asked for land: he was given the *muang*, the whole territory from Thong Lo to Kiu Sala. But the Khmu could not live on this plain because they had killed the spirit of the place and so their attempts to cultivate the land failed. That is why they let the Lao live there. Times have changed since 1975 but the Khmu continue to live on the periphery of the *muang*.

The second version is taken from a small book published in 2008 in Lao in Vientiane by Boualay Pengsengkham, a member of the Institute for Cultural Research, who collected three oral versions of the original myth and wrote a compilation of them. This text now constitutes, in a way, the 'official' legend of the history of Vieng Phu Kha (see Figure 8.1). The following is a summarised translation:

> Once upon a time there was a princess, the sole daughter of the king of U Neua, who was named Nang On Am. Her beauty was unequalled on earth and all the princes of the neighbouring kingdoms wanted to take her as their wife; but her father would not accept any of them as his son-in-law. The prince of U Tai also wanted to try his luck and asked for the help of his parents in this process. With his son, the king of U Tai sent a procession of officials and soldiers and horses and elephants carrying gold, silver and betel for Nang On Am's father. However, he still refused to give his daughter's hand in marriage. The prince of U Tai decided, therefore, to use trickery. He organised a feast and invited the entourage of the beautiful girl. The officials and soldiers of U Neua ate and drank for seven days and seven nights. Taking advantage of their drunkenness, the prince of U Tai kidnapped the girl, took her on a raft and fled with her and his soldiers. The king of U Neua went after them, fought the soldiers and killed them, but the prince of U Tai managed to

14. Depending on the version, the name of the second village is sometimes different. The name Kmpre, formerly Ban Saphai (today Nam O Tai), is mentioned in the versions collected in Ban Nong Kham.

escape with Nang On Am. One day, she took advantage of her captor sleeping to escape. She walked alone for long days, exhausted, hungry, her clothes in tatters.

One day, she met a hunter from Phu Lan village. After listening to her story, he promised to take her home. However, ashamed of what had happened and afraid that her father would reject her, she refused the hunter's offer and asked him to keep her with him and to consider her as his own daughter. One day, as she looked down on the valley from the heights of Phu Lan village, she asked her adoptive father why the people of this area did not settle in this valley which seemed so fertile and pleasant to live in. He explained that no one could settle there because of three terrible man-eating animals: an elephant, a tiger and a snake. She decided to announce that she would marry anyone who could kill these three animals. Three volunteers of exceptional courage responded to the challenge. Their names were Saen Krin, Saen Pharb and Men Krao.[15] They managed to kill the wild animals and then returned to stand before Nang On Am. However, Nang On Am could not marry all of them, so she decided to challenge them by holding a competition to find the biggest and fastest meat-eater. Only Saen Krin and Meuan Krao agreed to participate, while Saen Phab withdrew from the competition and asked for three gold necklaces in compensation. It was Saen Krin who was the winner and he received the right to marry Nang On Am.

Figure 8.1: Booklet published in Vientiane in 2008 about the legend of Vieng Phu Kha.
→ Colour version on page 380.

Once married, Nang On Am took the villagers of Phu Lan to live on the plains. Their village became a town called Phu Kha, or Phu Kha Ya Tai because their ancestors are Saen Krin, a Kha, and Nang On Am, a Lue from U Neua. During the Burmese invasions, the inhabitants dug a moat around the town to protect themselves and for this reason the term Vieng is used today before the name of the town.

15. These are the transcripts used in Boualay Phengsengkham 2008.

In addition to these two versions, there are many other variants, between which there is a whole series of shifts or losses of meaning, of contamination and/or of inversions operating either from one ethnic group to another or between oral and written traditions. For the sake of simplicity, however, we shall first observe that the two versions presented above are opposed to each other on several levels. In the first version, a foreign conqueror from the north, Chao Muen Sin, entrusts a local hero and his descendants with the custody of the town that his men have just built in gratitude for the help they have given in hunting the wild animals that used to infest the place. In the second, a Tai woman exiled from her native region is at the origin of the establishment of the town through her marriage to a local hero. Although in both versions the coming of humans and the foundation of the *vieng* stem from an encounter, this leads to the maintenance of an irreducible otherness in the first version and to the fusion of differences in the second. In the narrative collected in Ban Phu Lan, the Khmu are custodians of an essentially ritual right granted by the foreign founder, who has now become the tutelary figure of the *muang*: however, they cannot live in the valley with the Tai because they have killed the guardian spirits of the place. In the second version, the foreign founder of the first story, Chao Muen Sin, becomes a Khmu villager whose name is transformed by the Lao narrator (Saen Krin). He now also appears as a secondary character vis-à-vis his wife, the Tai foreigner whose charms and intelligence make possible the construction of the town and the establishment of villages deriving from the mountains in the valley.

The myth maps out the world order and either confirms or abolishes a genealogical and geographical distance. As such it has has strong and very contemporary political connotations. The 'official' version, written and published in Vientiane, of the legend of Vieng Phu Kha has, for obvious political reasons, retained the themes of shared ancestry and shared residence, while the narrator of the first version, who comes from a mountain village that has moved to the valley, insists on maintaining distinct geographical and ritual identities as well as the idea of patronage – of the delegation of power by foreign founders to indigenous populations. The two versions refer to two distinct political and cultural 'models' and to two different interpretative historical grids for local populations: the first emphasises a principle of dissimilation (creation of a more or less voluntary distance within the same society) and inclusion (hierarchical positioning and inclusion); the second, by contrast, emphasises the assimilation of mountain people and their domestication by the civilisation of the lowlands.

It is tempting to regard the structural and ideological opposition between the two narratives as the result of an historical and ethnic overlap – between an ancient and indigenous narrative of the founding of the town explaining the eminent right of the Khmu to the territory, on the one hand, and a later narrative of Tai origin, on the other. The first is reinterpreted and a feminine motif is added to it – one that is very widespread in Lan Na, Lang Xang and Sip Song Panna literature (for example in classic novels by Nang Phom Hom or Nang Taeng On). This opposition should, in fact, be regarded as a nuanced one; it is likely that these two mythical themes have coexisted for a long time and that they have been nourished both by the vicissitudes of local history and by shared representations and tales among the local populations.

The 'Town of the Savages'

Vieng Phu Kha is located at the intersection of zones of historical influence on the part of the main regional powers (Burmese, Siamese, Chinese and Lao) and also at the intersection of a network of trade routes. It has gone through periods when it was under the tutelage of different powers, as well as periods of conflict, abandonment and then re-foundation, all of which may have constituted episodes in the context of which the myth of the founding of the town by a foreign conqueror has been reactivated several times and condensed into a single narrative.

Two Tai populations, the Yuan and the Lue, appear to have alternately controlled and occupied the site. The earliest written records indicate that Vieng Phu Kha was within the cultural and political orbit of the Tai Yuan principalities of the Upper Mekong. The Chiang Mai Chronicle, for example, indicates that this area was one of the 'outer Panna' recognised during the founding of the town of Chiang Saen (also known as Muang Roy, or Chiang Lao) in 1329 by King Saen Phu (Wyatt and Aroonrut Wichienkeeo 1998: 60). In Vieng Phu Kha itself, the only written record consists of a silver leaf that can be dated to 1509, a date that coincides with the period when it was under the political and cultural influence of Lan Na (northern Thailand today). It is very damaged but appears to contain *tham* writing from Lan Na. This includes a reference 'to a dignitary of Chiang Khong (*chao nang khoa [khua] muang chiang khong*), to an ordinance (*atya*) and to a sovereign (*somdet phra pen chao*) who can only be that of Chiang Mai' (Lorrillard 2008: 134).[16] Tai Yuan settlements probably accompanied the political expansion of the Lan Na principalities on the right bank of the Mekong up to the present town of Luang Nam Tha, which the Tai Yuan would have founded at the end of the 16th century (in 1587) according to the local chronicle,[17] then abandoned in the 18th century (1718) before settling there again at the end of the 19th century (1890) (Inpan Chanthaphon 1994: 14). The Lue, on the other hand, migrated to Vieng Phu Kha from the north and the principalities of the Sip Song Panna, again reflecting the regional political situation and economic opportunities, interspersed with phases of conflict and deportation. The Tai Lue settlement as it is today does not predate the end of the 19th century, with the immigration of populations from U Neua and U Tai, in what is now Phongsaly province, who spread out along the road and founded several villages, including the present-day village of Ban Vieng Mai in Vieng Phu Kha but also Tha Fa and Don Chai in Bokeo province.

We also know that this region was affected by the 'Burmese' wars in the 17th and 18th centuries, which were generally accompanied by destruction and mass deportations (Grabowsky 2008: 48–49). In the case of Vieng Phu Kha, however, oral tradition indicates that they also gave rise to the construction of religious buildings (the Vat Mahaphot and Vat Bo Kung are attributed to the Man[18]) and the arrival of new populations,

16. Sarassawadee Ongsakul mentions another dignitary of the same period by the name of Moen Khwa – perhaps the husband or a relative of the dignitary referred to in the inscription found in Vieng Phu Kha? – who was killed in 1523 during a military campaign against the principality of Keng Tung (Sarassawadee Ongsakul 2005: 82).

17. A series of manuscripts in tham Yuan belonging to Cao Noi Si Langka Caiñavong were copied out in the Lao language by his son, Maha Khamsaen Caiñavong, and summarised by Inpan Chanthaphon (1997).

18. Taking up local accounts, Boualay Phengsengkham asserts that the ramparts of Vieng Phu Kha were also built during the 'Burmese wars' but it is not clear by whom – defenders or invaders (Boualay Phengsengkham 2008: 16). Moreover, it is not certain that the conquering armies were, strictly speaking, Burmese; it is much more likely that they were made up of different groups coming from the right bank of the Mekong and culturally close to those already installed in Vieng Phu Kha.

particularly those now living in the village of Ban Thiao, near the ruins of the Vat Mahaphot, who claim a Samtao identity.[19] This ethnonym, which is rare in Laos, refers to populations that are culturally and linguistically close to the Palaung and found mostly west of the Mekong. The term seems to have originated as a political category[20] for a semi-autonomous mountainous territory near the town of Kengtung in the Shan States, which Francis Garnier reported in 1870 as having a population of about 10,000 (Garnier 1873: 416). It was known throughout the region as a place where firearms were made from iron bars brought by Chinese caravanners: 'the Doï [Doi] Samtao produced 3,000 rifles a year and gave about 200 to the King of Xieng Tong [Kengtung] as a sign of allegiance' (Garnier 1873: 416). During his visit to Vieng Phu Kha, Alfred Raquez (2000 [1902]: 270) noted that Samtao men were 'seriously armed' and described a New Year's ceremony 'in which a monk blessed the rifles and swords placed before him'. The Samtao now settled in Vieng Phu Kha may have been originally mountain mercenaries recruited by the invaders and then left in the area after its conquest to ensure control.[21] It is, in any case, remarkable that the use of this ethnonym has continued despite the fact that these groups have largely assimilated to the Tai and Khmu and have even lost their original language. Their role in the ritual for the tutelary spirit of Vieng Phu Kha (see below) undoubtedly contributed to this, as did their practice of Buddhism, which they attribute to their Burmese heritage.

While little is known about the consequences of the long 'Burmese' domination of this region, more is known about the events of the 19th century. The armies of the principality of Nan, in Siam, conducted three large-scale military operations in 1804–1805, 1812–1813 and 1830–1831 in the north-western regions of Laos, each time involving massive population displacements. The 1812 campaign in particular contributed to a demographic disaster, with more than 6000 prisoners

19. The Phunoy, a Tibeto-Burmese speaking group most of whom now live in Phongsaly province, have also kept the memory of their move to Vieng Phu Kha (Bouté 2005: 74).

20. In Burmese, the term 'Sam' refers to the Shan.

21. Some inhabitants of Ban Thiao say that they were once called Kha Khet or Kha Khang because of their migration history: having arrived in Vieng Phu Kha with other groups, they did not go with them when they left, and they thus remained 'in the middle of the path'.

'brought to Siam from Muang La, Muang Phong, Chiang Khaeng and Muang Luang Phukha' (Grabowsky 1999: 238).[22] Thus, when the first Western travellers and explorers arrived in Northern Laos at the end of the 19th century, they found that the region was still very much affected by the depopulation that followed the Siamese wars. In Vieng Phu Kha, where, in 1894, 'only one or two unhabited wooden huts remained' (Lefèvre-Pontalis 1902: 153), they mentioned abandoned rice fields (McCarthy 1994 [1900]: 156; Lefèvre-Pontalis 1902: 153), the insalubrity of the place and the threat of tigers (Raquez 2000: 237). They also underlined the instability of the settlements along the track and in particular the multiple displacements of the Tai Yuan and Tai Lue villages, which had alternately occupied the region, in response to factors arising from conflicts between the regional powers. Pierre Lefèvre-Pontalis noted, for example, that the Tai Yuan, who had resettled in Vieng Phu Kha shortly before his first visit in 1893, had already left on his return a few months later, and that at the same time Tai Lue migrants had begun to cultivate old rice fields again on various sites nearby (Lefèvre-Pontalis 1902: 153–155).

Being a commercial crossroads as well as a place of geostrategic significance (the French colonisers briefly made it the command centre of the Upper Mekong region between 1896 and 1901), the Vieng Phu Kha region was thus also in recent history characterised by what may be called 'thwarted sedentariness', where political conditions never allowed for the emergence of any stable and prolonged occupation of the plateau. The area was periodically emptied of its inhabitants and then reoccupied by enslaved populations (*Kha*, a term designating a status rather than an ethnic identity) installed by the conquering armies or by refugees from war zones.[23] These alternating phases of depopulation and repopulation have resulted in a profusion of ethnonyms, some referring to a geographical origin, others to a particular migratory history and many referring to linguistic mixtures. Thus, when Lefèvre-Pontalis

22. It is likely that the text refers here not only to Vieng Phu Kha but also to Luang Nam Tha, which was sometimes called Luang Phu Kha in the 19th century (Grabowsky 1999: 249).

23. Miao-Yao (Yao, Hmong) or Tibeto-Burmese (Lahu and Akha) speaking populations also arrived during the 20th century from the regions of Muang Sing and Muang Long. However, local oral literature does not attribute to them any role in the founding of the city of Vieng Phu Kha.

went through the village of Ban Yang Neua in 1894, he noted that the inhabitants were Tai Lue refugees (Lefèvre-Pontalis 1902: 153), while in the village of Ban Yang Tai, located a few kilometres further south, the villagers told him that they were 'Kiorr whose ancestors were Khas from the country of Xieng Kheng [Chiang Khaeng] who had taken refuge in Vieng Phu Kha in the face of a Burmese invasion' (ibid.: 290).[24] Alfred Raquez, who passed through the region a few years later, stated that the inhabitants of a village then called Ban Thakhat, close to the current village of Ban Nam Fa, were 'Kha Tiol', that is to say 'Kha belonging to no race', who had arrived in 1870 from Xieng Kheng (Chiang Khaeng) and who spoke a 'mixed patois of Lue and Khmu' (Raquez 2000: 237). It is possible that these constant waves of migrations are partly responsible for the town's name, or at least contributed to its fact that Vieng Phu Kha came to be the name of the town. However, it is to the mountain dwellers, rather than to the inhabitants of the lowlands, that oral tradition relating to the name refers.

In fact, while wars and deportations periodically ravaged the lowlands, they had comparatively little impact on the villages settled on the surrounding ridges (McCarthy 1994 [1900]: 156). Their inhabitants did not take over the rice fields left vacant by their previous occupants near the main track; instead, they continued to practice swidden agriculture on the heights (Lefèvre-Pontalis 1902: 153). Political instability even contributed to the increased autonomy granted to certain Khmu populations, especially those formerly known as Kha Khwaen or those known today as Khmu Khwaen. Within the Khmu populations of Laos, there are subdivisions (called *tmoy* in Khmu language) that sometimes include linguistically distinct but culturally close groups (Rmeet, Samtao for example) and these often correspond, at least in the north-western regions, to relatively precise territories as well as to differences in dialect, technical knowledge, clothing and even religion. I have previously shown (Évrard 2003, 2006 and 2007) that these subgroupings constitute a kind of imprint left by the Tai political systems in these regions, where the zones of influence of different principalities (Lan Xang for the Lao; Lan Na and the principality of Nan for the Tai Yuan; Sip Song Panna for the Tai Lue in particular) have long overlapped.

24. Kiorr is an ethnonym unknown today in the region.

The case of the Khmu Khwaen 'subgroup' is particularly interesting because their territory circled the town of Vieng Phu Kha[25] and they seem to have long held the role of guardians of the margins, in charge of the surveillance of this border region. Alfred Raquez notes that in 1900 the term *khwaen* in Siam refered to an administrative unit, 'a subdivision of the *monthon*' and that 'no one can move without the authorisation of the chief of Khwaen' (Raquez 2000: 247). Pierre Lefèvre-Pontalis observed that the principal Khwaen chiefs, several of whom bear the title of *phanya*, did not hesitate to change the locations of their swiddens and villages to better monitor population movements along the main roads (Lefèvre-Pontalis 1902: 290). Their geographical position, close to a junction of caravan trails and at the intersection of Tai Lue and Tai Yuan political influence, seems to have allowed them to retain a great deal of autonomy. Thus, at the end of the 19th century, when they were theoretically under the tutelage of the principality of Nan, the Khwaen chiefs no longer paid taxes and occasionally came into conflict with the Tai Yuan of Luang Nam Tha but also with the Tai Lue of Muang Sing when the latter moved the boundary markers or claimed to control more directly the territory of Vieng Phu Kha. On the other hand, they sometimes gave their help to migrant populations, notably to the Lue families (the ancestors of the current inhabitants of Ban Vieng Mai) who at the end of the 19th century arrived from Muang La by way of the river Nam Se and settled in the region to cultivate the rice fields abandoned by their previous occupants (ibid.: 162).

Today, the Khwaen are still distinguished from the other Khmu sub-groups by their elaborate ritual practices and the fact that there are three religious officiants in most of their villages, whose functions are hereditary along the male line: the first (*lkun*) in charge of the village spirit, the second (*cha*) in charge of spirits outside the village, and the third (*tanang*) explicitly considered to be a medium. While the *lkun* performs the rituals for the village spirit (*roy kung*) at harvest time and for the

25. The ancient Khmu Khwaen territory once occupied the area between the basin of the Nam Ha, a tributary of the Nam Tha, and the basin of the Nam Ngao, which flows into the Mekong. Bounded to the south by the town of Vieng Phu Kha, it extended northwards towards Muang Long, Muang Sing and Luang Nam Tha. It was almost completely emptied of its inhabitants after 1977, during the military operations carried out by the Lao army to secure the area. The northern part of this territory has today been reoccupied by Akha immigrants.

altar spirit (*roy rong*) at sowing time, the *cha* is in charge of the rituals for the mountain spirit (*roy mok*) and for the border spirit (*roy met*), both performed after sowing. The border spirit ritual traditionally brings together a main village and its satellite localities (called *pang* or *sakha*). The rite involves a cow sacrifice and the placing of bamboo stars (*tal-aeo*) at the boundaries of the territory. On such occasions, the priest in charge of the 'outside' spirits invokes pairs of guardian ancestors (which may also include pairs of mountain names), for whom the villagers often recognise a non-Khmu origin, either Rmeet or, more frequently, Tai. Thus in Ban Nongkham the altar of the border spirit hosts the spirits of Chao Un Kaeo and Nang Ole as well as that of their son-in-law Chao Mai and daughter Nang Khamking. The villagers consider them all to be protective spirits of Tai Yuan origin. These spirits, they say, 'descend' periodically into the body of the medium, speak in Lao, say they come from the Nan region of Thailand and ask that the villagers deposit rice bran in front of the village ritual house (*hnting nam*) for their horses.

All of these elements suggest that Vieng Phu Kha has experienced a series of abandonments and refoundations over the last few centuries, accompanied by major movements of enslaved, fugitive or refugee populations and that, at the same time, non-state groups, whether immigrant mercenaries (Samtao) or indigenous highlanders (Khmu), have played the role of allies or observers, who have been more or less autonomous depending on the circumstances. In this context, the story of the founding of the town by a foreign leader who then entrusted it to a mountain hero has been updated several times until it has become a common reference for all the inhabitants. Rather than being a story specific to mountain people and appropriated by the lowland populations in the course of their successive migrations, it should therefore be considered to be a shared narrative whose elements are compatible with the different local cultures and that can be manipulated and interpreted in the context of political discourse.

The 'Town of the Kha and Tai Ancestors': The Myth of a Shared Ancestry

A second story was grafted on to this first mythical framework, which takes up and transforms the first one while at the same time modifying the transcription and the meaning of the toponym. This transformation is probably recent as the new version is mainly found in the oral literature of the Tai Lue populations now settled in Ban Vieng Mai (see Map 8.2), whose ancestors came from the region of U Neua and U Tai (now Phongsaly province) in the 19th century. By contrast with the first mythical framework, this one attributes the main role to a female character and her alliance with a mountain hero.[26] The stories collected from storytellers all follow more or less the same progression: they first describe the curse that strikes a young princess from Muang U, her exile on the water and in the forest, then her meeting with the mountain people and finally her marriage to one of them. They all make explicit reference to the story of Nang Phom Hom ('the young woman with fragrant hair'), a classic novel of which there are many oral and written variants.[27] Here is one of the versions collected in Ban Vieng Mai:

> Our village is named after the story of Phu Kha Ya Tai. We are Lue de Ñot U. Originally the woman was a Tai Lue and the man was a Kha, or Khmu. She was the daughter of the local ruler, Chao Muang U. As she was born with 32 teeth, she was put on a bamboo raft and abandoned. The raft went down the Nam U, up the Mekong, up the Nam Fa, up the Nam Chuk and finally ran aground near a cave not far from our old vil-

26. This theme is unusual in the region. While it is certainly relatively common to find, in Tai language chronicles or legends, mention of a union between a conquering prince and the daughter of a local ruler (see, for example, the account of Chao Fa Dek Noi given by Volker Grabowsky 2008), the opposite pattern is usually mentioned, only to be immediately contradicted. In the legend of Camadevi, for example, the story revolves partly around the foreign princess's refusal to marry Vilangkha, the Lawa chief who is in love with her (Swearer and Sommai 1998). There are also stories about a love affair between a Tai woman and a Kha mountain man, such as the Nang Ua-Nang Malong legend cycle (Archaimbault 1973), but the tragic outcome of these stories underscores the prohibition against such unions. The atypical character of the Vieng Phu Kha legend is further reinforced by the fact that only the Tai Lue versions (and now the 'official' Lao version of the legend printed in Vientiane) clearly mention the marriage of the perfumed-hair princess with the local hero, while in the versions collected from Khmu storytellers this episode is generally omitted.

27. The Lao version tells of the thwarted marriage of a Lao prince with the daughter of the king of elephants, the latter being ousted by an ogress and exiled to the forest with the monkeys before the usurper is unmasked and the spouses are reunited. A similar plot is found in the Yuan and Isan (north-eastern Thailand) versions. However, in the Lue, Khwaen and Shan versions, Nang Phom Hom becomes the wife of the hero, an orphan whose cowardice and stupidity contrast with his wife's courage and intelligence. Variations are also present in Siamese and Khmer environments (Peltier 1995: 26–29).

> lage. One of the Kha villagers saw this beautiful young girl near the entrance of the cave and alerted the others. They all gathered around her, all wanted to marry her. The chief of the Kha calmed them down and told them that whoever wanted to marry this beautiful young woman must first rid the area of the three terrible wild animals that were preventing people from living there in peace. Three hunters collaborated to kill the wild animals and then a buffalo sacrifice was organised. Of the three hunters, only Chao Muen Sin managed to finish the meat he had been served.[28] He became the husband of Nang On Am. Old Thongsi is the descendant of the union of these two. He is the *chao cham* of our village.

In Bun Neua, where the inhabitants of Ban Vieng Mai say they come from, Vanina Bouté collected the following version in the village of Ban Yo (Bouté 2005: 120):

> The King of the Sipsong Panna had two daughters. The younger one had scented hair, so she was called Nang Phom Hom. One day she cut off a lock of her hair, wrapped it in a leaf and let it drift on the Mekong; the lock arrived in Luang Prabang. The son of the king of Lan Xang, who found it, decided that the one to whom the lock of hair belonged would be his wife. After much searching, he was told that she was one of the daughters of the Sipsong King Panna. The king sent an emissary to ask for the princess' hand in marriage. However, the father of the princess did not want to marry off his younger daughter before his elder daughter, so he concocted the following scheme: the younger daughter's fragrant hair was cut off and the eldest was made to look like her. She left for Luang Prabang accompanied by a large party of Ban Yo people whose specialty was weaving and many Kha (slaves) [...]. But after a few months, the princess' hair lost its perfume and she still had no children. The king's son repudiated her and the princess left with her retinue up the Nam U and settled in Ban Yo.

The transformation of the myth between the points of departure and arrival of the migration of the Tai Lue villagers takes place through a series of inversions and tricks. While the Ban Yo version tells of the failed marriage of Nang Phom Hom's elder sister to a Lao prince, the Ban Vieng Mai version develops the theme of the successful marriage

28. Hence his name: 'Chao Meun Sin' in Lao and 'Chao Meun Chin' in Tai Lue – literally 'the one who can eat several *meun* (1 *meun* = 1.2 kg) of meat (*sin/chin*)'.

of Nang Phom Hom herself (now Nang On Am[29]) to a native Khmu. The first presents exile on the river as the ultimate consequence of a usurpation of identity (an act of culture) and of a broken alliance, the second as the consequence of a physical trait (an act of nature) and as the preamble to a happy alliance.[30] Simultaneously, the initial version of the myth of Vieng Phu Kha is also altered: Chao Muen Sin, the foreign conqueror, is now presented as one of the Khmu hunters (they are now three instead of two) and the future husband of the Tai princess. These modifications clearly reflect the need felt by newcomers to link two very different mythical frames, one imported from their region of departure, the other found on their arrival in Vieng Phu Kha. Several clues suggest, however, that elements of the new version were already present in the local culture. In other words, the success of this mythical graft can be explained not only by the ingenuity of the Tai Lue storytellers but also by the existence of an imaginary common to several populations.

The theme of an exiled princess on a raft is the local version of a theme widely used in mythology throughout Southeast Asia: one of female power exerted first over the aquatic world before extending over the male, terrestrial world (Przyluski 1925: 283). This idea appears to be particularly prevalent in Tai societies, but it is also found in the oral literature of (present-day) mountain populations. Among the Khmu of the Nam Tha basin and of the Vieng Phu Kha Plateau, it gave rise to the myth of Ya Phan Phaeng.[31] The numerous versions collected in this region deserve a comprehensive study that would go beyond the limits of this chapter. Here I will present only a broad outline of the myth. Ya Phan Phaeng is presented as a stranger with supernatural powers who ar-

29. None of the storytellers we met knew the origin of this name. According to some, it would come from the onomatopoeia pronounced by the princess tai in front of the winner of the competition of the biggest eater: 'am lae!' a contraction of 'am laeo' (แล้ว) literally 'well, it's over!' or 'he's done with everything!'

30. Exile on a raft from Nang On Am echoes other Tai myths: for example, that of Chao Fa Ngum, left adrift on the Mekong due to a malformation (he was born with 33 teeth); and that of Chao Fa Dek Noi, son of a king of Chiang Rung, who had to leave his native region on a boat and married a Kha princess (Grabowsky 2008).

31. *Ya* in Khmu: mother's mother or father's mother and any female person of equivalent rank. By extension: female ancestor. The term also exists in Lao, pronounced ñya, but it refers specifically to the father's mother, while the mother's mother is called *mae thu* or *mae thao*.

rives in the region by going up the river. She prepares (*phaeng* in Khmu) or repairs (*paeng* in Lao, ແປງ) the landscape and shares (*phan*) the territory between the multiple villages. Her encounter with the inhabitants is associated with a challenge (and a feast) from which the inhabitants of Mongklang, a Khmu village now settled not far from the banks of the Nam Tha, in the district of Nalae (Luang Nam Tha province), emerge victorious. It is in that village that the following version was recorded:

> The men received a message from heaven one day telling them that an important person was coming, that they had to find a buffalo and take out the bronze drum to welcome him. It was at this time that Ya Phan Phaeng went up the Nam Tha. His brother, Ai Tramal, and his sister, Ya Phan Kluep, caused havoc everywhere they went. The first went up the Mekong and never stopped making war with his seven-bladed sword. The second went up the Nam Baeng valley from Pakbaeng, bringing with her seven tigers that devoured men and destroyed everything. But Ya Phan Phaeng went up the Nam Tha with a seven-handled spade to dig and find tubers to share with everyone, because there was a famine! She shaped the landscape, created the rivers and mountains, and shared the land among the inhabitants. She showed us how to follow the cycle of the seasons and how to share tasks between men and women. [...]
>
> When she arrives, the villagers gather and prepare a feast. They have a contest for the biggest eater and the best jar of alcohol, and each time we (the villagers of Monklang) win the challenge with our cunning. Ya Phan Phaeng then decides to put us all to the test and asks us to close our eyes. She raises her skirt, sits down on the sand of the bank and, after lowering her skirt, asks around who will be able to recognise the footprint on the ground. A smart guy from our village, Ta Saeng Ngan, who had cheated and looked between his fingers, answered that it was the imprint of her vulva. Ya Phan Phaeng gave him her metal helmet as a gift and before she left, she asked the villagers of Mongklang to sacrifice a white buffalo for her every three years. And so we continue to this day to drink and eat in her honour.

There are two distinct parts to the story. The first is a poem in verse (*trnem*[32]) that emphasises the creative actions of Ya Phan Phaeng, which are in contrast to the destructive actions of her brother and sister in the nearby river valleys. The poem tells how the world was created and

32. On poems and their sung versions in Khmu culture, see Lundström and Damrong Tayanin 2006 and Lundström 2010.

organised. It attributes to this female character the configuration of the landscape, the agrarian calendar and the sexual division of tasks. It echoes other accounts collected from Khmu story tellers in the same region in which men owe to women or a woman (in this case almost always a grandmother or widow) the invention of housing, animal husbandry, funeral rites or the sharing of meat and fish (Lindell et al. 1995: 12–18). The second part, in prose, uses the register of the saucy farce and involves a frequent character in Khmu oral literature: the joker or malicious person, here called Ta Saeng Ngan, who is also found in Lao tales under the name of Siaeng Miaeng. This part explains, in comic fashion, the origin of the rite performed in the past every year for the spirit of Ya Phan Phaeng in the village of Mongklang (now Ban Phou Khang).[33] This took place after sowing near a rocky hill where the helmet once offered by Ya Phan Phaeng to the villagers is said still to be found today. The meat of the buffalo was then shared among all the participants, and pieces were also sent to numerous villages, Khmu but also Rmeet.

As one moves away from the village of Mongklang, the content of the myth changes. Towards the east, in Khmu Rok territory, the emphasis is on the magical powers of Ya Phan Phaeng and in particular on her ability to 'cook the earth' to make it more fertile.[34] Towards the west and the plateau of Vieng Phu Kha, on the other hand, a link is made with the story of the princess with fragrant hair. The following version, collected in Ban Phu Lan, is particularly valuable from this point of view because it is a link between the two mythical frames.

> There was once a Khmu king in Luang Prabang named Chao Luang Mung Lang Moi. He had three children, two girls and a boy: Nang On Am, Nang Phan Phaeng and Ai Phama. One day, he decided to go up the Nam U and ask for the hand of Nang Phom Hom, daughter of the king of the Muang U, whose hair, which had floated in the river to Luang Prabang, had bewitched him. When he arrived there, he was refused by the beauty and failed to seduce her. He then made the princess' entou-

33. No longer practiced since the early 1980s, this rite used to involve at least two villages, Ban Mongklang and Ban Saensrae. Damrong Tayanin (1994: 28) mentions the practice of the rite but says nothing about the myth related to it.

34. The magical powers attributed to Ya Phan Phaeng explain why the land in the Khmu villages of eastern Nam Tha is 'black' and fertile, while the land in the villages west of the river is 'white' and poor. Some versions connect with other myths, such as the creation of opium.

> rage drink for three nights and three days, then kidnapped her while her protectors were drunk. When they came to their senses, they went after her. They offered a feast to the kidnapper, but the kidnapper ate and drank for seven days and seven nights without getting drunk and without giving them the opportunity to take the princess back. So they had to resolve to fight; and they won the battle. The king was killed and the princess returned to her kingdom. The children of Chao Long Mung Lang Moi had to flee from Luang Prabang. The son went up the Mekong river, Nang Phan Phaeng went up the Nam Tha river, Nang On Am went up the Nam Fa river and came to our region.
>
> She stopped at different places, and each time she challenged local villagers with riddles. For example, in Ban Punahiaen, she asked a man to climb a tree halfway up and then she asked, 'Will he keep going up or will he go down?' A villager from Kon Tlong replied, 'No matter what happens, he will come down eventually', and he was the winner. Further on, she asked everyone to put their hands over their eyes. She took off her skirt, sat down in the sand and then put her skirt back on and asked who could identify the print in the sand. A man from Ban Mongklang, who had cheated by looking through his spread fingers, answered correctly and said it was the imprint of her vulva.
>
> So Nang On Am arrived in the Phu Kha area and asked for two volunteers to free the area of the three terrible man-eater animals, a tiger, a snake and an elephant, who prevented people from living there. Two men, Saen Khun Kuen from Phu Lan village and Muen Klao Klao from Kon Tlong village, volunteered and, after being offered a feast during which Saen Khun Kuen managed to eat three *meun* [around 3.6 kg] of meat, succeed in killing the three animals. As a reward, the Kon Tlong man asked for and received a golden necklace which was wrapped around his throat three times. This was a ruse because he had a goitre. The man from Ban Phu Lan asked for an elephant, but as he could not tame it, he finally obtained the whole territory of Vieng Phu Kha, from Kiu Sala to Thong Lo.

This account of Nang On Am's peregrinations is clearly inspired by the myth of Ya Phan Phaeng: it includes the idea of two sisters and a brother in exile travelling up the major river valleys, the theme of the enormous feast (as a ruse, as a challenge or as a substitute for war), as well as naughty or comical episodes in which a Mongklang villager plays the role of the joker. The narrative also includes elements specific to the Nang Phom Hom myth (geographical origin and royal status of the female character, mention of fragrant hair) and takes up in its last part the theme of the hunting heroes that led to the founding of the town of Vieng Phu Kha. The teller of the myth thus proceeds to a synthesis between a local theme or warp (the development of a territory free of the animal spirits that haunt it) and two peripheral wefts which, although conceived by the inhabitants as being typically Khmu for the first (Ya Phan Phaeng) and Tai for the second (Nang Phom Hom or Nang On Am), are in fact part of the same transethnic imaginary.

There is little doubt that the appearance, in its present form, of the story of Nang On Am in the mythology of the people of Vieng Phu Kha is relatively recent and that it is directly related to Tai Lue immigration. On the other hand, the character of Ya Phan Phaeng, although attributed solely to the Khmu oral tradition, occupies a more ambiguous position and clearly stems from a common heritage shared by the Tai and Khmu populations. She is always a foreign character coming from a distant place; and her role in Khmu mythology echoes several of the legends, oral or written, of the Northern Tai people. Cholthira Satyawadhna reports, for example, that the legend of Suvana Khom Kham (on the east bank of the Mekong River, opposite the present-day town of Chiang Saen) attributes to a woman, Nang Indapathana, the creation of a town named Muang Indapatha Nagara Krom Luang, the invention of flooded rice cultivation and the sharing of cooked rice (Cholthira Satyawadhna 1991: 303).[35] The idea of a foreign woman with extraordinary powers founding a town or 'civilising' the natives is also present in the legend of Camadevi as it was written down in the 15th century by a Lamphun monk (Swearer and Sommai Prenchit 1998). Closer to Vieng Phu Kha, in the town of Luang Nam Tha, a Tai Yuan legend mentions two sisters, Nang Khankham and Nang Suthamma, younger daughters of the local sovereign, who perished in the Nam Tha River when they cut down the giant liana that was obstructing its course and causing floods.[36] Finally,

35. The same author mentions that oral tradition in the Nan and Uttaradit regions speaks of a vanished city (Muang Laplae) led by a woman, Nang Phaya Muang Laplae (Cholthira Satyawadhna 1991: 302).

36. A cow sacrifice takes place every year in Ban Vieng Neua (Luang Nam Tha) on the seventh night of the rising moon of the seventh month, for the spirit of the two sisters. A version of the local chronicle collected in this village has been translated into English with the help of Chiang Mai University students. Charles Archaimbault also mentions this legend (Archaimbault 1973: 127).

the very name Ya Phan Phaeng itself resonates in a surprising way with the story of the princess with fragrant hair as it is given in the Isan and Tai Yuan versions of the classic Lao novel: the daughter of Queen Sita and the king of elephants, Nang Phom Hom, had a younger sister, named Nang Phueng Phaeng, who was killed by their pachyderm father, who did not recognise her as his daughter.[37]

The myths about Ya Phan Phaeng and Nang On Am thus seem to belong to the same 'group of transformations', to use the term coined by Claude Lévi-Strauss (1955), the details of which vary according to place and time. In this sense, they refer to a shared cultural background from which contemporary ethnic identities have been nourished and against which they have positioned themselves. They constitute two sides of the same tradition, one oral, mythical and sometimes saucy, the other more literary and Buddhist; this does not exclude the possibility of independent and localised developments, rediscoveries and successive cross-contaminations in the course of history. We can thus understand how the last Tai Lue immigrants who arrived in Vieng Phu Kha at the end of the 19th century were able to import the narrative of Nang Phom Hom from their region of origin and adapt it to the local context. They proceeded to a 'grafting' that altered the form and meaning of the original myth while renewing and extending an older framework already present in the imagination of the local population.

It might be argued that as well as examining the abstract relationships between myths, it is also important to interrogate the local historical conditions that have given rise to them and without which the stories cannot make any real sense. Indeed, the existence of an imaginary common to the Tai and Khmu populations is not enough in itself to explain why the notion of a founding female power has imposed itself in the mythology of Vieng Phu Kha. This idea must also have been nourished by certain events in local history with which the myth has, so to speak, resonated. At least two of these can be highlighted. The older one is reported in the only inscription found in Vieng Phu Kha, already mentioned above, that refers to the visit of a dignitary named Chao Nang Khua Muang Chiang

37. In the version provided by Anatole Peltier (1995: 16–23), the two sisters meet the elephant in the forest and have to balance on its tusks to prove to it that they are indeed its daughters. Nang Phueng Phaeng fails and ends up being eaten by the wild elephant. In the Yuan version of Chiang Mai, the story is known as Jang Prong–Nang Phom Hom, Jang Prong being the king of elephants (ibid.: 23–24).

Khong.[38] The inscription, dated 1509, confirms the long-standing influence exerted by the Tai principalities of the west bank of the Mekong River on this area. It is also the first testimony of the political role that noble women could play at that time, even in remote areas. It should also be noted that the beginning of the 16th century coincides with a period of strong political and cultural influence on the part of the Lan Na polity and with the production of a significant number of Buddhist writings by the monks of Chiang Mai, notably the legend of Queen Camadevi.

There is a second, better-documented and more recent piece of historical evidence of political power being not simply associated with a woman but held and exercised by a woman in this region. When Lefèvre-Pontalis stayed in Vieng Phu Kha in 1893–94, a Khmu Khwaen chief told him that, according to tradition, Vieng Phu Kha and Muang Sing had, in a distant era, 'obeyed the same queen' (Lefèvre-Pontalis 1902: 290). The principality of Muang Sing did indeed exert direct political influence over the Vieng Phu Kha region, particularly in the 18th century, and a track, now abandoned, used to link the two cities directly, avoiding the Luang Nam Tha plain, which was empty of inhabitants for most of the 18th and 19th centuries. The words of the Khmu Khwaen chief most certainly alluded to the widow of the ruler of Chiang Khaeng, Nang Khemma, who, in 1792, led a group of Tai settlers who came to repopulate the Muang Sing plain, deserted after being occupied earlier, in the 16th century. According to local sources, she established a town called Vieng Fa Ya five kilometres south-west of present-day Muang Sing and she was also responsible for the construction of That Chiang Thung, a monument that is still the centre of an important festival at the first full moon in November (Grabowsky 1999: 235).[39]

The myth of a foreign conqueror-builder delegating his authority to the mountain dwellers has been updated several times in the course of

38. Michel Lorrillard, who translated the contents of this inscription, remains cautious about the gender of the visitor. He writes that the inscription refers 'to a dignitary of Chiang Khong (Chao Nang Khoa [Khua] Muang Chiang Khong)' (Lorrillard 2008: 134). Given the title of the character, it seems reasonable to think that the dignitary in question was a woman.

39. Local tradition also mentions another lesser female figure, Nang Bua Kham, a secondary wife of the Prince of Chiang Khaeng, who came to establish new villages in Muang Sing as leader of a group of Tai Neua settlers in the 1860s (Grabowsky and Renoo Whichasin 2008).

the many conquests and abandonments that the region has experienced. Similarly, the idea of a founding female power also echoes certain events in local history. The two intertwined mythical frames must therefore be considered less as a transformation from one to the other (or a replacement of one by the other) than as two distinct conceptions of the territory, one focusing on a historical and geographical separation of identities, the other on an idea of shared ancestry and common residence on the plain. We find here, expressed in the language of myth, the idea of a symbiosis between a political and economic power centred on the lowlands on the one hand and its mountainous peripheries on the other. The former sought to assert itself and expand, not through military conquest but by proposing a cultural model accessible to all those who, regardless of their origin, wished to conform to the geographical, religious and linguistic model that it provided. This universalist impulse was contradicted by historical circumstances (instability, displacement, rejection of the model) and, symbolically, by the need to maintain a frontier, both geographical and civilisational (Scott 2009: 111). This symbiotic relationship is illustrated by the ritual, which, until the early 1970s, gathered all of the villages located near the geographical and historical heart of the *muang* of Vieng Phu Kha.

Table 8.1: Villages participating in the ritual for the *samao* spirit

Current Name	Identity	Former name
Ban Phu Lan	Khwaen	Thong Poch
Ban Nam Sing	Khwaen	Om Sueng
Nam O Tai	Khwaen	Kmprae (or Saphai)*
Nam Aeng	Khwaen	Prlui
Nam O Neua	Khwaen	Ruet
Nong Kham	Khwaen	Tlahon
Pha Daeng	Khwaen	Sanghung
Ban Prang	Khwaen	Kontlong
Ban Thiao	Samtao	Thiao*
Ban Vieng Mai	Read	Vieng (or Lavae)*
To Bokèo	Khwaen	On
To Bokèo	Khwaen	Oich

* Villages from which the three main priests of the ritual came (major priest, chanting priest, sacrificing priest)

An Abandoned Ritual: *Roy Samao*

Until the early 1970s, a ceremony was held every three years (or every seven years, according to informants) for the guardian spirit of Vieng Phu Kha. This was called *phi samao* (Tai) or *roy samao* (Khmu).[40] It took the form of a buffalo sacrifice followed by a procession through the Thong Lo plain that ended not far from the ruins of the Vat Mahaphot. The ritual originally involved about 10 Khmu villages, a Tai Lue village and a Samtao village (Table 8.1), all of which have since changed location and, with the exception of Ban Thiao, have been renamed in recent decades. The Khmu Khwaen villages that once stood on the heights on the outskirts of Vieng Phu Kha are now all located in the valley, at the roadside, following complex migrations, most of which occurred in the mid-1970s and were marked by multiple regroupings, splits and name changes.[41]

The only Tai Lue village involved in the ritual, formerly called Ban Vieng or sometimes Ban Vieng Phu Kha, was originally located on the site of the current village of Ban Nam O, at the junction of the tracks leading to Luang Nam Tha and Muang Sing. It was founded at the end of the 19th century by people from U Neua who had first lived briefly on the banks of the Mekong River (in Hat Vai, a little north of the present-day town of Chiang Khong), before moving to Vieng Phu Kha.[42] Ban Vieng then moved a little to the west during the 20th century, to the site of the present Ban Nong Kham (whose relocated Khmu Khuaen inhabitants now cultivate the rice fields once developed by the Tai Lue immigrants). Like the previous site, it is a strategic one, because it is at the

40. The meaning of the term *samao* is unknown.

41. It would take too long and to a large extent it would irrelevant to provide an exhaustive description of these migrations here, especially since each village consisted of a ritual centre and several satellites, sometimes temporary, and each of these localities may have had different trajectories (for the villages of Pha Daeng and Phu Lan, see Évrard 1996). As a result of these migrations, the former Khmu Khwaen territory has been completely emptied of its inhabitants, who nevertheless continue to travel to the old sites (three to six hours' walk from the road where their current settlements are located) in order to cultivate their swiddens. The new names of their settlements have been chosen with reference to local streams (Nam O, Nam Sing), or cliffs (Pha Daeng) close to the new sites. In some cases, the new toponym is a translation of the old Khmu name (Phu Lan for Mok Potj: 'mountain of bamboo shoots'); more rarely, it is an invention (Ban Nong Kham).

42. Other groups who came from the same region at the same time followed a similar path. See, in particular, Karl Gustav Izikowitz's account of the founding of the village of Tafa, some 50 km south of Vieng Phu Kha (Izikowitz 2004 [1944]: 54).

confluence of the Nam Chuk and Nam Ching streams, allowing control of irrigation for all the rice fields of the Thong Lo plain. In 1962, fleeing insecurity and war, the inhabitants of Ban Vieng settled further south, near a tributary of the Nam Fa, the Nam Lavae, where they founded a village of the same name (Ban Lavae) and gradually developed new rice fields reclaimed from the forest. In 2002, following a flood, the villagers moved again: they settled on the opposite bank of the Nam Fa and the place became Ban Vieng Mai, the name by which it is known today.

For the *roy samao* ritual, all these villages would contribute to the purchase of a buffalo and prepare the various offerings, and each settlement would send one or two male representatives to participate. There were, ideally, 12 officials (see list in Table 8.2) and the same number of assistants. An accurate and complete list is difficult to obtain orally today because few villagers have themselves attended the ceremony. Therefore, the total number of officiants (sometimes 12, sometimes seven) and the terms used to designate them vary from one informant to another. However, there is a consensus on the three most important functions, the only ones that were theoretically transmitted down the patrilineal line: the chief officiant (*mo luang*), considered to be the descendant of Chao Muen Sin and Nang On Am; the sacrificial officiant (*mo hok*, 'master of the spear'); and the reciter (*mo uen* or *mo an chatue*, 'master of incantations'). The first of the three, who was also called *mo cam* (because he 'dipped', (*cam*) the rice in the blood of the sacrificed buffalo before placing it on the altar for the *samao* spirit), came from the Tai Lue village of Ban Vieng Mai. The second came from the village of Ban Saphai, a Khmu Khwaen village formerly known as Kmprae in the Khmu language and which today constitutes the 'downstream' part of the village of Nam O (Nam O Tai).[43] Finally, the reciter came from the Samtao village of Ban Thiao and performed the incantation accompanying the offering to the *samao* spirit using a manuscript written in *tham* script. This manuscript has since been lost but the part containing the incantation as well as the list of officiants and offerings had been copied out by the lay leader of the temple of the present-day village of Ban Vieng Mai. Curiously, the reciter does not appear in the list, although this role is mentioned in the oral tradition.

43. Nam O was formed by the joining together of several villages or segments of villages: Kmprae in 1977, Ruet and Nam Lung in 1978 and finally Saklang in 1994.

The ritual itself lasted only one day, but it was preceded and followed by a day when all participating villages were closed and agricultural ac-

Table 8.2: List of officiants and order in the procession (from the manuscript of Ban Vieng Mai)

Title	Translation
Mo lak, mo choung (a)	Pole Master
Mo sè (b)	Whip Master
Mo dong (c)	Master of the winnowing basket
Mo tang	Chair Master
Mo nam ton khan mak	Betel Master
Mo kup sad	Master of mats
Mo luang	Senior Officer
Mo pha kang (c)	Curtain master
Mo khay	Egg Master
Mo kay	Pool master
Mo khuan	Axe Master
Mo hok (d)	Master of the spear

(a) He 'pulled' (*chung*) the buffalo behind him

(b) He chased away evil spirits with a whip.

(c) He carried a basket for winnowing which was attached to his turban by cotton threads in which the offerings were placed.

(d) He sacrificed the buffalo with a spear.

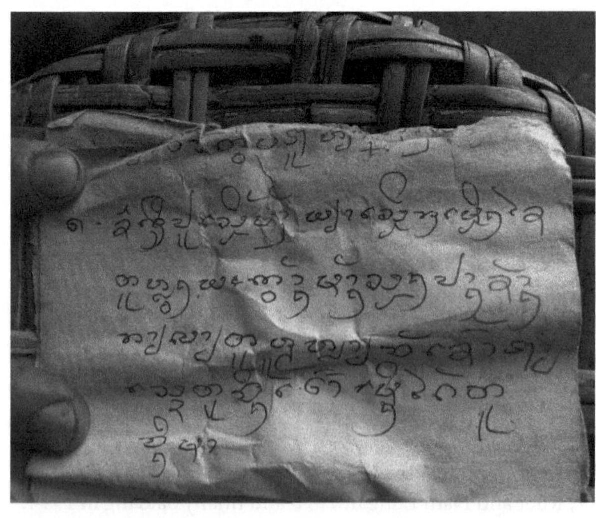

Photo: O. Évrard, 2011

Figure 8.2: Portion of a manuscript kept by the lay leader of Ban Vieng Mai that was used during the *roy samao* ritual. → Colour version on page 380.

tivities stopped. It took place in the eighth month of the Tai Lue calendar (June), just after sowing in the swiddens and at the time of transplanting in the wet rice fields, during the series of three days called *rvai set, moeng kai* and *plek chai.*[44] Officials met in Ban Vieng and then marched in a procession, with the main officiant dressed in yellow. They were followed by the assistants in charge of carrying the various offerings and utensils used during the ritual.

The procession was to the top of a small hill between the present-day villages of Nong Kham and Nam O, at the eastern end of the Thong Lo plain. There is a flat space here, where the participants would erect a sacrificial pole, 12 small altars (or seven depending on the version) and a ritual house (*sala*) decorated with cloth, in which the three officiants from Ban Vieng, Ban Saphai and Ban Thiao sat. The buffalo chosen for the sacrifice had to be black and the first in a line of four (*khuai dam sam nong*). The officiants made three series of three circumambulations around the buffalo, successively passing an egg, a black chicken and an axe over its forehead, and then the animal was sacrificed with a spear. When the meat was shared, the chief officiant of Ban Vieng and the reciter of Ban Thiao each received a thigh, while the Khmu officiant of Ban Saphai kept the head and tail of the animal. An offering of meat, blood, rice, and alcohol was placed on each of the 12 altars by the chief officiant, while the reciter invoked a series of guardian spirits and invited them to participate in the feast.[45] However, the buffalo sacrifice was performed

44. The Tai and Khmu people count and name days and years using two sets of words. The first set consists of 10 terms and the second of 12, which may be pronounced differently depending on the group and region. The decimal cycle is combined with the duodecimal one to produce a series of 60 terms used to refer to specific days and years (Évrard 2006: 383). A similar principle can be found in the Chinese tradition, where the decimal signs are arranged in a cross and referred to as 'heavenly trunks', while the duodenary signs, arranged in a circle, are referred to as 'earthly branches' (Granet 1999 [1934]: 131–133).

45. The text of the prayer, as it was copied out in the manuscript found in Ban Vieng Mai (see Figure 8.2), is difficult to understand, even when transcribed into modern Lao. References to the main characters of the original myth of Vieng Phu Kha, Cao Meun Chin and Nang One Am, are not always obvious and they are mixed up with other names, male or female, and sometimes with toponyms. For example, the names of Nang On Am and Ya Phan Phaeng merge to produce the name Nang Amphaeng, which is linked to the name Nang Ai Kham (or Khamlae), who is presented as her sister. This is obviously a combination of a local theme (Ya Phan Phaeng/Nang On Am) with that of the two sisters who became guardian spirits

Table 8.3: List of offerings (manuscript of Ban Vieng Mai)

Twelve pairs of candles with their holders
A red shirt and a curtain
Mat and pillow
A basket to be woven, a chair, a woven hat
Silver 1,000, gold 100 (a)
A shirt, a skirt, a new headband.
Arec nuts
1,000 cowries, 1,000 arec nut quarters (b)
Alcohol bottles with medicinal plants
One egg, two chickens
A roll of two fathoms of white cotton yarn
An axe, a spear
Wax 1,000, water 10,000 (c)

(a) 1.2 kg of silver and 100 g of gold.

(b) The arec nuts were cut into quarters and strung in a garland.

(c) 1.2 kg of wax and 1.2 l of water.

primarily for the spirit of Chao Muen Sin, while the spirit of Nang On Am was invoked only by the Tai Lue after their return to their village.

Once the meal was over, the procession would return to its starting point, near the 'head' of the Thong Lo plain (*hua thong lo*), to the village of Ban Vieng. There, a small cannon called *lamok*, 'as big as a thigh, as long as an arm', was fired, its lower third sunk into the ground, mouth towards the sky, and its inside filled with a mixture of sawdust, coal and bat guano. The object can still be seen today in the Provincial Museum of Luang Nam Tha, and Raquez witnessed its firing during the Buddhist New Year Festival in April 1900 (Raquez 2000 [1902]: 270). The sound of the detonation resounded throughout the valley and marked the end of the ceremony (some informants report that the *lamok* was fired twice, at the departure of the procession and upon its return). Several villages in the surrounding area apparently had this type of object, but they were often simple bamboo tubes, for single use only, while the barrel used for

of Luang Nam Tha (Nang Khankham and Nang Suthamma), as the name Nang Thammasusada also occurs several times in the text.

Photo: O. Évrard, 2011

Figure 8.3: The cannon used during the *roy samao* ritual.
→ Colour version on page 380.

the *samao* ritual was made of cast iron. It belonged to the village of Ban Thiao and the inhabitants consider it to be a 'Burmese' (*man*) heirloom, which is plausible since the use of cannons called *amrok* or *mibok* is attested in the Burmese archives from the beginning of the 15th century (Sun Laichen 2003: 501–504).

In short, the ritual for the *samao* spirit constituted a common language that established or recreated a reference territory within which identity differences unfolded. Both in concrete terms (through the route taken by the procession) and symbolically (through the geographical origin of the participants) the procession traced out the contours of the Thong Lo plain, the economic and geographical heart of the ancient town, and its mountainous dependencies at a key moment in the agrarian cycle (the beginning of the rainy season). At the same time, the sharing of the meat at the end of the sacrifice resembled a mythopraxis (Sahlins 1981) – that is, a staging of the myth, in which a Khmu hero takes a Tai princess as his wife. The chief officiant, of Tai Lue origin, would receive a thigh from the animal, which, in Khmu ritual terms, placed him, symbolically, in the position of 'wife-giver' (*em*), while the sacrificial officiant, of Khmu Khwaen origin, received the head and tail of the animal, which are associated with the position of 'wife-taker' (*khuey*).[46] The fact that either the reciter or the master of incantations, of Samtao origin,

46. In the Khmu naming system, the term for a mother's brother, *em*, also refers to all members of her lineage, who are considered to be 'donors' of a wife because the ideal spouse is the matrilateral cross-cousin (mother's brother's daughter), real or classificatory. In theory, the symmetrical term *kuñ* (husband of the father's sister)

was also cast as a 'wife-giver', since he received a buffalo leg, indicates the way in which the ritual structure, although based on a dialectical scheme (Tai/Kha, plain/mountain, town/forest, civilisation/wildlife, wife-givers/wife-takers), integrated the accidents of history and the multiple migrations, abandonments and refoundations that had shaped Vieng Phu Kha social landscape. The Tai Lue of Ban Vieng Mai, who arrived late in this area, explicitly took over a pre-existing ritual system in which another Mon-Khmer-speaking Buddhist population had for a time occupied a dominant position, as evidenced by the existence of the prayer book that the new arrivals sought to copy.

Conclusion

An abandoned ritual, lost manuscripts, various scattered and mostly unexplored ruins: Vieng Phu Kha's past has still, to date, largely escaped the scrutiny of historians. The study of oral literature allows some cross-checking with elements drawn from the written tradition, but further research on local sources and comparisons with fortified sites found in northern Thailand and Burma (Berliet 2010) are necessary to establish more precise chronological milestones.

However, the true interest value of origin myths and ritual acts lies less in what they allow us to reconstruct of the past than in what they say about how local populations think about it, with their own language and categories and with reference to specific political or social issues. A myth is not presented as a historical truth but as an 'interpretative scheme' (Sahlins 1985), as an interactive narrative: it offers a grid for interpreting history and at the same time it is constantly altered and updated by events. The latter must therefore be considered 'an interpreted occurrence modifying in return the categories of interpretation' (Naepels 1991: 159). Like a ritual, it plays the role of 'common operator' (Robinne and Sadan 2007), a role through which ethnic identities are positioned and co-constructed in relation to each other. In this context, Vieng Phu Kha offers an example of a transethnic rather than an interethnic system – that is, a context in which ethnolinguistic categories cannot constitute starting points for analysis but, on the contrary, must be related to the common matrix that defines their relevance.

---

could designate the wife-takers, but it is the Lao word *khuey* that is most often used.

CHAPTER 9

The End of Rituals

A Dialogue between Theory and Ethnography in Laos[1]

GUIDO SPRENGER

Some predict that ritual will inevitably disappear, for better or worse, due to the growth of science or rationalism. Others claim that ritual persists or even proliferates, as it is a necessary part of human society or cognitive order. Yet others argue that the disappearance of ritual and religion is only illusory, and that what presents itself as non-religious, even as scientific, is in fact religious and ritual by nature. Yet, although anthropologists are frequently confronted with the disappearance of rituals and cosmological ideas, this is acknowledged far more than it is discussed, being either treated as obvious or ignored.

This chapter offers a perspective within which the discontinuance of ritual is taken seriously as a source of anthropological insight. It has two aims. Firstly, it attempts to specify and formulate a specific question and to situate it within anthropological discourse. Secondly, the question posed is explored in a frame provided by an ethnography of the Rmeet in northern Laos; it is this data that has inspired the formulation of the question. The issue is complex in both regards, the answers presented here at best sketchy and tentative. The dialogue presented here between

1. Initial research was conducted for twelve months (2000–2001) then three months (2002) in Takheung village, Nalae District, with funding from the Deutsche Forschungsgemeinschaft and Münster University. Four additional months (2005) in Takheung, Mbling and Hangdeun (Houeisai) were funded by the Frobenius Institute, Frankfurt am Main and the Institute of Ethnology, Academia Sinica. Thanks for their help in Laos to Chanthaphilith Chiemsisuraj and Khammanh Siphanxay, Institute of Cultural Research. A first version was presented at the conference of the Deutsche Gesellschaft für Völkerkunde in Halle in 2005. Thanks for their comments to Volker Gottowik, Annette Hornbacher and Philip Silverman.

theory and ethnography serves to heighten the level of abstraction in order to make comparison possible.

The questions that are posed here are the following: What are the conditions for the discontinuance or diminution of rituals from the perspective of a specific society? How can the reduction of a ritual system be explained by the ideas at the core of the system?

Definitions and Approaches

The Rmeet (Lamet) are mostly swidden farmers living in the northern provinces of Laos. They are non-Buddhists, speak a Mon-Khmer language and have no traditional organisation above the village level. Rmeet ritual addresses a pantheon of spirits, the most important being the ancestors, house spirits (which are aspects of ancestors), village spirits and diverse spirits of the wilderness. Rituals integrate these cosmic entities with the kinship system, the social structure and the rules of asymmetric marriage alliance (Sprenger 2006).

In using the term 'ritual system', I am referring to the entirety of these integrated forms of social reproduction. My definition of ritual is thus as follows: a ritual is an activity that a particular community acknowledges as being effective in the maintenance or creation of social or cosmic relationships that are vital for the reproduction of this community; this creative or maintaining force gains its efficacy with reference to a higher level in the social or cosmological hierarchy than that represented by the persons or groups for whom the ritual is being performed (Barraud et al. 1994; Barraud and Platenkamp 1990; Iteanu 2005).

This definition hinges very much on the social function of rituals, which, although it has been regarded as debatable (Handelman 2005), nonetheless applies to the phenomena I am concerned with here and highlights those features that need to be taken into account in addressing the question at hand. It is therefore both heuristic and analytical. It stresses that rituals have to be acknowledged – although not unequivocally – but need not be traditional. The 'higher level' is not restricted to metaphysical beings; a marriage in town hall is clearly a ritual, the higher level being the state.

But although the above definition identifies the structural features of ritual, one crucial point for the argument is that social reproduction by ritual can only be achieved through practice, and practice is highly contingent (Tambiah 1985a). Thus, a ritual system should be seen as a set of rules that enables communications, these communications being the individual ritual and social events and also the discourse that surrounds them. One must distinguish between normative statements and explicit rules on the one hand, and those that emerge from observation and analysis on the other. The latter are more complex, as the rules are applied to the specificity of each ritual occasion. While normative statements seem to outline 'structure', observation reveals 'process'. However, from the perspective of a general theory of systems, the difference is less fundamental than it seems. Structures only emerge as repeated practice; they consist of a series of events that is reversible. Processes, on the other hand, consist of irreversible events (Luhmann 1984: 73–74). Both are subject to the same rules in relation to the production of events.

There are many reasons for rituals to be discontinued, and my focus is on the less obvious ones. I will not focus here on straightforward prohibition by officials or missionaries, the decimation or dispersal of communities, or the dying out of specialists. Conversion to a codified, non-ethnic religion is closer to what I will be looking at here. Conversion as a reason for the disappearance of ritual is mainly found among so-called minorities, and it is often promoted by an identity as a disadvantaged people. Although I will not be dealing with the literature on conversion, the problems associated with conversion, and their possible solutions, are comparable to what I am looking at here.[2] Another, related, issue is growing orthodoxy in communities that already belong to a codified religion, but that practice a synthesis of canonical and local ritual. Here, outside influences from authoritative religious centres and leaders may cause the discontinuance of the more local rituals.[3] But the question I am asking is most urgent in cases in which there is no obvious replacement for the system. This is the case for the Rmeet: a minority with a specific ritual system, which gives up part of it without conversion or strong outside pressure.

The discontinuance of ritual is rarely analysed in anthropology because it is usually seen in negative terms: certain things do not happen any more. This is supported by a tendency to stress the passive role of those who stop doing these things – they are often seen as succumbing

2. See, for example, Horton 1971; Cusack 1996.

3. For a general discussion, see Shaw and Stewart 1994.

to outside influence, or as simply falling victim to tedium.[4] Rarely is ceasing ritual considered in active terms, as a motivated decision and an act of cultural creativity. For this reason, the discontinuance of ritual lies in a dead centre of most theorising. Anthropologists tend to fall into two categories with respect to ritual. Those who are interested in understanding it stress its fundamental importance and are hard pressed to account for its disappearance; they tend to focus on the persistence of ritual in either form or meaning, against the odds of historical change (Højbjerg 2002; Platenkamp 1992). Others, less interested in ritual meaning, integrate it instead into general trends of transformation in a given society, often conceptualised in terms of globalisation, culture change or modernisation. These studies engage much less in an analysis of the internal coherence of meaning systems. The two positions represent a more abstract problem: if a system of rituals and representations is meaningful, largely coherent and essential for the maintenance of the society, how could it be stopped or shrink without society and meaning systems themselves falling apart? And if, on the other hand, religion and ritual are nothing but cognitive form and tradition without coherent meaning attached to their detail, why is there any attention to detail among practitioners, and what does the obvious integration of relations and ideas rest on?

To Secularise or Not to Secularise?

The following model attempts to unify these two opposing approaches to ritual – which are, respectively, meaning-centred and transformative. Let us start with the second, which stresses transformation over meaning. With regard to the relationship between the socialist Laotian government and Buddhism, Grant Evans (1998a) speaks of 'secularist fundamentalism'. Theories of secularisation do indeed come to mind in addressing the issue at hand. But can they be extended to the type of ritual systems being discussed here? After all, they are designed to deal with the dwindling influence of codified, non-ethnic religions on social life. The phrase 'non-ethnic, codified religions' serves a mostly heuristic purpose. It covers the traditions of Christianity, Islam, Buddhism, Judaism and Hinduism, often called 'world religions' due to their crossing of national and ethnic boundaries. There are, of course,

4. See, for example, Kroeber 1948: 403.

problems with the term itself – for example, Judaism has a strong ethnic element – but what I would like to emphasise here is the fact that the term serves mainly to differentiate these religions from less codified systems of rituals and representations that are bound up with a specific ethnic identity. In mainland Southeast Asia, for example, the boundary runs between Buddhism, Christianity and Islam on the one hand and the cosmologies of many minority groups on the other. 'Animism' is often used for the latter, but in its generic use, the term is often hardly more than a residual category that depends on its differentiation from so-called world religions.

Beyond this difference, it is difficult to discern characteristics of such systems that are not only defined in negative terms. I would like to suggest some shared characteristics of these systems, features that are relevant both to the Rmeet and to other groups in the region. The first is that ethnic, localised systems often lack written accounts of ritual practices and beliefs. Sometimes, written texts are used for recitals during rituals or as ritual objects, though they do not describe the rituals themselves.[5] This supports change: older versions disappear without a trace as soon as the actual witnesses have died.

Another important characteristic is that these ritual systems are not only associated with metaphysics, but with a 'way of life', covering, for example, types of social relations, economic practices, notions of organisation and leadership that differ from the state. This connecting of ritual or 'religion' with everyday practice is accomplished both by practitioners and by outsiders. A well-known example is the *Akha zang*, the system of rules of behaviour and rituals associated with Akha identity (Kammerer 1990; Tooker 1992). Even when strong links and similarities with neighbouring ritual systems are recognised, the systems are, so to speak, 'ethnicised' and integrated into the identity of a society. Unlike the subjects of secularisation theory, the practice of 'religions' in minority scenarios is often bounded by cultural identity on the outside, while not being functionally differentiated from other aspects of social life on the inside. Among the Rmeet, ritual roles are tied up with kinship degrees, which themselves are determined by marriage rules. Therefore we can say that societies such as the Rmeet are what may be described as socio-cosmic societies, which have a tight integration between social

5. See, for example, Holm 2003; Müller and Obi 1996.

and cosmological relations (Barraud and Platenkamp 1990; Barraud et al. 1994).

But functional differentiation is crucial to the processes that secularisation theories describe. Even when formulated in general terms, like 'disenchantment of the world', these theories are geared to describing the replacement of codified and institutionalised religions by secularist ideologies and practices. This is often thought to be a modern phenomenon. Yet repudiation of ritual is not unique to modernity, but can be found in other societies and historical periods as well. It is clear that these repudiations are based on processes that probably cannot be compared with what secularisation theories describe (Bell 1997: 255). Secularisation under conditions of functional differentiation means that fields like politics, economics, education and medicine develop institutions and terminologies independent of the encompassing cosmology that is provided by religion (Dobbelaere 2002). Even if these subsystems relate in their entirety to religion – for example, when nation-states seek metaphysical legitimation – they are themselves structured by principles that do not immediately relate to some cosmic whole. In this way, religion loses its function as an embracing umbrella structuring the entire society and its cosmology, and is increasingly restricted to a specific section of social life. In a socio-cosmic system such as that found among the Rmeet and other groups, this is not the case.

The necessity of functional differentiation for secularisation theory highlights another difference between what it deals with and the problem at hand here – ethnic diversity. This issue plays a role in all states with regional differences in ritual, even when these rituals are accounted for in terms of a nation-wide religion. This differentiation is not functional; the ritual systems of different groups may relate to each other, but not in the sense of any functional unity at a higher level. Here, the shift from ritual to secular practices is not only a shift from one functional subsystem to another, but also from local practices to (supra-) national ones, from 'old tradition' to (seemingly) universal solutions.

However, there is something to be learnt from secularisation theory about the conditions under which rituals are discontinued. As Peter L. Berger has pointed out, in modern societies functional differentiation was preceded by cosmological differentiation.[6] European secularisation

6. Berger 1967, quoted in Dobbelaere 2002: 36–39.

has its roots not only in a general trend towards rationalisation, but also in the Christian religion itself. Christianity established the idea of a distinction between the sacred and the world: 'the autonomy of the secular "world" was given a *theological* legitimation' (Berger 1967: 124 [original emphasis]). If we look for secularisation in other societies, we may find similar distinctions, but we have to remember that there is no one, single, universal understanding of the 'secular', while 'religion' is contingent. When the realm of the sacred is differentiated from the world, the notion of 'world' is just as specific as is that of 'the sacred'. Therefore, it is the overall cosmological system that initiates the changes that finally reduce its influence and dissolve it. The weakening of religious ideas does not originate outside the cosmological order and then intrudes upon it, as a rationalist, 18th-century ideology would have it. As Berger argues, the separation of religion and non-religion is a product of the encompassing religious ideology itself.

Conditions Under which Rituals are Discontinued

Rituals and social relations form a system in socio-cosmic societies. Elements of this system can only be changed or removed in the context of the system. This ties in with the understanding of ritual, structure and process outlined above. Socio-cosmic systems are not at their core either repetitive or rigidly traditional. In fact, they have to accommodate an almost infinite variety of specific cases, in particular where social relations are concerned. Each performance of a ritual varies with the specifics of the situation and the relations involved, even when the performers identify it as a repetition of a 'traditional' pattern. This is mirrored in the extensive discussions on the correct way of doing things that accompany Rmeet rituals. The potential for change emerges from the cosmology itself because the terms of the cosmological system demand variation. This variation is pushed to its limits when rituals are changed or discontinued. Still, changes must be performed and explained as part of the system. Therefore, even irreversible discontinuances are, at the moment at which they are realised, part of the reproductive pattern that they are supposed to end.

A classic example is Marshall Sahlins' analysis of the abolition of the *tapu* system in Hawaii early in the 19th century (1981, 1985). In 1819, about 40 years after the first – and, for James Cook, fatal – encounter with Europeans, and before the arrival of missionaries proper, the Hawaiian court put an end to the system of ritual and taboos in favour of Christianity. Sahlins explains this as a political calculation made in terms of cosmological power. The decision made sense within the existing system of socio-cosmic representations, although it finally led to its disappearance. This was only possible because ideas about and representations of Europeans were integrated into the system. It was thus not the active influence of Europeans themselves that led to the abolition, but the meaning that was attributed to them by the Hawaiians, especially their ruling class. Rulers competed for Europeans items and identities, but these were couched in terms of spiritual power. Sahlins describes the process as 'an extension from ritual to practical purposes' (1985: 142). This may sound like a major upheaval, a shift from ritual imagination to pragmatic utilitarianism, from structure to agency. But the rift is not as deep as it seems from the point of view of functionally differentiated societies such as in Euro-America: ritual always has practical purposes, and it is only the conception of ritual as practical and useful that opens it up to uses within the entire field of social reproduction, both 'traditional' and 'creative'. There is no substantial break in Sahlins' statement – the extension he mentions is a relatively easy one.

On this basis, we can identify, in the case studies that follow, several modes or conditions for the diminution and discontinuance of rituals. Not all possibilities are covered here; I focus on those cases in which the actors locate the intention to give up rituals with themselves, not with some outside force.

The Rmeet, History and the State

Data on the Rmeet were collected in both rural and suburban villages. The discontinuance and diminution of ritual is evident in both settings, although more so in the suburban one. Everywhere this is a phenomenon that is clearly perceived and reflected upon by the Rmeet themselves. The Lao term *loblang* is used for it, meaning 'to abolish', 'to do away with'; this term is also used in official administrative discourse to describe the ending of 'unmodern' features of society, like illiteracy. The term is complemented by another one: *riid Rmeet* (Rmeet tradition), often employed to explain ritual by referring to the distinctiveness of Rmeet ethnicity.

The major sources relating to the past are the writings of Karl Gustav Izikowitz (1979 [1951], 1985, 2004 [1944]) who conducted research among the Rmeet (whom he called Lamet) from 1937 to 1938. Compared to what I witnessed, he describes the ritual life of the Rmeet as more elaborate in some respects and less so in others. But historical reconstruction offers little in terms of an understanding of how the Rmeet themselves perceive their history. Only their own accounts can elucidate the significance of the discontinuances that have occurred within the meaning system of the rituals itself. The same is true in relation to outside forces. Thus, when speaking about government policies, I do not refer to official documents but to Rmeet depictions of these (Sprenger 2004).

The Rmeet acknowledge both external and internal motivations for ritual change. The external ones are also stressed by scholars dealing with ritual change in Laos (Evans 1998a, 2003a, Goudineau 2000a). The Laotian state officially recognises its multi-ethnic composition and grants each group the right to its own culture (Pholsena 2002). However, there is a certain pressure towards mainstream Buddhism or secularism, which was most explicit between the revolution in 1975 and the end of the 1980s. During this period, the expensive animal sacrifices that were part of ritual practice among many highland groups were strongly discouraged by government agents, who came from both lowland Lao and highland minority backgrounds. A number of better educated people who worked with the administration – village and parish (*tasseng*) headmen – went from village to village both to report the end of the war and to explain the new government's policies. Among these explanations were arguments against ritual, especially animal sacrifice. Although the government was firmly socialist in its early years, it seems that the campaign in highland villages did not employ ideological arguments of the 'religion is the opium of the people' type. The approach taken was, instead, pragmatic: rituals are expensive and destroy valuable livestock; instead of killing animals people should take medicine. An informant who was involved in the campaign explained that the government started it because of its awareness of people's poverty – it wished to give people a chance to decide for or against the sacrifices.

The campaign did, however, also have a political dimension. Today the Rmeet say that the former rulers supported and prescribed rituals. The old government, although actually that of the King of Laos, is strongly associated with the French colonial regime and with American influence during the Second Indochinese War. In these Rmeet accounts, the French and Americans appear as agents of ritual conservatism. The past and its foreign regimes are thus contrasted with the current one, usually casting the latter in a favourable light. Most Rmeet do not see themselves as the passive subjects of historical change and government policies, and their positive attitude towards reform and the government that was evident in the statements I heard could easily be a kind of defence mechanism against the foreign anthropologist. However, I have reason to believe that the positive position of many Rmeet is genuine – even though it is expressed in the form of official rhetoric. Most Rmeet I talked to do not stress their allegiance to the government when talking about ritual change, stressing instead that they make their own choices. Only a few say that the government is forbidding rituals; indeed it would be an impossible task for it to do this, given the remoteness of many villages and the relative weakness of the administration in many highland areas. What the government has done, from my informants' point of view, is that it has opened up new possibilities in terms of decision-making. Thus, the Rmeet have been able to decide what, from the 'old tradition' (*riid priim*), they will keep and what they will abandon. These decisions have sometimes been made at the village level, sometimes at the level of individual households.

An example of this decision-making relates to the keeping of buffalo and pig skulls in the house after a sacrifice to the house spirit. In traditional households, these objects are kept on the site where the house spirit is located and they have the effect of strengthening its presence – there is more protection by the spirit, but there are also more restrictions and taboos. In the mountain village of Takheung, all households except one throw the skulls away after the ritual, but many households in neighbouring villages keep them. The discontinuance of this practice in Takheung seems to have been gradual, with one household after another deciding to give it up. By now, throwing away the skulls has become part of the village's identity. This does not mean that change in general has always been smooth, without conflict with the administration or power-holders or with other households within villages. However, besides the obvious use of government rhetoric, the discursive framework of the changes emphasises Rmeet agency and decision-making.

It is important to note that the discontinuance of this practice has not destroyed the entire system. Skulls are removed in order to decrease taboos, not as demonstrations of disbelief. People who throw away buffalo and pig skulls after rituals continue to take the house spirits into account, but handle their relationship with them differently. In fact, individual belief has little to do with the discontinuance of ritual. People often perform rituals even if they do not believe in the cosmology that they represent. On the other hand, people may cease performing rituals even though they continue to believe in the beings to whom these rituals are addressed. Changes in personal attitude must be translated into communications before they can affect socially acknowledged practice. In their turn, these communications must be framed by the respective system; otherwise, attitudes and social life remain pretty much separate.

The second type of motivation for discontinuing rituals is more internal and derives from personal and reflected experience, though it still relates to the nation state. Compared to earlier times, the Rmeet today find themselves in close contact with various cultural traditions and ethnic groups. Migrations during the war, the peace that followed it and the re-emergence of economic networks all facilitated the experience of ethnic variety. Another important factor is army service: platoons in the army are multiethnic, a policy probably designed with an eye on the ethnic politics of rebellion in Laos and neighbouring countries. Also, there are more multiethnic villages emerging along the trade routes, in the lowlands and near the towns, composed of migrants from various areas. The number of young people going to lowland or mixed villages for schooling has increased. The argument of the Rmeet regarding these changes goes like this: in earlier times, the Rmeet did not know about other ethnic groups, but now they have been around and watched them. They now see that others do not perform the rituals and do not observe the taboos that the Rmeet know.

This argument reflects the motivations and experience of the Rmeet, but it must be qualified. Certainly the channels through which interethnic contact is possible have multiplied. Still, the situation is gradually growing different, rather than being absolutely different, from that in the past. According to Izikowitz, the Rmeet were involved in labour migration and trade in the 1930s. Trade was more restricted than it is today and seldom seems to have caused people to leave their villages for any prolonged period of time: the traders went to the villages, or close to them, in order to buy rice, and then left. Although trading villages and the Rmeet co-existed in close vicinity, as in the Nam Tha river valley, there seems to have been little interaction (Izikowitz 1979: 310–311; 2004: 63, 182). Labour migration to Siam was the most important form of migration, with numerous young Rmeet staying in this neighbouring country in order to acquire wealth. Izikowitz notes that the Upper Lamet, among whom migration was more frequent, have rules that are not as strong (Izikowitz 1979: 352) – an observation that supports the Rmeet interpretation of ritual change.

But intercultural contact does not necessarily lead to the discontinuance of rituals; the point made by the Rmeet is valid in this case, but it is not an inevitable development. In fact, there are hints that Rmeet shamanism originates from or was strongly influenced by Northern Thai ritual healing (ibid.: 23). This would mean that there is an elaborate and frequently performed set of rituals that has come from another group in fairly recent times; the Yuan settled in the Rmeet area for only a brief period in the 19th and early 20th centuries. The intensification of interethnic contacts may thus lead either to an elaboration or a discontinuance of rituals, depending on one's own perception and the representations of others.

From the Rmeet point of view, both types of change imply a comparison of their own practices with those of others. They conceive of their rituals and ideas as a way of understanding and handling the world, not just as a marker of cultural identity. They therefore acknowledge that other people's practices are functional equivalents of their own. These functional equivalents emerge in the Rmeet's perception – they are not statements that the anthropologist makes about the universal functions of social systems (such as 'all religions need to deal with death'). But the perception of functional equivalence forms a kind of relay by which outside features can be translated into the language of the system. There is thus the potential to conceive outside elements or systems as the functional equivalents of inside elements or sub-systems. This, although in need of more research, provides the basis for a comparison of own and other practices.

The perception that there is such an equivalence might seem paradoxical, given that there is a relational dependence between elements within the (social and cosmological) system. In socio-cosmic societies, social reproduction depends on rituals that connect relations among the living to those with spirits, gods, the dead and other forces. Given this integration of social and cosmic relations, discontinuance not only affects relations with the metaphysical within the confines of institutions that are specialised on ritual; it directly or indirectly also concerns the maintenance of social relations in general. The perception and practice of functional equivalence between elements of the Rmeet system and elements of neighbouring systems requires the isolation of elements from the system that gives meaning to them. Their relatedness is suspended so that comparison becomes possible. But in the event of reintegration, or of the integration of new elements as a result of the comparison, relations with the rest of the system have to be established. Therefore, the discontinuance of rituals indicates redefinitions of the concept of society and the categories of relations that are necessary to maintain it. It implies that other, new types of social relations are available that may, if not neatly replace, at least take on a number of the functions of former relations. This would include relations outside the socio-cosmic society, such as trade, employment, state administration, non-ethnic religion. But it would be misleading to conclude that the closed system of socio-cosmic relations now opens itself up to the wider world. Socio-cosmic systems, like all meaning systems, are always closed. Only meaning determined by the system can produce meaning, even when it integrates outside influences. Insofar as new relations replace older ones, they become part of this closed system; whatever their nature outside of it, they have to be translated or transformed at the boundaries of the system in order to become effective within it. This means that, although the persons or institutions involved are situated on the outside, their involvement in the form of acts and communications is only relevant insofar as they are operationalised by the system. The fact that this does occur can be seen in Rmeet statements that the altering of their rituals was inspired, but not implemented, by outside forces.

The inside–outside relationship can also be formulated in terms of a system–environment relationship. Systems depend on their environment, but they are themselves marked off by specific types of relations between their elements. Social systems consist of communications or social relations. However, the environment can only have an effect upon the workings of the system if the system in question is able to produce a system-specific response to the environmental input (Luhmann 1984: Chapter 1, especially p. 69).

Healing and Efficiency

How, then, are functional equivalents conceived of? What makes comparison possible in local discourse and practice? The practical side of ritual creates important inroads for non-ritual types of action. In relation to my material on the Rmeet, the element of power, which is crucial to Sahlins' analysis, retreats, and the element of efficiency steps to the fore. One must differentiate here between rationality and rationalism. Rationality, in the sense of Weber's *Zweckrationalität* (instrumentally rational action), can be defined as the effort to optimise means–end relations: to design and employ means to come to certain ends in the most efficient manner. It must be stressed that, in the sense in which I use 'efficiency' here, it has nothing to do with scientific empiricism, as is often assumed. But instrumentally rational action becomes a central value in modern ideology, pairing up with the rejection of metaphysics and an exclusive positivism to form rationalism.

The fact, however, that rational efficiency is prominent in modern ideology – although it is not the organising principle of the functional differentiation of modern society (Luhmann 1994 [1982]: 69) – does not mean that efficiency is unimportant in non-modern societies and their rituals.[7] Among the Rmeet, at least, there is a difference between rituals and actions with externally measurable, differentiated efficiency and those with non-measurable, absolute efficiency. The latter concerns rituals that reproduce certain crucial relationships, such as annual sacrifices to village spirits, weddings and funerals. There is no measure to describe them as more or less efficient, as their performance is seen as necessary and sufficient to create or maintain the relationships involved. The effect is inherent in their performance. Therefore, they cannot be replaced by more efficient practices.

But other rituals do have an external measure for efficiency. Healing rituals, which may fail or succeed, are one example.[8] Their effect is, for

7. Despite what Whitehouse (2004: 3–4) suggests.

8. Of course, this is not a universal distinction. There are societies in which weddings may cause infertility if they are performed incorrectly; it is also conceivable that

the Rmeet, not entirely part of the ritual. This type of efficiency, which can be measured against events external to the ritual, creates the possibility for practices from outside the system to influence it.

The role of efficiency as a mode of functional equivalence is highlighted by the fact that there is a reduction in the number of sacrifices made among the Rmeet when medical services become available. Modern pharmaceuticals are on sale in the mountain villages, but often there are no village health workers or other specialists to supervise their proper use. Illness is frequently treated by ritual, usually consisting of a performance by a shaman and a sacrifice. Shamans differ from lay healers in that they heal through their relationship with spirit familiars. This relationship, along with their knowledge of lengthy chants, is usually acquired through initiation. The chants are sung in a largely incomprehensible idiom identified as a lowland language or Lao; it may be a corrupt form of Buddhist or Yuan origin (Izikowitz 1979: 252; Tambiah 1970: 323–324). The biggest sacrifices involve buffaloes. These are occasions at which the sick person and his family are integrated into a socio-cosmic whole that consists of ancestors, relatives and spirits. This integration brings about healing (Sprenger 2005).

Yet the Rmeet are equally ready to accept medical services, which are often considered more effective. In Hangdeun, a suburban village in Bokeo Province, hospitals are only a few minutes away by car, and people often prefer them to sacrifices. Medical cures are not associated with socio-cosmic wholeness; in fact, the Rmeet are usually not able to explain the basics of modern medicine, including germ theory or pharmacy. Their belief in the efficiency of medicine derives partly from experience, and partly from a general sense of the superiority of technological advance, sophisticated organisation and the means of the modern state. Still, the efficiency of medicine does not itself eradicate the necessity for a ritual. After all, efficiency is not a cosmology itself, but is situated within one. Both rural and suburban Rmeet differentiate between illnesses caused by spirits and those called *beñad*, a category that comprises what we may call naturally-caused diseases. Even in a single case, both medicine and ritual may be required to fight all the causes of the illness, both spiritual and natural. There is no conflict

healing rituals to expel spirits are always considered effective, the ongoing disease being covered by a different explanation.

of cosmologies involved here; a concept of externally-measurable efficiency is part of the cosmology that shapes the rituals, and as such it is applied to modern medicine.

However, there is an important difference between the two systems involved. As mentioned earlier, measurable efficiency is a central value in modern societies, not just one possible mode of action. This, under conditions of functional differentiation, creates a medical system with exclusive claims to heal. But in the Rmeet system, the idea of efficiency and its related practices are integrated differently. There is a measure of efficiency regarding healing rituals or those that promote human fertility, and many are considered successful: the sick do better, women do become pregnant after rituals. These are fields where rituals and outside practices compete in terms of the system itself. But this inroad or form of functional equivalence, which I describe here as 'measurable efficiency', is limited, and efficiency cannot claim sole validity in relation to the entire system, as it does in regard to 'rationalist' medicine.

Efficiency as part of the system also contributes to the acquisition of ritual. The Rmeet say that they learnt shamanism from the Shan early in the 20th century, and at that time it was probably considered to be more efficient than earlier local rituals. However, it was not introduced simply by copying. Today, shamanism is not only regarded as a Rmeet tradition; its practices are more often than not well integrated into the rest of the ritual system. The ritual use of colonial silver coins, wrist-tying and the smearing of shins with sacrificial blood all play major roles in both shamanistic and non-shamanistic rituals. New techniques have, thus, only been accepted as part of the existing system of ideas and practices.

Rejecting Lightning

The reduction of healing rituals after the arrival of medical care was not in itself a ritual act. But the discontinuance of rituals has sometimes taken a more obviously active and ritualised form. I shall focus on two examples, both of which stress the creativity of the Rmeet themselves, though they are related to external representations. The first concerns the invention of a much shorter and smaller scale ritual, catalyzed by government secularism; the second exemplifies the gradual diminution and marginalisation of ritual, derived from a general pattern in mainland Southeast Asia.

The first example is the discontinuance of buffalo sacrifices for lightning spirits. When lightning strikes a house or a field, a household that follows 'old custom' has to perform a series of rituals. First, the members of the household visit the site of the strike, which is usually one of the few tall trees left after clearing a rice field, where they sacrifice a white chicken on a rack. After this, the household has to observe a lengthy taboo period of up to a year, which virtually isolates it from the rest of the community. Its members are not allowed to speak to those outside the household, nor can they partake in their rituals. There are also a number of restrictions relating to behaviour, everyday activities and food. During this period, the members of the household 'have' a lightning, that is, a spirit identified with an ancestor, whose coming is regarded as punishment for some misdeed. The spirit becomes a guest of the household, making it dangerous. In particular, the members of this household cannot talk to people in whose houses there has recently been violent death or suicide. Lightning spirits and the spirits of suicides are both spirits of the dead, and both are dangerous, but the two types of spirit are in opposition to each other. The human who committed suicide died a bad death (*yóóm sa'ieb*)[9]; the other spirit is a proper ancestor who has become angry. Conflict between the two spirits would bring fresh death to the households concerned. The end of the taboo period is reached either after a year or at the beginning of the new agricultural year in spring, when the household performs a large ritual, spanning three days. At its centre is the sacrifice of a white buffalo, a pig and a chicken. Buffaloes are highly prized animals and it is almost exclusively buffaloes that are killed in rituals. A sacrifice to a lightning spirit, which is much less urgent than a healing sacrifice or the payments of buffaloes as bride-price, is seen as a major expenditure.

Some Rmeet households and villages responded willingly when the government demanded the abolition of large-scale sacrifices. The changes were introduced over a long period, some houses starting in the 1970s, others only in recent years. Today, the village of Takheung and a number of houses in other villages practise a very much abbreviated

9. The way of dying is more important for the fate of a spirit than any amount of good or bad deeds in lifetime. Victims of violence (including suicide) or accidents turn into permanently needy spirits that may attack the living, make them ill, or kill them. This basic idea is found in numerous variations in the region (Formoso 1998).

version of the ritual. When lightning strikes, the village headman writes a letter, using the official rhetoric of the socialist state, announcing that the 'rules of the old society and the affairs of the sky spirits will not be respected any more'. The accompanying ritual is performed after one or two months. A crowd of young men and women, not restricted to members of the afflicted house, gathers at the site of the strike. The house father brings along a dish with banana leaf rolls and an egg for the lightning spirit. After the headman has read the letter, he places it on the burnt tree, and everybody dances around the site in lowland Lao *lamvong* style. Back at the village, a pig is killed for the house spirit, and there is some drinking and singing. Afterwards, some houses may observe certain taboos – in particular, avoiding other people's rituals – but they are less strict, taboo periods are shorter than before, and at their close a pig is sacrificed instead of a buffalo.

As the incomplete discontinuance of the ritual demonstrates, the relationships it reproduced are still thought to exist. After all, lightning is understood to be an enraged ancestor; completely disregarding it would risk the protective relationship between the dead and the living. But it is not only the persistence of the ritual that demonstrates the enduring nature of the socio-cosmic system. The diminution is only possible through the ritualisation of an originally non-ritual object. The letter that denounces the ritual signals secularism and politically-conceived rationalism, in form – as a written document – content and style. But it is still ineffective. It is only through its use in a ritual modelled upon the older practice that the text alters the ritual system. The model is the initial chicken sacrifice made to the lightning immediately after the strike is discovered. In the modified form of the ritual, the letter, instead of a rack with offerings, is left on the tree. The fact that lightning is a spirit is not denied, but a superior force is invoked, represented by the letter, which is a symbol of the power of the new state. The socialist government is linked to the sphere of ritual, as was – in hindsight, at least – the royal government. The earlier rulers supported ritual, but the new ones do not, the Rmeet argue. In this way, a place is claimed for the state in the ritual system.

The relationship between the living and the dead, fundamental to Rmeet social reproduction, is not called into question. It is just that one specific representation of it is limited in its influence. There is no other way of relating to the ancestors but ritual; but changing the ritual reshapes the relationship. The continuation of the ritual allows repetition, while its diminution is irreversible: both variations are present within the confines of a single system of meaning and value. An anecdote from Takheung illustrates this point. During an interview, a householder in his late twenties said that it was observing other groups that had led to the diminution of lightning rituals. A few minutes later he mentioned, without voicing doubt, that the hiding-place of such a spirit had been discovered in a neighbouring village; it resembled that of a goat.

It is also worth noting that the active role of the state is contested: some people, including the headman of Takheung, said that the new ritual and the use of the letters had been invented by the Rmeet themselves, although others claimed that they had been adopted at the instigation of the government. It seems that the impulse to abridge the ritual originated with the state, but the specific form of the abridging was created through the creativity of some Rmeet leaders. This allows personal choices with regard to whose agency is deemed to be decisive. In any case, the state is accepted as a higher level in the value hierarchy of the ritual ideology. As such, this is also a way to identify functional equivalence.

Displacing the Ancestors

The second case of an active, ritualised form of diminution concerns the spatialisation of ritual. This also touches upon another aspect of discontinuance that, although it is not that prominent, nevertheless permeates the entire process: the way in which a people like the Rmeet themselves describe their ritual system. As already noted, systems such as this do not differentiate themselves from other systems on the basis of functional specialisation; the difference between such a system and what lies outside it usually relates to the entirety of existence. Therefore, their forms of self-description are different from those of the sub-systems of modern society. The perception of functional equivalence with regard to certain elements and sub-systems of the socio-cosmic system is already self-referential. More engrained in practice are references to the inside–outside dichotomy in rituals, common in Southeast Asian societies, such as the construction of certain kin degrees as outsiders, or the ritual integration of foreign goods or unsocialised spirits (Sprenger 2007; Luhmann 1984: 64).

Members of these societies like these also use ideas of ethnic and cultural identity that encompass the entire society to describe the differences between themselves and others. 'Because it is our custom (and different from those of our neighbours)' is the paradigmatic and usual explanation of differences, and the most explicit form of reflexivity. The nature of these differences depends on how the others are defined – whether they consist of immediate neighbours; the state; or foreigners from other countries. Definitions of the other have changed over history; and it is very likely that one or another method of creating cultural difference has always been an element of such systems, especially in the context of the complex ethnic makeup of mainland Southeast Asia. The relationship between a system and its environment always implies specific definitions of system and environment. The socialist state provides a different environment than the royal government did, and this is directly reflected in the production of meaning within the system.

How does awareness of the distinctiveness of a system as part of the system itself contribute to change? One point to be made here relates to the seemingly paradoxical nature of ethnic identity: its development, at least in a modern setting, may go along with the destruction of features that partially make up the identity. When the members of a group enter a new arena for ethnic identity, whether this is created by nation-states, tourism or developers, they often find it necessary to present their specificity in a censored or reduced manner. As Evans (1998b) and Dru Gladney (1994) have observed, minorities are allowed to dance and dress colourfully, but not to practise anything that is regarded as harmful or irrational, such as destroying valuable livestock in bloody sacrifices. Giving up rituals may thus be considered the price for maintaining distinctiveness in the context of minority/majority identification. But the same dynamic that leads to the discontinuance of rituals may also fuel the revitalisation and continuation of traditions in other areas of society.

Another aspect of this development is that the perception of rituals and taboos as a pragmatic necessity dictated by the world order is increasingly complemented by a concept of 'tradition' as a marker of ethnic difference. One might even say that the 'outsourcing' of the pragmatic aims of certain rituals and the recognition of efficiency outside the system go hand in hand with an intensification of ethnic identity – the reflexive elements of the system.

The following, and final, case study highlights this point, but it also shows how models that are used in a repetitive practice of ritual can also be used in an irreversible process. It comes from Hangdeun, a migrant village close to the provincial capital, Houeisai, and it concerns the relationship of the ancestors to space. Ancestral spirits reside in two different forms in the house: as 'house spirits', the spirits of a line of male ancestors with their wives, and as the spirits of lightning. The spirits are located in a specific place inside the house, called *sekä ña* ('the taboo of the house'). There are numerous restrictions that must be observed for them, and these vary from village to village. In some villages one may not make loud noises in the house; in others, strangers may not enter the central room; in yet others, one must leave the building through the same door that one used to enter it; and in others, roasting chilli or steaming rice is not allowed during taboo periods; and so on.

One of the most widespread taboos concerns birth, although here too there are significant differences between villages. In Takheung it is the house spirit that demands the restrictions, while in Sepriim and those houses in Hangdeun that originate from there, the restrictions are only observed by houses who 'have' a spirit of lightning. Except in Takheung, the rituals for this spirit do not expel it entirely from the house; it has, rather, be to treated separately on all major ritual occasions as long as the house as a building continues to exist. However, the taboos are similar whether or not the spirit of lightning has been expelled from the house. For ten days after a woman has given birth, she and the newborn child are not allowed to enter the house. They usually stay between the house posts beneath it, where a bedstead is set up, or in a shack belonging to the house. The newborn baby is gradually integrated into the house by both ritual and care, so its *klpu*[10] will become part of the pool of *klpu* that is protected by the house spirit. Before that, the *klpu* roams around and is in constant danger. A number of taboos prevent it from leaving. The father is not allowed to hunt because the child's *klpu* would accompany him and get ill from the sound of gunshots. No knots should be tied in the forest because that would tie up the *klpu* as well; instead, knots are

10. The *klpu* is an immaterial and personalised aspect of all human beings; it sees the future in dreams, may leave the body and thereby cause illness, and turns into the spirit of the dead person after death. Binding *klpu* to the body, for example by wrist-tying, is a major objective of many rituals (Sprenger 2006a).

tied into the sheets where the baby lies. All these taboos acknowledge the uncertain position of the child's *klpu* in the socio-cosmic space defined by the inside and outside of the house.

However, many people feel that the demands the spirits make are bothersome and they try to diminish their influence in their everyday lives. The throwing away of skulls after sacrifices has already been mentioned. Another method of avoiding the bother of responding to the demans of a spirit is to relocate the spirit. After rebuilding their houses and replacing wooden structures with stone ones, many Hangdeun villagers moved their 'taboo of the house' to the kitchen, called the 'small house', which is often a separate structure, either within a short distance of the main building or linked to it by a door. In most cases, there is a clear architectural distinction: kitchen houses are made of bamboo, while the main building is made of wood or stone. Relocation has a similar effect to throwing away skulls: the house spirit is still present, but its power does not reinforce the taboos within the house. Now the house may be freely visited by guests who may 'play' (that is, party and drink) there. A reason that is often given for doing this is that the owners would be 'ashamed' of visits by Lao during spirit sacrifices, which are much more frequent in Hangdeun than in Takheung. The girls in particular would, it is said, be repelled by the sight of the blood-stained 'house taboo'. In this way, the maintenance of cultural identity in front of outsiders leads to change and 'censoring'.

But for those households in Hangdeun that 'have lightning' [spirits], relocation sets off another process. If a woman does not give birth in hospital, she will also not do it within the house, because the spirit of lightning would be angered by the blood. But because of the extended presence of the spirits, she cannot give birth in the kitchen either. Retreating under the house is equally impossible, as most buildings in Hangdeun are low or even built directly on the ground. This necessitates the building of a bamboo hut near the house, one that is only maintained for the duration of the birth taboos.

This is a rather special case, but it makes visible a general idea that the removal of the spirits represents their marginalisation. It is not simply an exchange of positions: the kitchen is an important site of transition, of mediation between the inside of the house, which is governed by taboos and the ancestors, and the outside, associated with foreigners and alien spirits. But in the new arrangement, the kitchen is not a zone where the rules of the house spirit can be ignored. Therefore giving birth necessitates a further extension of the margin into a space away from the spirit. This marginalisation is considered an irreversible shift in the practice of ritual among the Rmeet.

However it should be noted that similar procedures can be found in both Rmeet and lowland Lao rituals. In both, there is a pattern of centre–margin relations that may be used for both repeated and irreversible events in the ritual system. Among the Rmeet, this relationship is played out in the rituals for the village spirit. Like the house spirit, this spirit is a composite, this time of all the house spirits and the sky and earth spirits. During its actualisation at the annual sacrifices, the centre and the margin of the village are connected. The spirit is addressed in two forms, one located in the village centre, in a ritual shack called a *cuông*, the other at the village boundary, in a particular tree or rock. The spirits at these two locations have different names, but are either identified with each other or considered to be related. What is important is that the spirit on the outskirts is integrated into the village during the ritual, but expelled and confined to the border again at the end of the ritual. Without the shift in position, the spirit would become dangerous: hungry and demanding without a ritual, but equally bringing death and illness if kept within the village after it.

Similar shifts can be found among the Lao. After building a new house, the spirits in the ground, which own the site, must be ritually removed to its margins (Platenkamp 2004). Here too, the power of the spirits is weakened and their influence no longer affects the house members. Unlike the Rmeet house and village spirits, these spirits are not representations of social units – like patrilines – but exist independently of humans. However, the process of weakening through marginalisation is comparable: the relationship with the spirit is translated into spatial arrangements, with a focus on centre–margin distinctions.

The existence of this pattern in several ethnic settings makes it likely that it stems from a more general concept of spaces and spirits that is shared by numerous groups in mainland Southeast Asia. The 'galactic polities' of the past were built on comparable notions of centre and margin, which are often articulated in terms of the spirits of various encompassed domains (Tambiah 1985b; Tanabe 1988). Deborah Tooker

(1996) has demonstrated how these models work at several levels of social organisation, such as the village and the house, even in groups without large polities. As these concepts have an important function in relating different communities and spiritual realms, they certainly worked as a communicative model between groups in mainland Southeast Asian. It can therefore be expected that the model, in its many variations, infuses the way in which spatial relations are conceived, including the mapping of socio-cosmic relations. In the Rmeet case this means that although the Lao are the dominant ethnic group, the centre–margin model may not be a simple borrowing, but rather a general means used in the region to communicate about social space across ethnic boundaries. In any case, the process of marginalisation follows local conceptions of socio-cosmic order, even in the context of modern influence.

It seems clear that these models work as modes for the identification of functional equivalence, in this case both within a ritual system (the model is transferred from the village ritual to the house) and across its borders (similar processes are found in non-Rmeet ritual). The tool that makes discontinuance possible comes from the system itself. At the same time, as the shame felt in front of Lao visitors suggests, such revisions are made in the light of the differentiation of the system from its environment.

Conclusion

In order to make sense of rituals, one has to assume a degree of coherence in the representations of which they consist and that link them to other domains of culture and society. Even if their meaning and practice are debated, there has to be a set of terms and ideas that informs such debates. This implies that rituals are best understood as forming one of several systems or as being part of a system. The systems in question are systems of values and ideas, or even entire systems of social reproduction, including elements of social morphology beyond the immediate field of ritual. These systems are adaptive and productive at the same time, reacting to specific inputs and producing specific responses. Each performance of a ritual has to adapt to a particular occasion. The same is true of the entire system when large-scale changes affect communities, whether these are economic, political, demographic or some other type of change. Structure and process are only two manifestations of the same meaning-producing system.

The system/environment relationship is crucial for the way a ritual system works. The system itself is to a large extent defined by its relation to the outside, being shaped by the relay points at which outside forces are translated into the language of the system. These relay points are themselves part of the system and reproduce or change its specific form. One important relay point is the acknowledgement of functional equivalence of elements inside and outside of the system. Paradoxically, this acknowledgement demands that the definition of elements through their relatedness be ignored, thus reifying these elements. Identifying functional equivalents reduces the complexity of the system, but it also makes it and its elements comparable. The Rmeet data suggest several ways to identify functional equivalence. One is the measuring of efficiency in rituals and medicine. Another is the juxtaposition of certain higher levels in the cosmology, as in the comparison of state power and ancestral power in the discontinuance of rituals for lightning. A third method uses general models for ritual process shared among neighbouring groups, and is found in the centre-margin relations employed to marginalise house spirits. These models of ritual and social space are applied, in irreversible processes, to reduce spirit influence.

In this perspective, the discontinuance of ritual is an act of cultural creativity that can be described in the terms of the ritual system itself. Revitalisations at a later stage notwithstanding, discontinuance is conceived of as irreversible, and thus different from the repeated events of 'traditional' ritual. At the same time, the discontinuance of particular rituals does not necessarily imply the disappearance of entire ritual systems,[11] nor is it a reliable indicator regarding personally held beliefs. Ritual is a structured means of communication within communities and should be understood independently from individual attitudes.

11. But see the abolition of local ritual in Hawaii that, as Sahlins (1985) argues, developed from its own internal operations when processing European influence.

CHAPTER 10

Buddhism and Spirit Cults among the Phunoy of North Laos[1]

VANINA BOUTÉ

Ethnological studies of people practising Theravada Buddhism invariably involve a debate about the existence of Buddhist practices alongside spirit cults, commonly described as 'animist' cults. While some authors have maintained that certain societies have been moving too far away from doctrinal Buddhism for them to be considered authentically Buddhist, other authors have attempted to analyse the interaction between Buddhist components and non-Buddhist components. However, their conclusions diverge: for some authors, these two components form a single religious system, while others see the two as separate religious systems.[2] When I worked among the Phunoy,[3] one of the few minorities in Laos to have a longstanding practice of Buddhism, I found myself faced with this problem: how to characterise the relationship between Buddhism and spirit cults?

During my initial investigations, the Phunoy forestalled any question on this subject by presenting what they conceived to be the articulation

1. I would like to thank Yves Goudineau, Guillaume Rozenberg and Grégoire Schlemmer for their comments on this chapter.

2. On the nature of these debates and their authors, see Tambiah 1970, Kirsch 1977 and Gellner 1990.

3. Most of the Phunoy are settled in the extreme north of the country, in a mountainous zone of the Phongsaly district, crossed from north to south by one of the country's largest rivers, the Ou river. Their livelihoods are based on shifting cultivation and cattle breeding, although this way of life has recently been jeopardised by national politics.

between their practice of Buddhism on the one hand and their relationship with the spirits on the other. Using what amounts to a quasi-official terminology in Laos, they distinguished between the 'religion of the Buddha' (*sasana phout*) and the 'religion of the spirits' (*sasana phi*).[4] And they sought to convince me that although 40 years ago they had practised Buddhism whilst performing a considerable number of rituals to spirits – the two forming a set called 'Phunoy religion', *sasana khong Phunoy* – they had since abandoned the 'religion of the spirits', to only practise 'pure Buddhism'. They told me that in the 1960s monks from the capital had come and demonstrated to them that spirit-related practices were ineffective, and since then these cults – and their officiating priests – have been banned from Phunoy villages. However, in the course of my fieldwork it became clear to me that the spirits were still considered to be present and that they were held responsible for many of the problems confronting the villagers. I came to understand this in the course of many discussions with villagers, through witnessing rituals performed semi-clandestinely and through the fact that spirit-related prohibitions were respected by some people, although they did not admit that they were doing this. So what, today, is the exact status of representations and practices relating to the 'religion of the spirits' in the context of what the villagers now conceive of as (a single) 'religion' (*sasana*)?

In this chapter, I intend to consider this question by examining rituals for allaying misfortune. These were formerly carried out by the officiating priests in charge of worship of the spirits, but now, since the religious reforms, include Buddhist officiants. Through an ethnography of these rituals, we will throw light on the place now occupied by the spirits, how they are treated, and the nature of the officiating priests responsible for them. The review should allow us to specify the nature of the relationship between Buddhism and spirits in the case of the Phunoy.

Ritual Functions among the Phunoy before the 1960s and the Impact of Religious Reforms

The Phunoy, a group of about 35,000 people who speak a Tibeto-Burman language, are one of the few non-Tai language groups in Laos

4. Terms in the Phunoy language are followed by a 'P'. The transcription I have used is based on a free system of equivalence. To simplify reading, the tones (six in Phunoy) and the differences between consonants and vowels (long or short), have not been transcribed.

who adopted Theravada Buddhism a relatively long time ago. They probably discovered it through their lowland neighbours, the Tai Lue, from whom they borrowed the monastic disciplinary code and the scheduling of ceremonies, as recorded in manuscripts written in Lue. Until the 1960s, every village had a pagoda (*vat*) occupied by monks and novices who carried out various ceremonies in honour of Buddha, to gain merit for the whole community, as a means of ensuring prosperity in this world and beyond. The Phunoy villagers also performed many rituals addressed to spirits (*dat*, P). These were linked to the dead (both the dead of the community – ancestors – and others) and/or were related to inhabited places. These rituals were meant to incur the favour of the dead or to expel the misfortunes of which they were said to be the cause.

These rituals were carried out by two main celebrants: the *tjaocam* and the *maphê*. The *tjaocam* (whose name, of Tai origin, means 'master of worship') belonged to the clan of the primary founder of the village, who was regarded as having become the guardian spirit of the community. The *tjaocam* conducted rituals for that spirit each time a change took place in the composition of the village (birth, death, departure), when a problem threatened the integrity of the entire village (epidemics, fire, etc.) and at sowing time. The *maphê*, an officiant whose function was also hereditary and who was also the village blacksmith, was in charge of two collective rituals related to the agricultural cycle addressed to the spirits of Heaven and Earth, and to the spirits of the forge. One was carried out at the time of clearing of swiddens, the other before harvest. He also had to solve problems occurring in the fields, he performed funeral rites and he carried out healing rituals for individuals.

Ceremonies held at the pagoda by monks coexisted, therefore, with rituals addressed to spirits. The Phunoy argue that, within this set of rituals, there was an opposition between, on the one hand, the monks and the lay leader of the pagoda (*atjan vat* or *atjan*), who were associated with Buddhism and the inside of the village; and the *maphê*, who was linked to dangerous spirits and to the outside, on the other (the *tjaocam*, who was on the side of the spirits but of an ancestor-spirit protecting the village territory, had a sort of intermediate position). This opposition was reflected in the fact that the monks could not attend the rituals performed by the *maphê* (because, villagers maintained, of the greater vulnerability of monks to attacks by spirits), while the pagoda was forbidden to the *maphê* – 'Buddha does not like people who make sacrifices, let alone those who handle metals and are in contact with telluric spirits, his enemies', I was told.

These characteristics of Phunoy socio-religious organisation applied up to the 1960s, when religious reforms radically transformed it. Phongsaly province was placed under the control of Pathet Lao communist forces after the Geneva Accords of 1954, and the new administration of the district and of the province termed 'superstitions' the religious practices of people in the region (*kan sùa sok sùa lang*), because they combined spirit cults and Buddhist ceremonies. In 1962–1963, groups of monks and *atjan*, supporters of the Pathet Lao from Huaphanh province and Vientiane, were sent to Phongsaly district. Initially, re-education sessions were organised in the town of Phongsaly, to which elders, monks and *atjan* from Phunoy villages were summoned. The monks explained how and why the Phunoy must abandon spirit worship and strengthen their practice of Buddhism. Emphasis was placed on the excessive number of rituals performed by the Phunoy and the cost that this involved. It was explained to villagers that the poor could become equal to the richest if they would abandon the costly sacrifices, and it was also argued that the priests led the rituals for the sole purpose of enriching themselves personally.

Having prepared the ground beforehand in this fashion, the team of monks began a campaign to put reforms into practice in Phunoy villages. Accompanied by dozens of soldiers, they exhorted the villagers to 'throw the spirits back into the forest' (*thim phi yu pa*). Permanent altars dedicated to ancestors and to *maphê* were the primary targets. The altars were burned, along with the costumes, jewellery and other ritual accessories used by the *maphê*. Lao monks compelled the villagers to now go and feed their ancestors at the pagoda, during Buddhist festivals dedicated to the dead (Khao Padapdin and Khao Salak).

Most of the villagers alive today did not experience these events, or were very young when they occurred, but they contend that the cessation of sacrifices actually satisfied the poorest, and that the villagers spontaneously stopped performing a number of rituals addressed to the spirits. Echoing the orders of monks to 'throw the spirits back into the forest', the Phunoy assert that now only Buddhist ceremonies are performed in the village, that there is no more worship of ancestors and that the officiating *maphê* and *tjaocam* have disappeared. The Phunoy were therefore not only the main recipients of these religious reforms but also the most receptive to the changes they have involved – similar actions conducted among neighbouring populations (Tai Lue, Khmu) having had little effect. For the Phunoy, joining a Buddhism purged of its 'superstitions' does not only mean meeting the expectations of those in power by embarking on the path of progress; it also means distinguishing themselves from other mountain peoples of the region. By adopting not only their practices but also their representations of what 'religion' must be (Bouté 2011a) the Phunoy somehow feel that they are becoming more similar to the Lao, the dominant population of the country.

These changes have been accompanied by the expansion of the ritual role of officiants related to Buddhism – the monks and the lay leader of the pagoda, the *atjan*. These officiants traditionally celebrated religious ceremonies held in the pagoda, which are, as elsewhere in Laos, the Lao New Year (*Pimay*), the beginning and the end of Buddhist Lent (*Khao Phansa, Ok Phansa*), and the two celebrations for the dead. Moreover, Buddhist monks and *atjan* are now also consulted in relation to various actions, procedures for which are recorded in books in Lue: the choice of a name for a baby according to the day of his or her birth; the determination of auspicious days for weddings, funerals or the building of a house; the scheduling of a trip; the construction of little houses used to make offerings to the deceased (*than phasat*); or the foundation of a new village (*tang ban*). In the wake of the religious reforms, Buddhist monks have come to be involved in most rituals designed to ward off misfortune, referred to as *kê kro* ('to deliver from bad luck'), which may be carried out for the entire village community, for a household, or for an individual.

Phunoy Rituals to Ward off Misfortune

Rituals to treat misfortunes can take many forms: regular or exceptional, therapeutic or prophylactic, performed for an individual or on behalf of the community. They are presented here according to their sociological importance and the seriousness of the problem to which they respond, starting with the treatment of minor individual misfortunes and finishing with the rituals for the entire village community.

Rituals for Minor Individual Misfortunes: The Recall of Souls

When a person feels weak, he calls on a soothsayer, who must determine the origin of the problem. Divinatory procedure is always the same. Crouched at the bedside of the patient, the diviner holds in one hand a piece of clothing belonging to the latter. He asks a series of questions, hypotheses on the cause of the illness. For each question, he takes a pinch of rice, which he throws into the middle of a dish. An even number of rice grains falling into the dish is considered to be a positive response, and an odd number is regarded as a negative response. If the diviner diagnoses the departure of one or more souls[5] – which is usually the case when the state of the individual is not deemed serious, when he is not considered sick (P, *deuleu bia*) but feels depressed, has no more enthusiasm for life, or has a poor appetite – this requires that a therapeutic ritual called *tu-kong la ku ni* (P, 'to bring back the souls of the head') be carried out. This ritual is performed at night, either by a monk, the *atjan* or an elder who has been a monk. The officiant crouches close to the patient, takes his wrist, applies an object (a stone or an egg) and begins a recitation in Lue to transfer into the object the dread, fear or apprehension of the patient, regarded as the cause of the loss of souls. He then turns to the souls of the patient and makes threats – this time in Phunoy language – against the spirit that the soothsayer has proven to be responsible for the shock, the violent vexation or the sudden fear that has caused the departure of the patient's souls. Then he places three rice balls (for the three souls of the head) on the tripod in the centre of the hearth of the home if the patient is a man, on on the transversal beam of the floor if the patient is a woman. He pours some alcohol on the ground and on the balls, calling the souls to come and eat. These balls are ultimately consumed by the patient, who by doing this reincorporates his or her souls.

As well as the ritual recalling the souls, there is also a ritual 'inviting the souls' (*su khuan*) following each of the operations for warding off misfortune (whether from the village, from a household or from the

5. The Phunoy say they have nine souls or *la* (the souls of the head, mouth, heart, eyes, chest, hands, ears, back, feet); women are said to have an additional soul, that of the breasts. These souls are attached to the body of the individual but are also present in his clothes, in certain everyday objects in the house, and in the hearth. While the departure of a soul can be countered with a ritual (described below), the departure of all of a person's souls is thought to cause the death of that individual.

body of an individual). For the Phunoy, as for the Lao, the main objective of the ritual is to 'give strength' (P, *gatchanibeu*) and bring prosperity to people by strengthening the presence of their souls in their bodies.[6] These rituals to invite the souls, carried out during the day, all therefore have a prophylactic character: they mark a transition to a new state (e.g. construction of a house, passage from one stage of life to another via the 'increase of years', see below), or the strengthening of souls in rituals that may have accidentally put men and spirits into contact. This ritual is not performed by monks, but jointly by several elders (who must have been monks), who sometimes officiate with the *atjan*.

A Response to Serious Individual Misfortune: 'Increasing the Years'

When an individual is affected by a series of misfortunes (such as the death of several children in succession or of several animals or repeated problems related to crops),[7] a ritual to recall his or her souls is not enough. At divination, the diagnosis is usually that a monk or an *atjan* will have to perform a ceremony called *sip* (or *sut*, or *sup*) *say ta*, which some gloss in Lao as meaning 'instilling a vision' or 'increasing [the] years' (*to agnu*) – understood as 'of the patient's life.'[8] It is considered that the patient's life may be coming to an end and a fixed number of additional years is requested, according to the year, the month and the day of his birth.[9] The ritual consists of two parts: the first takes place at the pagoda, the second outside the village.

---

6. The ritual to invite the souls can also be done before a journey, three months after the burial of a deceased person, before marriage ceremonies, after childbirth or to honour a guest.

7. However, there are instances when it is possible to be touched by misfortune without going through a divinatory diagnosis, such as where a person is permanently and seriously ill, or following an accident that causes blood to flow.

8. But it is possible that the name of this ritual is, in fact, the Lue way of pronouncing *sut sa ta*, 'prayer for existence', which M. Zago (1972: 274) mentions in relation to the Lao. C. Archaimbault also refers to a ritual called *süp sata* (no translation given), which seems to aim, by increasing the years of the sovereign, at perpetuating the fertility of the territory (the *muang*; see Archaimbault 1971: 122). See also R. Renard (1996: 167). A more complete description of this rite is given by R. Pottier (2007). A. Eon also describes this ceremony in a Lao urban environment (2019).

9. For example, a patient may be 45 years old and, according to his birth horoscope, the monk will ask for 14 more years; when the number of additional years has elapsed (when the patient reaches the age of 59), it will be necessary to carry out

During the first part, the parents of the person concerned prepare four wooden sticks of the same height as the patient, four other smaller ones, and bits of wood and threads of cotton the length of which equals different measurements of the patient's body (arms, head circumference, head to toe, hand to chest, head to navel) and the number of which must match the number of additional years requested. The eight pieces of wood are assembled in pairs and arranged so as to form a pyramid, at the foot of which are deposited various small pieces of wood.[10] The trunk of a banana plant is placed at one corner of the pyramid and a sugarcane stalk in another. In the third corner, a chick supposed to represent a wild bird is placed, tied by the leg, and a bow is placed in the fourth corner. All of these are partially covered with white fabric. A cotton thread goes from the top of the pyramid to the altar (*alam*) of the Buddha. A large rice sieve is placed before the altar, containing a piece of the patient's clothing, eggs or a chicken, silver, red flowers, a spindle, a spool of cotton and a bottle of alcohol, as well as different trays called *kê kro* by the assistants at the ceremony, but which the monk calls *kê kam leut* (the Tai Lue name for this ceremony). These trays, which are also used in other rituals, as we will see, to ward off misfortune, are a central element of such rituals. Made especially for this occasion, they are fitted with a bamboo frame and a base of banana leaves. There may be several with a single compartment (the monk determines the number according to the horoscope of the patient) or just one with nine compartments. They contain cooked rice, unhusked rice, chicken bones, fish bones, crab shells, a fragrant grass (unidentified), sugar cane and pieces of fruit. The primary function of these trays is to trap the spirits responsible for misfortunes.

The patient is placed under the pyramid and the monk begins to read a prayer in Lue. In his hand he holds a glass of water, into which he dips leaves with which he sprinkles the patient. When the prayer is

---

the operation again. This ritual can only be carried out on Buddhist holidays (*van sin*), that is to say, the 8th and 15th days of waxing and waning moons.

10. This 'pyramid' may actually represent a *that* (although the Phunoy do not give it a name); in this context, the treatment may be read as a re-centring of the patient in the cosmic order through his position in the centre of the *that*, which is also an axis of the world. According to Zago (1972: 350), the *that* is 'a cosmic centre [...] access to it is equal to an initiation, a complete renewal, a new life, because it is a space for creation'.

finished, the patient burns the cotton threads, takes the glass of water from which the monk has sprinkled him with water, drinks some of the water and washes his face with the rest. The monk then takes the thread connecting the pyramid to the altar, ties it to the wrists of the patient and recalls the souls of the latter. Then the pyramid is dismantled, the chick is released near the forest next to the pagoda, and the trays are taken away, to be used in the second part of the ritual.

The second part essentially aims at feeding and then chasing away the spirit responsible for the weakening of the patient.[11] It is carried out outside the confines of the village, in a place deemed representative of the patient's birth element.[12] It is believed that the patient will be able to regain his strength here, and the spirits that might prevent him from prolonging his lifetime are also fed here. The details of the ritual depend on the individual for whom the ritual is carried out. I will now give details of what was done at one such ritual, which was carried out for a patient who is under the influence of the element water.

The ritual was performed close to the spring and was addressed to the 'spirits of the forest' (P, *chichong dat*) responsible for the illness of the patient. The patient and the monk brought along the four sticks that had formed the pyramid built at the pagoda. When they came to the spring, they planted the sticks, placing a protective bamboo lattice (P, *kra bia*; literally, 'the eye of the eagle') above them. Then they linked the four sticks with a cotton thread and formed a square, in the centre of which the patient sat and where the trays were placed. The aim of placing the trays here was to nourish the spirit. The patient had also brought various common objects (including a pot and a rice basket) belonging to his household, so that the whole family would benefit from the ritual. Finally, he wound one of his garments around his neck to transfer any evil influences to it. The monk called the spirit responsible

11. If the ritual is being performed because the number of years requested in a previous ritual is about to expire, the second part of the ritual is not necessary; the patient is not considered to have been subject to any malign influence.

12. The year of birth of an individual is, according to astrological treatises (*horasat*), under the influence of one of the five elements (water, wood, earth, metal, fire) and under that of one of 12 animals (Rat, Pork, Ox, Tiger, Dragon or Naga, Snake, Horse, Rabbit, Dog, Goat, Monkey and Rooster). For someone born under the influence of metal, the Phunoy ritual is carried out at the forge; for someone born under the influence of water, it is carried out near the river; etc. For a discussion of *horasat*, see Gagneux, 1973.

for the illness to consume the offerings (the bamboo latticework was designed to prevent other spirits from coming). After the monk's first recitation, the patient left the square, breaking the cotton thread, knelt by the stream and burnt the garment he had put around his neck, which he threw into the water. He then returned to his place in the square. The monk resumed his recitation, then knocked over a bottle of alcohol, thus terminating the act of warding off misfortune. The trays were thrown into the river. The patient went to the pagoda and placed pieces of wood at the four corners of the building. This final phase of the ritual, which is called *sia kro* or *kê upatihét* ('warding off accidents'),[13] closes the ritual performed at the pagoda.[14]

Rituals to Ward off Misfortunes for the Community

In addition to rituals aimed at resolving individual misfortunes (rituals to recall souls and to 'increase years'), Buddhist officiants perform rituals for households or for the village community as a whole. The rituals of expulsion of misfortune for the village are performed each year at the time of New Year ceremonies (Boun Pimay) and when an exceptional and harmful event occurs in the community (epidemics, fire, violent death[15]). When carried out for the New Year ceremonies, the ritual simply involves the monk making a tray of nine compartments (*kro tang kao*) that allows the expulsion of all the misfortunes of the previous year. When the ritual takes place following an exceptional event, it is held in two stages. The *tjaocam,* accompanied by the villagers, goes to the tree where the guardian spirit of the village sits and here he deposits offerings and says a prayer. Then the *atjan* and some of the elders go to the pagoda to make a nine-compartment tray; the *atjan* and the monks then jointly officiate, to imprison the spirits. The tray with nine compartments built for the occasion is more complex than one that is made in the case of an individual misfortune. In each compartment, black rice, white rice, dried meat, small bones, flowers, gold and silver

13. According to S. J. Tambiah, among the Isan the terms *sia kro* or *gae ubab* (*kê upath*) refer to rituals to ward off bad luck when abnormal events occur, causing a disruption of the order of things. On rituals of exorcism of the spell (*sia kro*) in southern Laos, see also the descriptions provided by C. Archaimbault (1971: 104–114).

14. Regarding new rituals to question the future that have recently appeared in urban contexts, see Bouté 2021.

15. On the treatment of bad death in Northern Laos, see Bouté 2011b.

(represented by pieces of shiny paper) and the effigy of an animal in clay (buffalo, chicken, pig, dog, horse, naga, cow, elephant) are placed. In the central compartment a figurine in the shape of a human is placed, which is called the Lord of Days (Phanya Van).[16] It is said that the old Lord, responsible for past evils of the community, should be thrown away, so that the new Lord can come in. This tray, which has a door on each side, is made to trap spirits. Attracted by the figurines of animals and of the man placed in the compartments, they rush to feed themselves. The 'doors' of the tray are then destroyed and, under the influence of a prayer recited by the monk, then by the *atjan,* the spirits are trapped in the tray, which is then thrown out of the village, towards the setting sun.

The monks also perform rituals to remove misfortune when a problem occurs that affects all of the members of a household, since, in such cases, it is considered that the whole village community is involved. Indeed, certain offences committed by individuals (such as not informing the village guardian spirit of the building of a new house, visiting the cemetery when a funeral is not taking place, chopping wood in the sacred forest, having an incestuous relationship, and bringing a live wild animal into the village) may trigger the wrath of the guardian spirit of the village. The sanction will be collective and, it is said, terrible: people and livestock will die, the village will burn, etc.

These rituals are performed with a prophylactic intent, such as when a house has been built (or its roof changed, which is likened to building a new house), or when an exceptional event that is considered to be a reversal of the natural order occurs in a house or in a field (such as the intrusion of wild animals – say, a snake nesting under a stone in a house or a wasps' nest under the roof). In the first instance, the first to officiate is the *tjaocam,* who comes to the new house on the last day of work to recite protective formulae. He then goes to the altar of the guardian spirit of the village to inform him of the presence of the new house and asks him to place the occupants under his protection. A few days later, the monk is in turn invited. He must chase away the evil spirits

16. Similar rituals of expulsion of misfortune at the end of the ceremony of the new year have also been carried out in the principality of Bassak (Southern Laos); the figurine that was supposed to draw to itself the misfortunes of the inhabitants of the *muang* was, in that case, that of the sovereign of the principality, which 'draws on his person all the plagues and thus diverts all malevolent attention that could be directed to his subjects' (Archaimbault 1971: 70).

that might be found in building materials. Wooden sticks, on which the protective bamboo latticework is hung, are planted at the four corners of the house and connected by a cotton thread to protect the place from outside evil influences. The monk recites the *kê mangkala* prayer, drawn from texts read in Lue, in front of a nine-compartment tray to attract the misfortunes that might reside in the materials. The tray is then thrown outside the village.

When something that disturbs the natural order has occurred in a household, a similar ritual is carried out. In this case, the ritual is split into two parts carried out simultaneously, one led by the great soothsayer,[17] the other by the monk. The participants are divided into two groups: one is made up of the consanguineous relatives of the master of the house, who install themselves, with the monk, inside the house; the other group is made up of affineal relatives who gather, with the great soothsayer, near an altar to the spirits of the forest, which is built for the occasion near the house. On this altar, the great soothsayer sacrifices a chicken, deposits alcohol and candles, and invites the spirits to come and feed themselves. Then, one of the members of this group hits a small gong, while another picks up a fishing net, and the whole group throw stones toward the house, asking those inside to let them in. They then climb the stairs to the open door and crouch down on the landing; on the other side of the door are the monk and the master and mistress of the house. Through the door, which is left ajar, a small table is passed, with flowers, alcohol and a bowl of rice containing a silver bracelet and an egg on it, to the group outside. Then, from the two sides of the door, the two groups say prayers to ask for prosperity. Finally, the great soothsayer pours some alcohol near the offerings, and from the other side of the door, the master of the house gives him a cloth containing a little

17. The function that I translate using the term 'great soothsayer' (*mo–ê*, from Lao *mo*, 'healer') seems to arise from the disappearance of the former *maphê*. Previously, say the Phunoy, the soothsayers (*bioba*, from *bio*, 'seek'), present in all the villages, conducted only divinations, with sacrifices being carried out by the *maphê*. Today, when there are no longer any *maphê*, only soothsayers regarded as the most powerful (i.e. those I call the 'great soothsayers') can make sacrifices. However, unlike the *maphê*, the soothsayers are never in direct communication with the spirits during the cures, and they are considered less powerful than the former *maphê* were.

money.[18] The outside group may be regarded as representing the spirits of the forest, while the master and mistress of the house represent the spirits of the house; the ritual aims, among other things, to restore order through an alliance between villagers on the one hand and elements alien to the village community on the other.

When something that disturbs the natural order has occurred in a field, a ritual performed by the *maphê* at the site of the disorder precedes the other parts of the ritual. He offers a sacrifice to the spirit of rice (Apitchaba) and chases away the spirits of the forest. A ritual to remove misfortune is then performed by the monk in the house belonging to the owner of the field.

The Distribution of Functions in Relations with the Spirits

This ethnographic overview of new ritual functions related to the treatment of misfortune since the 1960s allows us to make two observations. Firstly, non-Buddhist officiants continue to be regularly involved in rituals relating to spirits. Secondly, Buddhist celebrants are always also involved in these rituals, both in prophylactic and in therapeutic rituals; and in rituals concerning both individuals and the wider community. While the presence of a monk is not required during rituals to recall souls, just as the presence of the *atjan* is not essential, the elders who preside over the ceremony are, I observed, always monks. Their time in the pagoda has given them mastery of the formulae in Tai Lue.

My observations clearly show – no matter what the Phunoy say – that non-Buddhist officiants have not completely disappeared, since they can be seen officiating alongside monks and *atjan*. Despite reforms carried out in the 1960s, there is always, in every village, someone who officiates in the fields and whom the villagers call *maphê*. However, when I discovered that such an officiant was still alive, they hastened to tell me that, although he is described as a *maphê*, this person does not have much in common with the old *maphê*. He actually has no important power, or costume, or auxiliary spirit, and the function is no longer hereditary. In addition, the *maphê* is now no longer a blacksmith. Villagers told me that he only occasionally leads rituals in the fields; and he is, I was told, a

18. The same ceremony of removal of misfortune for the house among ethnic Lao (Vientiane and Luang Prabang) was described in the 1970s by Clément-Charpentier and Clement 1990.

good Buddhist (an interesting observation, bearing in mind the fact that there was a time when the *maphê* could not go to the pagoda). Finally, he is no longer involved in any way in the regular ceremonies that are officiated over by several different individuals: the ritual performed before the felling of trees before burning (as part of swidden cultivation) is carried out by three elders, and the rituals formerly performed within the village to the spirits of the house are led by the *atjan*, the monks and, exceptionally, by the great soothsayer.

It was also clear that the *tjaocam* still has a function. This has also changed, albeit to a lesser extent. Now that a ritual is no longer performed at sowing time, the role of the *tjaocam* is limited to performing occasional rituals addressed to the guardian spirit of the village (which is no longer conceived of as an ancestor, but as a conglomerate of forces of the place). This relative continuity in the function of the *tjaocam* is perhaps explained by the fact that the rituals he carries out, unlike those of the *maphê*, are, for the Phunoy, those that appear to be the least opposed to Buddhism: the *tjaocam* does not make any sacrifices, the communication he establishes with the guardian spirit of the village is limited to prayers and the offerings he deposits (flowers and candles) are identical to those brought to the pagoda.

As well as continuing to carry out some of their old functions, these officiants are involved in rituals for warding off misfortune performed by the monk. We have seen that, during the construction of a house or when problems threaten a household or the village, the first ritual performed is that of the officiating *tjaocam*; the ritual performed by the monk is complementary to this. The angry spirit of the village, of the house, or of the rice is soothed by the *tjaocam* and nourished by the great soothsayer or by the *maphê*. It is only later that the monk traps the unwanted spirits, which, attracted by the reigning lack of order (in the case of the village) or by the sacrifice (in the case of the house), are likely to make an appearance. It is only in healing rituals that the monk officiates alone; in these rituals the tray to remove misfortune is less complex than that involved in putting right a lack of order in the village and is said to be less powerful. Even then, however, the intervention of a non-Buddhist officiant is sometimes required, especially when the divination reveals that the problem needs to be resolved through a ritual performed by the great soothsayer. It can therefore be said that there is no misfortune the resolution of which would be exclusively entrusted to the monks, and the more important the issue addressed by the ritual, the more the role of the monk is secondary and requires the involvement of another, non-Buddhist, officiant.

How should the fact that officiants involved in the spirit cults continue to participate in rituals to ward off misfortune be understood, given that, as we have seen, the religious reforms imposed by the authorities have been well accepted by the Phunoy, eager to consider themselves as practitioners of 'genuine' Buddhism? The roles played by the *maphê*, the *tjaocam* and the 'great soothsayer' in the rituals to ward off misfortune may, at first glance, appear to be related to the presence of spirits. These – and the sacrifices they require – are indeed omnipresent in these rituals, either indirectly, as the cause of the departure of souls, or directly, as being responsible for disease. But there are instances, as we have seen, when the monk feeds and traps the spirits by himself. Why, then, would the monk not be able to perform all the rituals to ward off misfortune on his own? An answer to this question means taking into account the characteristics associated with ritual officiants among the Phunoy – be they monks, *atjan*, or specialists in rituals related to the spirits.

The Power of the *Atjan*: A Necessary Heritage

As we have seen, monks never perform rituals to ward off misfortune on their own – rituals that are held to be the most important and most dangerous. This appears to be related to the fact that they are regarded as devoid of the 'power' (*yi*, P) necessary for ritual treatment of spirits. The fact that monks lead all the regular ceremonies at the pagoda does not imply that they are regarded as being endowed with special powers. 'The religion of the spirits means having experience and power; the religion of the Buddha just means reading from a book', a Phunoy told me one day. While rituals performed in the temple or in homes are performed amidst the cries of children and conversations among the curious, villagers say that those who address rituals to the spirits outside the village must have good concentration: 'If people come to see the ritual outside the village and they ask questions, the officiant must not answer, otherwise people will die.' It should be remembered that the monk never attends rituals performed in the fields by the *maphê*; as for the elders, despite all the prestige they enjoy, they would not risk trying to solve a problem that has occurred outside the village. As one of them explained to me, 'the spirits are more dangerous than Pali [the language used in the Theravada Buddhism liturgy]'. The Phunoy therefore consider that powerful authorities are required to manage the relationship between spirits and men. It is the fact that specialists associated with spirit cults – the *maphê*, the *tjaocam*, the great soothsayer – are known to have power that guarantees their ability to achieve the recovery of a patient or the resolution of a problem.

Therefore the status of monk is far from being regarded as prestigious and it is common to hear villagers holding critical conversations about the religious: 'The monks? They are lazy! They do nothing but ask peasants for food.' And although the Buddhist celebrants have been responsible for more functions since the 1960s, most Phunoy pagodas no longer have any monks. This vocational crisis can be explained by the fact that nowadays young people are all in school and the pagoda no longer has exclusive responsibility for education, which was one of its major attractions in the past. Entering the pagoda is not very popular and the only young men who do enter are individuals whose inclusion within the village society would otherwise not be guaranteed: today, most novices or monks are orphans, men afflicted with disabilities that do not allow them to work the fields or to start a family, or men in conflict with their families. In short, this is a far cry from the observation that S. J. Tambiah made in relation to the north east of Thailand: 'The monks are as well human mediators who have access to mystical powers, deriving from sources which represent negation of life, but which are pre-eminently of a life-intensifying character when transferred to the laity' (1970: 211).

Unlike the monk, the *atjan* enjoys substantial prestige. In some villages, he will lead Buddhist ceremonies, his knowledge of the texts being greater than that of recently ordained monks, who simply assist them. The prestige that surrounds him is rooted in the fact that his role lies between that of the monk he was in the past and that of the non-Buddhist officiant he now is. Within a given village, it is the ex-monk who has mastered not only Buddhist ceremonies but also tradition – of which he is considered to be the custodiam – who will be appointed *atjan*. It is the *atjan*'s role to handle interpersonal conflicts, to know the rules relating to marriages, births, funerals and legacies and to perform rituals to ward off misfortune. He must also be able to supplement the functions of the *maphê* or the *tjaocam,* when these are lacking. This eclecticism and the importance of the knowledge that he is able to mobilise, both in the field of Buddhism and in that of tradition and communication with spirits, make the *atjan* a central officiant within the village community.

But given that the *atjan* defines himself as a former monk, where does his supposed power in dealing with spirits come from? Before the 1960s, the role of *atjan* was not hereditary – whereas all the ritual roles of non-Buddhist officiants were (like political roles) handed down within the same lineage. In theory, the role of *atjan* continues to be non-heritary: the successor to an *atjan* is supposed to be appointed by his predecessor when the latter is very old or is about to die and must give up his office. However, in all the villages where I conducted research, the function of *atjan* is always passed, *de facto,* within the same lineage. Furthermore, it appears that these families and lineages are almost systematically the descendants of the holders of ritual functions related to spirit cults in the past. In other words, virtually all of those occupying the role of *atjan* are descendants of *maphê* or *tjaocam.* In the 20 villages in which I investigated this role, 14 *atjan* were descended from a line of *tjaocam,* five from a line of *maphê,* and only one had no ancestry linked to one of these two roles.

The fact that the vast majority of *atjan* are descended from *tjaocam* and not from *maphê* needs to be understood in the context of the fact that *atjan* and *tjaocam* are at the intersection of Buddhist rituals and rituals to the spirits. The role of *tjaocam* has, in fact, been strongly buddhicised, a growing trend that is even more pronounced in Phunoy communities that have emigrated to the lowlands and to cities (Bouté 2018). In lowland Phunoy villages, the *tjaocam* regularly officiates at ceremonies and on Buddhist holidays (the 8th and 15th days of the waxing and waning moon), and he is always the *atjan* of the village. In the town of Phongsaly, the provincial capital, there is no longer a *tjaocam;* but the *atjan* of the city has taken on the functions performed by the *tjaocam,* even re-introducing, for those who cultivate a few patches of land, a small ceremony at planting time, similar to the one conducted by the *tjaocam* before the 1960s.

One might be tempted to interpret this over-representation of descendants of *tjaocam* – and also of *maphê* – among *atjan* as being due to a desire on the part of members of lineages that were important in the past to regain their dominant position by adapting to ritual reconfigurations and adopting the role of *atjan*. Let us recall that the lineage of the *tjaocam* is said to descend from the primary founder of the village, and that, as such, one of its members held political power in the past. This hypothesis, although probable, is not easily verifiable. In any case, the fact that the *atjan* is recognised as having the ability to carry out rituals involving communication with dangerous spirits is no surprise. The *atjan*, as descendants of the celebrants of the past, are recognised as holders of the power (*yi*) that allowed their ancestors to celebrate great collective rituals addressed to the spirits.

The fate of the lineage of a *maphê* from Thongpi village is an illustration of this. Following the religious reforms of the 1960s, the *maphê* Achien, faced with the destruction of ritual instruments he owned and the disapproval of the villagers, left Thongpi and settled in the village of a neighbouring non-Buddhist population, the Akha, where he remarried and was honoured as a powerful officiant. His son, Paseuth, who remained in Thongpi, found it difficult to be accepted. Even though he did not hold the role of *maphê*, because the role is considered to be inherited, the villagers regarded him as being endowed with the same powers as his father, and they feared that the guardian spirits of his lineage, which were no longer worshipped, would retaliate. Even today, aged 70 and having spent over 60 years in the village, Paseuth is still considered undesirable and is marginalised. He is not part of the council of elders and what he says is routinely criticised. He is also excluded from the religious sphere due to the ambivalence of his position: son of the *maphê* and, like it or not, heir to his powers, he cannot, any more than can his father, go to the pagoda, as this could 'anger the Buddha'. At the same time, he refuses to assume the powers vested in him or to claim any relationship with the spirits (which he could have done in another form, some of the old *maphê* officiants from other villages having become diviners). This complete exclusion from the religious sphere makes him, for the Phunoy, subject to potential misfortune from two directions: he is deprived of the protection of the Buddha and the spirits take revenge on his abandonment by persecuting him and his family.

However, Thitsouk, Paseuth's son and Achien's grandson, is attempting to escape the suspicion surrounding his father by trying to take on important positions in his village. On the one hand, through the support of his relatives on his mother's side, he has entered the political sphere, as a party member and then as assistant to the village chief. On the other hand, he has tried to become an important religious specialist. At a time when there were very few applicants to enter the monastic order, Thitsouk lived in the pagoda for 12 years as a novice and then as a monk – a particularly long time among the Phunoy. When he left the pagoda to get married, he continued to dedicate himself to the study of Buddhist texts in the evening. In 1987 he was appointed by the lay leader of the pagoda (his maternal grand-uncle) as his successor, e.g. as the *atjan* of the village. Thitsouk thus became a key figure in the religious life of the village. For example, in 1992 he organised a Buddhist festival, the feast of the Kinari, that is not usually held because it is so expensive.[19] His entry into the pagoda as a monk, ensured that he developed a knowledge of texts and of scheduling ceremonies, and it also allowed him to get rid of the stigma that had surrounded his family since the days of the religious reforms. However, he also continues to dedicate significant time to completing his knowledge of rituals to the spirits. He has made regular visits to the former *maphê* of the neighbouring village (his maternal uncle) and to great diviners. He has now become a powerful officiant whose fame extends beyond Phunoy villages. Akha neighbours who once hosted his grandfather now come to see Thitsouk to solve problems for which the spirits are held accountable.

By taking on the role of *atjan,* Thitsouk has assumed an important ritual position, re-assuming a central role that his lineage had lost after the collapse of the former role of *maphê*. Thus, this descendant of *maphê* is no longer excluded from the pagoda as his father and grandfather were, but has become an indispensable part of it.

Conclusion

What can be learned from this review of rituals to ward off misfortune in relation to the role of spirits in Phunoy religion today? First of all, it is clear that the religious reforms of the 1960s did not so much aim to

19. This festival is also called Boun Than Ba ('The Great Ritual'). It is held when a new statue of the Buddha is enthroned (a heart of gold is placed on the statue to bring it to life on this occasion). The term 'Feast of the Kinari' derives from the fact that on this occasion two dancers put on masks and long claws, which represent birds' claws. The *kinari* are bird-women who appear in some episodes of the Ramayana.

eliminate spirits and their worship as evict them from the space inhabited by humans – the village, which was to be placed under the exclusive rule of Buddhist law. But even once they are ejected into the forest, the spirits continue to appear – this is, for the Phunoy, a fact that they feel in their flesh, with the main effect of this being illness and misfortune. It is necessary to prevent this happening and, where appropriate, to respond to spirit attacks. As the village is supposed to be placed under Buddhist law, it is monks or the lay leader of the pagoda (*atjan*) that the Phunoy call upon to perform the necessary rituals. Having failed to eliminate the spirits, the reforms to 'buddhicise' Phunoy practices have actually meant that Buddhist officiants have taken on the handling of misfortunes attributed to spirits.

But the presence of these Buddhist officiants is not sufficient: not being holders of the power necessary to make contact with spirits, monks officiate jointly with 'spirit specialists,' whose function has not disappeared, although their role has been diminished. Most of the Phunoy admit, with some discomfort, that these specialists continue to be involved in rituals as officiants. In some sense they regard them as a necessary evil, essential in the fight against the misfortunes with which the spirits torment them. In many rituals to ward off misfortune, *atjan* can, in fact, replace non-Buddhist celebrants, as they are also capable of performing everything a monk can do (the reverse not being true).

An analysis of these rituals to ward off misfortune reveals that it is only through the conjunction of two domains, Buddhism and spirit worship – through two types of officiants, or their union in one (the *atjan*) – that the ritual resolution of evils can be accomplished. The considerable prestige now enjoyed by the *atjan* results from this conjunction. The fact that it is the descendants of *maphê* or of *tjaocam* who almost always take on the role of *atjan* is rooted in the fact that they have the inherited ability to relate effectively to the spirits.

The Phunoy example illustrates the changing practices of a population who have been subjected to a policy of imposing a supposedly orthodox Buddhism. It shows that this attempt has not led to the demise of previous religious elements, nor to their mere perpetuation behind a 'Buddhist veneer.' In fact, as we have seen, rather than leading to a buddhicisation of these practices, the reforms have caused the monks, who are having to deal with rituals involving the spirits, to be 'animised'.

My aim in this chapter has been to move beyond the ways in which the relationship between Buddhism and spirit cults has been analysed to date. My intention has been to display the diachronic dimension of this relationship and to look at the logic involved in the transformation of the previous system. The Phunoy case is interesting because it enables us to do this. The relationship between Buddhism and spirit worship in a given society does not have an invariable form; it is subject to history. It is this historicity of religious systems, and therefore the consideration of their successive re-articulations, which, in my view, still needs to be introduced into studies of religion among the people of Laos and, more broadly, of Buddhist societies of Southeast Asia.

CHAPTER 11

Huaphanh – Revolutionary Heritage and Social Transformations in the 'Birthplace of Lao PDR'

OLIVER TAPPE

Huaphanh province in north-east Laos assumes two roles in Grant Evans's work on the history and cultures of Laos. First, as an obscure hiding place of the Pathet Lao leadership – a rugged frontier from which the revolutionary movement emerged, spreading throughout the Lao uplands and finally reaching the Mekong basin, culminating in the seizure of power in 1975 (as outlined in his 2002 *A Short History of Laos*). Secondly, the province became his anthropological fieldsite in which to study processes of asymmetric cultural assimilation for which he coined the term 'Tai-isation' (2000; also see Évrard 2019). Here, Grant Evans anticipated later debates on Zomia, the uplands of Southeast Asia as multicultural zones of conflict and interactions and complex relations across cultural difference (cf. Scott 2009; Jonsson 2014).

In this chapter, I would like to highlight the significance of Huaphanh for understanding the historical and sociocultural dynamics of past and present-day Laos. My discussion of the caves of Viengxay as a revolutionary heritage site is of course inspired by Evans's seminal works on the politics of history and memory in post-1975 Lao PDR (Evans 1998b). I extend the scope of analysis through a couple of sections dedicated to the social and economic transformations that have taken place in Huaphanh since the 1990s, when the province was opened for tourism and other development incentives. Observations in the provincial capital Sam Neua and remote places such as the new district Muang Kuon next to the Vietnamese border are also informed by Grant Evans's early studies on agrarian change (in particular the failure of collectivisation) in lowland Laos (Evans 1990a; also see the insightful works by Robert Cole on recent trends of agrarian change in Huaphanh: Cole 2021 and forthcoming). The concluding section on interethnic relations and interactions in Huaphanh takes Evans' 2000 study on Tai-isation processes as its vantage point and aims to find new perspectives on transcultural dynamics in multi-ethnic Laos using the lens of mimesis (Tappe 2018).

The aim of this chapter is to show how the history and landscape of Huaphanh has shaped the lifeworlds of the different people (including Lao, Tai Daeng, Tai Dam, Khmu, Phong, Ksingmul, Hmong and Yao) living in the hills and valleys of the Lao–Vietnamese borderlands. Since my first visit in 2008, the region has witnessed social transformations and new interethnic dynamics – processes that have accompanied the ongoing efforts of the Lao government to make Huaphanh a showcase of revolutionary memory and Party–State legitimacy.

Viengxay, a Revolutionary Heritage Site

Siphone was aware that I was particularly interested in the caves of Viengxay, the place in the northwestern mountains of Laos where the leaders of the communist revolution endured the daily bombings of the Americans during this sideshow of the Vietnam War (Tappe 2013a). And yet the skinny Hmong guide from the 'Viengxay Caves Visitor Centre' insisted on taking me to another brand-new attraction, which was – according to official historiography – the 'birthplace of the Lao PDR' (Lao National Tourism Administration 2010). Leaving the cool shadows of the vertical karst rocks behind, we passed the periphery of the town of Viengxay with its small houses, reminiscent of the time when this area was just an agglomeration of villages.

Like a rocket base in the Kazakh steppe, a huge concrete platform emerged. In the middle, encircled by Lao national and red socialist flags, the five-metre high statue of Kaysone Phomvihane (1920–1992), the late strongman of the Lao People's Revolutionary Party, raises his right arm in a benevolent greeting pose. Icon of the socialist Party–State (see Evans's 1998b discussion of the 'cult of Kaysone'; and Tappe 2017), he represents the ongoing claim to power of the Lao one-party regime at

Photo: O. Tappe, 2010

Figure 11.1: The politburo meeting room in the Viengxay caves.

this important *lieu de mémoire* (Nora 1989). My companion, who had accompanied me during previous tours in the area, stressed Kaysone's historical importance for modern Laos and proudly stated that this statue 'was as tall as the one in Vientiane!' He was referring to the identical statue at the Kaysone Memorial in the capital, clearly expressing local pride and ongoing revolutionary devotion.[1]

The monument to Kaysone was sponsored by the Vietnamese government as a token of recognition of the 'special relationship' between the two socialist regimes (see Evans 2002a). It is the most recent addition to the landscape of revolutionary memory associated with Kaysone, marked by a number of caves where Kaysone and other leaders of the so-called 'national liberation struggle' (*kantosu ku sat*) maintained their political and military base during the years of the US 'secret war' in Laos (1964–73). Kaysone's own cave complex, which included the politburo meeting room, is usually the starting point of the guided cave tours (Figure 11.1). Incense sticks in front of a small bust of the revolutionary

1. Interview with Siphone Vangduayang, 2011. This chapter uses material gathered on many field trips to Huaphanh between 2008 and 2019 (also see Tappe 2013a/b, 2017, 2018).

leader indicate ongoing veneration, which is fuelled by heroic accounts of his deeds in school books, newspapers and TV documentaries.

The standard tour around the caves of Viengxay includes detailed information about the 'American War', provided through information plates, by well-informed local guides – mainly of Hmong ethnic origin – and through an English-language audio tour with original voices of witnesses of the American bombings (Lao National Tourism Administration 2010). All the recorded voices somehow unanimously hint at the righteousness of the revolutionary struggle, emphasising the solidarity of party cadres, soldiers, and civilians facing foreign aggression, and thus help the Party–State to perpetuate the narrative of the valiant 'Lao multi-ethnic people' fighting under the leadership of selfless patriots against foreign oppressors (Tappe 2013a, 2013b).

Parallel to the heroic narratives, there remains a competing discourse of hardship and suffering, as reflected in the frequent description by many locals of their 'poor' (*thuk nyak*) livelihoods. Despite the growing local pride and recognition by lowland Lao and foreign visitors, there is still a sense of marginality and inequality in Huaphanh, as far as my interviewees in Viengxay were concerned. To a large extent this is due to high levels of poverty – many districts in Huaphanh are officially classified as 'poor districts' – which some persons whom I talked to blamed on the devastation of war. Thus, Viengxay is a site of 'spatial melancholia' (Navaro-Yashin 2009: 16) and sad memories, as well as revolutionary nostalgia, discharged by the very materiality of the physical landscape.

Meanwhile, the violent death of the last Lao king, Sisavang Vatthana (1907–1980) in a re-education camp in Huaphanh is hushed up. Evans (2009) presents telling pictures from shortly before and after the communist revolution, one showing the king on an official visit to the 'liberated zone' in front of respectfully kneeling Pathet Lao soldiers, and another more notorious one, displaying the king and his wife now themselves sitting on the ground in a devout posture, apparently in a re-education camp. This episode remains officially silenced so as to obscure the fact that the birth of the Lao PDR was attended by acts of violence and brutality (also see Pholsena 2012). What was a traumatic journey with no return for members of the royal elite and the 'Vientiane side' of the civil conflict that tore apart the country from the late 1950s until 1975 is now an exciting new adventure for the urban middle classes, who enjoy the rugged landscape and the simple lifestyle of the countryside as offered by the commemorative/touristic site of Viengxay (in recent years often combined with a tour to Phu Phathi mountain, where North Vietnamese sappers captured a secret US American radar station in 1967).

Viengxay as revolutionary commemoration site underscores an increasing local pride and development aspirations that present a contrast to the narrative of the poor peripheral provinces. The new central monument of Sam Neua, built in 2008 and locally just called *anousavali* ('monument'), making it analogous to the Patu Xay (Arc de Triomphe) in Vientiane (Evans 1998b), is considered a key element in making Sam Neua a 'modern' city (see Petit 2020). According to an official of the local tourism office (interview in 2011), the stylised gemstone on the top refers to the 'indestructible' Sam Neua and its brave people, despite the fact that Sam Neua was razed to the ground by American bombs. Along with other recent development initiatives (see below), this monument marks a re-centralisation of this first 'liberated zone' (*khet potpoi*) and revolutionary 'centre' (*sunkang*) of Laos.

As Phill Wilcox (2021) has recently observed, the UNESCO heritage site of Luang Prabang is marked by a tension between preservation and development. In the case of Viengxay, development is part of the story, too. As a party cadre highlighted in a speech on the occasion of the opening ceremony for the new Buddhist temple in Viengxay in 2011, Viengxay had risen from the ashes to become a modern *muang*, a bright example of the farsighted direction of the revolutionary Party. However, Viengxay has yet to fulfil the government's promise of economic prosperity. Before I discuss the ambiguities of development, I will go more deeply into discourses relating to local memory.

Huaphanh as Ambiguous Landscape of Memory

Viengxay is certainly the key element of the memorial landscape palimpsest of Huaphanh. So far, hopes of triggering tourism beyond the caves tour have not been fulfilled. Although the province witnesses a constant flow of visitors, this mainly consists of private Lao tours or groups from schools and ministries, and the occasional Vietnamese delegations. As Siphone and his father Siphanh, former head of the caves tours office, complained in 2015, their private initiatives to establish trekking tour-

Photo: O. Tappe, 2019

Figure 11.2: Lao tourists on Phu Phathi. → Colour version on page 381.

ism in the hills around Viengxay could not be realised due to lack of Western customers and lack of interest on the part of the Sam Neua department of tourism. Neither Lao nor Vietnamese tourists like the idea of following the old mountain trails of the Hmong (at least not yet). The hike up to Phu Phathi seems to be the most adventurous expedition undertaken, so far (Figure 11.2).

In consequence, the region by and large remains a landscape of ossified revolutionary commemoration. Governmental historiographic hegemony is not interested in a more polyphonic local memory (which I perhaps should not have expected in 2013). Still, Huaphanh offers many different perspectives on local history, which hide beneath the neat surface of the Lao People's Revolutionary Party master narrative. Viengxay and Sam Neua have more to tell.

In 2008 and 2013, I carried out long interviews with Siphanh, back then head of the Viengxay caves tourism office (later officially named 'Kaysone Phomvihane Caves Tour Office'). Besides outlining the process of making Viengxay a national heritage site and appealing to tourists, the renovation of the caves and development of the guided tours,

Siphanh integrated his own biography into the history of Viengxay, and Huaphanh more generally. In conversations like this with older people in Huaphanh, I was able to get an idea of the strength of the imprint that the rugged landscape and the years of the war have left in the individual memories of the people.

Siphanh's childhood memory of his Hmong village in the mountains of Xieng Kho province suggests an idyllic rural life with hard but rewarding work on the upland rice fields and a generous number of livestock ('we had cows and buffaloes, 50–60 pigs, 200–300 chickens…'). The war, especially the American bombings, put an end to this prosperous Hmong livelihood. One day, a huge bomb destroyed many of the houses in Siphanh's village and killed his grandfather and other villagers. The following years, in the late 1960s, were shaped by hardship and a precarious existence in makeshift, mobile forest villages, with most of the young men recruited by the Pathet Lao. Siphanh insisted that his father had already joined the 'Lao Front' (*naeo lao*) before this, and not the 'Vang Pao Hmong' around Phu Phathi, who were the 'enemy' (*satu*).[2]

His story is only one example of many such narratives. Some of them, including Siphanh's account, were printed in the book *Voices of Viengxay* (Lao National Tourism Administration 2010; also see Tappe 2013a: 68). These narratives show how the people of Huaphanh were mobilised (or radicalised?) in the course of the arbitrary US bombings (for a time directed from the radar station on Phu Phathi; Castle 1999). People did not dare to cultivate their fields during the daytime and avoided making fires, as the smoke would attract American planes. Up to 20,000 people sought shelter in the caves around Viengxay, while villagers in other regions just dug out hideouts in the forest, eating roots and tubers and sometimes scavenging in an abandoned maize field.

These narratives have certainly been shaped by the revolutionary master narrative of the 'national liberation struggle' (*kantosu ku sat*) of the 'Lao multi-ethnic people' (*pasason lao banda phao*) (see Tappe 2013b; Ministry of Information and Culture 2000). This standard view of the 'birthplace of the Lao PDR' glosses over the internal tensions and ruptures that marked Huaphanh province, beyond the internecine

2. See Benson 2018 for a detailed account of the (civil) war in Huaphanh.

conflicts of the Hmong. The ambiguous role of the Lao and Tai *phya*[3] and other former elite families, and of the Catholic Tai Daeng communities in eastern Huaphanh, most of which had been loyal to the French beforehand, seem to have been erased from local memory.

An old man from Ban Houaxieng (near Sam Neua) spoke of the social tensions that existed due to the rampant paranoia about spies informing the US forces about potential targets. Initially, the villagers tried to avoid taking sides, accepting guests from both sides ('like a bird with two heads', as he put it), but they became more cautious when revolutionary soldiers began aggressively searching the villages for 'traitors'. He remembered one incident when Vietnamese soldiers came to the village and claimed to be from a nearby communist garrison while in fact reporting to the US radar post on Phu Phathi. With a shrug, the old man explained apologetically that it was difficult for the local villagers to tell the different garrisons and troops as at that time they were very busy just surviving...

While 'traitors' and 'enemies' occasionally pop up in the heroic and/or victimising historical narratives of Huaphanh, there is one notable absence: the fate of the last king of Laos, Sisavang Vatthana, as represented by the uncanny photographic couplet in Evans 2009. His tragic story is either silenced or only mentioned in somewhat apologetic accounts such as the following one, told by Siphanh in 2013:

> They brought the old king to Samneua and built a house for him at Ban Na Ngoua, Xieng Kho district. [...] The old king was very sad and unhappy with the incredible living conditions because when he was a king in Vientiane [sic] he led a plentiful life, had a great house for living and nice car for riding, but later to be here his life changed very much. He worked hard, cared for the vegetable gardens. He became ill, headache, and then he passed away.

In fact, the king's 'house' was located in one of the notorious re-education camps where many members of the old elite met their deaths. Some published memoirs written by former inmates of these camps (see, e.g., Bounsang 2006; Khamphanh 2004) tell of the brute force of

3. An honorific title for the heads of what people today call the 'feudal administration' (*bokkhong khong sakdina*), who governed the commoners. Interestingly, Kaysone's cave had previously been used as a secret hideout by the *phya* of Xiengluang, a major Lao settlement during colonial times.

a paranoid regime; of humiliation, violence and death from maltreatment, illness and undernourishment. This is the 'other' landscape, the 'dissonant heritage' (Tunbridge and Ashworth 1996) of Huaphanh: not the caves of heroism and solidarity, but the fields of hatred and violence enclosed by barbed wire.

But the local people also suffered from the aftermath of war. Following the brief period when Viengxay was the 'resistance capital' in 1973, the town became almost deserted, when almost everyone moved to Vientiane after the revolution of 1975 – not only the families of the new leaders of the country but also a large part of the already displaced population of the area. Only a few people remained in the war-torn landscape and even fewer planned to stay on longer term. Siphanh spoke of people living in poor-quality, makeshift houses, ready to move on somewhere else at any time. It was only in the 1990s that things improved, when roads, electricity, and public services made the town more attractive (and a key destination for Hmong resettlement).

Aspects of 'Progress' in Sam Neua and Viengxay

The promise of development, reflected in the ashes-to-*muang* story, is perhaps even more relevant for Sam Neua, the provincial capital of Huaphanh since 1905. Completely erased during the US bombing campaign, it has only recently started to become a prosperous town, benefiting mainly from Vietnamese investment and corresponding development initiatives. Besides the aforementioned new new city pillar monument, a big park in the town centre projects Sam Neua's new self-image, linking the 'birthplace of Lao PDR' and 'land of heroes' revolutionary narratives with the rich cultural heritage of the region (included in the narratives only recently, though). A replica of the 3,000-year-old megaliths in Houameuang province[4] and statues representing the different ethnic groups – displaying 'traditional' dress and handicraft[5] – represent the cultural wealth of Huaphanh (Figure 11.3).

4. The *sao hintang* ('20 standing stones') in Houamuang district constitute one of the most important archaeological sites of Laos (see Colani 1935; Källéen 2016). Locals proudly stress the fact that the megaliths are older than the famous stone jars of Xieng Khouang province.
5. See Goudineau's (2015) discussion of the increasing official exhibition of ethnic diversity that is taking place, against a background of accelerated standardisation of social and cultural diversity.

Photo: O. Tappe, 2019

Figure 11.3: Displaying multi-ethnic heritage in Sam Neua. → Colour version page 381.

This all forms part of the general climate of economic development and modernisation that is currently shaping the changing urban landscape of Sam Neua. In an interview in 2019, the guesthouse manager Bounhom – of mixed Tai Daeng and Chinese origin – discussed recent urbanisation initiatives with me, such as new infrastructure and a large Chinese market complex offering all kinds of consumer goods (imported from China and Vietnam). He made an interesting connection with the legacy of Chinese traders of precolonial and colonial times, who intermarried locally and represent the origin of the small Lao/Tai-Chinese business elite in Sam Neua (who venerate their ancestors annually at the Chinese cemetery in the north of town). Chinese influence notwithstanding, Bounhom highlighted the fact that it is Vietnamese investment and trading activity that fuel economic development and make Sam Neua a *chaleun* (prosperous) town.

The Vietnamese have been a significant demographic element in the area for more than a century. Recent Vietnamese labour migration into the local construction sector, in particular infrastructure, is reminiscent of the colonial practice of recruiting Vietnamese labour for road construction in upland Laos. In order to 'unblock' Huaphanh in the direction of Hanoi, and to foster the flow of natural resources downhill, the French ordered Vietnamese 'coolies' (and a smaller number of local hands) to build two key routes linking Sam Neua with the Vietnamese lowlands (Foropon 1927).

As was the case with the Chinese merchants, Vietnamese workers and petty traders have intermarried locally, as have the Vietnamese soldiers who have increasingly operated in the region since the 1940s. When in 1953 the Vietminh and a small group of Lao Communists under the leadership of Kaysone managed to seize Sam Neua from the French – a prelude to Dien Bien Phu (Lentz 2019) – the North Vietnamese had established a number of military posts in the borderland and they have remained an important political and economic factor ever since.

Despite the celebrations of the Lao–Vietnamese 'special relationship' (see Evans 2002a) and the promising economic opportunities linking Huaphanh with Thanh Hoa province (Pierre Petit 2020 describes a dancing performance in the cultural hall enacting this relationship), locals in Sam Neua expressed some resentment of increasing Vietnamese in-migration. The aggressive behaviour of Vietnamese traders particularly annoyed the many local people (mainly women) who engage in very low levels of petty trade to help support their families.

I recently (September 2021) asked a local friend via WhatsApp if the Covid19 pandemic has affected this issue. He was quite upbeat in his response, telling me that due to the stricter border regime fewer Vietnamese migrants have been coming to Laos, thus opening up new opportunities for trade and work for locals. At least that was his view. He underscored this observation by mentioning that there is an ongoing flow of commodities from Vietnam – but without the involvement of the Vietnamese themselves. The importance of agriculture in Huaphanh's economy arguably also provides a safety net against the disturbances caused by the pandemic.[6]

Vietnamese work migration is certainly connected to Vietnamese investment in a range of infrastructure projects in Sam Neua. The new

6. I have learnt from what I have seen and been told in the border areas with Thailand that people in Laos suffer more from restrictions that hamper the flow of goods and people (given that work migration to Thailand and corresponding remittances used to be a key factor for local subsistence).

bridge across the Nam Sam, the new market buildings, the cultural hall, and finally the huge concrete madness of a new revolutionary memorial: such projects form part of a wider Lao–Vietnamese economic collaboration as part of which 'gifts' like these are made, together with tax exemptions and other incentives for Vietnamese investors.

Another visible expression of this collaboration are the guesthouses, restaurants and entertainment venues that are created to cater for Vietnamese customers in Sam Neua and Viengxay. Signs in the Vietnamese language are an unmistakable marker of this development (and were not very common a couple of years ago). My Lao interlocutors seemed ambivalent about this recent trend. A few welcomed the fact that there is now some action going on (e.g. Vietnamese karaoke bars) – something to offer visitors from Vientiane and other urban places. More people, however, pointed to the rise of prostitution (which was, of course, already present beforehand) and other moral problems. An over-the-top party in one of the Viengxay caves went viral on Facebook; it was, again, the allegedly immoral Vietnamese who were blamed for this.

Thus it seems that the revolutionary heartland faces the ambiguous and contingent effects of development and modernisation. This is also true for the countryside.

Muang Kuon: A New District, Old Connections and Upland Development

I met Siphone again seven years after our first encounter, while I was doing some research using oral history methods in the districts that border Vietnam, Sam Tai and Muang Kuon. In Muang Kuon, a small town that has been turned into a new district capital, he showed up during an interview with the head of the Department of Information and Culture, Bountong, and his colleague from Sam Tai, Somsouk. Siphone seemed unhappy with his new office job, and said that his plans for tourism in Viengxay had not, beyond the occasional cave tour, been successful. Although his new job means a stable, if low, income and a certain social mobility and prestige (see High 2021), he had apparently had other plans for his life. This reflects the dilemma faced by ambitious young cadres, who still find themselves in a rigid system where you move mainly by being moved, for better or worse, within the complex clientelist system that marks Lao society today.

In 2012, Muang Kuon was separated from Sam Tai district of which it formed a large part south of Sam Tai town, bordering Xieng Khouang province and Vietnam. What emerged on the maps as Muang Kuon District was, in fact, an underdeveloped periphery of a periphery. Sam Tai itself had long been a dead end at which one arrives after a journey of several hours from Sam Neua. Muang Kuon was only connected by dirt roads, and was basically inaccessible during the rainy season. Around 2010, a development programme by the Asian Development Bank (ADB) brought a paved road between Sam Tai and Muang Kuon, and further discussions of rural development in this remote region.

Siphone's office mates claimed that it was Nouhak Phoumsavan's (1910–2008) initiative to develop these areas of Huaphanh. Interestingly, the former Party–State's 'Number Two', after Kaysone, had initiated one of the first development projects in the region that was funded by non-socialist countries, namely an Australian project in Ban Tao by the Sam river near the Vietnamese border (Kathryn Sweet, personal communication). Every now and then during my stays in Huaphanh province, local people talked fondly about Nouhak, who regularly stayed at his 'cave house' until he was very old, and engaged with issues of food security and agrarian development in the poor districts of Huaphanh. Rumours have it that he had a *mia noi* (mistress) in Ban Tao. Nouhak was certainly among the Party leaders (*phak-lat*) who maintained a particularly close bond with the revolutionary heartland in the uplands – regions that in recent decades have often been bypassed by lowland economic growth.

Initiatives to develop this remote (in many respects) area were soon followed by the idea of making Muang Kuon the centre of a new district (in 2012). The local authorities in Sam Tai district had been facing administrative challenges in this vast, mountainous and sparsely populated district – echoing the complaints of French colonial administrators of a century ago. Dividing Sam Tai District would have the advantage of separating the administration of Sam Tai town and the larger Nam Sam area on one side from that of the rugged, allegedly underdeveloped terrain further south, which would be administered from a new focal centre. The division would also have other advantages. To quote from the interview I carried out in the Department of Information and Culture:

> Bountong: The idea of dividing Sam Tai district was first proposed by the district authorities to the central government.

> Somsouk: Because of the difficulties of development.
>
> Bountong: The development process is very slow and uneven as the territory of Sam Tai is too large.
>
> Somsouk: And the budget we receive for district development is also limited... so if we have two districts then we can receive a double annual budget!

This was a smart move on the part of the district authorities at Sam Tai, intended to get the provincial government of Huaphanh to allocate additional funding from the central government for local development. In 2017, the results were visible: more roads, electricity, office facilities (still rudimentary, though), and a new 'government' quarter with large houses, where only a few years before wooden stilt houses had dominated the landscape. Simultaneously, Muang Kuon became a focal site for the resettlement of upland villages, so that the population of the town doubled within five years (to almost 5,000 inhabitants by 2017; the whole district has 25,000 inhabitants).

As Muang Kuon is located on a plateau, water supply is the main challenge in relation to development there. Costly large-scale irrigation schemes have been introduced by the ADB, with pump systems bringing water up from the rivers that pass the plateau a few kilometres away. Paddy land is scarce, and the growing population mainly relies on swidden cultivation. Local authorities are aware of the pressure on natural resources but they turn a blind eye to rampant deforestation. As one official told me in a similar context near Viengxay: 'People must eat rice.'

In anticipation of irrigation and available land, large numbers of Hmong and Khmu people were attracted to Muang Kuon, following in the footsteps of others from the same communities who had already been resettled there. Later on the same day that I carried out the interview in the Department of Information and Culture, I talked to a Hmong woman who was waiting by the roadside for her son (a soldier in the nearby military base) to pick her up. She informed me that she moved to Muang Kuon in 2002 (when the resettlement campaign was already in full swing; see Évrard and Goudineau 2004). Nine households had, she told me, moved there from her village, which was called Houay Bouay, but five of them had returned, after realising that there was not enough farmland available. She had decided to stay. Her main reason for staying was the fact that there was a school in Muang Kuon: a future for her children. Many resettled Hmong mentioned the school as a reason for remaining. They also said that they resent the fact that there are either no schools in remote villages or a lack of teachers. Thus, the Hmong are, in practice, accepting precarious livelihoods for the sake of access to education and other forms of infrastructure.[7]

The Hmong in Muang Kuon form separate neighbourhoods around an 'urban' core consisting mainly of Lao and Tai Daeng houses – called 'Tai Kuon' by the Hmong woman – as is the case in many towns in Huaphanh that have recently expanded in size. A similar spatial configuration can be seen in the Hmong village Ban Phu Say, which is located just outside Viengxay town. In the Tai Daeng village of Ban Kho (near Sam Tai town), the demographic situation has changed immensely, with resettled Hmong now making up half of the population, the rest of which is predominantly made up of Tai Daeng. In Muang Kuon, the spatial demarcation between the 'old' Tai village and the Hmong part, further up the hill, is striking. The integration or non-integration of Hmong households into village communities deserves further scrutiny, and Muong Kuon would be a good test case.

The reason why Muang Kuon was chosen as a new 'centre', in spite of water supply problems, was mainly its geographic location and its existing, albeit rudimentary, infrastructure. The town is located at the junction of historic trading routes linking Sam Tai with Nong Het in Xieng Khouang province and southern Huaphanh with Nghe An in Vietnam. In colonial times benzoin resin and shellac were key commodities in trade with the lowlands, and opium was also an important source of income for decades ('many hectares!' [were planted with opium], as Somsouk exclaimed) before the eradication campaigns of the 2000s. As will be discussed below, maize is the number one cash crop now.

Livelihood Transitions – the Examples of Agriculture and Weaving

In an early issue of the journal *Anthropos*, the French missionary Antoine Bourlet claimed to have observed a strange form of 'socialism' in

7. Interestingly, a Lao friend from the Ministry of Information and Culture suggested half-jokingly that the Hmong will outpace the Lao soon as they have more children and take proper care of education (unlike the Khmu, he said, as they prefer their children to start working, at the expense of their school education; as Stolz [2021] points out, there is a strong work ethic in Khmu society, despite the fact that they are poor and marginalised).

Huaphanh: '[...] une manière de communisme, mais un communisme qui ressemble fort à de la féodalité' (Bourlet 1906: 525). Every couple of years the village land was redistributed according to household size. In addition, anyone who cleared a tract of new land for cultivation could claim proprietary rights as long as he cultivated it.

Interestingly, this system is still used in some Tai and Lao villages, while others have subsequently moved to a system of private land titles – and an even smaller number of villages still have land that is cultivated cooperatively. There are overlaps between customary forms of land organisation and different forms of state-controlled cultivation. Village maps of previous land allocation programmes, which demarcate farmland from (different kinds of) forest land, are often ignored by local committees faced with dealing with integrating resettled communities and other challenges relating to local land organisation.

An old man, a former *nai khet* ('head of area', meaning the head of a village group, reminiscent of the older Tai title *nai kong*) of Muang Kuon before it became a proper town, told me about the various transformations in land use since colonial times. He highlighted the fact that in the 'feudal' (*sakdina*) system, there had indeed been a practice of land redistribution, as documented by Bourlet. However, the Tai or Lao *phya* ('lord') owned most of the paddy land, on which he could conscript villagers to work. Labour conscription was also usual for tasks like house construction and the organisation of festivals. Finally, at least two servants recruited from among the villagers took weekly turns to stay at the *phya*'s house and to accept any assignments (they even had to bring their own food).

This, together with arbitrary taxation – no one knew how many of the *piastres* collected by the *phya* were really passed on to the French authorities – gave fodder to the anticolonial and antifeudal propaganda disseminated by the Vietminh in the region. The last 'feudal' leader of Muang Kuon, Phya Leu, was chased away after the revolutionary takeover in 1953, briefly returned during the period of the coalition government in 1956 (probably thanks to what was still a functioning network of patronage) but was ousted again when the civil war escalated – 'and then no *phya* anymore', as the elderly *nai khet* whom I interviewed said.

The collectivisation of the 1970s (see Evans 1990a), when all the harvest was collected and redistributed, was considered a failure by most villagers. The old man identified the main problem as being the fact that people became lazy as you got the same ration according to a certain score that depended on your family size, independent of how hard you worked. This led to severe food shortages and hunger, a downward spiral and eventually abandonment of the system (the old man laughed at how ridiculous it all was...). In the late 1980s, not only was the paddy land divided again but it was even reclaimed by the former landowners, thus reproducing old hierarchies.

All of the 50 ha of paddy land in Muang Kuon have been divided up, with land titles to all land, with no communal land remaining – except swidden land, which is used according to demand and availability. However, since 2003 it has not been possible to divide the land any further, according to the old man, because too many people have settled in Muang Kuon and land has become scarce. In 2005, the authorities decided that if people want to settle in Muang Kuon they can only come as businesspeople. Not surprisingly, most newcomers still cultivated swidden land in the vicinity, with resulting pressure on the forest base.

People in Huaphanh still claim that *het hai het na* (making swiddens and growing rice in paddy fields) is the basis of agriculture there. Cash crops like maize and other income opportunities have, in fact, meant that livelihoods in rural Laos have become more complex. However, rice-growing continues to be the focus of many villagers' livelihoods in the valleys of Huaphanh. But, as a Vietnamese maize trader quoted by Robert Cole (forthcoming) argues: 'If all of you only grow rice, you cannot get out of poverty.'

In his recent studies on livelihood change in Huaphanh, Cole (2021; Cole and Rigg 2019) discusses the way in which villages have experienced a rapid livelihood transition from what was primarily subsistence rice farming before 2006 to increasingly commercially-oriented livelihoods combining rice with hybrid maize thereafter. This transition has reflected government policies that are aimed at fulfilling the development objectives of economic growth and modernisation. This includes controlling and harnessing peripheral space and making 'productive' use of it (Barney 2009; Hirsch and Scurrah 2015).

Export-oriented production has been made possible through contract farming arrangements, which have helped to extend commodity crops further into marginal spaces, connecting cross-border traders with farmers, opportunity-seeking Vietnamese traders and a cross-border expansion of the Vietnamese feed sector fuelled by increasing demand for maize (Cole forthcoming). This appeared to be a solution for food insecurity after the opium eradication campaigns of the 2000s. Farmers belonging to the different ethnic groups in Huaphanh learned quickly from the Vietnamese farmers-turned-traders, as Cole reports from his fieldsite in northern Huaphanh (see Lu 2017 for a similar example relating to rubber cultivation).

Vietnamese sold fertilisers, chemical sprayers and rice-mills, and the farmers would pay with maize production after the harvest. Thus, villagers depended on the trader to purchase their output and to build and maintain the feeder roads each year (this is what I learnt in Sam Tai district as well). Longstanding contacts implied trust, but also risk, as the villages in Huaphanh remained highly dependent on their Vietnamese trading partners. In 2017 people in Houamuang district (which is further from the Vietnamese border than are Sam Tai and Muang Kuon) complained that a drop in market prices resulted in Vietnamese traders not showing up to collect the harvest, leaving the villagers with rotting corn and no money to buy food.

The farming households of Huaphanh displayed a pioneering spirit in experimenting with new and sometimes risky crops. The female members of many of these households demonstrated a similar spirit in professionalising the production and distribution of handwoven textiles (Stolz and Tappe 2021). Lao and Tai Daeng weavers in particular are renowned throughout Laos for their excellent weaving skills. Silken scarves and skirts from Huaphanh are highly esteemed by both domestic and international customers, and are sold in the boutiques of Vientiane and Luang Prabang or exported abroad.

In her inconspicuous wooden house, a well-established weaver from Sam Tai told me in 2017 about her customers in countries such as Japan, Australia, and USA, often diaspora people who appreciate what are regarded as the authentic weaving traditions of Huaphanh. However, her main customers are well-off urban people from Vientiane, especially the 'daughters-in-law of the elite' (*phu nyai*) who can afford these handmade silk textiles (instead of the cheaper fake ones from China). She mentioned in particular the daughter-in-law of Thongloun Sisoulith, who was at that time Minister of Foreign Affairs, later prime minister, and who comes from Sam Neua.

One pioneer of this translocal business and an example of female mobility was Ms. Souksayphone, who inspired many local women to increase their production of textiles in order to generate income. There is such a high demand for these textiles that Ms. Souksayphone is able to maintain a network (extending into remote rural villages) of 200 weavers who work for her. She also runs two guesthouses in Sam Tai. She has, through all of this, established a profitable female socioeconomic network (also see Vallard 2017) that challenges the male *phu nyai* patronage system.

During the interview, the weaver called her daughter and her neighbours on the phone, asking them to bring products to sell to me. It was only when I listened to the recordings later that I realised that in one of these conversations she had said: 'Bring XY, as the *falang* [Westerner] is interested in traditional Tai Daeng patterns.' These are successful businesswomen, generating most of income that comes into the households to which they belong. Not surprisingly, looms are a common sight in virtually any Tai and Lao house, and also in Phong houses that have appropriated their neighbours' techniques and patterns (see below). Girls start weaving from the age of seven and eight, in the evening after school.

A young neighbour of the weaver showed me a particularly fine piece of weaving, with a very detailed pattern, the result of two months' work. She calculated a sale price for it of 500,000 Kip [around 50 euros]. This would imply a monthly income of 250,000 Kip if she made regular sales like this. She claimed that the amount she earns is not much, and that it is quickly spent on rice if there is a bad harvest; however, households in this area usually have enough rice, as well as having some maize to sell. If you compare standard salaries for civil servants, teachers etc. in Laos (which range from 250,000 to 500,000 Kip), this is quite a good income and it is easy to see how important weaving is for household subsistence. That said, it increases the massive workload for females, who also do most of the household labour, tending the chickens, weeding gardens and fields, etc.

Another interesting aspect of this amazing development of textile production in Huaphanh was the fact that successful weavers claim to master the different techniques and patterns of different ethnic groups.

Lao and Phong women highlighted their skills in emulating 'traditional' Tai Daeng styles, which are particularly in demand in Vientiane and Luang Prabang. This is only one aspect of mimetic appropriation in this multi-ethnic context, as the concluding section will show.

Processes of Mimetic Appropriation in a Multi-Ethnic Society

As I have discussed elsewhere (Tappe 2018), mutual mimetic appropriation is a key phenomenon of interethnic relations in upland Laos. The Austroasiatic Phong of Huaphanh are a case in point. Almost 100 years ago, the French administrator Lagrèze (1925) speculated that the Phong (like all 'Kha') showed 'a tendency to leave their customs and even their religion'. By this he probably meant certain animist ritual practices – 'their ancient customs'. Only 10 years later, French archaeologist Madeleine Colani (1935: 27) described the Phong as 'a race close to extinction'. Conversion to Buddhism and a lack of significant local material culture are put forward as key markers of this.

The Phong do indeed constitute a good test case for a process of sociocultural transformation that Grant Evans (2000) and Olivier Évrard (2019) discuss as Tai-isation or Lao-isation. Besides conversion to Buddhism – which had already taken place in precolonial times – the (mimetic) appropriation of Tai/Lao material culture, loanwords and sociopolitical structures exemplify this process (see Tappe and Badenoch 2021; Ladwig and Roque 2020; Jonsson 2010). A replica of the Sam Neua city pillar monument located next to the Buddhist temple suggests a self-consciously mimetic *muang*. And yet, even if they increasingly call themselves 'Lao Phong', indicating belonging to the Lao 'multi-ethnic' nation (see Évrard 2019), the Phong stress their specific Phong-ness and a sense of place, as the proud village community in Ban Saleuy demonstrates.

Besides cultivating their own language within the village community, the Phong have specific cosmological beliefs and ritual practices that even today distinguish them from their Lao Buddhist ('Lao Phut') neighbours. As with Austroasiatic speaking groups on the Boloven Plateau (Sprenger 2018), conversion to Buddhism produces shifts concerning the temporality and spatiality of the ritual cycle but does not completely transform these original systems. Conversion to Buddhism did not lead to cultural assimilation, and neither did the adoption of silk weaving from the Phong's Tai and Lao neighbours. Such cultural borrowings have been vernacularised and constitute key markers of Phong local identity today (Tappe and Badenoch 2021; also see Évrard 2019; and Bouté 2018 on the Phunoy of Phongsali).

Grant Evans (2000) has proposed a one-sided process of Tai-isation of the Ksingmul (who are Austroasiatic speakers, like the Phong and the Khmu) through contact with the Tai Dam, especially with regard to their material culture, which is now virtually indistinguishable from Tai Dam material culture. Nathan Badenoch (forthcoming) criticises Evans's conclusion that the Ksingmul are on an inevitable cultural merger with the Tai Dam, since the persistence of the Ksingmul language suggests that there is at least some resistance to hegemonic Tai culture. Badenoch adds that a Tai Dam discourse of alleged Ksingmul laziness is central to Evans' argument. Unfortunately, Evans seems to confuse laziness with alleged un-productiveness, thus reproducing socialist narratives of unproductive uplands that contrast with the work ethos that is cultivated among many upland groups (see Stolz 2021for the Khmu example).

Even if the Phong appear by and large indistinguishable from their Tai-speaking neighbours with regard to material culture – which seems to confirm Evans's argument regarding cultural assimilation – their oral history suggests a creative process of cultural appropriation that aims to strengthen Phong identity (Tappe 2021; Tappe and Badenoch 2021). The increasing use of the autonym 'Lao Phong' links self-identification to a specific positionality within the Lao PDR context, in particular as 'civilised' Buddhists. The politics of belonging and recognition are also evident in the 'official register' (Badenoch 2018), which uses the term 'Lao Mai' ('new Lao') as an ethnonym for the Ksingmul. As I learned from Siphanh in Viengxay, the Ksingmul hid Kaysone in the forest during the early insurgency against the French, and apparently received Lao Mai as an honorific and apparently inclusive ethnonym (also see Badenoch forthcoming).

Lao Buddhism also seems to function as an integrating principle vis-à-vis non-Buddhist people in the context of Lao-isation in the sense of national building. The opening ceremony of Viengxay's Buddhist temple in 2010 – in a region with a non-Buddhist majority of Tai Daeng and Hmong – managed to mobilise a large part of the population under the umbrella of national 'solidarity' (*samakkhi*). Following Lao and Tai music and dance performances, a dozen Hmong schoolchildren performed a 'traditional' group dance – an ambiguous performance of inclusion and recognition, but also of cultural difference and even infantilisation of the minorities. During my conversations with Hmong observers of the ceremony, it appeared that most of them are either indifferent or pragmatic in their attitude to the Buddhist temple. As one old man put it: 'Our grandchildren will be Buddhists, anyway.'[8]

Besides Lao-isation in the Lao PDR context, long-term processes of mutual cultural borrowings (and different registers thereof) remain under-researched. Two interesting examples of the diffusion of specific elements across ethnolinguistic boundaries are the practice of ritually sharing a jar of rice beer (*lao hai*); and the demarcation of villages and fields with a *talaeo* – an ornamental structure made from rattan or bamboo – to ward off strangers and spirits or simply to ritually indicate taboo spaces. As these cultural phenomena appear among all the different ethnic groups of Huaphanh, this is less an asymmetric assimilation process than a series of mutual borrowings without a clear starting point, which eventually lead to the development of a transethnic ritual language operating in a culturally diverse and multilingual setting.

In 2010, on my first visit to Muang Kuon, a group of young Lao and Tai Daeng teachers invited me to talk about local history in one of their houses, a typical Lao house on wooden stilts. They produced a jar of *lao hai* for us to drink together – something that I still associated at that time with the 'ethnic' imagery on stamps and tourism brochures, where it is mainly used to represent 'Lao Theung' ('Uphill Lao', an outdated name for Austroasiatic groups; see Schlemmer 2017) culture. When I mentioned this, they insisted that this was a 'Lao Loum tradition' (*papheni Lao Loum*).

It would seem that the Lao of Huaphanh – described as Tai Neua ('Northern Tai') in French colonial sources – have incorporated certain elements usually associated with upland cultures. Still claiming to be 'Lao of the Lowlands', they have adopted livelihood patterns typical of other mountain-dwelling groups such as the Khmu or the Hmong – in particular swidden agriculture, due to the scarcity of land suitable for

8. This accords with Patrice Ladwig's (personal communication) recent observation of an increasing number of Hmong novices in the temple in Luang Prabang – another option for education and mobility for the children of rich Hmong families.

wet rice cultivation. Moreover, the *lao hai* – from which I have since been invited to drink in many villages belonging to different ethnic groups and to all ethnolinguistic categories – is a means of communication intelligible to everyone in Huaphanh: it is a means of integrating outsiders into an ephemeral (ritual) community (see Lissoir 2017 for an excellent study of the Tai Dam practice).

This reminded me of Edmund Leach's famous statement that 'people may speak different languages, wear different kinds of clothes, live in different kinds of houses, but they understand each other's ritual' (Leach 1954: 279). As Stéphane Gros (2007: 259) points out, Leach conceived of ritual mainly as a system of symbolic communication and a way of expressing the otherwise abstract social structures of a given society. Although Leach focused mainly on the circulation of wealth in the context of *mayu–dama* (wifegiver–wifetaker) relations, the underlying idea of a transethnic symbolic language can be transferred to different contexts such as the *lao hai* ritual of village hospitality.

There is no question that the *lao hai* creates a sense of solidarity that encompasses 'civilised' Lao Buddhists and their culturally different neighbouring groups. In this case the civilising process has included the adoption by the dominant group of cultural elements that used to be characteristic of the Other and that function as a means of interethnic communication. The *lao hai* expresses a temporal situation of communality despite difference, a performance of hospitality and temporal integration of a stranger into a village community. Moreover, it points to the fact that the upland groups of Huaphanh are more often than not spatially isolated and that essential networks of good exchange can only function through a specific ritual system of hospitality that permits strangers to enter other villages and create or reproduce social and economic relations. Latent hostilities are softened through common drinking. At the same time, hierarchies within the groups and are enacted and visualised.

Another case in point is the *talaeo* (see for example Formoso 2018; Anuman Rajadhon 1967), a bamboo ornament that marks areas as (temporally) taboo, e.g. graveyards. This symbol is so widespread among the different ethnic groups in upland Laos that one can only speculate about its origins and patterns of cultural diffusion. What matters here is that the *talaeo* is intelligible in various cultures with animist backgrounds –

including even the Buddhist Lao, whose cosmology is characterised by a manifold pantheon of ghosts (Holt 2009; Ladwig 2017). The belief in ghosts among many different ethnic groups arguably constitutes a transethnic 'moral milieu' (Durkheim and Mauss 1971: 811), although animist practices are frowned upon today as 'uncivilised' according to official *sivilai* ('modern', 'civilised') discourse. However, even the Lao and other Tai groups living in the uplands still perform buffalo sacrifices at important ritual occasions. This common ritual or symbolic language unites the different groups in the region. Thus, the upland frontier of Huaphanh is a centre in itself or at least a multi-centric region with diverse civilisational influences and internal interethnic dynamics where certain forms of symbolic communication create a sense of belonging to a common life-world.

Conclusion

As Gustav Izikowitz (1969: 142) once noted, interethnic interaction 'depends on the nature of the relations, the accepted evaluation of the different ethnic groups etc., and can lead to war, rebellion, persecution, flight, the imitation of customs, peaceful trade, and many other types of action'. I have discussed some aspects of the lifeworlds of Huaphanh in this paper. The region offers various vantage points from which to study interethnic dynamics, and also from which to study livelihood transformations and the dynamics of state integration with the discourses around memory that accompany these.

Huaphanh, in particular Viengxay, has been defined as the 'birthplace of the Lao PDR' and is thus a keystone of revolutionary historiography. Local discourses around memory are shaped by the master narrative of the Lao People's Revolutionary Party, which highlights the valiant struggle of the 'Lao multi-ethnic people' against foreign oppressors. Alternative views hardly contest this narrative, as my discussion of the caves of Viengxay has shown. And yet different layers of this specific historical palimpsest remain, hidden under the heroic story of party and people enduring the war in the caves.

Meanwhile, urbanisation in Sam Neua and the processes of agrarian change also reflect another dynamic within the region, beyond the ossified commemorative politics of the government. Promised by the Party–State since the incipient of socialist Laos, economic change has only recently been felt to any significant degree by the people of Huaphanh; and this has included unexpected consequences that are not always positive, such as increasing Vietnamese migration and new risks such as those that have accompanied the boom in maize-growing. With all these changes, the Lao People's Revolutionary Party's claim to power, with its associated imagery (as displayed in the Viengxay caves tour), is put into question. It remains to be seen how this will all play out in the coming years.

CHAPTER 12

The Ongoing Invention of a Multi-Ethnic Heritage in Laos[1]

YVES GOUDINEAU

How does one assert a 'national culture' and, within this national culture, what role should be given to different specific ethnicities? To a greater or lesser degree, almost every modern country faces this issue and choices stemming from it, in terms of management of a multi-ethnic society. Depending on what choices are made, the issue may become either an asset or a liability. While some countries are willing to publicly debate this topic, others implement coercive policies that are not supposed to be discussed (see Brown 2004a; 2004b).

In this respect, Laos – officially a multi-ethnic nation (*paxaxon Lao banda phao,* 'the multi-ethnic Lao people') – is in an experimental phase. Authorities face the difficult task of having to invent distinct cultural traditions for the 49 officially registered ethnic groups, almost 50% of which belong to 'ethnic minorities,' and of actively involving people in their assigned self-presentation (Goudineau and Évrard 2006; Pholsena 2006a).

Discussion of the invention of the social or the cultural is nothing new. Since the influential writings of Eric Hobsbawm, Terence Ranger (1983) and Benedict Anderson (1983), there have been countless books, articles or projects with titles such as 'The invention of', 'The making of' or 'The fabric of,' or with titles that use present participles such as 'Creating,' 'Imagining', 'Building' or 'Configuring.'[2] The main

1. This chapter is based on the slightly modified text of a keynote lecture given at the Fourth International Conference on Lao Studies at the University of Wisconsin-Madison on April 19, 2013. I am grateful to Grant Evans and Vanina Bouté for their insightful comments and to Ian Baird for his meticulous reading.
2. For Southeast Asia, see, among others, Horstmann and Wadley 2006; Michaud and Forsyth 2011; Ivarsson 2008; Harms 2011.

idea behind these titles is that process is involved – the idea of social construction. Everything is 'in the making' and a multitude of actors and networks participate together in building, inventing or imagining the cultural and the social. Laos seems particularly well suited to this kind of approach at present, as an attentive observer can witness, almost from month to month, the enactment of new policies, the emergence of new themes and debates and the invention of new cultural emblems, both at a national level and in the provinces, districts and villages (Berliner 2010; Grabowsky 2011; Ladwig 2008; Tappe this volume, Chapter 11).

On the other hand, common sense is generally resistant to this idea that culture is an 'invention', and would instinctively favour an 'essentialist' approach based on various forms of culturalism. There is an increasing desire among tourists today to encounter 'real, authentic cultures'. And Laos, a country whose borders were long closed to outsiders, appears to offer guarantees of the authenticity that many travellers seek among 'ethnic minorities' (Petit 2008; Tappe 2011). Actually, for a long period, this had not been entirely unfounded, when compared with some neighbouring countries. Until fairly recently, local culture has been able to survive in many villages in Laos better than elsewhere in the Mekong region.[3] It has sometimes been challenging for anthropologists to work out what the conditions are under which certain social structures or certain 'patterns of thought' are able to resist the ups and downs of history for long periods of time.[4]

But the situation has changed dramatically over the past 20 years. The development policies that have been adopted, aimed at permanently erasing any traces of what are regarded as archaic ways of life, have gradually banished much of what remained of traditional social organisation and ancient systems of belief from the culture of ethnic minorities. And there is clearly a certain degree of misapprehension among visitors today, who think they are seeing 'traditional villagers', not realising the dramatic changes that most of these people have experienced in their way of life. Over the past 10 years, in particular, the cultural landscape of entire regions has been transformed, due to the massive displace-

3. On the politics of neighbouring states' attitudes towards minorities, see McCaskil and Kampe 1997; Turton 2000; Duncan 2004; Masako 2013.

4. See Goudineau 2008 and 2009 for a discussion of the resilience of a circular model in Austroasiatic villages.

ment of villages across the country. As a result, in southern Laos most of the villages where I worked some 15 or 20 years ago no longer exist.

It is against the background of these tremendous social and economic changes, which have affected all the provinces of the country, from north to south, that I will consider the recent development of multiculturalism in Laos, one of the aims of which has been, paradoxically, to satisfy the desire for authenticity sought by visitors.

From Archaism and Backwardness in the 1990s to the 'Opening Up' of Remote Areas in the 2000s

Mainly because of the political splits and war-related dislocations that Laos has experienced over a period of almost 50 years, few outside observers have been able to witness the full evolutionary process over the period. Most have observed only certain periods, and often in particular regions. Some experienced the country before the war, others during the war, a few others in the years just following 1975, and many researchers and experts have only been able to work in Laos for the past 10 or 15 years (Goudineau this volume, Introduction). Although it is not unique in the world, a situation such as this, involving very fragmented knowledge, in time and space, about the contemporary history of a country, is not common. The idea of 'Laos Studies' reflects the difficulty of creating a whole picture from so many scattered points of view. My own knowledge of Laos is rooted in the 1990s, and I will begin with a brief overview of my own experience, which will explain 'where I am coming from'.

The peoples living in the region of Upper Sekong in the provinces of Saravane and Sekong, among whom I lived in the 1990s,[5] were all of Austroasiatic (or Mon-Khmer) 'stock'. They were the Ta Oi (Ta-Oih), the Katang and the Pacoh on the right bank of the Sekong River,

5. I spent two years in Saravane in 1993–1994, where I carried out an extensive ethnographic fieldwork in the remote districts of Toumlan, Ta Oi and Samui – at that time extremely difficult to access. Because local authorities would not allow me to spend more than two nights in the same village at first, I had to walk from village to village for many weeks. This did give me an overview of the whole region, which was crossed by one of the branches of the Hô Chi-Minh trail during the war. Then, in Sekong, after 1995, I progressively gained the confidence of the provincial Governor who, after I had carried out a number of visits to different ethnic villages, let me settle down for eight months in a remote Kantu village in Kaleum District.

and the Alak (Arak), the Ngé (Ngkriang) and the Kantu/Katu on the left bank. They all spoke languages from the same Katuic family, and formed a sort of 'cultural continuum'.[6] Village life, with its intense ritual activity, seemed to have started up again at the end of the conflict. In Samui District, Pacoh villages were made up of two or three magnificent longhouses, each one housing, on occasion, more than 100 people. In Kaleum, the Ngé or Kantu villages were circular, with a communal house in the centre (see Goudineau 2009). All these villages had remarkable architectural features. The black and white photos that I took at that time gave the impression of a far distant past, as they were so similar to the very rare photographs of these almost inaccessible regions taken in the 1920s or 1930s. However, although a traditional way of life had resumed that followed some old patterns in terms of social structure and religious practices, this was largely an illusion of archaism (Goudineau 2009, and this volume Chapter 6).

Even if they looked ancient, these villages were recent; most were less than eight years old. They were, in fact, the result of a preliminary phase in the reorganisation of the territory after the war, which was implemented with different policies depending on the province. In Saravane, before 1990, a proactive policy had favoured certain groupings of multi-ethnic villages, while in Sekong the policy had been different. Sekong was established in 1984 and has long been considered a 'Lao Theung'[7] province, because 98% of the population is from ethnic Austrasiatic groups. In gratitude for their contribution during the war, many villagers in Sekong were allowed to return to their previous sites after 1985 and to rebuild villages in the style of their 'ancestors'.

At that time, any anthropologist attached to a foreign research institution was highly suspect (except for the Vietnamese), so I was officially labelled an 'ethnic minorities expert' (*xiaoxan sonphao* in Lao), and I worked as such, first as a consultant to medical non-governmental or-

6. On the 'cultural continuum' in southern Laos, see Goudineau, this volume, Chapter 6.

7. 'Lao of the mountain slopes', a generic term referring to ethnic minorities speaking Austrasiatic (Mon-Khmer) languages. For a discussion of the common – but unofficial – classifications 'Lao Loum', 'Lao Theung' and 'Lao Soung', see Stuart-Fox and Kooyman 1992.

ganisations (NGOs),[8] and then with the United National Development Programme (UNDP) and the United Nations Educational, Scientific and Cultural Organization (UNESCO), working on informal education projects. As a consultant for UNESCO and UNDP, I also carried out several specific missions in the north of the country, to Oudomxay and Luang Nam Tha, which enabled me to compare the situations of minorities in the south with those in northern Laos. I was therefore confronted very early on with the issue of 'multi-ethnicity' and cultural diversity; and I became particularly disturbed by the obvious contempt shown by many officials in the provinces toward ethnic minorities, who were generally regarded as embodying different types or degrees of social and cultural backwardness.

In 1996, with the moral support of the late Professor Georges Condominas and in cooperation with the Institute of Research on Culture (IRC), I agreed to coordinate an International UNESCO Conference on 'The Intangible Heritage of Ethnic Minorities' in Vientiane (Goudineau 2003). The conference was more political than scientific, and the Lao government had been put under diplomatic pressure to recognise the need to promote and preserve 'minority heritages'. However, it did open the way for foreign researchers to study non-Lao-Tai ethnic groups, something that had hitherto (at least since 1970) been almost impossible.

I had witnessed, with some concern – almost at the outset, in 1994 and 1995 – the unexpected and sudden relocation of a number of ethnic minority villages in Sekong and Muang Sing, where I was working, and I decided to note the economic and cultural effects of the displacement and of the regrouping of villages during the first months of relocation. In 1997, when I realised that the relocation was the consequence of an unspoken and generalised rural planning policy, coordinated at the central level, I initiated the first survey research on the resettlement of villages on a national scale. The survey took place in 6 provinces in 22 districts and involved over 1,000 families. I was able to carry out this enquiry with the support of UNDP and UNESCO and with the help of a young team of researchers and local education officials. When published, the survey report came as a shock, both for some foreign donors and stake-

8. Notably MSF (Médecins Sans Frontières / Doctors without Borders) in Saravane and ACF (Action Contre la Faim) in Sekong.

holders who had financed and developed projects in relocated villages and for the provincial authorities, who often admitted, reluctantly, that they were facing many difficulties in applying the resettlement scheme (Goudineau [ed.] 1997, 2000b; Évrard and Goudineau 2004).

I left Laos at the end of 1999 and returned to work and live there at the end of 2011 (with only short stays of a few weeks to three months in between). When I did return, I found a very different country from the one I had left nearly 12 years earlier, and I was stunned by the changes, especially in the districts in the south where I had previously worked. In Ta Oi district, a huge road had been constructed, and long lorries loaded with logs now drove directly towards Vietnam. Electricity had been installed in Samui. And the district town of Kaleum – just a few shacks and small houses on stilts in 1999 – had become a real, small town with a market, schools and brick houses.

The political challenge of 'opening up' remote areas may appear to have been overcome, but the reason behind it has often been the implementation of national or provincial 'plans' involving dams, infrastructure or mining projects. These changes have led to a profound territorial transformation – with a wide redistribution of populations and a new type of village organisation. The questions asked by the 1996 UNESCO conference, and even more so, the concerns expressed in the report that I edited on resettlement (Goudineau [ed.] 1997) remain completely valid some 15 years later; and the issue of multi-ethnicity is central to both.

What Does Heritage Mean in a Multi-Ethnic Country?

The national debate on the topic of 'Lao multi-ethnic heritage' (*paxaxon Lao banda phao moladok* in Lao) has developed considerably since 1990. Among the developments related to this debate are certain state innovations in the presentation of multi-ethnicity, particularly some recent initiatives in the provinces, such as 'cultural villages' (*ban vatthanatham* in Lao), which attempt to combine development and heritage.

In a statement to the United Nations Committee on the Elimination of Racial Discrimination in Geneva in February 2012, the Minister of Justice of Laos, Dr. Chaleun Yiapaoheu, who is ethnic Hmong himself, outlined what 'a multi-ethnic nation' might be in the Lao People's Democratic Republic (Lao PDR). He noted that 'In the Lao PDR all Lao people, regardless of their ethnicity, hold Lao citizenship.' He added that '[...] the preservation of the culture of all ethnic groups, large and small, is recognised by the government as a driving force for the development and preservation of national identity in the country.' But before acknowledging this, he also stated that national development is the priority and that 'the relocation policy is [...] a crucial component in poverty reduction programmes', although the government 'is well aware that the establishment of development villages and cluster villages in the rural areas affects the traditional livelihoods of the people in the mountainous areas'.[9]

In fact, this speech about multi-ethnicity and the priority given to national development could apply to all the countries neighbouring Laos, except for the recognition of citizenship, which must still be negotiated in countries such as Thailand.[10] However, such a discourse and its implications do not have the same significance in Laos and elsewhere, because Laos is distinctive in having a population that is roughly two-fifths ethnically and culturally non-Lao-Tai.[11] This puts the Lao cultural majority in a very different position from the Kinh (Viêt) in Vietnam, the Han in China[12] or the Khmer in Cambodia. In these countries,

9. 'Opening Statement by H.E. Dr. Chaleun Yiapoaheu, Minister of Justice, Head of the Lao Delegation, at the Eightieth Session of the UN Committee on the Elimination of Racial Discrimination,' February 28, 2012, Geneva, Switzerland.

10. See McCaskill and Kampe 1997; Turton 2000; Tanabe 2008; King and Wilder 2003 (cf. especially chapter 6, 'Ethnicity, Identity and Nationalism'); Masako 2013.

11. Any calculation remains largely arbitrary, given the lack of any systematic and reliable ethno-linguistic surveys carried out nationwide. However, if we accept the now official classification of the population of the country into four major ethno-linguistic families as in the latest census (2015), the Lao-Tai family, which includes Lao but also Tai Neua, Tai Dam, Tai Daeng, Lue, Phuan and others, accounts for around 60% of the population (so the actual 'Lao' represent a much lower percentage). For their part, those speaking Austroasiatic languages – the oldest and most diverse language family – comprise approximately 35% of the population, Yao and Miao (Hmong) almost 10%, and the Tibeto-Burmans around 3%. For the classification to be complete, we would need to add urban minorities, mainly Vietnamese and Chinese, plus many groups belonging to ethno-linguistic 'minority' families mentioned above who have migrated to the city after leaving their villages.

12. I include China here, even though it is not considered to be part of Southeast Asia, partly because many minority ethnic groups present in the Indochinese Peninsula (for instance, Yao, Hmong, Tibeto-Burmese, and Tai) originate directly from China and occupy large areas in Yunnan, Guangxi and Guizhou, and partly because there is a comparison to be made with the Lao situation in terms of a political model regarding ethnicity.

minorities represent a relatively small, even very low (in Cambodia) percentage of the population. Laos also has another distinctive feature, which is that the 'Isan' population living in north-east Thailand, which is linguistically and culturally Lao, is three times as large as the entire population of Laos itself. In a way the Lao majority is in an uncertain cultural space, in between cultures. As a nation, before envisaging a 'multi-ethnic' culture, Laos first had to invent a 'Lao' culture.

Several researchers have shown to what extent the Lao PDR continues to reinforce a national identity largely based on Lao history and on Lao Buddhism, in other words based on the culture of what is considered to be the majority group.[13] The École française d'Extrême-Orient (EFEO; French School of Asian Studies), which is the oldest research institution in Laos, was at the heart of this fabrication of a Lao culture during the colonial period. From 1901 onwards, its scholars were actively involved in the reconstruction of the monumental emblems of Vientiane, particularly That Luang and Vat Phra Keo. They also wanted – in opposition to the long-term Siamese influence – to identify a 'Lao' literature and a 'Lao' art, and they established a Buddhist institute to train monks in 'Lao' Buddhism.[14] It should be noted, however, that outside of the colonial context, their work, which was generally based on quality research, also served as a scientific guarantee of the emergence of Lao nationalism and is still the basis of some current research in Laos itself.

The most striking contribution, in this context, is that of Charles Archaimbault, also an EFEO scholar. Archaimbault was a philologist and ethnologist who did research in Laos in the 1950s, particularly in Xieng Khouang and Champassak. A former resistance fighter against the Nazis during World War II and an anti-colonial activist, he worked deliberately to promote Lao nationalism after independence. His very extensive research aimed to demonstrate – on a historical, religious and social level – the existence and coherence of original structures that were specifically 'Lao,' and he provided a considerable amount of information to this end (Goudineau 2001b, 2002). He studied Lao traditions and legends in many villages across the country and he also translated local chronicles and compared cycles of rituals in a number of

13. See, for instance, Evans 1998b, 1999 (ed.), cf. Introduction; Pholsena 2006a.

14. See Finot 1917; Parmentier 1954; Evans (ed.) 1999; Kourilsky 2006; Ladwig 2018.

Lao towns along the Mekong.[15] Yet, perhaps because he is rather difficult to read – his writings mix very detailed ethnography with a structuralist perspective and some psychoanalytical interpretations – Archaimbault has never been very influential locally, although the aim of his work was precisely to contribute to the project of constructing a national and essentially Lao culture. This may also be because he chose to work in places that were not central to the social construction of a Lao national identity, Xieng Khouang and Champassak.

It must be kept in mind that 'the invention of a national culture' is not a continuous process that relies on a gradually collated corpus of knowledge. There are times within the process where contradictions are faced, and it is those who hold political power who decide on the selection of the emblematic items to be associated with the national culture. This is particularly true in Laos, where there are few local researchers, who are, for the most part, poorly informed about international research and have very limited capacity to intervene effectively in the shaping of state policy. Although there are other actors, it is the state that is principally responsible for the 'presentation' of national culture; and some of the research projects currently underway in relation to Lao culture are not considered very helpful by the Lao government in terms of the meta-narrative relating to Lao culture that it wishes to present. Some of these projects are even regarded by the government as quite disturbing.

Some scholars have expressed regret that the Lao authorities have shown little interest in the work on manuscripts or archaic inscriptions, which has principally been led by international experts.[16] Although these studies relate to an ancient Lao cultural heritage, the fact is that they can hardly be staged in front of a wide audience. Moreover, they often show evidence of external influences – from Lanna, Khmer or even Mon culture – and for this reason they are of little use in the context of national ideology. This is less true of famous archaeological sites such as Vat Phou or the Plain of Jars. Although these two sites cannot really be linked to Lao culture itself – as one is proto-Khmer and the origin of the other remains obscure and controversial – spectacular 'presentations' are

15. See, for instance, Archaimbault 1961, 1967, 1971, 1973.

16. See École française d'Extrême-Orient 1999. However, some projects have been successfully developed, such as the German-led 'Preservation of Lao Manuscripts Programme', which thrived, in cooperation with the National Library, over a 10-year period (1994–2004).

organised by the state and the provinces, such as the Vat Phou festival in Champassak, which is attended by thousands of participants every year.[17]

The State and Discourse on Multi-Cultural Heritage

In its relationship with 'Lao history' the state has shown a marked capacity to innovate. Martin Stuart-Fox, Grant Evans, Vatthana Pholsena, Oliver Tappe and Volker Grabowsky have shown how the Lao PDR has both indulged itself with the reputation of being a protector of Buddhism by reinstating certain ceremonies and fabricated a historical legitimacy by appearing to follow in the footsteps of the great defender kings of the nation, whose statues are now located in the four corners of Vientiane.[18]

One of the latest innovations on the part of the state, and one that is highly visible in Vientiane, is the Lak Muang city pillar of the capital, also called the Ho Lak Muang ('City Pillar Sanctuary'). Located near Vat Si Muang, it was officially opened in October 2012 and consecrated during an impressive ceremony, which was led by dozens of monks and attended by a huge audience.[19] However, for the population of Vientiane, the nearby Vat Si Muang has housed the town's Lak Muang since the time of King Setthathirath, in the 16th century. Vat Si Muang is known to be a special, popular shrine, and this has been reinforced by the legend concerning its origin, when a pregnant woman was said to have been sacrificed and placed at the base of the stone post that became the central pillar of the city.

Why then are the state authorities building the new 'Ho Lak Muang'? With this monument, the State seeks to somehow regain control of the former 'Muang' city pillar, a symbolically important space. There is no suggestion that the Ho Lak Muang is replacing the Lak Muang that is still located in Vat Si Muang. Instead, the new monument is presented as a sanctuary and as a museum that contains relics of the ancient history of Laos. As the Minister of Information and Culture stated during the

17. See http://www.vatphou-champassak.com/index.php/events-gb/events-at-vat-phou-gb (consulted on the 21 Feb., 2022); and 'Boun Wat Phou – An experience like no other', *Laotian Times*, January 16, 2019, https://laotiantimes.com/2019/01/16/boun-wat-phou-experience-like-no/.

18. See Stuart-Fox 1996; Evans 1998b; Pholsena 2006a; Tappe 2012; Grabowsky 2011.

19. 'Thousands To Attend Vientiane City Pillar Shrine Consecration', *Vientiane Times*, 13 November 2012.

inauguration of the monument: 'It must be a vital cultural reference for future generations.'[20]

The construction of the monument was decreed on the occasion of the 450th anniversary of the city of Vientiane. It houses hundreds of different stones extracted from archaeological excavations. Some come from the ancient wall of Vientiane, which was constructed in the 16th century, but others are from proto-historical sites around the city.[21] In any event, the State is willing to establish its current patronage on the city's Lak Muang, as well as its place in history, with the support of ancient and indisputable emblems – far more ancient than those in Vat Si Muang. The state is responsible for this 'cultural innovation,' but through the selection of archaeological evidence, is attempting to show that it also relies on scientific expertise.

It was also widely rumoured that the monument had been largely financed by private funds, suggesting that the whole of Lao society had supported this project. In fact, it turns out that the funds provided by the state were supplemented primarily by large national companies and some foreign firms. A few months after its inauguration, popular fervour was still concentrated at Vat Si Muang, while the new Ho Lak Muang seemed deserted.

This example shows that there are three primary types of actors involved in the invention of the national culture. First, there is the state, which is usually the main player or actor in Laos today. By 'the state', is meant here the government that embodies it and *ad hoc* committees of officials and party members at central level and in the provinces and districts. The second type of actor is the 'expert'. This is a very broad and varied category and includes national and international researchers and consultants as well as some NGOs or associations whose work can be exploited but who also have the ability to intervene, often through contacts outside the country, particularly via international networks and the media. The third, and most crucial, actor is the 'Lao people', or 'Lao society' in the broadest sense, although its 'agency' – the capacity to propose, react or resist – is obviously not the same in large cities like

20. 'Fin des travaux du Musée du pilier de Vientiane', *Le Rénovateur,* 15 October 2012.

21. More than a dozen articles in the Lao newspapers, as well as in the *Vientiane Times* and the *Rénovateur,* were devoted in 2012 to the 450th anniversary of Vientiane and to these archaeological findings.

Vientiane or Pakse as it is in remote village districts.[22] Society also makes choices among proposals. In Vientiane, we can see that the That Luang festival is growing larger every year and is attended by hundreds of thousands of people. Observers have also been surprised by the nationalist and popular devotion expressed in relation to the statue of Chao Anou in Vientiane, which receives offerings of flowers, while other royal statues or famous presidential busts are virtually ignored.[23]

The role of models should also be emphasised in order to understand the sources of official cultural innovation in Laos. Regarding the new Ho Lak Muang in Vientiane, one is struck by the similarity of the building with comparable monuments found in Thai cities. As Vientiane is the capital, one would assume the San Lak Muang in Bangkok to have been a possible source of inspiration. But looking more closely, it is evident that long before Vientiane built the new Lak Muang, several major cities in Isan had built similar monuments. And today all provincial capitals are encouraged to build a collective stupa symbolising the unity of the people. In this fabrication of a Lao culture, it is particularly important to note all the new exchanges of cultural symbols now developing between the two banks of the Mekong.

A Multi-Ethnic National Culture Underpinned by a Majority Culture

The creation of a multi-ethnic national culture is grounded very firmly in the creation of a so-called 'majority culture.' In contrast to the Lao, who are culturally dominant, non-Lao-Tai groups are referred to as 'minorities' or 'ethnic minorities', for this terminology is always and above all a political reality in the context of the Lao nation-state, even if this terminology is debatable from an anthropological point of view.[24]

The management of ethnic diversity has been an important and visible theme since 1975. This began when the Lao People's Revolutionary Party, the Pathet Lao, came to power with the help of the Vietnamese army, and established a communist-type regime. Under the previous

22. Social control in Laos is generally stronger in villages than in cities, tending to prevent any strong local reaction on the part of people in rural areas. The same may not be true elsewhere in the region, notably in Cambodia or Thailand, where rural associations or local NGOs are good at supporting the dissemination of villagers' claims.

23. Tappe 2012. On Lao nationalism, see also Creak 2015.

24. In this regard, some non-Buddhist Tai groups can be seen also as 'ethnic minorities'.

Royal Lao Government (RLG), there had been a committee dealing with inter-ethnic relations, but the division of the country by almost 30 years of war moved this concern into the realm of military matters, with each side trying to get the support of minorities who occupied mountainous positions that were considered to be strategically important.

After 1975, it was a question of reuniting the country and making its multi-ethnicity viable. The formulation of the ethnic question in Laos is based, with some variations, on the Vietnamese model, which was itself dependent on Soviet and Chinese experience. Two major issues came to the fore: firstly, whether or not to grant a form of autonomy to certain regions on the basis of ethnic criteria; and secondly, a positivist concern – representative of a form of socialist scientism – with labelling and classifying the ethnic groups of the country.[25]

However, the government of Kaysone Phomvihane, Secretary General of the Pathet Lao, made it clear upon taking power that he would make the unity of the country a priority. He promised that all minorities could retain their 'ancestral customs' and that the Party would ensure that all ethnic groups were treated equally. But, in contrast to the early revolutionary positions of the Chinese or Vietnamese, he refused to recognise any 'nationality' (as in China) or regional autonomy on an ethnic basis and defended poly-ethnic solidarity in the context of a single and indissoluble Lao nation.[26]

The emphasis was thus on national unity, supported by a national culture modelled on Lao-Tai cultural norms (Trankell 1998). The logic of this, for Kaysone, was only partly that the Lao-Tai formed the majority; it was mainly because they had the highest level of 'cultural development. 'Lao culture,' he said, during a speech in 1981 specifically devoted to the ethnic problem, 'must be the basic culture shared by all the ethnicities, and must be the one to provide the connections for the exchange of culture between all the ethnicities; spoken and written Lao is the common language and written Lao is the regular writing of all the ethnic groups' (Evans 1999a: 171).

It is not just ethnicity or history that defines the minority status of a group (or defines who are 'indigenous peoples') but also its economic

25. See Goudineau 2000b, and this volume Introduction; Schlemmer 2015a. On the politics of ethnic classification in Vietnam, see Masako 2013.

26. See 'Ethnic affairs' in Stuart-Fox 1986: 130–136.

and social condition. However, in the 1990s, when Laos began to develop, all indicators showed that the economic and social gap was widening between lowlanders and highland minorities (Pholsena 2005). It was initially a case of economic integration: while wanting to drastically reduce the practice of shifting cultivation, they also tried to move the villagers from a subsistence economy to a market economy. This was also a project of territorial and social integration: the aim was to reduce the isolation of some villages and to give them access to services (health and education, for instance). It was thought that this could be achieved through the displacement of villages and their relocation on the plains.

It was eventually decided to concentrate on cultural integration, with the promotion of a national culture. As mentioned earlier, it was first a question of promoting the common language, Lao, which was poorly spoken by many mountain peoples (the use of minority languages in education is not allowed by the Ministry of Education), and then of encouraging the creation of a national or regional ethnic folklore (e.g., dancing, singing and crafts). At the same time, many specific cultural practices, essential identity markers for certain ethnic minorities, were openly disparaged, to the point where some villagers gave them up of their own accord; this included religious practices (like domestic animal sacrifices) or material culture (such as architecture and statues).

The Evolution of the Debate on Multi-Ethnicity

The discourse on multi-ethnicity has not fundamentally changed, but its nature has evolved over recent years in Laos. Never before has so much importance been officially given to the cultural heritage of minority groups. Local officials are required to 'present' their local traditions. In addition, increasing numbers of villagers are mobilised to display their own 'ethnic characteristics' in new festivals or on new stages, and foreign experts – who were mistrusted before – are now offered to provide their knowledge of specific groups or to participate in the creation of museums in the provinces.[27] Actually, all the actors I mentioned above – the Lao government, its local officials, the experts and the ethnic groups concerned – are invited to participate in the presentation

27. See, for instance, the display of '*Posters on Ethnic Groups*' within the permanent exhibition of the Phongsaly provincial museum (Schlemmer 2015b). There are also some private initiatives allowed by the government, such as the Traditional Arts and Ethnology Center (TAEC) in Luang Prabang.

of the 'best' traditions of different ethnic minority groups. There is a strong demand for innovation; but in the context of this undertaking, two types of paradox emerge.

The first paradox is that at the same time as the push to display 'ethnic traditions' is taking place, the livelihoods of many minorities have been suddenly and drastically transformed. The second paradox is that the cultures of different ethnic groups are always presented as a kind of juxtaposition, as if they existed side-by-side, as seen on certain Lao banknotes. However, the reality corresponds less and less to this image, due to the territorial reorganisation that has taken place, with a sharp increase in the regrouping of villages, which has resulted in completely new situations of inter-ethnic relations everywhere.

It must therefore be recognised that the former basis for the cultural practices of many minorities has largely disappeared. In the past, distinct village cultures could be observed between one group and another in terms of architecture and religious and social organisation, but this has largely been erased since the 2000s. Without going into detail province by province, it can certainly be said that there is now a standardisation in domestic structure and dwellings, due to the incentive to build Lao-type houses. There has also been a reduction in collective rituals in non-Buddhist villages, in particular a decline in sacrificial rituals and shamanism.[28] The promotion of the nuclear family as the norm has significantly limited the multiplicity of forms of social organisation that existed in the past. This has resulted, for instance, in the disappearance, both in the north and in the south, of the longhouses that sheltered extended families or lineages.

In brief, the official exhibition of ethnic diversity is taking place, paradoxically, against a background of accelerated standardisation and a reduction of social and cultural diversity. Of course, in recent years Lao society as a whole has rapidly evolved as a result of modernisation and the growth fuelled by foreign investment. Lao-Tai groups have also experienced significant economic and social change (see Rehbein 2017); but they have not seen their livelihoods and their cultural or religious practices disrupted to the same extent as other groups. Above all, they have not been subjected to the development and resettlement policies

28. See Sprenger 2009 and this volume (Chapter 9); Bouté 2018.

that have been implemented in 'ethnic minority' villages, especially in upland areas, which account for about two-thirds of the territory of Laos.

Resettlements and Induced Changes among Inter-Ethnic Groups

Ironically, after surviving the vicissitudes of history for centuries, including recent wars, many ethnic groups in Laos now appear to be in an extremely precarious situation, at a time when the country is opening up to faster economic development. In addition, the mountain areas, where most of these groups live, are increasingly becoming an important factor in development, as it is here that the two main sources of the country's wealth are located: forests and hydroelectric power. The construction of large dams and the protection of forests, or the control of their exploitation through large market-oriented agricultural concessions (Dwyer 2017), has regularly led to conflicts with ethnic minorities over the occupation of space, especially for those still practising shifting cultivation in the uplands. Since the beginning of the 1990s, a solution has been adopted that calls for the permanent resettlement of mountain minorities in the plains, or close to main roads, recalling both some former migration dynamics and the forced displacement that occurred during the war years (Barber 1979; Taillard 1989).

In 2012, the Minister of Justice, quoted earlier, acknowledged that 'the relocation policy could affect traditional livelihoods', but said that it was, nevertheless, 'a crucial component of the poverty reduction programmes.' Unfortunately, since 1997, and the publication of the UNDP/UNESCO survey based on research that I led with my team (see Goudineau [ed.], 2 vol., 1997), there has been no new and systematic national survey on the social and cultural impact of the resettlement of displaced villages. However, several studies have, broadly, confirmed its findings and concerns, notably local surveys on some of the district resettlements and provincial internal migrations by Olivier Évrard, Steve Daviau, Ian Baird and Bruce Shoemaker, and Peter Vandergeest.[29] The aim of the first report had been to document the significant wave of relocations at a national scale that had occurred in the mid-1990s from mountain villages into valleys. These relocations were poorly organised,

29. See the following reports and summary papers on this issue, which are related to specific local areas: Goudineau 2000b; Évrard and Goudineau 2004; Vandergeest 2003; Romagny and Daviau 2003; Baird and Shoemaker 2007; Baird and Évrard 2017.

and, in the face of criticism following the publication of the report, the government has always fiercely denied at that time that the resettlements were part of a 'national relocation policy'. The only ideological justification for these relocations appeared to be a comprehensive sedentarisation of the upland communities through the establishment of so-called permanent occupations (*axip khong thi* in Lao). However, the initial official silence at the publication of the report was later followed by the explicit creation of several plans for the reorganisation of mountain territories. The first of these involved measures to establish 'focal sites' (*khet choutsoum phatthana* in Lao), and these were followed by plans to bring about 'village consolidation' and 'development of village clusters' (*khum phatthana* and *khum ban phatthana* in Lao).

All these village relocation measures were, in principle, driven by poverty reduction plans as well as by rural development policy. But, in reality, resettlement had very different objectives. Those more highlighted were purely social development, such as increasing access to public education and health facilities. But others were overtly coercive, notably the double objective to move swidden agriculturalists into more permanent agriculture – and to eradicate the cultivation of opium in the northern part of the country. Huge numbers of villages have also been displaced in the name of large provincial and national projects, including road building, dam construction and mining projects in many mountainous areas, as I witnessed in Ta Oi (Saravane) or Kaleum (Sekong) when I returned there after several years.

Overall, these resettlement and relocation measures have completely reorganised the map of villages in a large part of the country. It is not possible to obtain exact figures, but a reasonable estimate is that in many mountainous districts more than 75% of the population has been relocated since 1995. In addition, many families have chosen to move elsewhere in anticipation of their planned relocation into village clusters. These movements and regroupings of villages have resulted in complicated and sometimes conflicting neighborhood situations, and have created new configurations of inter-ethnic relations in all provinces. A large number of civil servants have been assigned to the districts concerned to steer the organisation of these new 'village clusters'.

These policies and actions are a form of social engineering, which is being deployed by the Lao government in the name of economic development, supposedly for the benefit of ethnic minorities. The model behind these current initiatives is quite clearly a Vietnamese one. Vietnam has offered assistance to the Lao PDR, drawing on their considerable expertise in the integration of ethnic minorities. This expertise not only concerns rural development or village relocation but has been applied in the field of education for ethnic groups, including specific measures, such as college funding reserved for children from families of mountain minorities in several provinces.

From Ethnic Minorities to 'Cultural Villages'

A Vietnamese model has also been the basis for one particular government innovation in the field of social engineering that deals directly with the issue of ethnicity and of a national multi-ethnic culture: the creation of 'cultural villages' (*ban vatthanatham* in Lao). The creation of these goes back to 1994 and, in principle, covers all ethnic groups, including the Lao-Tai; but it has mainly be since 2010 that the state has put a great deal of emphasis on the creation of these villages and has particularly targeted districts where many ethnic minorities have been displaced and relocated.

The Ministry of Culture, which is also the Ministry of Information and Tourism, stated in 2011 that more than 300,000 families and more than 1,500 villages had been granted the title 'models of culture.' The minister announced the target of granting this title to a further 160 villages and over 30 'cluster towns' during the period 2012–2014, and he stated that this would affect more than 120,000 families (*Vientiane Times*, November 9, 2011).[30] Following these instructions, the Sekong provincial government, which had already created 18 'cultural villages' since 2009, declared that it planned to create 24 new villages by 2014.[31]

30. This is a process that the authorities aim to expand considerably. In 2018 alone, 429 communities were declared to be 'cultural villages' and over 52,330 households were declared to be 'cultural families' (*Vientiane Times*, February 13, 2019). This injunction to label as many villages 'cultural villages' as possible now extends to the most remote provinces and to the district departments responsible for this work (see also High 2021).

31. In 2013, the head of culture in Phongsaly district told Vanina Bouté that the province wanted him to label up to 50% of the villages in the district 'cultural villages' – a task he considered impossible, as his job only allowed him to label one or two villages per year (personal communication).

A brochure was published in 2009 that lays out the rules that have to be followed by district and provincial officials in labelling a village a 'cultural village' (Ministry of Information, Culture and Tourism 2009). This brochure states that the village does not become 'cultural' unless at least 70% of the families in the village can be considered 'cultural families' (*khop khoua vatthanatham* in Lao). This means that families must comply with the 'five rules'. These are: that they respect the law and the instructions of the village committee; that they live in a settled home; that they have stable resources; that their children go to school; and that they 'reject irrational beliefs' (*tong loplang kan seua theu ngom ngoua sin seung* in Lao).[32] The village itself must also meet five conditions and follow five steps to be promoted to the status of 'cultural village'. Alongside standards of cleanliness and education and criteria for well-planned economic development, civic and political conditions are also stipulated, especially strong leadership of the Party and the ability to provide accurate statistics on the village. Rules to promote and consolidate a proper 'village heritage' are also issued in the brochure. Among these rules: the village must undertake to eradicate 'irrational beliefs'; that it must set up 'an information room' (*ho khao* in Lao) with posters in which the story of the 'liberation' of the country is recounted, and the good customs of the community, as passed down by the elders, are promoted. It should also, if possible, have an artistic action group that identifies, among other things, the costumes and traditional dances of the community.

The criteria for attaining model cultural village status relate to the fulfilment of a wide variety of conditions and norms: employment, healthcare, access to education, family unity, legal livelihoods, political awareness and community solidarity. The importance of the cultural transmission of the 'good and beautiful traditions' of the community to the family and the village is also stressed, as is the capacity to provide visitors with a self-presentation of the 'genuine' culture of the group. The cultural villages are key intermediaries of the state for the normalisation and standardisation of cultural events across the country.

32. See, for instance, the statement by the Governor of Sekong province that one of the obstacles to the development of the province is the continuing influence of ancient beliefs on uneducated populations (*Le Rénovateur*, April 2, 2012).

This leads to the abandonment of many collective rituals in model villages, to be replaced by festivals inspired by Lao culture. This is particularly the case at the New Year, when, alongside Pimai Lao or the Hmong New Year, each ethnic group is encouraged to organise its own equivalent New Year festival to replace its previous rituals.[33] Hence, there is Boun Greh for the Khmu, and Boun Vel (literally 'village festival' in a mix of the Lao and the Katuic languages) for the Kantu/Katu and the Ngé (Ngkriang). However, the buffalo sacrifices that were previously at the heart of rituals are banned or reduced.[34]

Model villages are to be an example to other surrounding villages, but they are more than that; they are supposed to establish new standards that will be disseminated within the ethnic group to which they belong, as 'true' tradition. In the 1990s, no Kantu/Katu or Ngé could say what a 'Boun Vel' was, and many Khmu did not practise 'Boun Greh,' but today people who are not aware of them are regarded as not knowing 'their' traditions. In contemporary Laos, the cultural villages are definitely at the heart of the reinvention of tradition. Villagers belonging to them are involved in a staging of multi-ethnic culture in the provinces, for tourists or during major national festivals.

Indeed, representations of the 'multi-ethnic Lao' are organised and folklorised by committees of civil servants from the Ministry of Information, Culture, and Tourism, from the central level to the districts. These civil servants have long been responsible for organising singing and dancing competitions between ethnic groups at the local level. They have also been largely responsible for the creation of texts and choreographies that are supposed to be representative of specific groups. On television, or when entertaining foreign VIPs, it was often the dancers from the National School who had to perform these so-called ethnic dances, whatever their ethnicity. However – as in the field of Lao culture – in recent years the state has dramatically increased 'multi-ethnic' cultural innovations, and it relies primarily on members of artistic committees in cultural villages in doing so.

These innovations are necessary because it has become clear that competitions and performances of songs and dances have bored both

33. On the politics of the folklorisation of local ethnic religions, see Bouté 2021b.

34. On Boun Greh, see Petit 2013. The Katu and Ngé (Ngkriang) examples are from my own observations in the field.

local people and tourists, particularly tourists from neighbouring countries, such as the Thai and the Chinese who have similar 'ethnic' entertainment. New presentations of multi-ethnicity can now be seen everywhere in Laos, especially during major festivals; for example, at the That Luang parade, the Vat Phou festival or at the Elephant festival in Xayaboury. This last festival has been described as 'The festival of the eight ethnic groups' since 2013, with the eight groups being the Lao, the Tai Dam, the Lue, the Hmong, the Khmu, the Phrai, the Yuan and the Iu Mien (*Le Rénovateur*, February 17, 2013).[35]

In these multi-ethnic presentations, each ethnicity must appear perfectly unique, and there has been an escalation in the folklorisation and exoticism of supposed ethnic traditions to reinforce this distinctiveness. In the Vat Phou festival, each of the southern minorities are presented wearing different ethnic clothes or headdresses, some of which are highly improbable. Some have attributes that are more or less warrior-like, depending on the group. The Ta Oi, Katu, Alak and Ngé are therefore presented as being highly differentiated, whereas in fact, as mentioned above, they are actually in a kind of cultural continuum, making differences in clothing or indeed anything else a product of pure fantasy. Their villages did have quite different characteristics in terms of social organisation – that was the real difference between the groups – but these differences have largely been erased due to the village relocations.

The Lak Muang of Sekong (Figure 12.1) is an impressive illustration of the positioning of national multi-ethnic culture under the guidance of Lao culture. This is especially striking in a province historically inhabited almost entirely by Austroasiatic-speaking minorities, in which ethnic Lao account for less than 2% of the population.

Photo: Y. Goudineau

Figure 12.1: The Lak Muang of Sekong. → Colour version on page 382.

35. 'The festival aims to promote the conservation and promotion of the fine traditions characteristic of the way of life of the multi-ethnic people, who have built a strong bond with elephants.' (Statement by Xayaboury Deputy Governor, *Laotian Times*, February 20, 2018)

The bizarre monument installed at the town entrance is called the Xouan Lak Muang Sekong – 'the garden of the Lak Muang of Sekong'. At the end of the garden is the new central pillar of Sekong, and in front of it statues of all the ethnic groups of the province stand in two lines – as if they are a guard of honour at the Lak Muang, and as a sign of respect and submission. Each group is represented by a couple, with distinctive differences in their costumes and, for some, warrior-like accessories. On the sides, assorted sculptures are intended to depict the specific ways of life of the different ethnic groups.

Photo: Y. Goudineau

Figures 12.2 (below) **and 12.3** (above): Line of couples belonging to different ethnic groups; and a Talieng (Triang) couple, one of the line of couples. → Colour versions on page 382.

Photo: Y. Goudineau

A small booklet has been published by the provincial government to explain the significance of the monument.[36] It says that the Lak Muang is the centre of the city and of the territory, that it unites all ethnic groups and that it is, at the same time, a concentration of all the sacrificial posts that can be found in the villages of the province. As such, it is more powerful than all the posts put together. The implication seems to be that it protects all the villagers, who no longer need to practice sacrifices and 'bad' customs. According to this booklet, the three circles at the top of the Lak Muang represent the *Tripitaka*, the sacred 'three baskets' of Buddhism (Buddha, Dhamma, Sangha), and the three stripes at the base represent weaving, which is one of the 'good' customs of the ethnic groups. This new Lak Muang, like the one in Vientiane, was consecrated by monks at its inauguration.

Conclusion: Anthropology and Competing Discourses on Ethnic Heritages

If the state appears to be primarily responsible for this invention of a multi-ethnic national culture, we must nevertheless consider whether alternatives to its initiatives exist, and what means of expression they may have in Lao PDR. There are two questions to be addressed in this regard: how much agency do the ethnic groups have in relation to presenting themselves? And what role can 'experts' play, even though they approach the issue from a different perspective?

Regarding the ethnic groups themselves, they certainly do not all have the same capacity for self-presentation. Some groups have the means to offer alternative ways of presenting their culture to those initiated by the state, while others do not. For a long time, the groups of a few thousand people each that I worked with in Saravane or Sekong had no specific discourse on what their tradition as an ethnic group might be. Many of them, however, had decided by the end of the 1980s' to return to their former lands and rebuild circular villages according to the instructions of their ancestors (see Goudineau this volume Chapter 6). But their culture essentially remained a 'village culture.' People regarded themselves first and foremost as being from a particular village. 'We were taught that we were Katu!' some old villagers told me, still amazed

36. *Xouan Lak Muang, khweng Sekong*, 2012. I thank Vatthana Pholsena for passing it on to me.

by this. In this context, having no sense of belonging to a specific 'ethnic' community, many villagers had, until recently, no clear idea of how to present their supposed ethnic group.

It is therefore clear that the inhabitants of these villages do not have a set of standards or values to hold up against the norms of the new 'cultural villages' – especially since their only links to the outside are relatives in the army or in local government, who are therefore part of the state apparatus and generally defend the official line of thought. When discussing with them during fieldwork, they can explain what has changed in recent years in the social life of the village and in their livelihoods. Some may approve it, and even express a desire for a new life, especially for young people, but others bitterly regret it. Villages or families can try to reject certain change, or even decide to continue to practice 'bad customs' such as sacrificial rituals, negotiating about them on the basis of a 'necessity' to be respected that may ultimately be tolerated (see High 2021: 163–164). Some may therefore operate locally and have some agency, but this appears very limited.

In contrast, if one considers the Hmong, the picture is completely different. Their ability of self-presentation and discourse as an alternative to the way in which they have been presented by the Lao is almost limitless. The Hmong are a large ethnic group in Laos and they have the means to negotiate at a political level, even to be controversial. They also have powerful communication links abroad, both in the media and in academic circles. They can therefore challenge, at least to some degree, the way in which they have been presented by the Lao State discourse, using strong arguments about their own community values, and they have many experts who are able to make articulate speeches about their culture.

These two contrasting cases serve to demonstrate that groups have more room to negotiate with the state about the presentation or invention of their culture if they are less remote, if they are involved in cross-border relationships, and/or if they are linked to diaspora communities in other countries.

But what about the 'experts' who are also involved in the invention of multi-ethnic culture through their work? What use that can be made of them? The range of such experts is wide, although some Christian organisations and indigenous NGOs that are instrumental elsewhere in the building of cultural communities are not allowed to work in Lao PDR or are under strict control from the State. Still – generally speaking – the experts are divided between the two sides, or two aspects of multi-ethnicity: those interested in ethnic diversity as cultural multiplicity, and those who are mainly concerned with the actual management of inter-ethnicity in Laos, and its social and economic effects.

These are also two main approaches among researchers, notably among anthropologists. On the one hand, there is an approach that can be called 'culturalist': an approach that seeks to highlight the cultural specificities of particular ethnic groups, either by studying certain musical, literary or artistic traditions, or by asking what it means to be Khmu, Hmong or Pacoh, for instance, sometimes at the risk of essentialising ethnic cultures. On the other hand there is an approach that can be described as 'localist,' which focuses on 'situations' and their history. This includes, for example, studying local inter-ethnic dynamics in the long run from an ethnohistorical perspective, or analysing how specific projects, policies or contemporary territorial dynamics affect different groups, and therefore have consequences on ethnicity and inter-ethnicity. These two approaches can, in fact, be complementary, as the two aspects of multi-ethnicity interact with each other. The state presentation of multi-ethnic culture tends to favour, though only to a certain extent, the culturalist approach, and to be wary of localist approaches.

Things are currently changing, as many provinces or districts want to assert their identities and to exhibit local multi-ethnic cultures that can be identified as their own. Here we are dealing with a kind of 'localist' or regionalistic perspective on the part of different provinces, which is often linked to the building of new museums, or the renovation of old ones. The idea is usually to illustrate the culture and the history of the province as a whole. Foreign experts are increasingly invited to participate in this staging. Sometimes they successfully widen the perspective and add information on the cultural history of minorities and on local inter-ethnic relationships. But the question of who these local museums are actually intended for remains. Tourists? Local civil servants? Schoolchildren? And an even more crucial issue is whether the villagers themselves will be able to take them over at some point. This might be in order to criticise (and change) the museums if they do not think they relate to them in an appropriate way – image and discourse –

giving a distorted picture of their culture, and not telling the right 'story'. Or it might be in order to look for elements of their own history in the museum – thus identifying memories for their own use.

To leave the last word here to Grant Evans:

> By placing particular ethnic groups within culture areas we are able to subvert or qualify the hegemonic discourse of nationalism, just as a focus on locality or context can do something similar. Through a combination of these levels of analysis with the reality of the modern state we can hopefully achieve a complex and dynamic understanding of ethnicity. Sensitivity to the complexities of ethnic identity and to the different levels at which notions of identity or matters of cultural similarity or difference are salient must become the hallmark of future anthropological research in Laos and in the region generally.
> (Evans 1999a: 186)

References

Ai Souliyasaeng, Khamphone Bounnadi, Visay Bobaykham, Somphay Phaysane, Pisa Siphandone, Sinya Thipphavong, Khemphet Philalak, Thongsi Simvongsane

2004. *Salub Songkham Pasason phaitai Kannampha khong Phak Pasason Pativat Lao 1945–1975* [Summary of the People's War under the Leadership of the LPRP 1945–1975]. Vientiane: Lao People's Revolutionary Party.

Althusser, Louis

1977. 'Ideology and ideological state apparatuses (Notes towards an investigation).' In Louis Althusser, *Lenin, Philosophy and Other Essays*, pp. 127–186. London: New Left Books.

Anderson, Benedict

1983. *Imagined Communities: Reflections on the Origin and Spread of Nationalism*. London: Verso.

Ang Cheng Guan

2002. *The Vietnam War from the Other Side. The Vietnamese Communists' Perspective*. London: RoutledgeCurzon.

Anonymous

1911. 'Historique de la province d'Attopeu.' CAOM/RSL D1, June 11, 1911. Laos: Attopeu.

———(2)

2004. *Pavat Khet Tai Lao* [Narrative of Southern Laos]. Vientiane: State Printing Press.

Anuman Rajadhon

1967. 'Notes on the thread-square in Thailand.' *Journal of Siam Society* 55(2): 161–187.

Archaimbault, Charles

1961. 'L'histoire de Campasak.' *Journal Asiatique* 249(4): 519–595.

1967. 'Les annales de l'ancien royaume de S'ieng Khwang.' *Bulletin de l'École française d'Extrême-Orient* 53(2): 557–673.

1971. *The New Year Ceremony at Basak (South Laos)*. New York, Ithaca: Cornell University, Department of Asian Studies, South East Asia Program, Data paper 78, XIV.

1972. *La course de pirogues au Laos. Un complexe culturel.* Ascona: Artibus Asiae Publishers.

1973. *Structures religieuses lao (rites et mythes)*. Vientiane: Vithagna.

1991. *Le sacrifice du buffle à S'ieng Khwang (Laos)*. Paris: École française d'Extrême-Orient, PEFEO, 164.

Århem, Kaj

2010. *The Katu Village. An Interpretative Ethnography of the Avuong Katu in Central Vietnam*. Göteborg: Göteborg University.

Århem, Nikolas

2015. *Forests, Spirits, and High Modernist Development. A Study of Cosmology and Change among the Katuic Peoples in the Uplands of Laos and Vietnam*. Uppsala Studies in Cultural Anthopology 55. Uppsala: Acta Universitatis Upsaliensis.

Asad, Talal

1993. *Genealogies of Religion. Discipline and Reasons of Power in Christianity and Islam*. Baltimore: John Hopkins University Press.

2003. *Formations of the Secular: Christianity, Islam, Modernity*. Stanford: Stanford University Press.

Asian Development Bank (ADB)

2002. *Cambodia. Indigenous Peoples, Ethnic Minorities and Poverty Reduction*. Manila: ADB.

Asian Development Bank (ADB), the Lao State Planning Committee and the National Statistical Centre

2001. *Participatory Poverty Assessment in Lao PDR*. Asian Development Bank (ADB), The Lao State Planning Committee and The National Statistical Centre: Vientiane.

Aymonier, Étienne

2003 [1885]. *La société du Laos siamois au XIXe siècle*. Paris: L'Harmattan. [*Notes sur le Laos*. Saigon: 1885].

Badenoch, Nathan

2018. 'Translating the state: ethnic language radio in the Lao PDR.' *Journal of Contemporary Asia* 48(5): 783–807.

2022. 'Speaking like a ghost: registers of intimacy and incompatibility in the forests of Northern Laos.' *Journal of the Siam Society*, 110(1): 103–115.

Baird, Ian G.

2000. *The Ethnoecology, Land-Use, and Livelihoods of the Brao-Kavet Indigenous Peoples in Kok Lak Commune, Voen Say district, Ratanakiri province, Northeast Cambodia.* Ban Lung, Ratanakiri, Cambodia: NTFP Project.

2003. 'Dipterocarpus Wood Resin Tenure, Management and Trade: Practices of the Brao in Northeast Cambodia'. MA thesis. Victoria: Department of Geography, University of Victoria.

2008. 'The case of the Brao: Revisiting physical borders, ethnic identities and spatial and social organization in the hinterlands of Southern Laos and Northeastern Cambodia.' In Y. Goudineau and M. Lorrillard (eds), *Recherches nouvelles sur le Laos*, pp. 595–620. Études thématiques n° 18. Paris: École française d'Extrême-Orient.

Baird, Ian G., Nattaya Tubtim and Monsiri Baird

1996. *The Kavet and the Kreung: Observations of Livelihoods and Natural Resources in Two Highlander Villages in the Districts of Veun Say and Ta Veng,Ratanakiri Province, Cambodia.* Livelihoods and Natural Resources Study Report. Ban Lung, Ratanakiri, Cambodia: Oxfam (UK and Ireland) and Novib.

Baird, Ian G. and P. Dearden

2003. 'Biodiversity conservation and resource tenure regimes: A case study from Northeast Cambodia.' *Environmental Management* 32 (5): 541–550.

Baird, Ian G. and Olivier Évrard

2017. 'The Political Ecoloy of Upland/Lowland Relationships in Laos since 1975.' In V. Bouté and V. Pholsena (eds), *Changing Lives in Laos: Society, Politics, and Culture in a Post-Socialist State*, pp. 165–191. Singapore: NUS Press.

Baird, Ian G. and Bruce Shoemaker

2005. *Aiding or Abetting? Internal Resettlement and International Aid Agencies in the Lao PDR.* Toronto: Probe International.

2007. 'Unsettling experiences: Internal resettlementand international aid agencies in Laos.' *Development and Change* 38(5): 865–888.

Barber, Martin

1974. 'Urbanisation' and religion in Laos – A comparative study.' In M. Barber and A. Doré (eds), *Sangkhom Khady San. Colloquium of researchers in the Human Sciences*, pp. 45–58. Vientiane: Vithagna.

1979. 'Migrants and modernization: A study of change in Lao society'. PhD dissertation, University of Hull, Hull.

Barney, Keith

2009. 'Laos and the making of a 'relational' resource frontier.' *The Geographical Journal* 175(2): 146–159.

Barraud, Cécile, Daniel de Coppet, André Iteanu and Raymond Jamous

1994. *Of Relations and the Dead: Four Societies Viewed from the Angle of their Exchanges.* Oxford and Providence: Berg.

Barraud, Cécile and Jos D.M. Platenkamp

1990. 'Rituals and the comparison of societies.' *Bijdragen tot de Taal-, Land- en Volkenkunde* 146(1): 103–123.

Barth, Fredrik (ed.)

1969. *Ethnic Groups and Boundaries: The Social Organisation of Culture Difference.* The Little Brown Series in Anthropology. Boston: Little, Brown and Co.

Baudenne, Antonin

1913. 'Les Khas de la région d'Attopeu.' *Revue indochinoise* 1: 261–274.

Baumann, Benjamin

2020. 'Reconceptualizing the cosmic polity: The Tai Mueang as a social ontology.' In B. Baumann and D. Bultmann (eds), *Social Ontology, Sociocultures and Inequality in the Global South*, pp. 42–66. London/ New York: Routledge.

Bechert, Heinz

1967. *Buddhismus, Staat und Gesellschaft in den Ländern des Theravada-Buddhismus* (Band II). Goettingen.

Bell, Catherine

1997. *Ritual: Perspectives and Dimensions.* New York and Oxford: Oxford University Press.

Benson, Frederic C.

2018. 'Turbulence in Sam Neua Province, Laos: 1953–1970.' In S. Sherman (ed.), *Indochina in the Year of the Pig – 1971*, pp. 131–210. Houston: Radix Press.

Berger, Peter L.

1967. *The Sacred Canopy: Elements of a Sociological Theory of Religion.* New York: Doubleday.

Berliet, Ernelle

2010. 'Kausambi, ancient royaume mao. Les traces archéologiques du peuplement shan sur les hauts plateaux de Birmanie.' *Aséanie* 26: 11–30.

Berlin, Brent

1992. *Ethnobiological Classification*. Princeton, NJ: Princeton University Press.

Berliner, David

2010. 'Perdre l'esprit du lieu. Les politiques de l'UNESCO à Luang Prabang (Lao PDR).' *Terrain* 55: 90–105.

Bernhard-Johnston, Jean

1993. 'Singing the Lives of the Buddha: Lao Folk Opera as an Educational Medium'. PhD dissertation, University of Massachusetts.

Bernstein, Henry and Terence J. Byres

2001. 'From peasant studies to agrarian change.' *Journal of Agrarian Change* 1 (1): 1–56.

Berval, René de (ed.)

1956. *Présence du Royaume Lao. Pays du million d'éléphants et du parasol blanc,* numéro spécial de *France-Asie,* tome XII, 118–120, mars-mai 1956 (trad. 1959. *Kingdom of Laos,* Saigon, Editions France-Asie).

Bloch, Maurice

1989. 'From cognition to ideology.' In M. Bloch, *Ritual, History, Power. Selected Papers in Anthropology,* pp. 106–136. London: Athlone Press.

Bottomley, Ruth

2002. 'Contested forests: An analysis of the highlander responses to logging, Ratanakiri province, Northeast Cambodia.' *Critical Asian Studies* 34 (4): 587–606.

Boualay Phengsengkham

2008. *Legend of Viangphoukhaa.* Vientiane: Sengsavan Press.

Bounsang Khamkeo

2006. *I Little Slave: A Prison Memoir from Communist Laos.* Washington: Eastern Washington University Press.

Bountavy Sisouphanthong and Christian Taillard

2000. *Atlas of Laos.* Chiang Mai: Silkworm Books and Copenhagen: Nordic Institute of Asian Studies.

Bourdieu, Pierre

1979. *Algeria 1960: The disenchantment of the world, The sense of honour, The Kabyle house or the world reversed. Essays.* Cambridge: Cambridge University Press.

1984. *Distinction.* London: Routledge and Kegan Paul.

1987. 'La dissolution du religieux.' In P. Bourdieu, *Choses dites,* pp. 13–46. Paris: Les Editions de Minuit.

1991. 'Genesis and structure of the religious field.' *Comparative Social Research* 13(1): 1–44.

1994. 'Rethinking the state: genesis and structure of the bureaucratic field.' *Sociological Theory* 12(1): 1–18.

1996. *Rules of Art: Genesis and Structure of the Literary Field.* Stanford: Stanford University Press.

1998. *Contre-feux. Propos pour servir à la résistance contre l'invasion néo-liberale.* Paris: Liber-Raisons d'Agir.

2000. *Pascalian Meditations.* Stanford: Stanford University Press.

2003. 'Participant Objectivation.' *Journal of the Royal Anthropological Institute* 9(2): 281–294.

Bourdieu, Pierre and Loïc Wacquant

1992. *An Invitation to Reflexive Anthropology.* Chicago: University of Chicago Press.

Bourlet, Antoine

1906. 'Socialisme dans les hủa phăn (Laos, Indo-Chine) [Socialism in Houaphan].' *Anthropos* 1(3): 521–528.

Bourotte, Bernard

1955. 'Essai d'histoire des populations montagnardes du Sud-Indochinois jusqu'à 1945.' *Bulletin de la société des études indochinoises* 30 (1): 1–116.

Bouté, Vanina

2005. 'Les Phounoy du Nord-Laos: ethnogenèse et dynamiques d'intégration'. PhD Dissertation. Paris: École Pratique des Hautes Etudes.

2008. 'Cultes aux esprits et bouddhisme chez les Phounoy du Nord-Laos.' In Y. Goudineau and M. Lorrillard (eds), *Recherches nouvelles sur le Laos,* pp. 579–593. Études thématiques n° 18. Paris: École française d'Extrême-Orient.

2011a. *En miroir du pouvoir. Les Phounoy du Nord Laos: ethnogenèse et dynamiques d'intégration.* Paris: École française d'Extrême-Orient.

2011b. 'Good death, bad death and ritual restructurings: the New Year ceremonies of the Phunoy in northern Laos.' In P. Williams and P. Ladwig (eds), *Buddhist Funeral Cultures of Southeast Asia and China*, pp. 99–118. Cambridge: Cambridge University Press.

2018. *Mirroring Power. Ethnogenesis and Integration among the Phunoy of Northern Laos*. Chiang Mai: Silkworm Books.

2021a. 'Soothsayers and horoscopes: New modes of inquiring into the future in northern Laos.' *Social Anthropology*, special issue 'Upland Pioneers: Future Aspirations, Moral Imaginaries and Emerging Religiosities in Upland Southeast Asia', 29: 748–762.

2021b. 'Religious Changes, Ethnic minorities and the State in Laos.' *Taiwan Journal of Southeast Asian Studies*, 16 (2): 79–110.

Bouté, Vanina and Vatthana Pholsena (eds)

2017. *Changing Lives in Laos: Society, Politics, and Culture in a Post-Socialist State*. Singapore: NUS Press.

Bowie, Katherine A.

1992. 'Unravelling the myth of the subsistence economy: Textile production in 19th century northern Thailand.' *The Journal of Asian Studies* 51(4): 797–823.

Boyd, Robert and Peter J. Richerson

2005. *The Origin and Evolution of Cultures*. Oxford: Oxford University Press.

Brown, MacAlister and Joseph J. Zasloff

1986. *Apprentice Revolutionaries: The Communist Movement in Laos, 1930–1985*. Stanford: Hoover Institution Press.

Brown, Michael

2004a. *Who Owns Native Culture?* Cambridge MA: Harvard University Press.

2004b. 'Heritage as Property.' In C. Humphrey and K. Verdery (eds) *Property in Question: Value Transformation in the Global Economy*, pp. 49–68. Oxford: Berg.

Cannell, Fenella

2010. 'The anthropology of secularism'. *Annual Review of Anthropology* 39(1): 85–100.

Casanova, José

1994. *Public Religions in the Modern World*. Chicago: The University of Chicago Press.

2006. 'Secularization revisited: A reply to Talal Asad.' In D. Scott and C. Hirschkind (eds), *Powers of the Secular Modern Talal Asad and His Interlocutors*, pp. 12–30. Stanford: Stanford University Press.

Castle, Timothy

1993. *At War in the Shadow of Vietnam: U.S. Military Aid to the Royal Lao Government 1955–1975*. New York: Columbia University Press.

1999. *One Day Too Long: Top Secret Site 85 and the Bombing of North Vietnam*. New York: University of Columbia Press.

Chagnon, Jacqui and Roger Rumpf

1982. 'Education: The prerequisite to change.' In M. Stuart-Fox (ed), *Contemporary Laos: Studies in the Politics and Society of the Lao People's Democratic Republic*, pp. 163–180. St. Lucia: Queensland University Press.

Chamberlain, James R.

1975. 'A new look at the history and the classification of the Tai languages.' In J. G Harris and J. Chamberlain (ed), *Studies in Tai Linguistics*, pp. 49–66. Bangkok: Office of State Universities.

Chamberlain, James R., Charles Alton and Arthur G. Crisfield

1995. *Indigenous Peoples Profile: Lao PDR*. Vientiane: CARE International.

Chamberlain, James and Panh Phomsombath

2002. *Poverty Alleviation for All. Prepared for Embassy of Sweden*. Vientiane: SIDA.

Chayanov, A. V.

1986 [1925, 1966]. 'Peasant farm organisation'. In A.V. Chayanov 1986 [1966]. *Theory of Peasant Economy*. Madison: The University of Wisconsin Press. Originally published separately in Russian 1925; republished, translated into English, in Chayanov 1986 [1966].

1986 [1966]. *Theory of Peasant Economy*. Madison: The University of Wisconsin Press.

Chazée, Laurent

1998. *Évolution des systèmes de production ruraux en République Démocratique Populaire Lao, 1975–1995*. Paris: L'Harmattan.

1999. *The Peoples of Laos: Rural and Ethnic Diversities*. Bangkok: White Lotus Press.

Chiengthong Jameree

2003. 'The politics of ethnicity, indigenous culture and knowledge in Thailand, Vietnam and Lao PDR.' In K-A. Mingsarn and J. Dore (eds), *Social Challenges for the Mekong Region*, pp. 147–172. Bangkok: White Lotus.

Cholthira Satyawadhna

1991. 'The Dispossessed. An Anthropological Reconstruction of Lawa Ethnohistory in the Light of their Relationship with the Tai.' PhD Dissertation. Canberra: Australian National University.

Christie, Clive J.

2000. 'Loyalism and 'special war': the montagnards in Vietnam.' In C. J. Christie, *A Modern History of Southeast Asia. Decolonization, Nationalism and Separatism*, pp. 82–106. London: I. B. Tauris Publishers.

2001. *Ideology and Revolution in South-East Asia, 1900–1975*. London: RoutledgeCurzon.

Clément-Charpentier, Sophie and Pierre Clément

1990. *L'Habitation lao dans les régions de Vientiane et de Luang Prabang*. Paris: Peeters.

Cohen, Paul A.

1997. *History in Three Keys. The Boxers as Event, Experience, and Myth*. New York: Columbia University Press.

2003. 'Three ways of knowing the past.' In *China Unbound: Evolving Perspectives on the Chinese Past*. London: Routledge Curzon.

Cohen, Paul T.

1998. 'Lue ethnicity in national context: a comparative study of Tai Lue communities in Thailand and Laos.' *Journal of the Siam Society*, 86 (1–2): 49–61.

2000. 'Resettlement, Opium and Labour Dependence: Akha-Tai Relations in Northern Laos.' *Development and Change* 31(1): 179–200.

Cohen, Paul T., and Olivier Évrard (eds)

2019. *The Australian Journal of Anthropology* (TAJA), Special Issue 'Grant Evans and Tai studies: Political Engagement and Intellectual Legacy' 30(2).

Cohen, Paul T., and Chris Lyttleton

2002. 'Opium-reduction programmes, discourses of addiction and gender in northwest Laos.' *Sojourn: Journal of Social Issues in Southeast Asia* 17(1): 1–23.

2008. *The Akha of northwest Laos: Modernity and social suffering*. Chiang Mai: Mekong Press.

Colani, Madeleine
1935. *Megalithes du Haut Laos*. Paris: École française d'Extrême-Orient.

Cole, Robert
(forthcoming). 'Commodity frontiers in motion: Tracing the advancing maize boom across the Lao-Vietnamese borderlands.' In O. Tappe and S. Rowedder (eds), *Extracting Development: Contested Resource Frontiers in Mainland Southeast Asia*. Singapore: ISEAS Publishing.

Cole, Robert and Jonathan Rigg
2019. 'Lao peasants on the move: Pathways of agrarian change in Laos.' *The Australian Journal of Anthropology* 30(2): 160–180.

Colonna, M.
1938. 'Monographie de la province de Saravane.' *Bulletin des Amis du Laos* 2: 81–121.

Condominas, Georges
1962. *Essai sur la société rurale de la région de Vientiane*. Vientiane: Ministère des Affaires rurales.
1990. *From Lawa to Mon from Saa' to Thai: Historical and Anthropological Aspects of Southeast Asia Social Spaces*. An occasional paper of the Department of Anthropology, Research School of Pacific Studies. Canberra: Australian National University.
1998. *Le Bouddhisme au village*. Vientiane: École française d'Extrême-Orient.

Condominas, Georges and Claude Gaudillot
2000. *La plaine de Vientiane: étude socio-économique*. Paris: P. Geuthner and Seven Orients.

Cook, Joanna
2010. *Meditation in Modern Buddhism: Renunciation and Change in Thai Monastic Life*. Cambridge: Cambridge University Press.

Cox, Peter and Boike Rehbein (eds)
2016. *Journal of Laos Studies (JLS)* 3(1). Special Issue 'Devoted to the work of Grant Evans.'

Cramb, Robert and I. R. Wills
1990. 'The role of traditional institutions in rural development: Community-based land tenure and government land policy in Sarawak, Malaysia.' *World Development* 18(3): 347–360.

Creak, Simon

2015. *Embodied Nation. Sport, Masculinity, and the Making of Modern Laos.* Honolulu: University of Hawai'i Press.

Crystal, David

2000. *Language Death.* Cambridge: Cambridge University Press.

Cupet, Captain P.

1998 [1891]. *Among the Tribes of Southern Vietnam and Laos. 'Wild' Tribes and French Politics on the Siamese Border (1891).* Bangkok: White Lotus Press.

Cusack, Carole M.

1996. 'Towards a general theory of conversion.' In L. Olson (ed.), *Religious Change, Conversion and Culture*, pp. 1–21. Sydney: Sydney Studies.

Cushman, Richard (translator)

2000. *The Royal Chronicles of Ayutthaya.* A translation of eight versions of Thai annals to English by Richard D. Cushman. David K. Wyatt (ed.). Bangkok: Siam Society.

Damrong Tayanin

1994. *Being Kammu. My Village, My Life.* Ithaca, N. Y.: Cornell Southeast Asia Program.

Đặng Nghiêm Van

1998. *Ethnological and Religious Problems in Vietnam.* Hanoi: Social Sciences Publishing House.

Đặng Nghiêm Vạn, Chu Thái Sơn and Lưu Hùng

1986. *Les Ethnies minoritaires du Vietnam.* Hanoi: Éditions en Langues Étrangères.

Dauplay, Jean-Jacques

1914. 'Les Kha Tahoï.' *L'Ethnographie* 3: 43–51.

1929. *Les Terres rouges du plateau des Boloven.* Saigon: Chambre d'agriculture de la Cochinchine.

Deacon, Roger

2006. 'From confinement to attachment: Michel Foucault on the rise of the school.' *The European Legacy* 11(2): 121–138.

Deuve, Jean

1999. *Le Laos 1945–1949. Contribution à l'histoire du mouvement Lao Issala.* Montpellier: Université Paul-Valéry.

Dianteill, Erwan.

2004. 'Pierre Bourdieu and the Sociology of Religion: A Central and Peripheral Concern.' In David Swartz and Vera Zolberg (eds), *After Bourdieu: Influence, Critique, Elaboration*. Dordrecht: Kluwer.

Diffloth, Gérard and Norman H. Zide

1992. 'Austro-Asiatic languages.' In W.O. Bright (ed.), *International Encyclopedia of Linguistics*, vol. 1, pp. 137–142. Oxford: Oxford University Press.

Dobbelaere, Karel

2002. *Secularization: An Analysis at Three Levels*. Brussels, Berlin: P.I.E.-Peter Lang.

Doré, Pierre-Sylvain

1972. 'De l'hibiscus à la frangipane. Essai de sociologie politique sur la notion d'autorité traditionnelle au Laos.' PhD dissertation. Paris: Université de Paris V.

Duangsai Luangphasi

1993. *Sam Bulut Lek haeng Meuang Thakhaek* [The Three Iron Men of Thakhek]. Vientiane: Lao Committee for Peace, Solidarity and Friendship with the Nations.

Duara Prasenjit

1995. 'Book review of Thongchai Winichalkul, *Siam Mapped: A History of the Geo-Body of a Nation*. Honolulu: Hawai'i University Press, 1994.' *American Historical Review* 100 (2): 477– 479.

Duncan, Christopher R. (ed.)

2004. *Civilizing the Margins. Southeast Asian Government Policies for the Development of Minorities*. Singapore: NUS Press.

Durkheim, Emile and Marcel Mauss

1971. 'Note on the notion of civilization.' *Social Research* 38(4): 808–13.

Dwyer, Michael B.

2017. 'The New 'New Battlefield': Capitalizing Security in Laos's Agribusiness Landscape.' In V. Bouté and V. Pholsena (eds), *Changing Lives in Laos: Society, Politics, and Culture in a Post-Socialist State*, pp. 192–220. Singapore: NUS Press.

École française d'Extrême-Orient (EFEO)

1949. *Carte ethnolinguistique de l'Indochine* (au 2.000.000e). collectif hors-série. Hanoi: Service Géographique de l'Indochine.

1999. *Laos. Restaurer et préserver le patrimoine national. Colloque sur la préservation du patrimoine artistique et historique du Laos.* Vientiane: Ministère Lao de l'Information et de la Culture, Editions des Cahiers de France.

Eisenstadt, Samuel
2000. 'Multiple modernities.' *Daedalus* 129(1): 1–30.

Elson, Robert E.
1997. *The End of the Peasantry in Southeast Asia: A Social and Economic History of Peasant Livelihood, 1800–1990s.* Great Britain: Macmillan Press.

Enfield, N. J.
1999. 'Lao as a national language.' In G. Evans (ed.), *Laos. Culture and Society*, pp. 258–290. Chiang Mai: Silkworm Books.
2002. *Ethnosyntax: explorations in grammar and culture.* Oxford: Oxford University Press.
2005. 'Areal linguistics and mainland Southeast Asia.' *Annual Review of Anthropology* 34: 181–206.
2006a. 'Languages as historical documents: The endangered archive in Laos.' *South East Asia Research*, 14(3): 471–488.
2006b. 'Laos – language situation.' In K. Brown (ed.), *Encyclopedia of Language and Linguistics, Volume 2*, pp. 698–700. Amsterdam, Boston, Heidelberg: Elsevier Science.
2010. 'Language and culture in Laos: An agenda for research.' *Journal of Lao Studies* 1(1): 48–54.

Engelbert, Thomas
2004. 'From hunters to revolutionaries: The mobilisation of ethnic minorities in southern Laos and north-eastern Cambodia during the First Indo-China War (1945–1954).' In T. Engelbert and H. D. Kubitscheck (eds), *Ethnic Minorities and Politics in Southeast Asia*, pp. 225–269. New York: Peter Lang.

Eon, Anne
2019. 'Le Bouddhisme socialement engagé dans le Laos contemporain'. PhD Dissertation. Paris: University Paris Descartes.

Evans, Grant
1983. *The Yellow Rainmakers: Are Chemical Weapons Being Used In South Est Asia?* London: Verso.
1986. *From Moral Economy to Remembered Village: the Sociology of James C. Scott.* Working Paper No. 40, Centre of Southeast Asian Studies.

Melbourne: Monash University.
1987. 'Sources of peasant consciousness in Southeast Asia.' *Social History* 12(2): 193–211.
1990a. *Lao Peasants Under Socialism*. New Haven: Yale University Press.
1990b. 'Millennial rebels in colonial Laos.' *Peasant Studies* 18(1): 53–57.
1991. 'Reform or revolution in heaven? Funerals among upland Tai.' *The Australian Journal of Anthropology [TJA]* 2(1): 81–97.
1993a. 'Buddhism and Economic Action in Socialist Laos'. In C. M. Hann (ed.), *Socialism: Ideals, Ideologies, and Local Practice*, pp. 123–140. ASA Monograph 31, London: Routledge.
1993b. 'Asia and the Anthropological Imagination.' In G. Evans (ed.), *Asia's Cultural Mosaic. An Anthropological Introduction*, pp. 1–19. Singapore: Prentice-Hall.
1995a. *Lao Peasants Under Socialism and Post-Socialism*. Chiang Mai: Silkworm Books.
1995b. 'Central highlanders of Vietnam.' In R. H. Barnes, A. Gray and B. Kingsbury (eds), *Indigenous Peoples in Asia*, pp. 247– 271. Ann Arbor: Association for Asian Studies, Inc., University of Michigan.
1998a. 'Secular fundamentalism and Buddhism in Laos.' In Oh Myung-Seok and Kim Hyung-Jun (eds), *Religion, Ethnicity and Modernity in Southeast Asia*, pp. 169–205. Seoul: Seoul National University Press.
1998b. *The Politics of Ritual and Remembrance: Laos since 1975*. Chiang Mai: Silkworm Books.
1999a. 'Apprentice ethnographers.' In G. Evans (ed.), *Laos: Culture and Society*, pp. 161–190. Chiang Mai: Silkworm Books.
1999b. 'Ethnic change in the highlands of Laos.' In G. Evans (ed.), *Laos: Culture and Society*, pp. 125–147. Chiang Mai: Silkworm Books.
2000. 'Tai-ization: Ethnic change in northern Indo-China.' In A. Turton (ed.), *Civility and Savagery: Social Identity in Tai States*, pp. 263–290. Richmond: Curzon.
2002a. *A Short History of Laos: The Land In Between*. Sydney: Allen and Unwin.
2002b. 'Between the Global and the Local, There are Regions, Culture Areas and National States. A Review Article of O. W. Wolters (1999).' *Journal of Southeast Asian Studies* 33(1): 147–161.
2003a. 'Laos: minorities.' In C. Mackerras (ed.), *Asian Ethnicity*, pp. 210–224. London: Routledge Curzon.
2003b. 'Urban minorities.' In Y. Goudineau (ed.) *Laos and Ethnic Minority Cultures. Promoting Heritage*, pp. 203–205. Paris: UNESCO.

Memory of Peoples collection.

2008. 'Lao peasant studies today.' In Y. Goudineau and M. Lorrillard (eds), *Recherches nouvelles sur le Laos*, pp. 507–531. Études thématiques n° 18. Paris: École française d'Extrême-Orient.

2009. *The Last Century of Lao Royalty: A Documentary History.* Chiang Mai: Silkworm Books.

Evans, Grant (ed.)

1999. *Laos: Culture and Society.* Chiang Mai: Silkworm Books.

Evans, Grant and Kelvin Rowley

1984. *Red Brotherhood at War: Indochina Since the Fall of Saigon.* London: Verso.

Evans, Grant, Christopher Hutton and Kuah Khun Eng (eds)

2000. *Where China Meets Southeast Asia. Social and Cultural Change in the Border Regions*. Singapore: ISEAS.

Évrard, Olivier

1996. 'New villages of Luang Nam Tha province.' In Y. Goudineau (ed.), *Resettlement and Social Characteristics of New Villages*, pp. 1–50 (Vol. 2). Vientiane: UNDP-UNESCO-IRD.

2003. 'Sens et actualité des 'sous groupes' khmou (tmoï) au Nord Laos.' *Aséanie* 11: 39–71.

2006. *Chroniques des cendres. Anthropologie des sociétés khmou et relations interethniques du Nord-Laos*. Paris: IRD.

2007. 'Interethnic systems and localized identities: The Khmu subgroups in North-West Laos.' In F. Robinne and M. Sadan (eds), *Social Dynamics in the Highlands of Southeast Asia. Reconsidering Political Systems of Highland Burma by E. R. Leach*, pp. 127–159. Leiden: Brill.

2019. 'From Tai-isation to Lao-isation: Ethnic changes in the longue durée in Northern Laos.' *The Australian Journal of Anthropology* 30: 228–242.

Évrard, Olivier and Yves Goudineau

2004. 'Planned resettlements, unexpected migrations and cultural trauma in Laos.' *Development and Change* 35(5): 937–964.

Évrard, Olivier, Oliver Pryce, Guido Sprenger and Chiemsisouraj Chanthaphilith

2016. 'Of myths and metallurgy. Archaeological and ethnological approaches to iron upland production in ninth century AD Northern Laos.' *Journal of Southeast Asian Studies* 47(1): 109–140.

Fall, Bernard B.

1966. *Vietnam Witness 1953–1966*. London: Pall Mall Press.

Feeny, David, Berkes Fikret, McCay J. and James M. Acheson
1990. 'The tragedy of the commons twenty-two years later.' *Human Ecology* 18(1): 1–19.

Ferguson, James
1999. *Expectations of Modernity: Myths and Meanings of Urban Life on the Zambian Copperbelt*. Berkeley and Los Angeles: University of California Press.

Ferlus, Michel
1974. 'Délimitation des groupes linguistiques austroasiatiques dans le centre-indochinois.' *ASEMI* 5 (1): 15–23.

Finot, Louis
1917. 'Recherches sur la littérature laotienne.' *Bulletin de l'École française d'Extrême-Orient* 17 (5): 1–221.

Flanagan, Caitlan
2004. 'How serfdom saved the women's movement.' *The Atlantic Monthly*, March.

Formoso, Bernard
1998. 'Bad Death and Malevolent Spirits among the Tai Peoples.' *Anthropos* 93: 3–17.
2018. 'Social and spatial organization of the Tai Deng of Mai-Châu (Viêt Nam) before 1954.' *Moussons* 31: 117–134.

Formoso, Bernard (ed.)
1997. *Ban Amphawan et Ban Han: Le devenir de deux villages rizicoles du Nord-Est thaïlandais*. Paris: CNRS Éditions.

Foropon, Jean
1927. 'La province des Hua-Phan (Laos).' *Extrême-Asie* 14: 93–106.

Foucault, Michel
1980a. 'Questions on geography.' In C. Gordon (ed.), *Power/Knowledge: Selected Interviews and Other Writings 1972–1977*, pp. 63–77. Brighton: Harvester Press.
1980b. *Power/Knowledge. Selected Interviews and Other Writings 1972–1977*. New York: Pantheon Books.
1994. 'La Naissance de la médecine sociale.' In M. Foucault, *Dits et écrits. 1954–1988*, pp. 207–228. Paris: Gallimard.

Fox, Jefferson

2002. 'Siam mapped and mapping in Cambodia: Boundaries, sovereignty, and indigenous conceptions of space.' *Society and Natural Resources* 15: 65–78.

Fraisse, André

1951. 'Les Villages du plateau des Boloven.' *Bulletin de la Société des Etudes Indochinoises* 26(1): 53–72.

Furseth, Inger

2009. 'Religion in the work of Habermas, Bourdieu and Foucault.' In P. Clarke (ed.), *The Oxford Handbook of the Sociology of Religion,* pp. 98–115. Oxford/New York: Oxford University Press.

Furuta, Motoo

1992. 'The Indochina Communist Party's division into three parties: Vietnamese communist policy toward Cambodia and Laos, 1948–1951.' In T. Shiraishi and M. Furuta (eds), *Indochina in the 1940s and 1950s,* pp. 143–163. Ithaca: Cornell Southeast Asia Program.

Gagneux, Pierre-Marie

1973. 'Eléments d'astronomie et d'astrologie laotienne'. PhD dissertation. Paris: École Pratique des Hautes Etudes.

Garnier, Francis

1873. *Voyage d'exploration en Indochine.* Paris: Hachette.

Gay, Bernard

1995. 'Notes sur le Laos sous le protectorat français (de 1893 à 1940).' In Nguyen The Anh and A. Forest (eds), *Notes sur la culture et la religion en Péninsule indochinoise – en hommage à Pierre-Bernard Lafont,* pp. 227–241. Paris: L'Harmattan.

Gellner, David N.

1990. 'Introduction: What is the anthropology of Buddhism about?' *Journal of the Anthropological Society of Oxford* 21(2): 95–112.

Gentner, Dedre and Susan Goldin-Meadow (eds)

2003. *Language in Mind.* Cambridge: MIT Press.

Gladney, Dru C.

1994. 'Representing nationality in China: refiguring majority/minority identities.' *Journal of Asian Studies* 53(1): 92–123.

Gombrich, Richard and Gananath Obeyesekere

1988. *Buddhism Transformed. Religious Change in Sri Lanka.* Princeton:

Princeton University Press.

Goscha, Christopher E.

1999. *Thailand and the Southeast Asian Networks of the Vietnamese Revolution, 1885–1954*. Richmond: Curzon Press.

2003a. 'La Guerre pour l'Indochine? Le Laos et le Cambodge dans le conflit franco-vietnamien (1948–1954).' *Guerres mondiales et conflits contemporains* 211: 29–58.

2003b. 'Revolutionizing the Indochinese past: Communist Vietnam's "special" historiography on Laos.' In C. E. Goscha and S. Ivarsson (eds), *Contesting Visions of the Lao Past. Lao Historiography at the Crossroads*, pp. 265–299. Copenhagen: NIAS Press.

2004. 'Vietnam and the world outside. The case of Vietnamese Communist advisers in Laos (1948–1952).' *South East Asia Research* 12(2): 141–185.

Goudineau, Yves

1997. 'Des survivants aux survivances: quelle ethnographie en zone démilitarisée? (Laos – Pistes Hô Chi Minh).' In M. Agier (ed.), *Anthropologues en dangers*, pp. 51–6. Paris: J.-M. Place.

2000a. 'Tambours de bronze et circumbulations cérémonielles: Notes à partir d'un rituel kantou (Chaine annamitique).' *Bulletin de l'École française d'Extrême-Orient* 87(2): 553–578.

2000b. 'Ethnicité et déterritorialisation dans la péninsule Indochinoise: considérations à partir du Laos.' *Autrepart* 14: 17–31.

2001a 'Intangible culture and development norms: the Katuic populations in the Annamese Cordillera.' In O. Salemink (ed.) *Viet Nam's cultural diversity: approaches to preservation*, pp. 213–226. Paris: UNESCO, coll. Memory of Peoples.

2001b. 'Le médium de Champassak.' *Aséanie* 8: 135–149.

2002, 'Charles Archaimbault (1921–2001).' *Bulletin de l'École française d'Extrême-Orient*, vol. 88, pp. 7–16.

2003. 'Managing the intangible cultural heritage.' In Y. Goudineau (ed.), *Laos and Ethnic Minority Cultures. Promoting Heritage*, pp. 33–38. Paris: UNESCO. Memory of Peoples collection.

2008. 'L'anthropologie du Sud-Laos et l'origine de la question Kantou.' In Y. Goudineau and M. Lorrillard (eds), *Recherches nouvelles sur le Laos*, pp. 639–663. Études thématiques n° 18. Paris: École française d'Extrême-Orient.

2009. 'Le Cercle des Kantou.' In J. Daniel (ed.), *Le Siècle de Lévi-Strauss*, pp.166–181. Paris: Editions du CNRS.

2015. 'The ongoing invention of a multi-ethnic heritage in Laos.' *The*

Journal of Lao Studies, Special Issue 2: 33–53.

Goudineau, Yves (ed.)

1997. *Resettlement and Social Characteristics of New Villages*. Volumes I & II, Vientiane: UNDP/ UNESCO.

2003. *Laos and Ethnic Minority Cultures. Promoting Heritage*. Paris: UNESCO, coll. Memory of Peoples.

Goudineau, Yves and Olivier Évrard

2006. 'Ethnicité et développement.' in D. Gentil and P. Boumard (eds), *Le Laos doux et amer. Vingt-cinq ans de pratique d'une ONG*, pp. 37–55. Paris: Karthala.

Goudineau, Yves and Michel Lorrillard (eds)

2008. *Nouvelles recherches sur le Laos / New Research on Laos*. Paris: Éditions EFEO, coll. Études thématiques n°18.

Grabowsky, Volker

1999. 'Introduction to the history of Mueang Sing (Laos) prior to French rule: The fate of a Lue principality.' *Bulletin de l'École française d'Extrême-Orient* 86: 233–291.

2001. 'On the social and political organization of Chiang Khaeng: A note on a Lü customary law text.' *Tai Culture* 6(1&2): 200–208.

2007. 'Buddhism, power, and political order in pre-twentieth century Laos.' In I. Harris (ed.), *Buddhism, Power and Political Order*, pp. 121–142. London: Routledge.

2008. 'The Tai polities in the Upper Mekong and their tributary relationships with China and Burma.' *Aséanie* 21: 11–63.

2011. 'Recent historiographical discourses in the Lao People's Democratic Republic.' In Volker Grabowsky (ed.), *Southeast Asian Historiography Unravelling the Myths: Essays in Honour of Barend Jan Terwiel*, pp. 52–69. Bangkok: River Books.

Grabowsky, Volker and Renoo Wichasin

2008. *Chronicles of Chiang Saen: A Tai Lue Principality at the Upper Mekong*. Honolulu: Center for Southeast Asian Studies, University of Hawai'i Press.

Granet, Marcel

1999 [1934]. *La Pensée chinoise*. Paris: Albin Michel.

Grenoble, Lenore A. and Lindsay J. Whaley (eds)

1998. *Endangered Languages: Current Issues and Future Prospects*. Cambridge: Cambridge University Press.

Grimes, Barbara F.

1996. 'Ethnologue: Cambodia.' In B. Grimes (ed.), *Ethnologue: Languages of the World* (13th edition). Dallas: Summer Institute of Linguistics.

Gros, Stéphane

2007. 'The missing share: The ritual language of sharing as a "total social fact" in the Eastern Himalayas (Northwest Yunnan, China).' In F. Robinne and M. Sadan (eds), *Social Dynamics in the Highlands of Southeast Asia: Reconsidering Political Systems of Highland Burma by E.R. Leach*, pp. 257–282. Leiden: Brill.

Gumperz, J. J. and S. C. Levinson (eds)

1996. *Rethinking Linguistic Relativity*. Cambridge: Cambridge University Press.

Gunn, Geoffrey

1990. *Rebellion in Laos. Peasant and Politics in a Colonial Backwater*. Boulder, Colorado: Westview Press.

1999. *Theravadins, Colonialists and Commissars in Laos*. Bangkok: White Lotus.

Gupta, Akhil and James Ferguson

1992. 'Beyond 'culture': Space, identity, and the politics of difference.' *Cultural Anthropology* 7 (1): 6–23.

Halpern, Joel M.

1961. 'Observations on the social structure of the Lao elite.' *Asian Survey* 5: 25–32.

1964. *Government, Politics, and Social Structure in Laos: A Study of Transition and Innovation*. New Haven: Southeast Asia Studies.

Handelman, Don

2005. 'Introduction: Why ritual in its own right?' In D. Handelman and G. Lindquist (eds), *Ritual in its Own Right*, pp. 1–32. New York and Oxford: Berghahn.

Hanks, Lucien

1975. 'The Thai social order as entourage and circle.' In G. W. Skinner and A. T. Kirsch (eds), *Change and Persistence in Thai Society*, pp. 197–218. Ithaca: Cornell University Press.

Hann, Chris

1980. *Tazlar: A Village in Hungary*. Cambridge: Cambridge University

Press.

Harmand, Jules
1994 [1887]. *L'Homme du Mékong*. Paris: Phébus.

Harms, Erik
2011. 'The critical difference: Making peripheral vision central in Vietnamese studies.' *Journal of Vietnamese Studies* 6 (2): 1–15.

Harvey, David
1990. *The Condition of Postmodernity: An Enquiry into the Origins of Cultural Change*. Blackwell: Cambridge, MA.

Helmers, Kent and Pia Wallgren
2002. *Indigenous Upland Minorities Impact Screening Study.* Interim Report. Washington DC: Cambodia Rural Investment and Local Governance Project, World Bank, East Asia and Pacific Region Rural Development and Natural Resources Sector Unit.

Hewison, Kevin
1995. 'Book Review of Thongchai Winichakul, *Siam Mapped: A History of the Geo-Body of a Nation*. Honolulu: University of Hawai'i Press, 1994.' *Australian Journal of International Affairs* 49 (1): 159–160.

Hickey, Gerald C.
1982. *Sons of the Mountains: Ethnohistory of the Vietnamese Central Highlands to 1954*. New Haven: Yale University Press.
2002. *Window on a War. An Anthropologist in the Vietnam Conflict.* Lubbock: Texas Tech University Press.

High, Holly
2014. *Fields of desire: Poverty and Policy in Laos*. Singapore: NUS Press.
2021. *Projectland. Life in a Lao Socialist Model Village*. Honolulu: University of Hawai'i Press.

Higham, Charles
1989. *The Archaeology of Mainland Southeast Asia*. Cambridge: Cambridge University Press.

Hill, Ann Maxwell
1998. *Merchants and Migrants: Ethnicity and Trade among Yunnanese Chinese in Southeast Asia*. Monograph 47, Yale Southeast Asia Studies. New Haven: Yale University Southeast Asia Studies.

Hinton, Peter

2000. 'Where nothing is as it seems: between Southwest China and mainland Southeast Asia in the "Post Socialist" era.' In G. Evans, C. Hutton and K.K. Eng (eds) *Where China Meets Southeast Asia. Social and Cultural Change in the Border Regions*, pp. 7–27. Singapore: ISEAS.

Hirsch, Philip and Natalia Scurrah

2015. *The Political Economy of Land Governance in Lao PDR*. Vientiane: Mekong Region Land Governance.

Hobsbawm, Eric and Terry Ranger (eds)

1983. *The Invention of Tradition*. Cambridge: Cambridge University Press.

Ho Chi Minh

1967. *On Revolution. Selected Writings, 1920–66*. London: Pall Mall Press.

Hoffet, Josué-H.

1933. 'Les Moïs de la chaîne annamitique entre Tourane et les Boloven.' *Terre, air, mer. La géographie* 59(1): 1–43.

Højbjerg, Christian Kordt

2002. 'Inner iconoclasm: forms of reflexivity in Loma rituals of sacrifice.' *Social Anthropology* 10(1): 57–75.

Holm, David

2003. *Killing a Buffalo for the Ancestors: A Zhuang Cosmological Text from Southwest China*. DeKalb: Center for Southeast Asian Studies.

Holt, John

2009. *Spirits of the Place: Buddhism and Lao Religious Culture*. Honolulu: University of Hawai'i Press.

Horstmann, Alexander

2002. 'Incorporation and resistance: Border-crossings and social transformation in Southeast Asia.' *Anthropologi Indonesia* 67: 12–29.

Horstmann, Alexander and Reed L. Wadley (eds)

2006. *Centering the Margin: Agency and Narrative in Southeast Asian Borderlands*. Oxford and New York: Berghahn Books.

Horton, Robin

1971. 'African conversion.' *Africa* 41(2): 85–108.

Hospitalier, Julien J.

1937. *Grammaire laotienne*. Paris: Geuthner.

Houmphanh Rattanavong.

1997. *On the Way to the Lolopho Land*. Vientiane: Institute for Cultural Research, Ministry of Information and Culture.

Hours, Bernard
1973. 'Un terrain d'étude des rapports inter-ethniques: la route de Paksé à Paksong (Sud-Laos).' *Cahiers Orstom*, série Sciences Humaines, 10(1): 31–45.

Hours, Bernard and Monique Selim
1997. *Essai d'anthropologie politique sur le Laos contemporain. Marché, socialisme et génies*. Paris: L'Harmattan.

Howell, Signe
2017. 'Two or three things I love about ethnography.' *HAU: Journal of Ethnographic Theory* 7 (1): 15–20.

Hudson, R. A.
1996. *Sociolinguistics*. Second edition. Cambridge: Cambridge University Press.

Hutton, Christopher and Dominique Blaettler
2016. 'From peasants to lords: The intellectual evolution of Grant Evans.' *Journal of Lao Studies (JLS)*, Special Issue 'Devoted to the work of Grant Evans', 3(1): 24–36.

Ingold, Tim
2014. 'That's enough about ethnography!' *HAU: Journal of Ethnographic Theory* 4(1): 383–395.
2017. 'Anthropology contra ethnography.' *HAU: Journal of Ethnographic Theory* 7(1): 21–26.

Inpan Chanthaphon
1994. ປະຫວັດຫຍໍ້: ເຜົ່າລາວຫຍວນ *(Lao Yuan Summary History)*. Typed document.

Inspection des Colonies
1938–1939. *Politique de contacts dans la Province de Saravane. Rébellion de groupements khas dans la délégation de la Haute-Sékong*. Archives d'Outre-Mer, Indochine NF, c. 290.

Institute for Cultural Research (ICR)
1995. *Round Table on Lao Language Policy*. Vientiane: Ministry of Information and Culture.

Inthasone Phetsiriseng
2003. *Lao PDR. Preliminary assessment of illegal labour migration and traf-*

ficking in children and women for labour exploitation. Bangkok: ILO Office.

Ireson, Carol J.

1996. *Field, Forest, and Family: Women's Work and Power in Rural Laos*. Boulder, Colorado: Westview Press.

Ireson, Carol J. and Randall W. Ireson

1991. 'Ethnicity and development in Laos.' *Asian Survey* 31(10): 920–937.

Ireson, Randall W.

1992. 'Peasant farmers and community norms: Agricultural labour exchange in Laos.' *Peasant Studies* 19(2): 67–92.

1994. 'Education prior to the Lao People's Democratic Republic.' In A. Savada (ed.), *Laos: A Country Study*. Washington: Library of Congress Federal Research Division. http://lcweb2.loc.gov/frd/cs/latoc.html [accessed on 15.12.2010].

1995. 'Village irrigation in Laos: Traditional patterns of common property resource management.' *Society and Natural Resources* 8: 541–558.

1996. 'Invisible walls: Village identity and the maintenance of cooperation in Laos.' *Journal of Southeast Asian Studies* 27(2): 219–244.

Ireson-Doolittle, Carol and Geraldine Moreno-Black

2004. *The Lao: Gender, Power, and Livelihood*. Boulder, Colorado: Westview Press.

Ironside, Jeremy and Ian G. Baird

2003. *Wilderness and Cultural Landscape: Settlement, Agriculture, and Land and Resource Tenure in and Adjacent to Virachey National Park, Northeast Cambodia*. Ban Lung, Ratanakiri, Cambodia: Biodiversity and Protection Area Management Project, Ministry of Environment.

Ishii, Yoneo

1986. *Sangha, State and Society: Thai Buddhism in History*. Honolulu: University of Hawai'i Press.

Iteanu, André

2005. 'Partial discontinuity: the mark of ritual.' In D. Handelman and G. Lindquist (eds), *Ritual in its Own Right*, pp. 98–115. New York and Oxford: Berghahn Books.

Ivarsson, Soren

1999. 'Bringing Laos into Existence. Laos between Indochina and Siam 1860–1945.' PhD dissertation, Copenhagen University.

2008. *Creating Laos: The Making of a Lao Space between Indochina and*

Siam 1860–1945. Copenhagen: NIAS Press.

Izikowitz, Karl Gustav

1962. 'Notes about the Tai.' *Bulletin of Far Eastern Antiquities* 34: 73–91.

1969. 'Neighbours in Laos.' In F. Barth (ed.), *Ethnic Groups and Boundaries*, pp. 135–149. London: George Allen and Unwin.

1979 [1951]. *Lamet: Hill Peasants in French Indochina*. New York: AMS Press.

1985. *Compass for Fields Afar: Essays in Social Anthropology*. Göteborg: Acta Universitatis Gothoburgensis.

2004 [1944]. *Over the Misty Mountain: A Journey from Tonkin to the Lamet in Laos*. Translated by Helena Berngrim. Bangkok: White Lotus.

Jacq, Pascale

2002. *A Description of Jruq (Loven): A Mon-Khmer language of the Lao PDR*. MA thesis, Australian National University, Canberra.

Jacques, Claude

1979. '"Funan", "Zhenla": The reality concealed by these Chinese views of Indochina.' In R. B. Smith and W. Watson (eds), *Early South East Asia*, pp. 371–379. New York, Kuala Lumpur: Oxford University Press.

Jerndal, Randall and Jonathan Rigg

1998. 'Making space in Laos: Constructing a national identity in a "forgotten" country.' *Political Geography* 17 (7): 809–831.

Jonsson, Hjorleifur

1997. 'Cultural priorities and projects: Health and social dynamics in northeast Thailand.' In D. McCaskill and K. Kampe (eds), *Development or Domestication? Indigenous Peoples in Southeast Asia*, pp. 536–567. Chiang Mai: Silkworm Books.

2010. 'Mimetic minorities: National identity and desire on Thailand's fringe.' *Identities* 17(2–3): 108–130.

2014. *Slow Anthropology: Negotiating Difference with the Iu Mien*. Ithaca, New York: Cornell University Press.

Johnstone, Patrick

1993. *Operation World*. Grand Rapids: Zondervan Publishing House.

Jullien, Rachel

1995. 'Les Restructurations économiques 1975–1992.' In M.-S. de Vienne and J. Nepote (eds), *Laos 1975–1995. Restructuration et développement*, pp. 7–72. Metz: Péninsule.

Källén, Anna

2016. *Stones Standing: Archaeology, Colonialism and Ecotourism in Northern Laos*. New York: Routledge.

Kammerer, Cornelia Ann

1990. 'Customs and Christian conversion among Akha highlanders of Burma and Thailand.' *American Ethnologist* 17: 277–291.

Kaysone Phomvihane

1985. *Niphon Luak Fen*. Vientiane: State Press.

Kearney, Michael

1996. *Reconceptualizing the Peasantry: Anthropology in Global Perspective*. Boulder, Colorado: Westview Press.

Keyes, Charles F.

1977. 'Millenialism, Theravada Buddhism and Thai society.' *Journal of Asian Studies* 36(2): 283–302.

1990. 'Buddhist practical morality in changing agrarian world. A case study from northeastern Thailand.' In R. Sizemore and D. Swearer (eds), *Ethics, Wealth and Salvation. A Study in Buddhist Social Ethics*, pp. 170–189. Columbia: University of South Carolina Press.

1995. 'Who are the Thai? Reflections on the invention of identities.' In L. Romanucci-Ross and G. A. De Vos (eds), *Ethnic Identity. Creation, Conflict and Accommodation*, pp. 136–160. Walnut Creek/London/New Delhi: Sage.

2002. 'Presidential address: "The Peoples of Asia' – Science and Politics in the Classification of Ethnic Groups in Thailand, China and Vietnam."' *Journal of Asian Studies* 61 (4): 1163–1203.

2019. *Impermanence. An Anthropologist of Thailand and Asia*. Chiang Mai: Silkworm Books.

Khambay Nyundalat (translator)

2000–2002 [1991]. *Pavat khong kan pativat khong khwaeng Sekong, 1945–1975* [History of the Revolution in Sekong Province, 1945–1975]. Unpublished manuscript.

Khamluan Sulavan and Nancy Costello

1998. *Katu-Lao-English Dictionary*. Vientiane: Institute of Research on Lao Culture.

Khamluan Sulavan, Thongpheth Kingsada and Nancy Costello

1995. *Aspects of Katu Traditional Medicine* [in Lao, Katu, English].

Vientiane: Institute of Research on Lao Culture.

Khampeuy Vannasopha
2003. *Religious Affairs in Lao PDR.* Vientiane: Ministry of Information and Culture.

Khamphanh Thammakhanty
2004. *Get to the Trunk, Destroy the Roots: The Fall from Monarch to Socialism.* Portland: Self-published.

Khampheng Thipmuntali
1999. 'The Tai Lue of Muang Sing.' In G. Evans (ed.), *Laos: Culture and Society*, pp. 148–60. Chiang Mai: Silkworm Books.

King, Victor T. and William D. Wilder
2003. *The Modern Anthropology of South-East Asia.* London: Routledge.

Kirsch, Thomas A.
1977. 'Complexity in the Thai religious system: An interpretation.' *Journal of Asian Studies*, 36(2): 241–266.

Kneer, Georg
2004. 'Differenzierung bei Luhmann und Bourdieu. Ein Theorienvergleich.' In A. Nassehi and G. Nollmann (eds), *Bourdieu und Luhmann. Ein Theorienvergleich*, pp. 25–56. Frankfurt: Suhrkamp.

Koret, Peter
2000. 'Books of search: Convention and creativity in traditional Lao literature.' In D. Smyth (ed.), *The Canon in Southeast Asian Literatures*, pp. 210–233. Richmond: Routledge.
1996. 'Past and present Lao perceptions of traditional literature.' In J. Butler-Diaz (ed.), *New Laos, New Challenges*, pp. 109–124. Temple, Arizona: Arizona University Press.

Kourilsky, Gregory
2006. 'Recherches sur l'institut bouddhique au Laos (1930–1949). Les circonstances de sa création, son action, son échec.' MA dissertation, École Pratique des Hautes Etudes, Paris.

Kroeber, Alfred L.
1948. *Anthropology.* Revised edition. New York: Harcourt and Brace.

Ladwig, Patrice
2008. 'Between cultural preservation and this-worldly commitment: Modernization, social activism and the Lao Buddhist sangha.' In Y.

Goudineau and M. Lorrillard (eds), *Recherches nouvelles sur le Laos*, pp. 465–490. Paris: École française d'Extrême-Orient.

2009. 'Prediger der Revolution: Der buddhistische Klerus und seine Verbindungen zur Kommunistischen Bewegung in Laos (1957–1975).' *Jahrbuch für Historische Kommunismusforschung* XV(1): 181–197.

2011. 'The genesis and demarcation of the religious field: Monasteries, state schools and the secular sphere in Lao Buddhism.' *Sojourn: Journal of Social Issues in Southeast Asia* 26(2): 196–223.

2013. 'Schools, ritual economies and the expanding state: The changing roles of Lao Buddhist monks as "traditional intellectuals".' In P. Kitiarsa and J. Whalen-Bridge (eds), *Buddhism, Modernity and the State in Asia. Forms of engagement*, pp. 63–91. New York: Palgrave Macmillan.

2016. 'Religious place making: Civilized modernity and the spread of Buddhism among the Cheng, a Mon-Khmer minority in Southern Laos.' In M. Dickhardt and A. Lauser (eds), *Religion, Place and Modernity. Spatial Articulations in Southeast Asia and East Asia*, pp. 95–124. Leiden: Brill.

2017. 'Contemporary Lao Buddhism. Ruptured histories.' In M. Jerryson (ed.), *The Oxford Encyclopedia of Contemporary Buddhism*, pp. 274–296. New York: Oxford University Press.

2018. 'Imitations of Buddhist statecraft. The patronage of Lao Buddhism and the reconstruction of relic shrines and temples in colonial French Indochina.' *Social Analysis* 62(2): 98–125.

Ladwig, Patrice and Ricardo Roque (eds)

2020. *States of Imitation: Mimetic Governmentality and Colonial Rule.* New York and Oxford: Berghahn.

Lafont, Pierre-Bernard

1962. 'Les écritures 'tay du Laos', *Bulletin de l'École française d'Extrême-Orient* 50(2): 367–393.

Lagrèze, Antoine

1925. *Dictionnaire Kha Pong*. Files of the Résidence Supérieure du Laos, Archives Nationales d'Outre-Mer, Aix-en-Provence; ANOM/RSL/Z.

Langer, Paul F.

1971. *Education in the Communist Zone of Laos*. Santa Monica: Rand Cooperation Report.

Langer Paul F. and Joseph J. Zasloff

1970. *North Vietnam and the Pathet Lao. Partners in the Struggle for Laos.*

Cambridge: Harvard University Press.

Lao Consulting Group of the Ministry of Finance
2002. *Existing Land Tenure and Forest Lands Study.* Vientiane: Ministry of Finance.

Lao Front for National Construction (LFNC)
2005. *The Ethnic Groups in Lao PDR.* Vientiane: LFNC.

Lao National Tourism Administration (LNTA)
2010. *Voices of Viengxay – Stories from the 'Hidden City' from Interviews with People who Lived under Bombardment in Northeastern Laos from 1964 to 1973.* Vientiane: LNTA.

Lavallée, Alfred
1901. 'Notes ethnographiques sur diverses tribus du Sud-Est de l'Indochine (Boloven, Naheun, Alak, Lave, Kaseng, Halang).' *Bulletin de l'École française d'Extrême-Orient* 1: 291–311.

Le Manh Hung
2004. *The Impact of World War II on the Economy of Vietnam 1939–45.* Singapore: Eastern University Press.

Le Pichon, Jean
1938. 'Les chasseurs de sang.' *Bulletin des Amis du Vieux Hué* 4: 353–409.

Leach, Edmund
1954. *Political Systems of Highland Burma: A Study of Kachin Social Structure.* London: G. Bell and Son.

Lebar, Franck M., Gerard C. Hickey and John K. Musgrave
1964. *Ethnic Groups of Mainland Southeast Asia.* New Haven: Human Relations Area Files Press.

Lefebvre, Henri
1974. *La Production de l'espace.* Paris: Anthropos.

Lefèvre-Pontalis, Pierre
1902. *Voyage dans le Haut-Laos et sur les frontières de Chine et de Birmanie.* Mission Pavie, tome V. Paris: Ernest Leroux.

Lemoine, Jacques
1972. *Un village hmong vert du haut Laos. Milieu technique et organisation sociale.* Paris: Editions du CNRS.

Lentz, Christian

2019. *Contested Territory – Đien Biên Phu and the Making of Northwest Vietnam*. New Haven and London: Yale University Press.

Lévi-Strauss, Claude

1955. 'The Structural Study of Myth.' *Journal of American Folklore* 68, 428–444.

Lindell, Kristina, Swanh Jan-Öjvind and Damrong Tayanin

1995. *Folktales from Kammu V: A Young Story-Teller's Tales*. Nordic Institute of Asian Studies Monograph Series, no. 66. Richmond: Curzon Press.

Lissoir, Marie-Pierre

2017. 'Boire, chanter et créer des liens. Ethnomusicologie et alcool chez les Tai Dam du nord Laos.' *Civilisations* 66: 159–175.

Lockhart, Bruce M.

2003. 'Narrating 1945 in Lao historiography.' In C. E. Goscha and S. Ivarsson (eds), *Contesting Visions of the Lao Past. Lao Historiography at the Crossroads*, pp 129–155. Copenhagen: NIAS Press.

Lorrillard, Michel

1995. *Les chroniques royales du Laos. Contribution à la connaissance historique des royaumes lao 1316–1887*. Thèse en Sciences historiques et philologiques. Paris: École Pratique des Hautes Études, 4e section.

2008. 'Pour une géographie historique du bouddhisme au Laos.' In Y. Goudineau and M. Lorrillard (eds), *Recherches nouvelles sur le Laos*, pp. 113–181. Études thématiques n° 18. Paris: École française d'Extrême-Orient.

Lu, Juliet N.

2017. 'Tapping into rubber: China's opium replacement program and rubber production in Laos.' *The Journal of Peasant Studies* 44(4): 726–747.

Ludden, David

2003. 'Presidential address: Maps in the mind and the mobility of Asia.' *The Journal of Asian Studies* 62(4): 1057–1078.

Luhmann, Niklas

1984. *Soziale Systeme. Grundriß einer allgemeinen Theorie*. Frankfurt am Main: Suhrkamp.

1985. 'Society, meaning, religion – based on self-reference.' *Sociological Analysis* 46(1): 5–20.

1994 [1982]. *Liebe als Passion. Zur Codierung von Intimität.* Frankfurt am Main: Suhrkamp.

Lundström, Håkan

2010. *I Will Send My Songs. Kammu Vocal Genres in the Singing of Kam Raw.* Copenhagen: NIAS Press.

Lundström, Håkan and Damrong Tayanin

2006. *Kammu Songs. The Songs of Kam Raw.* Copenhagen: NIAS Press.

Luu Hung

2007. *A Contribution to Katu Ethnography.* Hanoi: Vietnam Academy of Social Sciences, The Gioi Publisher.

Lyttleton, Chris

1999. 'Any Port in a Storm: Coming to Terms with HIV in Lao PDR.' *Culture, Health and Sexuality.An International Journal for Research, Intervention and Care* 1(2): 115–130.

Lyttleton, Chris and Yunxia Li

2017. 'Rubbers's Affective Economies: Seeding a Social Landscape in Northwest Laos.' In V. Bouté and V. Pholsena (eds), *Changing Lives in Laos: Society, Politics, and Culture in a Post-Socialist State,* pp. 301–324. Singapore: NUS Press.

Maffi, Luisa

2005. 'Linguistic, cultural, and biological diversity.' *Annual Review of Anthropology* 34: 599–617.

Maitre, Henri

1912. *Les Jungles Moi. Mission Henri Maitre (1909–1911) Indochine Sud-Centrale.* Paris: Emile Larose.

Malglaive, Joseph de, Cpt. (and A.J. Rivière)

2000 [1902]. *Mission Pavie, tome IV. Voyages au centre de l'Annam et du Laos et dans les régions sauvages de l'Est de l'Indochine par le capitaine de Malglaive et le capitaine Rivière.* Bangkok : White Lotus. (Original publication Paris: Leroux.)

Martin, John

2003. 'What is field theory?' *American Journal of Sociology* 109(1): 1–49.

Masako, Ito

2013. *Politics of Ethnic Classification in Vietnam.* Balwin North, Melbourne: Kyoto University Press, Trans Pacific Press.

Masuhara, Yoshiyuki

2003. *Economic History of the Lao Lan Xang Kingdom*. Bangkok: Mathichon. (In Thai).

Matras-Guin, Jacqueline (see Matras-Troubetzkoy, Jacqueline)

Matras-Troubetzkoy, Jacqueline

1975. 'Éléments pour l'étude du village et de l'habitation brou.' *ASEMI* 6(2–3): 201–228.

1983. *Un Village en forêt. L'essartage chez les Brou du Cambodge*. Paris: SELAF.

1992. 'Le cercle du village: orientation et hiérarchisation de l'espace chez les Brou du Cambodge.' In J. Matras-Guin et Ch. Taillard (eds), *Habitations et habitat d'Asie du Sud-Est continentale*, pp. 61–110. Paris: L'Harmattan.

Mayoury Ngaosyvathn

1995. *Lao Women Yesterday and Today*. Vientiane: State Publishing Enterprise.

McCarthy, James

1994 [1900]. *Surveying and Exploring in Siam*. Bangkok: White Lotus.

McCaskill, Don and Ken Kampe (eds)

1997. *Development or Domestication? Indigenous Peoples of Southeast Asia*. Chiang Mai: Silkworm Books.

McDaniel, Justin

2008. *Gathering Leaves and Lifting Words: Histories of Buddhist Monastic Education in Laos and Thailand*. Seattle: University of Washington Press.

McLeod, Mark

1999. 'Indigenous people and the Vietnamese revolution, 1930–1975.' *Journal of World History* 10(2): 353–89.

McMahan, David

2008. *The Making of Buddhist Modernism*. New York: Oxford University Press.

Michaud, Jean

2013. 'French Military Ethnography in Colonial Upper Tonkin (Northern Vietnam), 1897–1904.' *Journal of Vietnamese Studies* 8(4): 1–46.

Michaud, Jean and Tim Forsyth (eds)

2011. *Moving Mountains: Ethnicity and Livelihoods in Highland China,*

Vietnam, and Laos. Vancouver: University of British Columbia Press.

Mills, Mary Beth

1999. *Thai Women in the Global Labor Force: Consuming Desires, Contested Selves*. New Brunswick, N.J.: Rutgers University Press.

Ministry of Information, Culture and Tourism

2000. *Pavatsat lao*. Vientiane.

2009. *Banda matthan kan Sangkhon, Khobkhoua le ban vatthanatam* [Rules regarding cultural society, families and villages]. Vientiane.

Mitchell, Timothy

2000. *Questions of Modernity*. Minneapolis: University of Minnesota Press.

Molle, François and Srijantr Thippawal (eds)

2003. *Thailand's Rice Bowl: Perspectives on Agricultural and Social Change in the Chao Phraya Delta*. Bangkok: White Lotus Books.

Moppert, François

1981. 'La Révolte des Bolovens (1901–1936).' In P. Brocheux (ed.), *Histoire de l'Asie du Sud-Est: révoltes, réformes, révolutions*, pp. 47–62. Lille: Presses Universitaires de Lille.

Müller, Shing and Lucia Obi

1996. 'Religiöse Schriften der Yao: Überblick über den Bestand der Yao-Handschriften in der Bayerischen Staatsbibliothek.' *Nachrichten der Gesellschaft für Natur- und Völkerkunde Ostasiens* 67(1/2): 39–86.

Murashima, Eiji

2015. 'Thailand and Indochina, 1945–1950.' *Journal of Asia–Pacific Studies* 25: 166–167.

Murray, Martin J.

1981. *The Development of Capitalism in Colonial Indochina (1870–1940)*. Berkeley and Los Angeles: University of California Press.

Naepels, Michel

1991. 'L'anthropologie, science historique?' *Genesis* 4: 157–165.

Nassehi, Armin

2004. 'Die Theorie funktionaler Differenzierung im Horizont ihrer Kritik.' *Zeitschrift für Soziologie* 33(2): 98–118.

Navaro-Yashin, Yael

2009. 'Affective spaces, melancholic objects: Ruination and the production of anthropological knowledge.' *Journal of the Royal Anthropological Institute* 15(1): 1–18.

Nettle, Daniel and Suzanne Romaine
2000. *Vanishing Voices: The Extinction of the World's Languages*. Oxford: Oxford University Press.

Newman, David and Anssi Paasi
1998. 'Fences and neighbours in the postmodern world: Boundary narratives in political geography.' *Progress in Human Geography* 22(2): 186–207.

Nginn, Pierre S.
1965. *Eléments de grammaire laotienne*. Vientiane: State Press.

NGO Forum on Cambodia
2004. *Land Alienation from Indigenous Minority Communities in Ratanakiri*. Phnom Penh: NGO Forum on Cambodia.

Nguyên Thê Anh
1997. 'Les conflits frontaliers entre le Vietnam et le Siam à propos du Laos au XIXe siècle.' *The Vietnam Review* 2: 154–172.

Niti Pawakapan
2002. 'Consuming alien goods, digesting foreign culture : Complexity of new consumption in north-western Thailand.' *Aséanie* 10 : 85–104.

Nora, Pierre
1989. 'Between Memory and History: Les Lieux de Mémoire.' *Representations* 26: 7–24.

Nyo, Georges (Commandant)
1937. 'La pénétration française dans les pays moï.' *Bulletin de la Société des Études Indochinoises* 12 (2): 7–41.

Odend'hal, Prosper
1894. 'Les routes de l'Annam au Mé-kong (de Hué à Saravane et à Attopeu).' *Revue Indo-Chinoise illustrée* 4: 1–50.

Ovesen, Jan
1995. *A Minority Enters the Nation State: A Case Study of a Hmong Community in Vientiane Province, Laos*. Uppsala: Uppsala Research Reports in Cultural Anthropology, No.14.

Parmentier, Henri
1954. *L'art du Laos*. Hanoi: École française d'Extrême-Orient.

Pathammavong Somlith

1955. 'L'Obligation scolaire au Laos.' In C. Bilodeau, S. Pathammavong and Le Quang Hong (eds), *L'Obligation scolaire au Cambodge, au Laos et au Viet-Nam*, pp. 72–113. Paris: UNESCO.

Peltier, Anatole

1995. *Nang Phom Hom. The Woman with Fragrant Hair.* Chiang Mai: Ming Muang Nawarat Printing.

Peluso, Nancy Lee and Peter Vandergeest

2001. 'Genealogies of the political forest and customary rights in Indonesia, Malaysia, and Thailand.' *The Journal of Asian Studies* 60(3): 761–812.

Petit, Pierre

2008. 'Les politiques culturelles et la question des minorités en RDP Laos.' *Bulletin des séances de l'Académie royale des Sciences d'Outre-mer* 54(4): 477– 499.

2013. 'Ethnic performance and the state in Laos. The Bun Greh annual festival of the Khmu.' *Asian Studies Review* 37(4): 470–490.

2020. *History, Memory, and Territorial Cults in the Highlands of Laos: The Past Inside the Present.* London and New York: Routledge.

Pholsena, Vatthana

2002. 'Nation/representation: Ethnic classification and mapping nationhood in contemporary Laos.' *Asian Ethnicity* 3(2): 175–197.

2003. 'Narrative, memory and history: Multiple interpretations of the Lao past.' *Working Paper Series* No. 4. Singapore: Asia Research Institute.

2004. 'The changing historiographies of Laos: A focus on the early period.' *Journal of Southeast Asian Studies* 35(2): 235–259.

2005. 'A liberal model of minority rights for an illiberal multi-ethnic state? The case of the Lao PDR.' In W. Kymlicka and He Baogang (eds), *Asian Minorities and Western Liberalism*, pp. 80–109. Oxford: Oxford University Press.

2006a. *Post-war Laos: The Politics of Culture, History, and Identity.* Ithaca: Cornell University Press.

2006b. 'The early years of the Lao revolution (1945–1949): Between history, myth and experience.' *South East Asia Research* 14(3): 403–430.

2009. 'Nommer pour contrôler au Laos, de l'Etat colonial au régime communiste.' *Critique Internationale*, 45(4): 59–76.

2012. 'The (transformative) impacts of the Vietnam war and the communist revolution in a border region in Southeastern Laos.' *War and Society* 31(2): 163–83.

Phoumi Vongvichit
1967. *Veignakone Lao*. Vientiane: State Press.

Phoutong Phimmasone
1973. 'L'organisation du bouddhisme au Laos.' *Bulletin des amis du royaume Lao* 9(1): 121–129.

Platenkamp, Jos D. M.
1992. 'Transforming Tobelo ritual.' In D. de Coppet (ed.), *Understanding Rituals*, pp. 74–96. London and New York: Routledge.
2004. 'Über die gesellschaftliche Relevanz der Ethnologie.' In U. Bertels et al. (eds), *Aus der Ferne in die Nähe*. Neue Wege der Ethnologie in die Öffentlichkeit, pp. 21–32. Münster: Waxmann.

Plattner, Stuart
1989. 'Introduction.' In S. Plattner (ed.), *Economic Anthropology*, pp. 1–20. Stanford, California: Stanford University Press.

Popkin, Samuel
1979. *The Rational Peasant: The Political Economy of Rural Society in Vietnam*. Berkeley: University of California Press.

Potter, Sulamith Heins and Jack M. Potter
1990. *China's Peasants: The Anthropology of a Revolution*. Cambridge: Cambridge University Press.

Pottier, Richard
2007. *Yû dî mî hèng, 'être bien, avoir de la force'. Essai sur les pratiques thérapeutiques lao*. Paris: Ecole française d'Extrême-Orient.

Prados, John
1999. *The Blood Road: The Ho Chi Minh Trail and the Vietnam War*. New York: Wiley.

Proschan, Frank
1997. '"We are all Kmhmu, just the same": Ethnonyms, ethnic identities, and ethnic groups.' *American Ethnologist* 24(1): 91–113.

Przyluski, Jean
1925. 'La princesse à l'odeur de poisson et la *nagi* dans les traditions de l'Asie orientale.' *Études Asiatiques* 2: 265–284.

Raendchen, Jana and Oliver Raendchen

1998. 'Present state, problems and purpose of *baan-müang* studies.' *Tai Culture*, 3(2): 5–11.

Raquez, Alfred

2000 [1902]. *Pages laotiennes*. Vientiane: Institut de Recherche sur la Culture, Cercle de Culture et de Recherches Laotiennes.

Rathie, Martin

2017. 'The history and evolution of the Lao People's Revolutionary Party.' In V. Bouté and V. Pholsena (eds), *Changing Lives in Laos: Society, Politics, and Culture in a Post-Socialist State*, pp. 19–55. Singapore: NUS Press.

Rehbein, Boike

2004. *Globalisierung in Laos*. Münster: LIT.

2007. *Globalization, Culture and Society in Laos*. London/New York: Routledge.

2008. 'The modernization of Lao language.' In Y. Goudineau and M. Lorrillard (eds) *Recherches nouvelles sur le Laos*, pp. 453–464. Paris: Paris: École française d'Extrême-Orient.

2009a. 'Feld (champ).' In G. Froehlich and B. Rehbein (eds), *Bourdieu Handbuch. Leben-Werk-Wirkung*, pp. 99–103. Stuttgart/Weimar: JB Metzlar.

2009b. 'Religion und Globalisierung in Laos.' *Journal of Current Southeast Asian Affairs* 28(1): 9–29.

2017. *Society in Contemporary Laos: Capitalism, Habitus and Belief*. London: Routledge.

Rehbein, Boike and Sisouk Sayaseng

2004. *Laotische Grammatik*. Hamburg: Buske.

Renard, Ronald D.

1996. 'Blessing and northern Thai historiography.' In C. A. Kammerer and N. Tannenbaun (eds), *Merit and Blessing in Mainland Southeast Asia in Comparative Perspective*, pp. 159–180. New Haven: Yale University, Southeast Asia Studies.

Rey, Terry

2007. *Bourdieu on Religion: Imposing Faith and Legitimacy*. London: Equinox Publishers.

Robinne, François and Mandy Sadan

2007. 'Reconsidering the dynamics of ethnicity through Foucault's concept of "spaces of dispersion".' In F. Robinne and M. Sadan (eds), *Social Dynamics in the Highlands of Southeast Asia. Reconsidering Political*

Systems of Highland Burma by E. R Leach, pp. 299–308. Leiden: Brill.

Roder, Walter

1997. 'Slash-and-burn rice systems in transition: Challenges for agricultural development in the hills of northern Laos.' *Mountain Research and Development* 17(1): 1–10.

Roder, Walter, Bounthanth Keoboulapha, Khouanheuane Vannalath and Bouakham Phouaravanh

1996. 'Glutinous rice and its importance for hill farmers in Laos.' *Economic Botany* 50(4): 401–408.

Romagny, Laurent and Steeve Daviau

2003. *Synthesis of Reports on Resettlement in Long District, Luang Namtha Province, Lao PDR*. Vientiane: Action Contre La Faim.

Rowley, Kelvin

2016. 'The Genesis of *Red Brotherhood at War*.' In P. Cox and B. Rehbein (eds), *Journal of Laos Studies (JLS)*, Special Issue 'Devoted to the work of Grant Evans' 3(1): 12–23.

Russo, Manfred

2009. 'Differenzierung (différenciation).' In G. Froehlich and B. Rehbein (eds), *Bourdieu Handbuch. Leben-Werk-Wirkung*, pp. 69–72. Stuttgart/Weimar: JB Metzlar.

Sahlins, Marshall

1981. *Historical Metaphors and Mythical Realities: Structure in the Early History of the Sandwich Islands Kingdom*. Ann Arbor: University of Michigan Press.

1985. *Islands of History*. Chicago: The University of Chicago Press.

Salemink, Oscar

2003. *The Ethnography of Vietnam's Central Highlanders: A Historical Contextualization, 1850–1990*. London: RoutledgeCurzon.

Sarassawadee Ongsakul

2005. *History of Lanna*. Chiang Mai: Silkworm Books.

Schlemmer, Grégoire

2015a. 'Questionner la question ethnique. Lecture historique et politique des appartenances culturelles au Laos.' *Moussons* 25: 5–37.

2015b. 'La mise en place d'un musée d'ethnographie au Laos: démarches et questionnements.' In L. Vidal (ed.), *Les savoirs des sciences sociales: débats, controverses, partage*, pp. 33–50. Marseille: IRD Editions.

2017. 'Ethnic belonging in Laos: A politico-historical perspective.' In V. Bouté and V. Pholsena (eds), *Changing Lives in Laos: Society, Politics, and Culture in a Post-Socialist State*, pp. 251–280. Singapore: NUS Press.

Schneider, Andreas

2000. *Laos: Geschichte, Bildungswesen und Humankapitalentwicklung im 20 Jahrhundert. Untersuchungen zur personellen Entwicklungszusammenarbeit am Beispiel der Reintegration laotischer Absolventen deutscher Bildungseinrichtungen.* Frankfurt: Peter Lang Verlag.

Schober, Juliane

2007. 'Colonial knowledge and Buddhist education in Burma.' In I. Harris (ed.), *Buddhism, Power and Political Order*, pp. 52–70. London: Routledge.

Scott, James C.

1976. *The Moral Economy of the Peasant: Rebellion and Subsistence in Southeast Asia.* New Haven: Yale University Press.

1998. *Seeing Like a State. How Certain Schemes to Improve the Human Condition Have Failed.* New Haven: Yale University Press.

2009. *The Art of Not Being Governed. An Anarchist History of Upland Southeast Asia.* New Haven-London: Yale University Press.

Shanin, Teodor

1986. 'Chayanov's message: Illuminations, miscomprehensions and the contemporary "development theory".' In A. Chayanov, D. Thorner, B. Kerblay and R.E.F. Smith (eds), *A.V. Chayanov on the Theory of Peasant Economy*, pp. 1–4. Manchester: Manchester University Press.

Sharp, Lauriston

1987 [1951]. 'Steel axes for stone-age Australians.' *Human Organization* 11(2): 17–22.

Shaw, Rosalind and Charles Stewart

1994. 'Introduction: problematizing syncretism.' In C. Stewart and R. Shaw (eds), *Syncretism/Anti-syncretism: The Politics of Religious Synthesis*, pp. 1–26. London and New York: Routledge.

Shigetomi, Shinichi, Kasian Tejapira and Apichart Thongyou (eds)

2004. *The NGO Way: Perspectives and Experiences from Thailand.* Chiba: Institute of Developing Economies/Japan External Trade Organization (IDE-JETRO).

Sidwell, Paul

2005. *The Katuic Languages. Classification, Reconstruction and Comparative Lexicon*. Munich: LINCOM Studies in Asian Linguistics, 58.

2008. 'The Khom script of the Kommodam rebellion.' *International Journal of The Sociology of Language* 192: 15–25.

Sidwell, Paul and Pascale Jacq

2004. *A Handbook of Comparative Bahnaric: Vol. 1, West Bahnaric*. Canberra: Pacific Linguistics.

Sila Viravong (Maha)

1935. *Veignakone Lao* [Lao Grammar]. Vientiane: Imprimerie coloniale.

1964. *History of Laos* [translation]. New-York: Paragon Books.

1996. *Chau Maha Uparat Phetsarat* [Viceroy Phetsarat]. Vientiane: Phainan Publisher.

Siu, Helen F.

1989. *Agents and Victims in South China: Accomplices in Rural Revolution*. New Haven: Yale University Press.

Smalley, William A.

1994. *Linguistic Diversity and National Unity. Language Ecology in Thailand*. Chicago and London: University of Chicago Press.

Somphavanh Xainyavong, Khambai Nyounnalath, Soichi Hata and Futoshi Nishimoto

2003. *The Life and House of the Tariang People*. Vientiane: Institute for Cultural Research, Ministry of Information and Culture.

Souneth Phothisane and Nousai Phoummachan

2000. *Pavatsat Lao (Deukdamban-Pachuban)* [Lao History (Ancient Times to the Present)]. Vientiane: Ministry of Information and Culture.

Sprenger, Guido

2004. 'Encompassment and its discontents: Rmeet and lowland Lao relationships.' In G. Baumann and A. Gingrich (eds), *Grammars of Identity/Alterity: A Structural Approach*, pp. 173–191. New York and Oxford: Berghahn Books.

2005. 'The way of the buffaloes: Trade and sacrifice in Northern Laos.' *Ethnology* 44(4): 291–312.

2006a. *Die Männer, die den Geldbaum fällten. Austausch und Gesellschaft bei den Rmeet von Takheung, Laos*. Berlin: Lit Verlag.

2006b. 'The end of rituals: A dialogue of theory and ethnography in Laos.' *Paideuma* 52: 51–72.

2007. 'From kettledrums to coins: Social transformation and the flow of valuables in Northern Laos.' In F. Robinne and M. Sadan (eds), *Social Dynamics in the Highlands of Southeast Asia: Reconsidering Political Systems of Highland Burma by E.R. Leach*, pp. 161–186. Leiden: Brill.

2009. 'Invisible blood: Self-censorship and the public in uplander ritual, Laos.' *Asian Journal of Social Sciences* 37(6): 935–951.

2017a. 'Re-connecting the ancestors. Buddhism and animism on the Boloven plateau, Laos.' In M. Picard (ed.), *The Appropriation of Religion in Southeast Asia and Beyond*, pp. 95–121. Cham: Palgrave Macmillan.

2017b. 'Piglets are buffaloes: Buddhification and the reduction of sacrifice on the Boloven plateau.' In V. Bouté and Vatthana Pholsena (eds), *Changing Lives in Laos: Society, Politics, and Culture in a Post-Socialist State*, pp. 281–300. Singapore: NUS Press.

2018. 'Buddhism and coffee: The transformation of locality and non-human personhood in Southern Laos.' *Sojourn* 33(2): 65–90.

Stolz, Rosalie

2021. *Living Kinship, Fearing Spirits: Sociality among the Khmu of Northern Laos*. Copenhagen: NIAS Press.

Stolz, Rosalie and Oliver Tappe

2021. 'Upland pioneers: An introduction.' *Social Anthropology* 29(3): 635–650.

Stuart-Fox, Martin

1986. *Laos. Politics, Economics and Society*. London: Frances Printer.

1996. *Buddhist Kingdom, Marxist State. The Making of Modern Laos*. Bangkok: White Lotus.

1997. *A History of Laos*. Cambridge and Melbourne: Cambridge University Press.

1998. *The Lao Kingdom of Lan Xang: Rise and Decline*. Bangkok: White Lotus.

2002 [1996]. *Buddhist Kingdom, Marxist State: The Making of Modern Laos*. Bangkok: White Lotus.

2010. 'Review of Y. Goudineau and M. Lorrillard (eds), Recherches nouvelles sur le Laos/New Research on Laos.' *Journal of Lao Studies* 1 (1): 105–118.

Stuart-Fox, Martin and Rod Bucknell

1982. 'Politicization of the Buddhist sangha in Laos.' *Journal of Southeast Asian Studies* 13(1): 60–80.

Stuart-Fox, Martin and Mary Kooyman

1992. *Historical Dictionary of Laos.* N.J. and London: The Scarecrow Press, Inc. Metuchen.

Suksavang Simana and Elizabeth Preisig

1999. 'Kmhmu' Language Lessons – trial edition'. Vientiane (unpublished manuscript).

Sun Laichen

2003. 'Military technology transfers from Ming China and the emergence of northern mainland Southeast Asia (c. 1390–1527).' *Journal of Southeast Asian Studies* 34(3): 495–517.

Svantesson, Jan-Olof, Damrong Thayanin and Kristina Lindell

1994. *Kammu-Lao Dictionary.* Vientiane: Ministry of Information and Culture.

Swearer, Donald K. and Sommai Premchit

1998. *The Legend of Queen Cāma. Bodhiraṃsi's Cāmadevīvaṃsa, a Translation and Commentary.* New York: State University of New York Press.

Taillard, Christian

1974. 'Essai sur la bi-polarisation autour du vat et de l'école des villages lao de la plaine de Vientiane. Le bouddhisme populaire confronté au développement économique.' *Asie du Sud-est et Monde Insulindien* (ASEMI) 5(3): 91–104.

1977. 'Le village lao de la région de Vientiane, un pouvoir local face au pouvoir étatique'. *L'Homme.* 17(2–3): 71–100.

1979. 'Le dualisme urbain-rural au Laos et la récupération de l'idéologie traditionnelle.' *Asie du Sud-est et Monde Insulindien* (ASEMI), 10(2–4): 91–108.

1989. *Le Laos. Stratégie d'un Etat-tampon.* Montpellier: GIP Reclus.

Tambiah, Stanley J.

1968. 'Literacy in a Buddhist village in north-east Thailand.' In J. Goody (ed.), *Literacy in Traditional Societies*, pp. 86–131. Cambridge: Cambridge University Press.

1970. *Buddhism and Spirit Cults in North-East Thailand.* Cambridge: Cambridge University Press.

1985a. 'A performative approach to ritual.' In S. J. Tambiah, *Culture, Thought and Social Action*, pp. 123–166. Cambridge Massachussets: Harvard University Press.

1985b. 'The galactic polity in Southeast Asia.' In S. J. Tambiah, *Culture,*

Thought and Social Action, pp. 252–286. Cambridge Massachussets: Harvard University Press.

Tanabe, Shigeharu

1988. 'Spirits and ideological discourse: the Tai Lü guardian cults in Yunnan.' *Sojourn* 3(1): 1–25.

2008 (ed.). *Imagining Communities in Thailand. Ethnographic Approaches.* Chiang Mai: Mekong Press.

Tappe, Oliver

2008. *Geschichte, Nationsbildung und Legitimationspolitik in Laos: Untersuchungen zur laotischen nationalen Historiographie und Ikonographie.* Berlin: Lit Verlag.

2011. 'Memory, tourism, and development: Changing sociocultural configurations and upland-lowland relations in Houaphan Province, Lao PDR.' *Sojourn* 26(2): 174–195.

2012. 'Révolution, héritage culturel et stratégies de légitimation: Exemples à partir de l'historiographie et de l'iconographie officielles.' In V. Bouté and V. Pholsena (eds), *Laos. Sociétés et Pouvoirs*, pp. 69–92. Paris: IRASEC-Les Indes Savantes.

2013a. 'National *lieu de mémoire* vs. multivocal memories: The case of Viengxay, Lao PDR.' In V. Pholsena and O. Tappe (eds), *Interactions with a Violent Past: Reading Post-Conflict Landscapes in Cambodia, Laos and Vietnam*, pp. 46–77. Singapore: NUS Press.

2013b. 'Faces and facets of the Kantosou Kou Xat: The Lao "national liberation struggle" in state commemoration and historiography.' *Asian Studies Review* 37(4): 433–450.

2017. 'Shaping the national topography: The party-state, national imageries and questions of political authority.' In V. Bouté and V. Pholsena (eds), *Changing Lives in Laos: Society, Politics, and Culture in a Post-Socialist State*, pp. 56–80. Singapore: NUS Press.

2018. 'Variants of frontier mimesis: Colonial encounter and intercultural interaction in the Lao–Vietnamese uplands.' *Social Analysis* 62(2): 51–75.

2021. '*Phong* pioneers – Exploring the sociopolitics of mythology in upland Laos.' *Social Anthropology* 29(3): 763–777.

Tappe, Oliver and Nathan Badenoch

2021. 'Neither Kha, Tai nor Lao: Language, myth, histories, and the position of the *Phong* in Houaphan.' *Japan–ASEAN Transdisciplinary Studies Working Paper Series*, no. 12. Kyoto: Center for Southeast Asian

Studies (CSEAS), Kyoto University.

Taylor, Charles
2007. *A Secular Age.* Harvard: Harvard University Press.

Terwiel, B. J.
1983. 'Bondage and slavery in early nineteenth century Siam.' In A. Reid (ed.), *Slavery, Bondage and Dependency in Southeast Asia,* pp. 118–137. St. Lucia: University of Queensland Press.

Thapa, Gopal B.
1998. 'Issues in the conservation and management of forests in Laos: The case of Santhong district.' *Singapore Journal of Tropical Geography* 19(1): 71–91.

Thongchai Winichakul
1994. *Siam Mapped: A History of the Geo-Body of a Nation.* Honolulu: University of Hawai'i Press.
2000. 'The others within: Travel and ethno-spatial differentiation of Siamese subjects 1885–1910.' In A. Turton (ed.), *Civility and Savagery. Social Identities in Tai States,* pp. 38–62. Richmond, Surrey: Curzon.
2002. 'Writing at the interstices: Southeast Asian historians and post-national histories in Southeast Asia.' Paper presented to the panel on 'Boundary Margin and Local Autonomy in Thai History', 8th International Conference on Thai Studies, Nakhon Phanom, Ramkamhaeng University, January 9–12.

Thongphet Kingsada and Tadahico Shintani (eds)
1999. *Basic Vocabularies of the Languages Spoken in Phongsaly, Lao PDR.* Tokyo: Institute for the Study of Languages and Cultures of Asia and Africa.

Tooker, Deborah E.
1992. 'Identity systems of Highland Burma: "Belief", Akha *zang,* and a critique of interiorized notions of ethno-religious identity.' *Man N.S.* 27: 799–819.
1996. 'Putting the mandala in its place: a practice-based approach to the spatialization of power on the Southeast Asian 'periphery' – the case of the Akha.' *Journal of Asian Studies* 55(2): 323–358.

Trankell, Ing-Britt
1993. *On the Road in Laos: An Anthropological Study of Road Construction and Rural Communities.* Uppsala Research Reports in Cultural Anthropology 12. Uppsala: Uppsala University.

1998. 'The minor part of the nation: Politics of ethnicity in Laos.' In I-B. Trankell and L. Summers (eds), *Facets of Power and its Limitations*, pp. 45–64. Uppsala: Uppsala Studies in Cultural Anthropology.

Tunbridge, John E. and Gregory J. Ashworth
1996. *Dissonant Heritage: The Management of the Past as a Resource in Conflict*. Chichester: Wiley.

Turton, Andrew
2000. 'Introduction.' In A. Turton (ed.), *Civility and Savagery. Social Identity in Tai States*, pp. 3–31. Richmond: Curzon Press.

Tyrell, Hartmann
2008. *Soziale und Gesellschaftliche Differenzierung. Aufsätze zur Soziologischen Theorie*. Wiesbaden: VS Verlag.

Vallard, Annabel
2017. 'The textile economy in Laos: From households to the world.' In V. Bouté and V. Pholsena (eds), *Changing Lives in Laos: Society, Politics, and Culture in a Post-Socialist State*, pp. 374–91. Singapore: National University of Singapore Press.

Vandergeest, Peter
1993. 'Book review. *National Identities and Its Defenders: Thailand, 1939–1989*, edited by Craig J. Reynolds. Clayton: Centre of Southeast Asian Studies, Monash University, 1991.' *Journal of Southeast Asian Studies* 24(1): 205–207.
1996. 'Mapping nature: Territorialization of forest rights in Thailand.' *Society and Natural Resources* 9: 159–175.
2003. 'Land to some tillers: Development-induced displacement in Laos.' *International Review of the Social Sciences* 55(175): 47–56.

Vandergeest, Peter and Nancy Peluso
1995. 'Territorialization and state power in Thailand.' *Theory and Society* 24: 385–426.

Verdery, Katherine
1991. *National Ideology Under Socialism: Identity and Cultural Politics in Ceausescu's Romania*. Berkeley and Los Angeles: University of California Press.

Vitry, P.
1911, 1912. 'Rapports sur la situation dans la province de Saravane.' Archives d'Outre-Mer (AOM), Laos D2, E7, F5.

Vu Dinh Loi

2001. 'Brau and Roman cultures: Tradition and reality.' In O. Salemink (ed.), *Vietnam's Cultural Diversity: Approaches to Preservations,* pp. 169–176, 185–186. Mayenne, France: UNESCO.

Wadley, Reed L.

2003. 'Lines in the forest: Internatal territorialization and local accommodation in West Kalimantan, Indonesia (1865–1979).' *South East Asia Research* 11(1): 91–112.

Walker, Andrew

1999. *The Legend of the Golden Boat: Regulation, Trade and Traders in the Borderlands of Laos, Thailand, China, and Burma.* Honolulu: University of Hawai'i Press.

2000. 'Regional Trade in Northwestern Laos: An Initial Assessment of the Economic Quadrangle.' In G. Evans, C. Hutton and K.K. Eng (eds), *Where China Meets Southeast Asia. Social and Cultural Change in the Border Regions,* pp. 122–144. Singapore: ISEAS.

Wall, Barbara

1975. *Les Nya Hön. Étude ethnographique d'une population du Plateau des Bolovens (Sud-Laos).* Vientiane: Vithagna.

Weber, Max

1972. *Wirtschaft und Gesellschaft.* Tübingen: Mohr.

Westermeyer, Joseph

1983. *Poppies, Pipes and People: Opium and Its Use in Laos.* Berkeley: University of California Press.

Whitehouse, Harvey

2004. *Modes of Religiosity: A Cognitive Theory of Religious Transmission.* Walnut Creek: Altamira Press.

Wiegersma, Nancy

1988. *Vietnam: peasant land, peasant revolution: patriarchy and collectivity in the rural economy.* Basingstoke: Macmillan.

Wijeyewardene, Gehan

1991. 'The frontiers of Thailand.' In C. J. Reynolds (ed.), *National Identity and its Defenders: Thailand Today,* pp. 126–154. Chiang Mai: Silkworm Books.

Wilcox, Phill

2021. *Heritage and the Making of Political Legitimacy in Laos: The Past and Present of the Lao Nation*. Amsterdam: Amsterdam University Press.

Wittgenstein, Ludwig
1984. *Philosophische Untersuchungen,* Werke 1. Frankfurt: Suhrkamp.

Wolf, Eric
1966. *Peasants*. New Jersey: Prentice Hall.
1969. *Peasant Wars of the Twentieth Century*. New York: Harper and Row.
1982. *Europe and the People Without History*. Berkeley: University of California Press.

Wolters, O.
1999. *History, Culture, and Region in Southeast Asian Perspectives*. Ithaca/Singapore: Cornell University Press/Institute of Southeast Asia Studies.

Wright, Pamela Sue
2003. 'Singsali (Phunoi) speech varieties of Phongsali Province.' *Language and Life Journal* 1: 62–73.

Wuysthoff, Gerrit Van
1669. *Vremde Geschiedenissen in de Koninckrijcken Van Cambodia en Louwen Lant, in Oost-Indien, Zedert den Iare 1635, tot den Iare 1644, aldaer Voorgevallen* [Distant Journey in the Kingdom of Cambodia and the Lao Country, in East India, from the Year 1635 to the Year 1644, and What Happened There]. Haarlem: Pieter Casteleyn.

Wyatt, David K.
1966 'The Buddhist monkhood as an avenue of social mobility in traditional Thai society.' *Sinlapakorn* 10(1): 41–52.

Wyatt, David K. and Aroonrut Wichienkeeo
1998. *The Chiang Mai Chronicle*. Chiang Mai: Silkworm Books.

Zago, Marcel
1972. *Rites et cérémonies en milieu bouddhiste lao*. Roma: Universita Gregoriana.

Contributors

Ian G. Baird is Professor of Geography at the University of Wisconsin-Madison in the United States. He previously lived and worked in Laos and Thailand for over 20 years, and has extensive experience of conducting research in northeastern Cambodia. He has written extensively about ethnic minorities and nature–society relations in mainland Southeast Asia. He is particularly interested in large-scale land concessions and hydropower dam development in the Mekong River Basin, the concept of indigeneity in Southeast Asia, and political histories of ethnic Lao, Brao and Hmong peoples. His most recent book is titled *Rise of the Brao: Ethnic Minorities in Northeastern Cambodia during Vietnamese Occupation* (University of Wisconsin Press, 2020).

Vanina Bouté is Professor of Social Anthropology at the École des Hautes Etudes en Sciences Sociales (EHESS) and Director of the Centre Asie du Sud-Est in Paris (Southeast Asia Centre, CASE-CNRS). She has been conducting anthropological fieldwork in Northern Laos since 2000. She is the author or editor of numerous publications, including *Mirroring Power. Ethnogenesis and Dynamics of Integration among the Phunoy of Northern Laos* (Silkworm Books, 2018, translated from French) and *Changing Lives in Laos,* co-edited with Vatthana Pholsena (NUS Press, 2017). Her current research focuses on migration and the dynamics of change among highlanders living in the borders of Northern Laos.

Chiemsisouraj Chanthaphilith is a Lao historian who graduated from la Sorbonne in Paris and from Charles University in Prague. He was a researcher, then the director of the Department of History, at the Lao Academy of Social Sciences until 2017. He has co-authored several articles, including: 'Of myths and metallurgy: Archaeological and ethnological approaches to upland iron production in 9th century

CE northwest Laos' (*Journal of Southeast Asian Studies*, 2016) and 'An 8th–9th century AD iron smelting workshop near Saphim village, NW Lao PDR' (*Historical Metallurgy*, 2011).

N. J. Enfield is Professor of Linguistics at the University of Sydney. He has been conducting field research in Laos for 30 years, focusing on the Lao and Kri languages. His books include *A Grammar of Lao* (2007), *Dynamics of Human Diversity: the case of Mainland Southeast Asia* (2011), and *The Languages of Mainland Southeast Asia* (2021).

Olivier Évrard is a social anthropologist and senior researcher at the French Research Institute for Sustainable Development (IRD), France. He has worked in Laos since 1994 and in Thailand since 2005, mainly with upland populations. His main interests include land use systems, mobility patterns, heritage and myths. He is the author of *Chroniques des Cendres. Anthropologie des sociétés khmou et dynamiques interethniques du Nord-Laos* (IRD, 2006). Among his articles on oral literature among upland populations in Northern Laos is 'Of myths and metallurgy. Archaeological and ethnological approaches to iron upland production in 9th century AD Northern Laos,' *Journal of Southeast Asian Studies* 47(1) 109–140.

Yves Goudineau is Professor of Comparative Anthropology of Southeast Asia at the École française d'Extrême-Orient (EFEO) of which he was director from 2014 to 2018. He was formerly a visiting professor at the University of Oxford and an honorary research fellow at the University of Hong Kong. He has conducted extensive ethnographic fieldwork focusing on the ethnohistory and rituals of Austroasiatic ethnic groups, notably in Laos, where he has worked since 1991, and in northern Thailand, from Chiang Mai. His publications include *Laos and Ethnic Minority Cultures. Promoting Heritage* (UNESCO, 2003) and *New Research on Laos*, edited with Michel Lorrillard (EFEO Ed., 2008).

Patrice Ladwig studied social anthropology and sociology and obtained his PhD from the University of Cambridge. Currently, he works the Max Planck-Cambridge Centre for the Study of Ethics, Human Economy and Social Change. With a regional focus on Laos and mainland Southeast Asia, his widely published work in international journals covers the anthropology of Buddhism, death, death and funeral cultures, ghosts and spectrality, religion and communist movements and colonialism.

Vatthana Pholsena is Associate Professor and Head of the Department of Southeast Asian Studies at the National University of Singapore. She worked as a research fellow in the Centre National de la Recherche Scientifique (CNRS) for over a decade, based at the Institute of East Asian Studies in Lyon and at the Southeast Asia Centre in Paris. She is the author of *Post-War Laos: the Politics of Culture, History and Identity* (ISEAS, Cornell University Press, 2006) and *Laos. Un pays en mutation* (Belin, 2011). She has also co-edited *Interactions with a Violent Past. Reading Post-Conflict Landscapes in Cambodia, Laos and Vietnam*, with Oliver Tappe (NUS Press, 2013) and *Changing Lives in Laos*, with Vanina Bouté (NUS Press, 2017).

Boike Rehbein was Professor of the Sociology of Asia and Africa at Humboldt University Berlin prior to his untimely death in June 2022 while this volume was in production. He studied philosophy, sociology and history at Freiburg, Paris, Goettingen, Frankfurt and Berlin and received his PhD in 1996 and 'habilitation' in 2004 at the University of Freiburg. He was acting chair of sociology at Freiburg from 2004 to 2006 and director of the Global Studies Programme from 2006 before moving to Berlin in 2009. His areas of specialisation were social theory, globalisation, social inequality and mainland Southeast Asia. Recent books in English are: *Critical Theory after the Rise of the Global South* (Routledge 2015; translated from German), *Society in Contemporary Laos* (Routledge 2017), *Inequality in Capitalist Societies* (with Surinder Jodhka and Jesse Souza, Routledge 2017), *Inequality in Economics and Sociology* (edited with Gilberto Antonelli, Routledge 2018).

Guido Sprenger is Professor at the Institute of Anthropology, Heidelberg University. He has been doing research in the uplands of Laos since 2000. Among his publications are *Die Männer, die den Geldbaum fällten (The Men who cut the Money Tree: Concepts of Exchange and Society among Rmeet of Takheung, Laos)* (2006), *Animism in Southeast Asia* (co-edited with Kaj Århem, 2016), *Plural Ecologies in Southeast Asia* (*Sojourn* special issue, co-edited with Kristina Großmann, 2018) and numerous articles. His research interests include exchange, ritual, animism, kinship, human–environment relations, and cultural identity.

Oliver Tappe is Senior Researcher at the Institute of Anthropology, University of Heidelberg, working on a DFG-funded project on tin mining in Laos. His research interests include the historical anthropology of Laos, with a particular focus on labour relations, migration and mobility, and sociopolitical dynamics. He is editor of the forthcoming book *Extracting Development: Contested Resource Frontiers in Southeast Asia* (co-edited with Simon Rowedder and published by ISEAS/Singapore).

Photo: Y. Goudineau, 1996

Figure 6.1: Vel A-Rô, Kaleum (discussed on page 163).

Photo: Y. Goudineau, 1995

Figure 6.2: Ritual in Vel Kandon, Kaleum (discussed on page 164).

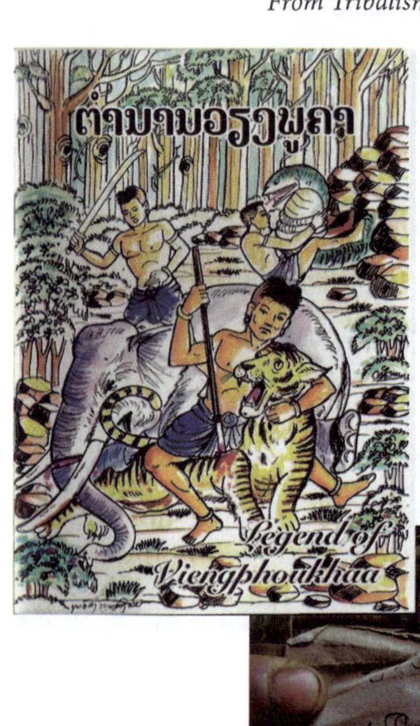

Figure 8.1 (left): Booklet published in Vientiane in 2008 about the legend of Vieng Phu Kha (discussed on page 205).

Figure 8.2 (below): Portion of a manuscript kept by the lay leader of Ban Vieng Mai that was used during the *roy samao* ritual (discussed on page 226).

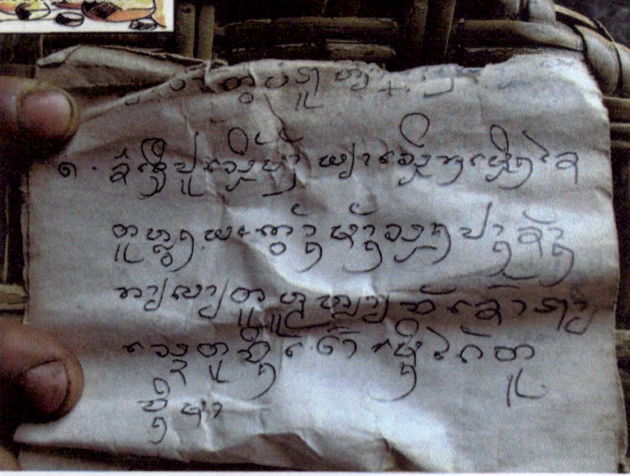

Photo: O. Évrard, 2011

Photo: O. Évrard, 2011

Figure 8.3 (left): The cannon used during the *roy samao* ritual (discussed on page 229).

Photo: O. Tappe, 2019

Figure 11.2: Lao tourists on Phu Phathi (discussed on page 282).

Photo: O. Tappe, 2019

Figure 11.3: Displaying multi-ethnic heritage in Sam Neua (discussed on page 286).

Photo: Y. Goudineau

Figure 12.1 (above): The Lak Muang of Sekong (discussed on page 322).

Figure 12.3 (right): A Talieng (Triang) couple (one of the line of couples discussed on page 323).

Photo: Y. Goudineau

Photo: Y. Goudineau

Figure 12.2: Line of couples belonging to different ethnic groups (discussed page 323).

Index

f = figure; n = footnote; t = table; * = map; **bold** = extended discussion or keyword

Critical Acclaim for *From Tribalism to Nationalism*

'This book is a fitting tribute to Grant Evans: a pioneer of Laotian studies and a penetrating and original intellect and, at the same time, an important contribution to the work he helped found and advance.'
– James C. Scott, Yale University

'The eminent contributions to this volume are not only testimony to the rich ethnic and religious diversity and complex history of Laos, but also a tribute to the pioneer of the field of post-1975 Lao studies, Grant Evans. An immensely inspiring figure to many of his friends and pupils, Evans remained the fountain of ideas after his move to Laos until his untimely death in 2014. This book salutes his many scholarly accomplishments that have made contemporary Lao studies possible.'
– Oscar Salemink, University of Copenhagen

From Tribalism to Nationalism is a valuable collection of ethnographic studies representing the 'anthropological turn' in Lao studies. It covers a long period of economic, political and cultural transformation in Laos, particularly the change of relationship between the state and ethnic minorities. The contributions of Grant Evans' colleagues and friends in this volume carry on his spirit, inspiration, and unparalleled work to further enhance current and encourage new research in the rich field of Laos Studies.
– Chayan Vaddhanaphuti, Chiang Mai University

'Grant Evans was generous with his time, wide in his interests, and deep in his knowledge of Laos. His work is the starting point for many of us working on agrarian change in the country, but rarely can we match his scholarship, nor his deft turns of phrase. This collection curated by Yves Goudineau and Vanina Bouté is a fitting and valuable tribute to Grant and his work.'
– Jonathan Rigg, University of Bristol